Gastrointestinal Diseases & Disorders
  Sourcebook
Genetic Disorders Sourcebook,
  1st Edition
Genetic D
  2nd Edit
Head Trau
Headache
Health Ins
Health Reference Series Cumulative
  Index 1999
Healthy Aging Sourcebook
Healthy Children Sourcebook
Healthy Heart Sourcebook for Women
Heart Diseases & Disorders
  Sourcebook, 2nd Edition
Household Safety Sourcebook
Immune System Disorders Sourcebook
Infant & Toddler Health Sourcebook
Injury & Trauma Sourcebook
Kidney & Urinary Tract Diseases &
  Disorders Sourcebook
Learning Disabilities Sourcebook,
  1st Edition
Learning Disabilities Sourcebook,
  2nd Edition
Liver Disorders Sourcebook
Lung Disorders Sourcebook
Medical Tests Sourcebook
Men's Health Concerns Sourcebook
Mental Health Disorders Sourcebook,
  1st Edition
Mental Health Disorders Sourcebook,
  2nd Edition
Mental Retardation Sourcebook
Movement Disorders Sourcebook
Obesity Sourcebook
Ophthalmic Disorders Sourcebook,
  1st Edition
Oral Health Sourcebook
Osteoporosis Sourcebook
Pain Sourcebook, 1st Edition
Pain Sourcebook, 2nd Edition

Pediatric Cancer Sourcebook
Physical & Mental Issues in Aging
  Sourcebook
Podiatry Sourcebook
                              Sourcebook

                              ebook

                              osmetic Surgery

Rehabilitation Sourcebook
Respiratory Diseases & Disorders
  Sourcebook
Sexually Transmitted Diseases
  Sourcebook, 1st Edition
Sexually Transmitted Diseases
  Sourcebook, 2nd Edition
Skin Disorders Sourcebook
Sleep Disorders Sourcebook
Sports Injuries Sourcebook, 1st Edition
Sports Injuries Sourcebook, 2nd Edition
Stress-Related Disorders Sourcebook
Substance Abuse Sourcebook
Surgery Sourcebook
Transplantation Sourcebook
Traveler's Health Sourcebook
Vegetarian Sourcebook
Women's Health Concerns Sourcebook
Workplace Health & Safety Sourcebook
Worldwide Health Sourcebook

Teen Health Series
Diet Information for Teens
Drug Information for Teens
Mental Health Information
  for Teens
Sexual Health Information
  for Teens

Depression
SOURCEBOOK

Health Reference Series

First Edition

Depression
SOURCEBOOK

*Basic Consumer Health Information about
Unipolar Depression, Bipolar Disorder,
Postpartum Depression, Seasonal Affective
Disorder, and Other Types of Depression in
Children, Adolescents, Women, Men, the Elderly,
and Other Selected Populations*

*Along with Facts about Causes, Risk Factors,
Diagnostic Criteria, Treatment Options,
Coping Strategies, Suicide Prevention, a Glossary,
and a Directory of Sources for Additional
Help and Information*

Edited by
Karen Bellenir

Omnigraphics

615 Griswold Street • Detroit, MI 48226

Bibliographic Note

Because this page cannot legibly accommodate all the copyright notices, the Bibliographic Note portion of the Preface constitutes an extension of the copyright notice.

Edited by Karen Bellenir

Health Reference Series

Karen Bellenir, *Managing Editor*
David A. Cooke, MD, *Medical Consultant*
Elizabeth Barbour, *Permissions Associate*
Dawn Matthews, *Verification Assistant*
Laura Pleva Nielsen, *Index Editor*
EdIndex, Services for Publishers, *Indexers*

* * *

Omnigraphics, Inc.

Matthew P. Barbour, *Senior Vice President*
Kay Gill, *Vice President—Directories*
Kevin Hayes, *Operations Manager*
Leif Gruenberg, *Development Manager*
David P. Bianco, *Marketing Consultant*

* * *

Peter E. Ruffner, *Publisher*

Frederick G. Ruffner, Jr., *Chairman*

Library of Congress Cataloging-in-Publication Data

Depression sourcebook : basic consumer health information about unipolar depression, bipolar disorder, postpartum depression, seasonal affective disorder, and other types of depression in children, adolescents, women, men, the elderly, and other selected populations; along with facts about causes, risk factors, diagnostic criteria, treatment options, coping strategies, suicide prevention, a glossary, and a directory of sources for additional help and information / edited by Karen Bellenir.-- 1st ed.
    p. cm. -- (Health reference series)
  Includes bibliographical references and index.
  ISBN 0-7808-0611-5
    1. Depression, Mental--Popular works. I. Bellenir, Karen. II. Health reference series (Unnumbered)

RC537 .D4455 2002
616.85'27--dc21

2002035495

Table of Contents

Part III: Treating Depression

Part IV: Depression and Common Co-Occurring Disorders

Part V: Suicide

Part VI: Depression-Related Research

Part VII: Additional Help and Information

Preface

About This Book

Depression, which affects more than 18 million Americans every year, is one of the most prevalent mental health conditions. Untreated, it can cause long-lasting problems in daily functioning and contribute to increased medical complications in patients with coexisting disorders such as heart disease, diabetes, and chronic pain. Treatment options include several different types of antidepressant medications, herbal therapy, exercise, and various forms of psychotherapy. Unfortunately, many who suffer do not know that depression is a treatable condition and fail to get the help they need.

This *Sourcebook* offers information about the various types of depression, including unipolar depression, bipolar disorder (manic depression), postpartum depression, seasonal affective disorder, and others. It includes facts about depression in children and adolescents, men, women, and the elderly. Readers will learn about warning signs, symptoms, treatments, coping strategies, and current research initiatives. A special section explains the link between depressive illnesses and suicide. A glossary of depression-related terms and directories of additional resources are also included.

How to Use This Book

This book is divided into parts and chapters. Parts focus on broad areas of interest. Chapters are devoted to single topics within a part.

Part I: Types and Causes of Depression describes the various kinds of depression including unipolar depression (major depression), bipolar disorder (manic depression), seasonal affective disorder, postpartum depression, dysthymic disorder, and schizoaffective disorder. It explains theories about the causes of depression and characterizes the relationship between substance abuse and depression.

Part II: Understanding the Experience of Depression offers information about how depression affects children, adolescents, young adults, women, men, and the elderly. It explains how certain life events and circumstances can increase the challenges faced by those suffering from depression, and it gives suggestions for people who want to help someone who is depressed.

Part III: Treating Depression describes the most commonly used tools in the battle against depression, including psychotherapy, antidepressants and other medications, electroconvulsive therapy, and exercise. Treatment challenges, such as managing the side effects of medications, avoiding drug interactions, and treating people with a history of alcohol dependency or other substance abuse problems, are also explained.

Part IV: Depression and Common Co-Occurring Disorders examines the relationship between depression and other illnesses that are often associated with it, including Alzheimer's disease, cancer, chronic pain, diabetes, eating disorders, heart disease, human immunodeficiency virus (HIV) infection, insomnia, Parkinson's disease, stroke, and thyroid disease.

Part V: Suicide presents facts about the role depression plays in suicide risk. It offers statistics about suicide and provides information about suicide prevention. The special challenges faced by teenagers and the elderly are described, and information is included for people seeking comfort after a loved one has been lost to suicide.

Part VI: Depression-Related Research explains current studies in areas such as brain function, depression medications, the role of psychotherapy in treatment and relapse prevention, hormones and other women's issues, and gender differences in the experience of depression.

Part VII: Additional Help and Information includes a glossary of depression-related terms and a list of books for further reading about depression. A directory of organizations able to provide more information is provided along with a directory of organizations able to assist in times of crisis. Help for people trying to locate support groups or financial assistance for depression-related medications is also included.

Bibliographic Note

This volume contains documents and excerpts from publications issued by the following U.S. government agencies: Agency for Healthcare Research and Quality; Centers for Disease Control and Prevention (CDC); National Cancer Institute; National Center for Complementary and Alternative Medicine; National Clearinghouse for Alcohol and Drug Information; National Institute of Mental Health; National Institute on Alcohol Abuse and Alcoholism; National Institute on Drug Abuse; National Institutes of Health; National Library of Medicine; Office of the Surgeon General; Substance Abuse and Mental Health Services Administration's Center for Mental Health Services; U.S. Department of Health and Human Services' Office on Women's Health; and the U.S. Food and Drug Administration's Center for Drug Evaluation and Research.

In addition, this volume contains copyrighted documents from the following organizations, publications, and individuals: About.com; American Academy of Child and Adolescent Psychiatry; American Academy of Family Physicians; American Association for Geriatric Psychiatry; American Diabetes Association; American Psychological Association; Cleveland Clinic; Expert Knowledge Systems/CNS, Inc.; Lippincott Williams and Wilkins; Medical Association of Atlanta; Medical College of Wisconsin/MCW HealthLink; *Midlife Passages*; National Alliance for the Mentally Ill; National Depressive and Manic-Depressive Association; National Foundation for Depressive Illness, Inc.; National Mental Health Association; National Parkinson Foundation; New York Online Access to Health (NOAH); New York-Presbyterian Hospital Behavioral Health Nursing Service Line; *Physician and Sports Medicine*; Tracy Pierson; Royal College of Psychiatrists; Stanford University; Suicide Awareness/Voices of Education (SA/VE); Thyroid Foundation of America; University of Oxford Centre for Evidence-Based Mental Health; University of Pennsylvania Health System; and Jerome Yesavage, MD.

Full citation information is provided on the first page of each chapter. Every effort has been made to secure all necessary rights to reprint the copyrighted material. If any omissions have been made, please contact Omnigraphics to make corrections for future editions.

Acknowledgements

Special thanks go to the many organizations who have provided materials that appear in this volume, to the staff in Omnigraphics' Detroit office, and to the following individuals who are vital to the editorial and production processes: medical consultant Dr. David Cooke, permissions specialist Liz Barbour, verification assistant Dawn Matthews, indexer Edward J. Prucha, and document engineer Bruce Bellenir.

Note from the Editor

This book is part of Omnigraphics' *Health Reference Series*. The *Series* provides basic information about a broad range of medical concerns. It is not intended to serve as a tool for diagnosing illness, in prescribing treatments, or as a substitute for the physician/patient relationship. All persons concerned about medical symptoms or the possibility of disease are encouraged to seek professional care from an appropriate health care provider.

Our Advisory Board

The *Health Reference Series* is reviewed by an Advisory Board comprised of librarians from public, academic, and medical libraries. We would like to thank the following board members for providing guidance to the development of this *Series*:

Dr. Lynda Baker,
Associate Professor of Library and Information Science,
Wayne State University, Detroit, MI

Nancy Bulgarelli,
William Beaumont Hospital Library, Royal Oak, MI

Karen Imarisio,
Bloomfield Township Public Library, Bloomfield Township, MI

Karen Morgan,
Mardigian Library, University of Michigan-Dearborn,
Dearborn, MI

Rosemary Orlando,
St. Clair Shores Public Library, St. Clair Shores, MI

Medical Consultant

Medical consultation services are provided to the *Health Reference Series* editors by David A. Cooke, MD. Dr. Cooke is a graduate of Brandeis University, and he received his MD degree from the University of Michigan. He completed residency training at the University of Wisconsin Hospital and Clinics. He is board-certified in Internal Medicine. Dr. Cooke currently works as part of the University of Michigan Health System and practices in Brighton, MI. In his free time, he enjoys writing, science fiction, and spending time with his family.

Health Reference Series *Update Policy*

The inaugural book in the *Health Reference Series* was the first edition of *Cancer Sourcebook* published in 1989. Since then, the *Series* has been enthusiastically received by librarians and in the medical community. In order to maintain the standard of providing high-quality health information for the layperson the editorial staff at Omnigraphics felt it was necessary to implement a policy of updating volumes when warranted.

Medical researchers have been making tremendous strides, and it is the purpose of the *Health Reference Series* to stay current with the most recent advances. Each decision to update a volume will be made on an individual basis. Some of the considerations will include how much new information is available and the feedback we receive from people who use the books. If there is a topic you would like to see added to the update list, or an area of medical concern you feel has not been adequately addressed, please write to:

Editor
Health Reference Series
Omnigraphics, Inc.
615 Griswold Street
Detroit, MI 48226
E-mail: editorial@omnigraphics.com

Part One

Types and Causes
of Depression

Chapter 1

Depression: An Overview

In any given 1-year period, 9.5 percent of the population, or about 18.8 million American adults, suffer from a depressive illness.[5] The economic cost for this disorder is high, but the cost in human suffering cannot be estimated. Depressive illnesses often interfere with normal functioning and cause pain and suffering not only to those who have a disorder, but also to those who care about them. Serious depression can destroy family life as well as the life of the ill person. But much of this suffering is unnecessary.

Most people with a depressive illness do not seek treatment, although the great majority—even those whose depression is extremely severe—can be helped. Thanks to years of fruitful research, there are now medications and psychosocial therapies such as cognitive/behavioral, "talk," or interpersonal therapies that ease the pain of depression.

Unfortunately, many people do not recognize that depression is a treatable illness. If you feel that you or someone you care about is one of the many undiagnosed depressed people in this country, the information presented here may help you take the steps that may save your own or someone else's life.

What Is a Depressive Disorder?

A depressive disorder is an illness that involves the body, mood, and thoughts. It affects the way a person eats and sleeps, the way one

"Depression," National Institute of Mental Health (NIMH), NIH Pub. No. 00-3561, 2000.

3

feels about oneself, and the way one thinks about things. A depressive disorder is not the same as a passing blue mood. It is not a sign of personal weakness or a condition that can be willed or wished away. People with a depressive illness cannot merely "pull themselves together" and get better. Without treatment, symptoms can last for weeks, months, or years. Appropriate treatment, however, can help most people who suffer from depression.

Types of Depression

Depressive disorders come in different forms, just as is the case with other illnesses such as heart disease. This chapter provides a brief overview of three of the most common types of depressive disorders. However, within these types there are variations in the number of symptoms, their severity, and persistence.

Major depression. Major depression is manifested by a combination of symptoms that interfere with the ability to work, study, sleep, eat, and enjoy once pleasurable activities. Such a disabling episode of depression may occur only once but more commonly occurs several times in a lifetime.

Dysthymia. A less severe type of depression, dysthymia, involves long-term, chronic symptoms that do not disable, but keep one from functioning well or from feeling good. Many people with dysthymia also experience major depressive episodes at some time in their lives.

Bipolar disorder. Another type of depression is bipolar disorder, also called manic-depressive illness. Not nearly as prevalent as other forms of depressive disorders, bipolar disorder is characterized by cycling mood changes: severe highs (mania) and lows (depression). Sometimes the mood switches are dramatic and rapid, but most often they are gradual. When in the depressed cycle, an individual can have any or all of the symptoms of a depressive disorder. When in the manic cycle, the individual may be overactive, over talkative, and have a great deal of energy. Mania often affects thinking, judgment, and social behavior in ways that cause serious problems and embarrassment. For example, the individual in a manic phase may feel elated, full of grand schemes that might range from unwise business decisions to romantic sprees. Mania, left untreated, may worsen to a psychotic state.

Symptoms of Depression and Mania

Not everyone who is depressed or manic experiences every symptom. Some people experience a few symptoms, some many. Severity of symptoms varies with individuals and also varies over time.

Depression

- Persistent sad, anxious, or "empty" mood
- Feelings of hopelessness, pessimism
- Feelings of guilt, worthlessness, helplessness
- Loss of interest or pleasure in hobbies and activities that were once enjoyed, including sex
- Decreased energy, fatigue, being "slowed down"
- Difficulty concentrating, remembering, making decisions
- Insomnia, early-morning awakening, or oversleeping
- Appetite and/or weight loss or overeating and weight gain
- Thoughts of death or suicide; suicide attempts
- Restlessness, irritability
- Persistent physical symptoms that do not respond to treatment, such as headaches, digestive disorders, and chronic pain

Mania

- Abnormal or excessive elation
- Unusual irritability
- Decreased need for sleep
- Grandiose notions
- Increased talking
- Racing thoughts
- Increased sexual desire
- Markedly increased energy
- Poor judgment
- Inappropriate social behavior

Causes of Depression

Some types of depression run in families, suggesting that a biological vulnerability can be inherited. This seems to be the case with bipolar disorder. Studies of families in which members of each generation develop bipolar disorder found that those with the illness have a somewhat different genetic makeup than those who do not get ill. However, the reverse is not true: Not everybody with the genetic makeup that causes vulnerability to bipolar disorder will have the illness. Apparently additional factors, possibly stresses at home, work, or school, are involved in its onset.

In some families, major depression also seems to occur generation after generation. However, it can also occur in people who have no family history of depression. Whether inherited or not, major depressive disorder is often associated with changes in brain structures or brain function.

People who have low self-esteem, who consistently view themselves and the world with pessimism or who are readily overwhelmed by stress, are prone to depression. Whether this represents a psychological predisposition or an early form of the illness is not clear.

In recent years, researchers have shown that physical changes in the body can be accompanied by mental changes as well. Medical illnesses such as stroke, a heart attack, cancer, Parkinson's disease, and hormonal disorders can cause depressive illness, making the sick person apathetic and unwilling to care for his or her physical needs, thus prolonging the recovery period. Also, a serious loss, difficult relationship, financial problem, or any stressful (unwelcome or even desired) change in life patterns can trigger a depressive episode. Very often, a combination of genetic, psychological, and environmental factors is involved in the onset of a depressive disorder. Later episodes of illness typically are precipitated by only mild stresses, or none at all.

Depression in Women

Women experience depression about twice as often as men.[1] Many hormonal factors may contribute to the increased rate of depression in women—particularly such factors as menstrual cycle changes, pregnancy, miscarriage, postpartum period, pre-menopause, and menopause. Many women also face additional stresses such as responsibilities both at work and home, single parenthood, and caring for children and for aging parents.

A recent National Institute of Mental Health (NIMH) study showed that in the case of severe premenstrual syndrome (PMS), women with a preexisting vulnerability to PMS experienced relief from mood and physical symptoms when their sex hormones were suppressed. Shortly after the hormones were re-introduced, they again developed symptoms of PMS. Women without a history of PMS reported no effects of the hormonal manipulation.[6,7]

Many women are also particularly vulnerable after the birth of a baby. The hormonal and physical changes, as well as the added responsibility of a new life, can be factors that lead to postpartum depression in some women. While transient "blues" are common in new mothers, a full-blown depressive episode is not a normal occurrence and requires active intervention. Treatment by a sympathetic physician and the family's emotional support for the new mother are prime considerations in aiding her to recover her physical and mental well-being and her ability to care for and enjoy the infant.

Depression in Men

Although men are less likely to suffer from depression than women, three to four million men in the United States are affected by the illness. Men are less likely to admit to depression, and doctors are less likely to suspect it. The rate of suicide in men is four times that of women, though more women attempt it. In fact, after age 70, the rate of men's suicide rises, reaching a peak after age 85.

Depression can also affect the physical health in men differently from women. A new study shows that, although depression is associated with an increased risk of coronary heart disease in both men and women, only men suffer a high death rate.[2]

Men's depression is often masked by alcohol or drugs, or by the socially acceptable habit of working excessively long hours. Depression typically shows up in men not as feeling hopeless and helpless, but as being irritable, angry, and discouraged; hence, depression may be difficult to recognize as such in men. Even if a man realizes that he is depressed, he may be less willing than a woman to seek help. Encouragement and support from concerned family members can make a difference. In the workplace, employee assistance professionals or worksite mental health programs can be of assistance in helping men understand and accept depression as a real illness that needs treatment.

Depression in the Elderly

Some people have the mistaken idea that it is normal for the elderly to feel depressed. On the contrary, most older people feel satisfied with

7

their lives. Sometimes, though, when depression develops, it may be dismissed as a normal part of aging. Depression in the elderly, undiagnosed and untreated, causes needless suffering for the family and for the individual who could otherwise live a fruitful life. When he or she does go to the doctor, the symptoms described are usually physical, for the older person is often reluctant to discuss feelings of hopelessness, sadness, loss of interest in normally pleasurable activities, or extremely prolonged grief after a loss.

Recognizing how depressive symptoms in older people are often missed, many health care professionals are learning to identify and treat the underlying depression. They recognize that some symptoms may be side effects of medication the older person is taking for a physical problem, or they may be caused by a co-occurring illness. If a diagnosis of depression is made, treatment with medication and/or psychotherapy will help the depressed person return to a happier, more fulfilling life. Recent research suggests that brief psychotherapy (talk therapies that help a person in day-to-day relationships or in learning to counter the distorted negative thinking that commonly accompanies depression) is effective in reducing symptoms in short-term depression in older persons who are medically ill. Psychotherapy is also useful in older patients who cannot or will not take medication. Efficacy studies show that late-life depression can be treated with psychotherapy.[4]

Improved recognition and treatment of depression in late life will make those years more enjoyable and fulfilling for the depressed elderly person, the family, and caretakers.

Depression in Children

Only in the past two decades has depression in children been taken very seriously. The depressed child may pretend to be sick, refuse to go to school, cling to a parent, or worry that the parent may die. Older children may sulk, get into trouble at school, be negative, grouchy, and feel misunderstood. Because normal behaviors vary from one childhood stage to another, it can be difficult to tell whether a child is just going through a temporary "phase" or is suffering from depression. Sometimes the parents become worried about how the child's behavior has changed, or a teacher mentions that "your child doesn't seem to be himself." In such a case, if a visit to the child's pediatrician rules out physical symptoms, the doctor will probably suggest that the child be evaluated, preferably by a psychiatrist who specializes in the treatment of children. If treatment is needed, the doctor may suggest that another therapist, usually a social worker or a psychologist, provide therapy while the psychiatrist will oversee medication if it is needed. Parents should not be afraid to ask questions: What are the therapist's qualifications? What kind of therapy will the child have? Will the family as a whole participate in therapy? Will my child's therapy include an antidepressant? If so, what might the side effects be?

The National Institute of Mental Health (NIMH) has identified the use of medications for depression in children as an important area for research. The NIMH-supported Research Units on Pediatric Psychopharmacology (RUPPs) form a network of seven research sites where clinical studies on the effects of medications for mental disorders can be conducted in children and adolescents. Among the medications being studied are antidepressants, some of which have been found to be effective in treating children with depression, if properly monitored by the child's physician.[8]

Diagnostic Evaluation and Treatment

The first step to getting appropriate treatment for depression is a physical examination by a physician. Certain medications as well as some medical conditions such as a viral infection can cause the same symptoms as depression, and the physician should rule out these possibilities through examination, interview, and lab tests. If a physical cause for the depression is ruled out, a psychological evaluation should be done, by the physician or by referral to a psychiatrist or psychologist.

A good diagnostic evaluation will include a complete history of symptoms: when they started; how long they have lasted; how severe they are; whether the patient had them before and, if so, whether the symptoms were treated and what treatment was given. The doctor should ask about alcohol and drug use, and if the patient has thoughts about death or suicide. Further, a history should include questions about whether other family members have had a depressive illness and, if treated, what treatments they may have received and which were effective.

Last, a diagnostic evaluation should include a mental status examination to determine if speech or thought patterns or memory have been affected, as sometimes happens in the case of a depressive or manic-depressive illness.

Treatment choice will depend on the outcome of the evaluation. There are a variety of antidepressant medications and psychotherapies that can be used to treat depressive disorders. Some people with milder forms may do well with psychotherapy alone. People with moderate to severe depression most often benefit from antidepressants. Most do best with combined treatment: medication to gain relatively quick symptom relief and psychotherapy to learn more effective ways to deal with life's problems, including depression. Depending on the patient's diagnosis and severity of symptoms, the therapist may prescribe medication and/or one of the several forms of psychotherapy that have proven effective for depression.

Electroconvulsive therapy (ECT) is useful, particularly for individuals whose depression is severe or life threatening or who cannot take antidepressant medication.[3] ECT often is effective in cases where antidepressant medications do not provide sufficient relief of symptoms. In recent years, ECT has been much improved. A muscle relaxant is given before treatment, which is done under brief anesthesia. Electrodes are placed at precise locations on the head to deliver electrical impulses. The stimulation causes a brief (about 30 seconds) seizure within the brain. The person receiving ECT does not consciously experience the electrical stimulus. For full therapeutic benefit, at least several sessions of ECT, typically given at the rate of three per week, are required.

Medications

There are several types of antidepressant medications used to treat depressive disorders. These include newer medications—chiefly the selective serotonin reuptake inhibitors (SSRIs)—the tricyclics, and the monoamine oxidase inhibitors (MAOIs). The SSRIs—and other newer medications that affect neurotransmitters such as dopamine or norepinephrine—generally have fewer side effects than tricyclics. Sometimes the doctor will try a variety of antidepressants before finding the most effective medication or combination of medications. Sometimes the dosage must be increased to be effective. Although some improvements may be seen in the first few weeks, antidepressant medications must be taken regularly for 3 to 4 weeks (in some cases, as many as 8 weeks) before the full therapeutic effect occurs.

Patients often are tempted to stop medication too soon. They may feel better and think they no longer need the medication. Or they may think the medication isn't helping at all. It is important to keep taking medication until it has a chance to work, though side effects may appear before antidepressant activity does. Once the individual is feeling better, it is important to continue the medication for 4 to 9 months to prevent a recurrence of the depression. Some medications must be stopped gradually to give the body time to adjust, and many can produce withdrawal symptoms if discontinued abruptly. For individuals with bipolar disorder and those with chronic or recurrent major depression, medication may have to be maintained indefinitely.

Antidepressant drugs are not habit-forming. However, as is the case with any type of medication prescribed for more than a few days, antidepressants have to be carefully monitored to see if the correct dosage is being given. The doctor will check the dosage and its effectiveness regularly.

For the small number of people for whom MAO inhibitors are the best treatment, it is necessary to avoid certain foods that contain high levels of tyramine, such as many cheeses, wines, and pickles, as well as medications such as decongestants. The interaction of tyramine with MAOIs can bring on a hypertensive crisis, a sharp increase in blood pressure that can lead to a stroke. The doctor should furnish a complete list of prohibited foods that the patient should carry at all times. Other forms of antidepressants require no food restrictions.

Medications of any kind—prescribed, over-the counter, or borrowed—should never be mixed without consulting the doctor. Other health professionals who may prescribe a drug—such as a dentist or other medical specialist—should be told of the medications the patient is taking. Some drugs, although safe when taken alone can, if taken with others, cause severe and dangerous side effects. Some drugs, like alcohol or street drugs, may reduce the effectiveness of antidepressants and should be avoided. This includes wine, beer, and hard liquor. Some people who have not had a problem with alcohol use may be permitted by their doctor to use a modest amount of alcohol while taking one of the newer antidepressants.

Antianxiety drugs or sedatives are not antidepressants. They are sometimes prescribed along with antidepressants; however, they are not effective when taken alone for a depressive disorder. Stimulants, such as amphetamines, are not effective antidepressants, but they are used occasionally under close supervision in medically ill depressed patients.

Questions about any antidepressant prescribed, or problems that may be related to the medication, should be discussed with the doctor.

Lithium has for many years been the treatment of choice for bipolar disorder, as it can be effective in smoothing out the mood swings common to this disorder. Its use must be carefully monitored, as the range between an effective dose and a toxic one is small. If a person has preexisting thyroid, kidney, or heart disorders or epilepsy, lithium may not be recommended. Fortunately, other medications have been found to be of benefit in controlling mood swings. Among these are two mood-stabilizing anticonvulsants, carbamazepine (Tegretol®) and valproate (Depakote®). Both of these medications have gained wide acceptance in clinical practice, and valproate has been approved by the Food and Drug Administration for first-line treatment of acute mania. Other anticonvulsants that are being used now include lamotrigine (Lamictal®) and gabapentin (Neurontin®): their role in the treatment hierarchy of bipolar disorder remains under study.

Most people who have bipolar disorder take more than one medication including, along with lithium and/or an anticonvulsant, a medication for accompanying agitation, anxiety, depression, or insomnia. Finding the best possible combination of these medications is of utmost importance to the patient and requires close monitoring by the physician.

Side Effects

Antidepressants may cause mild and, usually, temporary side effects (sometimes referred to as adverse effects) in some people. Typically these are annoying, but not serious. However, any unusual reactions or side effects or those that interfere with functioning should be reported to the doctor immediately. The most common side effects of tricyclic antidepressants, and ways to deal with them, are:

- **Dry mouth:** It is helpful to drink sips of water; chew sugarless gum; clean teeth daily.

- **Constipation:** Bran cereals, prunes, fruit, and vegetables should be in the diet.

- **Bladder problems:** Emptying the bladder may be troublesome, and the urine stream may not be as strong as usual; the doctor should be notified if there is marked difficulty or pain.

- **Sexual problems:** Sexual functioning may change; if worrisome, it should be discussed with the doctor.

- **Blurred vision:** This will pass soon and will not usually necessitate new glasses.

- **Dizziness:** Rising from the bed or chair slowly is helpful.

- **Drowsiness as a daytime problem:** This usually passes soon. A person feeling drowsy or sedated should not drive or operate heavy equipment. The more sedating antidepressants are generally taken at bedtime to help sleep and minimize daytime drowsiness.

The newer antidepressants have different types of side effects:

- **Headache:** This will usually go away.

- **Nausea:** This is also temporary, but even when it occurs, it is transient after each dose.

- **Nervousness and insomnia** (trouble falling asleep or waking often during the night): These may occur during the first few weeks; dosage reductions or time will usually resolve them.

- **Agitation** (feeling jittery): If this happens for the first time after the drug is taken and is more than transient, the doctor should be notified.

- **Sexual problems:** The doctor should be consulted if the problem is persistent or worrisome.

Herbal Therapy

In the past few years, much interest has risen in the use of herbs in the treatment of both depression and anxiety. St. John's wort (*Hypericum perforatum*), an herb used extensively in the treatment of mild to moderate depression in Europe, has recently aroused interest in the United States. St. John's wort, an attractive bushy, low-growing plant covered with yellow flowers in summer, has been used for centuries in many folk and herbal remedies. Today in Germany, *Hypericum* is used in the treatment of depression more than any other antidepressant. However, the scientific studies that have been conducted on its use have been short-term and have used several different doses.

Because of the widespread interest in St. John's wort, the National Institutes of Health (NIH) is conducting a 3-year study, sponsored by three NIH components—the National Institute of Mental Health, the National Center for Complementary and Alternative Medicine, and the Office of Dietary Supplements. The study is designed to include 336 patients with major depression, randomly assigned to an 8-week trial with one-third of patients receiving a uniform dose of St. John's wort, another third a selective serotonin reuptake inhibitor commonly prescribed for depression, and the final third a placebo (a pill that looks exactly like the SSRI and the St. John's wort, but has no active ingredients). The study participants who respond positively will be followed for an additional 18 weeks. After the 3-year study has been completed, results will be analyzed and published.

The Food and Drug Administration issued a Public Health Advisory on February 10, 2000. It stated that St. John's wort appears to affect an important metabolic pathway that is used by many drugs prescribed to treat conditions such as heart disease, depression, seizures, certain cancers, and rejection of transplants. Therefore, health care providers should alert their patients about these potential drug interactions. Any herbal supplement should be taken only after consultation with the doctor or other health care provider.

Psychotherapies

Many forms of psychotherapy, including some short-term (10-20 week) therapies, can help depressed individuals. "Talking" therapies help patients gain insight into and resolve their problems through verbal exchange with the therapist, sometimes combined with "homework" assignments between sessions. "Behavioral" therapists help patients learn how to obtain more satisfaction and rewards through their own actions and how to unlearn the behavioral patterns that contribute to or result from their depression.

Two of the short-term psychotherapies that research has shown helpful for some forms of depression are interpersonal and cognitive/behavioral therapies. Interpersonal therapists focus on the patient's disturbed personal relationships that both cause and exacerbate (or increase) the depression. Cognitive/behavioral therapists help patients change the negative styles of thinking and behaving often associated with depression.

Psychodynamic therapies, which are sometimes used to treat depressed persons, focus on resolving the patient's conflicted feelings. These therapies are often reserved until the depressive symptoms are significantly improved. In general, severe depressive illnesses, particularly those that are recurrent, will require medication (or ECT under special conditions) along with, or preceding, psychotherapy for the best outcome.

How to Help Yourself If You Are Depressed

Depressive disorders make one feel exhausted, worthless, helpless, and hopeless. Such negative thoughts and feelings make some people feel like giving up. It is important to realize that these negative views are part of the depression and typically do not accurately reflect the actual circumstances. Negative thinking fades as treatment begins to take effect. In the meantime:

- Set realistic goals in light of the depression and assume a reasonable amount of responsibility.

- Break large tasks into small ones, set some priorities, and do what you can as you can.

- Try to be with other people and to confide in someone; it is usually better than being alone and secretive.

- Participate in activities that may make you feel better.

- Mild exercise, going to a movie, a ball game, or participating in religious, social, or other activities may help.

- Expect your mood to improve gradually, not immediately. Feeling better takes time.

- It is advisable to postpone important decisions until the depression has lifted. Before deciding to make a significant transition—change jobs, get married or divorced—discuss it with others who know you well and have a more objective view of your situation.

- People rarely "snap out of" a depression. But they can feel a little better day-by-day.

- *Remember*, positive thinking will replace the negative thinking that is part of the depression and will disappear as your depression responds to treatment.

- Let your family and friends help you.

How Family and Friends Can Help the Depressed Person

The most important thing anyone can do for the depressed person is to help him or her get an appropriate diagnosis and treatment. This may involve encouraging the individual to stay with treatment until symptoms begin to abate (several weeks), or to seek different treatment if no improvement occurs. On occasion, it may require making an appointment and accompanying the depressed person to the doctor. It may also mean monitoring whether the depressed person is taking medication. The depressed person should be encouraged to obey the doctor's orders about the use of alcoholic products while on medication. The second most important thing is to offer emotional support. This involves understanding, patience, affection, and encouragement. Engage the depressed person in conversation and listen carefully. Do not disparage feelings expressed, but point out realities and offer hope. Do not ignore remarks about suicide. Report them to the depressed person's therapist. Invite the depressed person for walks, outings, to the movies, and other activities. Be gently insistent if your invitation is refused. Encourage participation in some activities that once gave pleasure, such as hobbies, sports, religious or cultural activities, but do not push the depressed person to undertake too much too soon. The depressed person needs diversion and company, but too many demands can increase feelings of failure.

Do not accuse the depressed person of faking illness or of laziness, or expect him or her "to snap out of it." Eventually, with treatment, most people do get better. Keep that in mind, and keep reassuring the depressed person that, with time and help, he or she will feel better.

Where to Get Help

If unsure where to go for help, check the *Yellow Pages* under "mental health," "health," "social services," "suicide prevention," "crisis intervention services," "hotlines," "hospitals," or "physicians" for phone numbers and addresses. In times of crisis, the emergency room doctor at a hospital may be able to provide temporary help for an emotional problem, and will be able to tell you where and how to get further help.

Listed below are the types of people and places that will make a referral to, or provide, diagnostic and treatment services.

- Family doctors
- Mental health specialists, such as psychiatrists, psychologists, social workers, or mental health counselors
- Health maintenance organizations
- Community mental health centers
- Hospital psychiatry departments and outpatient clinics
- University- or medical school-affiliated programs
- State hospital outpatient clinics

- Family service, social agencies, or clergy
- Private clinics and facilities
- Employee assistance programs
- Local medical and/or psychiatric societies

The end section of this book includes additional information about resources for further help and information.

References

1. Blehar MD, Oren DA. Gender differences in depression. *Medscape Women's Health*, 1997;2:3. Revised from: Women's increased vulnerability to mood disorders: Integrating psychobiology and epidemiology. *Depression*, 1995;3:3-12.

2. Ferketick AK, Schwartzbaum JA, Frid DJ, Moeschberger ML. Depression as an antecedent to heart disease among women and men in the NHANES I study. National Health and Nutrition Examination Survey. *Archives of Internal Medicine*, 2000; 160(9): 1261-8.

3. Frank E, Karp JF, Rush AJ (1993). Efficacy of treatments for major depression. *Psychopharmacology Bulletin*, 1993; 29:457-75.

4. Lebowitz BD, Pearson JL, Schneider LS, Reynolds CF, Alexopoulos GS, Bruce MI, Conwell Y, Katz IR, Meyers BS, Morrison MF, Mossey J, Niederehe G, Parmelee P. Diagnosis and treatment of depression in late life: consensus statement update. *Journal of the American Medical Association*, 1997; 278:1186-90.

5. Robins LN, Regier DA (Eds). *Psychiatric Disorders in America, The Epidemiologic Catchment Area Study*, 1990; New York: The Free Press.

6. Rubinow DR, Schmidt PJ, Roca CA. Estrogen-serotonin interactions: Implications for affective regulation. *Biological Psychiatry*, 1998; 44(9):839-50.

7. Schmidt PJ, Neiman LK, Danaceau MA, Adams LF, Rubinow DR. Differential behavioral effects of gonadal steroids in

women with and in those without premenstrual syndrome. *Journal of the American Medical Association*, 1998; 338:209-16.

8. Vitiello B, Jensen P. Medication development and testing in children and adolescents. *Archives of General Psychiatry*, 1997; 54:871-6.

Chapter 2

What Causes Depression?

Biological Factors

The brain is the control center for every part of the body. It controls our conscious behavior (walking and thinking) and our involuntary behavior (heartbeat and breathing). The brain also regulates our emotions, memory, self-awareness and thought processes. The brain receives information via nerve cells, called neurons, from every part of the body. The brain evaluates the information it receives and sends appropriate instructions via the neurons. Each one communicates with the cells around it through electrical signals. When a nerve signal reaches the end of one cell, it must pass over a gap to reach the other one. The nerve causes a release of chemicals called neurotransmitters. The improper relay of signals may be partly responsible for depression.

The underlying causes of depression are not well understood, although there are many clues suggesting various systems in the brain may cause depression or be affected by it. For example, major depression is characterized by excessive sleep. So, it is very likely that the brain stem, which controls sleep, plays a role in depression. Similarly, abnormalities in the cerebral cortex, which controls thinking, probably have something to do with the inability to concentrate and the negative thoughts that can be characteristic of depression.

"What Causes Depression?" *Depression: Health Topics*, University of Pennsylvania Health System, available online at www.pennhealth.com/health/hi_files/topics/depression/what_causes.html. Printed with permission from the Trustees of the University of Pennsylvania, © 2002.

Imbalances in neurotransmitters seem to play a key role in depression. Research into the way antidepressant medications function has provided the greatest insight in this area. For example, certain medications used to treat depression have been shown to increase amounts of neurotransmitters, such as norepinephrine, serotonin and dopamine, in the brain. This suggests that a chemical imbalance in the brain causes depressive symptoms. Abnormalities in the neuroendocrine system of the brain also seem to play a role in depression, including abnormalities linked to the thyroid, pituitary and, adrenal glands.

In some cases, a stroke may cause depression. Strokes that cause depression are more likely to occur in the left frontal lobe of the brain, but they can be found elsewhere. One study of older adults found that damage to specific areas of the brain (subcortical white matter lesions) were more likely to be found in people with major depression than in

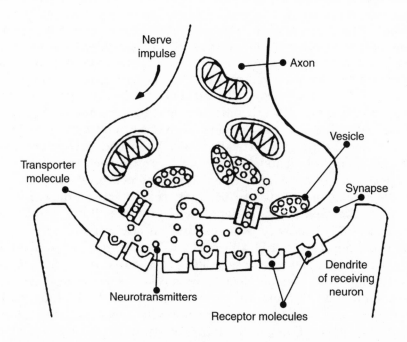

Figure 2.1. Each nerve cell communicates with cells around it through electrical signals which must pass over a gap called a synapse. Source: Mind Over Matter: Teacher's Guide, National Institute on Drug Abuse, NIH Pub. No. 98-3592.

healthy individuals, or patients with dementia (progressive decline in the ability to think and reason). These small, subcortical strokes are the type found in individuals with long-standing hypertension, diabetes, or other medical illnesses that affect blood vessels in the brain, heart and other organs.

Genetic Factors

Individuals with a family history of depression have a greater risk of becoming depressed than the general population. Some researchers believe a "single depression gene" exists, but there is mounting evidence to suggest that several genes may be responsible for causing depression.

Social and Environmental Factors

Social and environmental factors also may cause depression, but there are many conflicting scientific studies concerning this issue. For example, some studies suggest adverse life events, such as divorce, serious illness, or multiple episodes of misfortune, may cause depression. Other studies have found that no such relationship exists.

Chapter 3

Four Common Mood Disorders

In one year, about seven percent of Americans suffer from mood disorders, a cluster of mental disorders best recognized by depression or mania. Mood disorders are outside the bounds of normal fluctuations from sadness to elation. They have potentially severe consequences for morbidity (sickness) and mortality (death).

This chapter covers four mood disorders. As the predominant mood disorder, major depressive disorder (also known as unipolar major depression), garners the greatest attention. It is twice more common in women than in men, a gender difference that is discussed later. The other mood disorders covered below are bipolar disorder, dysthymia, and cyclothymia.

Mood disorders rank among the top ten causes of worldwide disability. Unipolar major depression ranks first, and bipolar disorder ranks in the top ten. Moreover, disability and suffering are not limited to the patient. Spouses, children, parents, siblings, and friends experience frustration, guilt, anger, financial hardship, and, on occasion, physical abuse in their attempts to assuage or cope with the depressed person's suffering. Women between the ages of 18 and 45 comprise the majority of those with major depression.

Depression also has a deleterious impact on the economy, both in diminished productivity and in use of health care resources. In the

From "Chapter 4: Mood Disorders," *Mental Health: A Report of the Surgeon General*, Office of the Surgeon General, 1999. The full text of this document, including references, is available online at www.surgeongeneral.gov/library/mentalhealth/.

workplace, depression is a leading cause of absenteeism and diminished productivity. Although only a minority seek professional help to relieve a mood disorder, depressed people are significantly more likely than others to visit a physician for some other reason. Depression-related visits to physicians thus account for a large portion of health care expenditures. Seeking another or a less stigmatized explanation for their difficulties, some depressed patients undergo extensive and expensive diagnostic procedures and then get treated for various other complaints while the mood disorder goes undiagnosed and untreated.

Complications and Comorbidities

Suicide is the most dreaded complication of major depressive disorders. About 10 to 15 percent of patients formerly hospitalized with depression commit suicide. Major depressive disorders account for about 20 to 35 percent of all deaths by suicide. Completed suicide is more common among those with more severe and/or psychotic symptoms, with late onset, with coexisting mental and addictive disorders, as well as among those who have experienced stressful life events, who have medical illnesses, and who have a family history of suicidal behavior. In the United States, men complete suicide four times as often as women; women attempt suicide four times as frequently as do men. Individuals with depression also face an increased risk of death from coronary artery disease.

Mood disorders often coexist, or are comorbid, with other mental and somatic disorders. Anxiety is commonly comorbid with major depression. About one-half of those with a primary diagnosis of major depression also have an anxiety disorder. The comorbidity of anxiety and depression is so pronounced that it has led to theories of similar etiologies, which are discussed below. Substance use disorders are found in 24 to 40 percent of individuals with mood disorders in the United States. Without treatment, substance abuse worsens the course of mood disorders. Other common comorbidities include personality disorders and medical illness, especially chronic conditions such as hypertension and arthritis. The mood disorders also may alter or "scar" personality development.

Clinical Depression Versus Normal Sadness

People have been plagued by disorders of mood for at least as long as they have been able to record their experiences. One of the earliest terms for depression, "melancholy," literally meaning "black bile," dates back to Hippocrates. Since antiquity, dysphoric states outside the range of normal sadness or grief have been recognized, but only within the past 40 years or so have researchers had the means to study the changes in cognition and brain functioning that are associated with severe depressive states.

At some time or another, virtually all adult human beings will experience a tragic or unexpected loss, romantic heartbreak, or a serious setback and times of profound sadness, grief, or distress. Indeed, something is awry if the usual expressions of sadness do not accompany such situations so common to the human condition—death of a loved one, severe illness, prolonged disability, loss of employment or social status, or a child's difficulties, for example.

What is now called major depressive disorder, however, differs both quantitatively and qualitatively from normal sadness or grief. Normal states of dysphoria (a negative or aversive mood state) are typically less pervasive and generally run a more time-limited course. Moreover, some of the symptoms of severe depression, such as anhedonia (the inability to experience pleasure), hopelessness, and loss of mood reactivity (the ability to feel a mood uplift in response to something positive) only rarely accompany "normal" sadness. Suicidal thoughts and psychotic symptoms such as delusions or hallucinations virtually always signify a pathological state.

Nevertheless, many other symptoms commonly associated with depression are experienced during times of stress or bereavement. Among them are sleep disturbances, changes in appetite, poor concentration, and ruminations on sad thoughts and feelings. When a person suffering such distress seeks help, the diagnostician's task is to differentiate the normal from the pathologic and, when appropriate, to recommend treatment.

Assessment: Diagnosis and Syndrome Severity

The criteria for diagnosing major depressive episode, dysthymia, mania, and cyclothymia are presented below. Mania is an essential feature of bipolar disorder, which is marked by episodes of mania or mixed episodes of mania and depression. The reliability of the diagnostic criteria for major depressive disorder and bipolar disorder is impressive, with greater than 90 percent agreement reached by independent evaluators (diagnostic criteria are presented in the American Psychiatric Association's *Diagnostic and Statistical Manual of Mental Disorders, Fourth Edition*; commonly abbreviated *DSM-IV*).

Major Depressive Disorder

Major depressive disorder features one or more major depressive episodes, each of which lasts at least two weeks (*DSM-IV*). Since these episodes are also characteristic of bipolar disorder, the term "major depression" refers to both major depressive disorder and the depression of bipolar disorder.

The cardinal symptoms of major depressive disorder are depressed mood and loss of interest or pleasure. Other symptoms vary enormously. For example, insomnia and weight loss are considered to be classic signs, even though many depressed patients gain weight and sleep excessively. Such heterogeneity is partly dealt with by the use of diagnostic subtypes (or course modifiers) with differing presentations and prevalence. For example, a more severe depressive syndrome characterized by a constellation of classical signs and symptoms, called melancholia, is more common among older than among younger people, as are depressions characterized by psychotic features (delusions and hallucinations). In fact, the presentation of psychotic features without concomitant melancholia should always raise suspicion about the accuracy of the diagnosis (vis-à-vis schizophrenia or a related psychotic disorder). The so-called reversed vegetative symptoms (oversleeping, overeating, and weight gain) may be more prevalent in women than men. Anxiety symptoms such as panic attacks, phobias, and obsessions also are not uncommon.

When untreated, a major depressive episode may last, on average, about nine months. Eighty to 90 percent of individuals will remit within two years of the first episode. Thereafter, at least 50 percent of depressions will recur, and after three or more episodes the odds of recurrence within three years increases to 70 to 80 percent if the patient has not had preventive treatment. Thus, for many, an initial episode of major depression will evolve over time into the more recurrent illness sometimes referred to as unipolar major depression. Each new episode also confers new risks of chronicity, disability, and suicide.

Criteria for Major Depressive Episode (DSM-IV)

- Five (or more) of the following symptoms have been present during the same two-week period and represent a change from previous functioning; at least one of the symptoms is either (1) depressed mood or (2) loss of interest or pleasure. (Note: Do not include symptoms that are clearly due to a general medical condition, or mood-incongruent delusions or hallucinations.)

26

- depressed mood most of the day, nearly every day, as indicated by either subjective report (for example, feels sad or empty) or observation made by others (for example, appears tearful). Note: In children and adolescents, can be irritable mood.

- markedly diminished interest or pleasure in all, or almost all, activities most of the day, nearly every day (as indicated by either subjective account or observation made by others).

- significant weight loss when not dieting or weight gain (for example, a change of more than 5% of body weight in a month), or decrease or increase in appetite nearly every day. Note: In children, consider failure to make expected weight gains.

- insomnia or hypersomnia nearly every day.

- psychomotor agitation or retardation nearly every day (observable by others, not merely subjective feelings or restlessness or being slowed down).

- fatigue or loss of energy nearly every day.

- feelings of worthlessness or excessive or inappropriate guilt (which may be delusional) nearly every day (not merely self-reproach or guilt about being sick).

- diminished ability to think or concentrate, or indecisiveness, nearly every day (either subjective account or as observed by others).

- recurrent thoughts of death (not just fear of dying), recurrent suicidal ideation without a specific plan, or a suicide attempt or a specific plan for committing suicide.

- The symptoms do not meet criteria for a mixed episode.

- The symptoms cause clinically significant distress or impairment in social, occupational, or other important areas of functioning.

- The symptoms are not due to the direct physiological effects of a substance (for example, a drug of abuse, a medication) or a general medical condition (for example, hypothyroidism).

- The symptoms are not better accounted for by bereavement, that is, after the loss of a loved one; the symptoms persist for longer than two months or are characterized by marked functional impairment, morbid preoccupation with worthlessness, suicidal ideation, psychotic symptoms, or psychomotor retardation.

Dysthymia

Dysthymia is a chronic form of depression. Its early onset and unrelenting, "smoldering" course are among the features that distinguish it from major depressive disorder. Dysthymia becomes so intertwined with a person's self-concept or personality that the individual may be misidentified as "neurotic" (resulting from unresolved early conflicts expressed through unconscious personality defenses or characterological disorders). Indeed, the onset of dysthymia in childhood or adolescence undoubtedly affects personality development and coping styles, particularly prompting passive, avoidant, and dependent "traits." To avoid the pejorative connotations associated with the terms "neurotic" and "characterological," the term "dysthymia" is used in *DSM-IV* as a descriptive, or atheoretical, diagnosis for a chronic form of depression. Affecting about two percent of the adult population in one year, dysthymia is defined by its subsyndromal nature (fewer than the five persistent symptoms required to diagnose a major depressive episode) and a protracted duration of at least two years for adults and one year for children. Like other early-onset disorders, dysthymic disorder is associated with higher rates of comorbid substance abuse.

People with dysthymia also are susceptible to major depression. When this occurs, their illness is sometimes referred to as "double depression," that is, the combination of dysthymia and major depression. Unlike the superimposed major depressive episode, however, the underlying dysthymia seldom remits spontaneously. Women are twice as likely to be diagnosed with dysthymia as men.

Diagnostic Criteria for Dysthymic Disorder (DSM-IV)

- Depressed mood for most of the day, for more days than not, as indicated either by subjective account or observation by others, for at least two years. Note: In children and adolescents, mood can be irritable and duration must be at least one year.

- Presence, while depressed, of two (or more) of the following:
  - poor appetite or overeating
  - insomnia or hypersomnia
  - low energy or fatigue
  - low self-esteem

- poor concentration or difficulty making decisions
- feelings of hopelessness

- During the two-year period (one year for children or adolescents) of the disturbance, the person has never been without the symptoms in the two criteria listed above for more than two months at a time.

- No major depressive episode has been present during the first two years of the disturbance (one year for children and adolescents); that is, the disturbance is not better accounted for by chronic major depressive disorder, or major depressive disorder, in partial remission. Note: There may have been a previous major depressive episode provided there was a full remission (no significant signs or symptoms for two months) before development of the dysthymic disorder. In addition, after the initial two years (one year in children or adolescents) of dysthymic disorder, there may be superimposed episodes of major depressive disorder, in which case both diagnoses may be given when the criteria are met for a major depressive episode.

- There has never been a manic episode, a mixed episode, or a hypomanic episode, and criteria have never been met for cyclothymic disorder.

- The disturbance does not occur exclusively during the course of a chronic psychotic disorder, such as schizophrenia or delusional disorder.

- The symptoms are not due to the direct physiological effects of a substance (for example, a drug of abuse, a medication) or a general medical condition (for example, hypothyroidism).

- The symptoms cause clinically significant distress or impairment in social, occupational, or other important areas of functioning.

Bipolar Disorder

Bipolar disorder is a recurrent mood disorder featuring one or more episodes of mania or mixed episodes of mania and depression. Bipolar disorder (which is also known as bipolar affective disorder and manic depression) is distinct from major depressive disorder by virtue of a history of manic or hypomanic (milder and not psychotic) episodes. Other differences concern the nature of depression in bipolar disorder. Its depressive episodes are typically associated with an earlier age at onset, a greater likelihood of reversed vegetative symptoms, more frequent episodes or recurrences, and a higher familial prevalence. Another noteworthy difference between bipolar and nonbipolar groups is the differential therapeutic effect of lithium salts, which are more helpful for bipolar disorder.

Mania is derived from a French word that literally means crazed or frenzied. The mood disturbance can range from pure euphoria or elation to irritability to a labile admixture that also includes dysphoria. Thought content is usually grandiose but also can be paranoid. Grandiosity usually takes the form both of overvalued ideas (for example, thinking "My book is the best one ever written") and of frank delusions (for example, thinking "I have radio transmitters implanted in my head and the Martians are monitoring my thoughts.") Auditory and visual hallucinations complicate more severe episodes. Speed of thought increases, and ideas typically race through the manic person's consciousness. Nevertheless, distractibility and poor concentration commonly impair implementation. Judgment also can be severely compromised; spending sprees, offensive or disinhibited behavior, and promiscuity or other objectively reckless behaviors are commonplace. Subjective energy, libido, and activity typically increase but a perceived reduced need for sleep can sap physical reserves. Sleep deprivation also can exacerbate cognitive difficulties and contribute to development of catatonia or a florid, confusional state known as delirious mania. If the manic patient is delirious, paranoid, or catatonic, the behavior is difficult to distinguish from that of a schizophrenic patient. Clinicians are prone to misdiagnose mania as schizophrenia in African Americans. Most people with bipolar disorder have a history of remission and at least satisfactory functioning before onset of the index episode of illness.

In *DSM-IV*, bipolar depressions are divided into type I (prior mania) and type II (prior hypomanic episodes only). About 1.1 percent of the adult population suffers from the type I form, and 0.6 percent from the type II form. Episodes of mania occur, on average, every two to four years, although accelerated mood cycles can occur annually or even more frequently. The type I form of bipolar disorder is about equally common in men and women, unlike major depressive disorder, which is more common in women.

Hypomania, as suggested above, is the subsyndromal counterpart of mania. By definition, an episode of hypomania is never psychotic nor are hypomanic episodes associated with marked impairments in judgment or performance. In fact, some people with bipolar disorder long for the productive energy and heightened creativity of the hypomanic phase.

Hypomania can be a transitional state (that is, early in an episode of mania), although at least 50 percent of those who have hypomanic episodes never become manic. Whereas a majority have a history of major depressive episodes (bipolar type II disorder), others become hypomanic only during antidepressant treatment. Despite the relatively mild nature of hypomania, the prognosis for patients with bipolar type II disorder is poorer than that for recurrent (unipolar) major depression, and there is some evidence that the risk of rapid cycling (four or more episodes each year) is greater than with bipolar type I. Women are at higher risk for rapid cycling bipolar disorder than men. Women with bipolar disorder are also at increased risk for an episode during pregnancy and the months following childbirth.

Criteria for Manic Episode (DSM-IV)

- A distinct period of abnormally and persistently elevated, expansive, or irritable mood, lasting at least one week (or any duration if hospitalization is necessary).

- During the period of mood disturbance, three (or more) of the following symptoms have persisted (four if the mood is only irritable) and have been present to a significant degree:
  - inflated self-esteem or grandiosity
  - decreased need for sleep (for example, feels rested after only three hours of sleep)
  - more talkative than usual or pressure to keep talking
  - flight of ideas or subjective experience that thoughts are racing
  - distractibility (attention too easily drawn to unimportant or irrelevant external stimuli)
  - increase in goal-directed activity (either socially, at work or school, or sexually) or psychomotor agitation
  - excessive involvement in pleasurable activities that have a high potential for painful consequences (for example, engaging in unrestrained buying sprees, sexual indiscretions, or foolish business investments)

- The symptoms do not meet criteria for a mixed episode.

- The mood disturbance is sufficiently severe to cause marked impairment in occupational functioning or in usual social activities or relationships with others, or to necessitate hospitalization to prevent harm to self or others, or there are psychotic features.

- The symptoms are not due to the direct physiological effects of a substance (for example, a drug of abuse, a medication, or other treatment) or general medical condition (for example, hyperthyroidism). Note: Manic-like episodes that are clearly caused by somatic antidepressant treatment (for example, medication, electroconvulsive therapy, light therapy) should not count toward a diagnosis of bipolar I disorder.

Cyclothymia

Cyclothymia is marked by manic and depressive states, yet neither are of sufficient intensity nor duration to merit a diagnosis of bipolar disorder or major depressive disorder. The diagnosis of cyclothymia is appropriate if there is a history of hypomania, but no prior episodes of mania or major depression. Longitudinal followup studies indicate that the risk of bipolar disorder developing in patients with cyclothymia is about 33 percent; although 33 times greater than that for the general population, this rate of risk still is too low to justify viewing cyclothymia as merely an early manifestation of bipolar type I disorder.

Diagnostic Criteria for Cyclothymic Disorder (DSM-IV)

- For at least two years, the presence of numerous periods with hypomanic symptoms and numerous periods with depressive symptoms that do not meet criteria for a major depressive episode. Note: In children and adolescents, the duration must be at least one year.

- During the above two-year period (one year in children and adolescents), the person has not been without the symptoms for more than two months at a time.

- No major depressive episode, manic episode, or mixed episode has been present during the first two years of the disturbance. Note: After the initial two years (one year in children and adolescents) of cyclothymic disorder, there may be superimposed manic or mixed episodes (in which case both bipolar I disorder and cyclothymic disorder may be diagnosed) or major depressive episodes (in which case both bipolar II disorder and cyclothymic disorder may be diagnosed).

- The symptoms are not better accounted for by schizoaffective disorder and are not superimposed on schizophrenia, schizophreniform disorder, delusional disorder, or psychotic disorder not otherwise specified.

- The symptoms are not due to the direct physiological effects of a substance (for example, a drug of abuse, a medication) or a general medical condition (for example, hyperthyroidism).

- The symptoms cause clinically significant distress or impairment in social, occupational, or other important areas of functioning.

Differential Diagnosis

Mood disorders are sometimes caused by general medical conditions or medications. Classic examples include the depressive syndromes associated with dominant hemispheric strokes, hypothyroidism, Cushing's disease, and pancreatic cancer. Among medications associated with depression, antihypertensives and oral contraceptives are the most frequent examples. Transient depressive syndromes are also common during withdrawal from alcohol and various other drugs of abuse. Mania is not uncommon during high-dose systemic therapy with glucocorticoids and has been associated with intoxication by stimulant and sympathomimetic drugs and with central nervous system (CNS) lupus, CNS human immunodeficiency viral (HIV) infections, and nondominant hemispheric strokes or tumors. Together, mood disorders due to known physiological or medical causes may account for as many as five to 15 percent of all treated cases. They often go unrecognized until after standard therapies have failed.

A challenge to diagnosticians is to balance their search for relatively uncommon disorders with their sensitivity to aspects of the medical history or review of symptoms that might have etiologic significance. For example, the onset of a depressive episode a few weeks or months after the patient has begun taking a new blood-pressure medication should raise the physician's index of suspicion. Ultimately, occult or covert medical illnesses must always be considered when an apparently clear-cut case of a mood disorder is refractory to standard treatments. Cultural influences on the manifestation and diagnosis of depression are also important for the diagnostician to identify.

Chapter 4

Seasonal Affective Disorder

Seasonal affective disorder (SAD) is a type of depression whose onset typically begins in late fall as daylight hours get shorter. It begins to lift as spring approaches with daylight hours growing longer. To be properly diagnosed as SAD, an individual must have experienced seasonal depression for at least two consecutive years. SAD can be a complicated diagnosis as the individual may have other depressive or anxiety disorders. SAD is seen more often in women, while children and adolescents are less likely to experience SAD. It has not yet been demonstrated that SAD runs in families, but depression, in general, often does.

Usually SAD symptoms are not as severe as a non-seasonal major depression, and they are not tied to a traumatic event as a major depression may be. SAD symptoms include those of a typical major depression, such as a depressed mood, anxiety, irritability and a general loss of interest or motivation. However, SAD patients usually sleep more, eat more, and may crave and binge on carbohydrates. As a result, they may gain weight. There are seldom thoughts of suicide.

In the northern hemisphere, the incidence of SAD appears to increase as one travels farther north to colder, darker climates. Individuals living in northern climates who travel south during the winter to sunnier locations may find their symptoms temporarily relieved.

"Seasonal Affective Disorder," by David B. Bresnahan, MD, *MCW HealthLink*, Medical College of Wisconsin Physicians and Clinics, January 2001, © 2001 Medical College of Wisconsin; reprinted with permission of the Medical College of Wisconsin/MCW HealthLink, http://healthlink.mcw.edu.

Causes of SAD

A change in the individual's circadian rhythms—brought on by reduced exposure to sunlight—may be related to SAD. Circadian rhythms are the body's natural 24-hour cycles that vary from individual to individual. This rhythm determines natural sleep/wake cycles, hormone secretion, and other functions. Circadian rhythms may be affected by light exposure, and normal circadian rhythms have been connected to a normal mood state.

SAD patients may have greater vulnerability to altered rhythms, particularly where brain chemicals called neurotransmitters are concerned. In particular, a reduced exposure to light causes the brain to secrete more melatonin, which may lead to SAD symptoms. Serotonin, too, may play a role, as might the natural steroid cortisol.

Treatment for SAD

The standard treatment for SAD is increased exposure to light— well beyond that of room lighting—with the use of a lightbox. A lightbox should offer a minimum lux value of 2,000–2,500. Some lightboxes have a lux value as high as 10,000. A lightbox should be situated within three feet of the patient and used for between 30 minutes and two hours per session. It is not necessary to stare at the light, but it must be possible for light to enter the eye to affect the brain and, in turn, mood. Many patients choose simply to read while using a lightbox.

About 80% of SAD patients have great difficulty waking in the morning. They should use the lightbox at that time. The remainder of patients may find they are alert in the morning but grow excessively tired later in the day. These individuals should use a lightbox in the late afternoon or early evening.

However, increased light exposure may not relieve symptoms. Some patients are prescribed anti-depressants (such as Prozac, Paxil, or Zoloft) or central nervous system stimulants (such as Ritalin). Regular exercise may be of great benefit to help regulate sleep, deal with anxiety and elevate mood.

Before diagnosing yourself as suffering from SAD and rushing to buy a lightbox, visit your physician to be thoroughly evaluated. A thyroid disorder and other medical conditions should be ruled out before a SAD diagnosis can be properly made.

Chapter 5

Postpartum Depression

Having a baby is one of the most exciting and joyous events in a woman's life. Life with a new baby can be thrilling and rewarding, but it can also be stressful and difficult for the new mother. The physical and emotional turmoil associated with pregnancy and childbirth leaves many new mothers feeling sad, anxious, afraid, or confused after delivery. These feelings are common and are often dismissed as "normal." However, many women who are experiencing these emotions have postpartum depression, and they need medical treatment.[1]

What Is Postpartum Depression?

The term postpartum depression describes the range of physical, emotional, and behavioral changes that many new mothers experience following the delivery of their babies. Symptoms of this condition can range from mild to severe. A new mother's depression may be a mild, brief bout of "baby blues"; or she may suffer from postpartum depression, a much more serious condition. In some cases, new mothers may have postpartum psychosis, a relatively rare but severe and incapacitating illness.[2]

The Range of Postpartum Conditions

The "Baby Blues"

This condition occurs in many new mothers in the days immediately following childbirth.[3] It is characterized by sudden mood swings,

"Women and Postpartum Depression," Office on Women's Health (online at www.4woman.gov/owh), June 2001.

which range from euphoria to intense sadness. Symptoms may include crying for no apparent reason; impatience; irritability; restlessness; anxiety; feelings of loneliness, sadness, and low self-esteem; increased sensitivity; and heightened feelings of vulnerability. The "baby blues" may last only a few hours or as long as one to two weeks after delivery. The condition may disappear as quickly and as suddenly as it appeared, without medical treatment.[4]

Postpartum Depression (PPD)

Roughly 10% of pregnancies result in postpartum depression,[5] which can occur a few days or even months after delivery. Postpartum depression can occur after the birth of any child, not just the first.[6] This condition is characterized by more intense feelings of sadness, despair, anxiety, and irritability. It often disrupts a woman's ability to function, which is the key sign that medical attention is necessary.

Left untreated, symptoms may worsen and linger for as long as a year. This physical disorder, however, can be diagnosed and its symptoms alleviated.[7]

Postpartum Psychosis

This serious mental illness affects approximately 1 in 500–1,000 new mothers.[8] Onset is severe and quick, usually within the first three months after delivery. Women who suffer from postpartum psychosis may completely lose touch with reality, often experiencing hallucinations and delusions.[9] Other symptoms may include insomnia, agitation, and bizarre feelings and behavior.[10]

Postpartum psychosis should be treated as a medical emergency. Patients need immediate medical assistance, which almost always includes medication. In many cases, women who are suffering from this condition are hospitalized.[11]

Who Is At Risk for Postpartum Depression?

Any woman who is pregnant, had a baby within the past several months, miscarried, or recently weaned a child from breast-feeding can suffer from postpartum depression. A woman can have this condition regardless of her age, socioeconomic status, or the number of children she has borne.[12]

Postpartum depression is more likely to occur if a woman had any of the following:

- previous postpartum depression

- depression not related to pregnancy

- severe premenstrual syndrome (PMS)

- a non-supportive partner; and stress related to family, marriage, occupation, housing, and other events during pregnancy or after childbirth.[13]

Symptoms of Postpartum Depression

Symptoms of postpartum depression include:

- restlessness, irritability, or excessive crying;

- headaches, chest pains, heart palpitations, numbness, hyperventilation;

- an inability to sleep or extreme exhaustion or both;

- loss of appetite and weight loss, or, conversely, overeating and weight gain;

- difficulty concentrating, remembering, or making decisions;

- an excessive amount of concern or disinterest in the baby;

- feelings of inadequacy, guilt, and worthlessness;

- a fear of harming the baby or one's self;

- a loss of interest or pleasure in activities, including sex.[14]

Women who have a previous history of mood disorders, such as depression, are at an increased risk of relapse after delivery.[15] At least 33% of women who have had postpartum depression have a recurrence of symptoms after a subsequent delivery.[16] As many as 60% of women with the psychiatric condition known as bipolar disorder have a relapse after childbirth.[17] Fortunately, prenatal screening can identify these women during their pregnancy.[18]

Some women may not be depressed, but they may feel very anxious. These women might suffer from postpartum anxiety or panic disorder. Symptoms can include intense anxiety and fear, rapid breathing, an accelerated heart rate, hot or cold flashes, chest pain, and shaking or dizziness.[19]

Factors Associated with Postpartum Depression

Postpartum depression is a complex mixture of biological, emotional, and behavioral changes. The exact cause of this condition is still unknown.[20]

A variety of hormonal changes may trigger its symptoms. Estrogen and progesterone levels—which increase tenfold during pregnancy to accommodate the growing fetus—suddenly and rapidly drop in the first 24 hours after childbirth. After delivery, these hormones fall to even lower levels, to pre-pregnancy levels.[21] These decreases may trigger depression, just as smaller hormonal changes can affect a woman's moods before menstruation.[22]

Thyroid levels may also drop sharply after birth. A thyroid deficiency can produce symptoms that mimic depression, such as mood swings, severe agitation, fatigue, insomnia, and anxiety. Simple thyroid tests can determine if this condition is causing a woman's postpartum depression.[23]

Aside from biological changes, a variety of physical, psychological, and environmental factors can lead to postpartum depression.

- Feelings of fatigue following delivery, broken sleep patterns, and insufficient rest often prevent a new mother from regaining her full strength for weeks, especially if she has had a cesarean delivery.[24]

- Taking responsibility for an expanding family can be overwhelming. Some new mothers have feelings of self-doubt and inadequacy. They may doubt their ability to be a good mother.[25]

- Many new mothers suffer from stress, which can be caused by changes in work and home routines. Stress can also be caused by the pressure a woman places on herself to be the "perfect mother," a highly unrealistic goal.[26]

- New mothers often experience feelings of loss. After the birth of a baby, many women feel a loss of identity, a loss of control, a loss of a slim figure, and a perceived loss of physical attractiveness.[27]

- In addition, their free time is suddenly restricted, they are confined indoors for long periods of time, and they have less time to spend with their baby's father.[28]

Treating Postpartum Depression

Postpartum depression is treated much like other types of depression. The most common treatments for depression are antidepressant medication, psychotherapy, participation in a support group, or a combination of these treatments. However, some antidepressants can contaminate breast milk. Women who breast-feed should talk to their doctors to determine the most suitable treatment option.[30]

40

The most appropriate treatment depends on the nature and severity of the postpartum depression and, to some extent, on individual preference. It is important to recognize that postpartum depression is both temporary and treatable.

New mothers with postpartum depression can practice a number of self-care strategies.

- Good, old-fashioned rest is important. Always try to nap during the baby's nap time.

- Relieve some of the pressure you may be feeling. Do as much as you can, and leave the rest. If possible, ask your husband or partner to share night-time feeding duties and household chores.

- To help you through the readjustment process, seek out emotional support from your husband or partner, family, and friends.

- Isolation often perpetuates the depression. Get dressed and leave the house for at least a short time each day.

- Make an effort to spend time alone with your partner.

- Ask your physician to advise you on possible medical treatments. Be assertive about your concerns. Not all health care professionals recognize the symptoms or seriousness of postpartum depression. Get a referral to a mental health professional who specializes in treating depression.[31]

- Talk with other mothers, so you can learn from their experiences.

- Join one of the many support groups that are now available to help women who suffer from postpartum depression. Call a hotline to access information and services.

For Further Information

National Women's Health Information Center (NWHIC)
Toll-free: 1-800-994-WOMAN (1-800-994-9662)
Toll-free TDD: 1-888-220-5446
http://www.4woman.gov

Additional resources for information and support can be found in the end section of this book.

Notes

1. Depression After Delivery, http://www.behavenet.com/dadinc.

2. Ibid.

3. The American College of Obstetricians and Gynecologists, Labor, Delivery, and Postpartum Care, (AP091), "Postpartum Depression," ACOG Patient Education Pamphlet, August 1990, Reviewed June 1995, http://www.acog.com.

4. Ibid.

5. National Institute of Mental Health, Office of Communications and Public Liaison, fax communication to OWH, 6/22/01.

6. ACOG, Postpartum Depression.

7. Ibid.

8. National Institute of Mental Health, Office of Communications and Public Liaison, fax communication to OWH, 6/22/01 and Kruckman, L., and Smith, Susan. "An Introduction to Postpartum Illness." In *Postpartum Depression Resource Guide* at http://www.chss.iup.edu/anthropology/projects/depression/postpart.html, p. 7.

9. Ibid.

10. Depression After Delivery, p. 2.

11. Ibid.

12. Ibid. p. 3.

13. "Postpartum Depression and the 'Baby Blues'," *American Family Physician*, April 15, 1999. http://www.aafp.org/afp/990415ap/990415e.html, p. 2.

14. An Introduction to Postpartum Illness, p. 6.

15. Epperson, C. Neill. "Postpartum Major Depression: Detection and Treatment." In *American Family Physician*, April 15, 1999, p. 4. http://www.aafp.org/afp/990415ap/2247.html

16. Ibid.

17. Ibid.

18. Postpartum Depression and the "Baby Blues," p. 4.

19. Depression After Delivery, p. 2.

20. An Introduction to Postpartum Illness, p. 7.

21. Ibid.

22. ACOG, Postpartum Depression.

23. Ibid.

24. Ibid.

25. Ibid.

26. Ibid.

27. Ibid.

28. Ibid.

29. Postpartum Depression and the "Baby Blues," p. 2.

30. Ibid.

31. Ibid.

Chapter 6

Dysthymic Disorder

What is dysthymic disorder?

Dysthymic disorder, or dysthymia, is a type of depression that lasts for at least two years. Some people suffer from dysthymia for years. The depression is usually mild or moderate, rather than severe. Most people with dysthymia can't tell for sure when they first became depressed.

Symptoms of dysthymic disorder include a poor appetite or overeating, difficulty sleeping or sleeping too much, low energy, fatigue and feelings of hopelessness. But people with dysthymic disorder may have periods of normal mood that last up to two months. Family members and friends may not even know that their loved one is depressed. Even though this type of depression is mild, it may make it difficult for a person to function at home, school or work.

How common is dysthymic disorder?

Dysthymic disorder is a fairly common type of depression. It is estimated that up to 3% of people have dysthymia. Dysthymia can begin in childhood or in adulthood. Like most types of depression, it appears to be more common in women. No one knows why depression is more common in women.

What causes dysthymic disorder?

No one knows for sure what causes dysthymia. It may be related to some changes in the brain that involve a chemical called serotonin (say "seer-o-tone-in"). Personality problems, medical problems, and ongoing life stress may also play a role.

How is dysthymic disorder diagnosed?

If you think you have dysthymia, discuss your concerns with your doctor. Your doctor will ask you questions to find out if you have depression and, if so, to identify the type of depression you have. Your doctor may ask you questions about your health and your symptoms, such as how well you're sleeping, if you feel tired all of the time, and if you have trouble concentrating. Your doctor will also consider medical reasons that may cause you to feel depressed, such as problems with your thyroid or a certain medicine you may be taking.

What is the treatment for dysthymic disorder?

Dysthymic disorder can be treated with an antidepressant medicine. This type of drug relieves depression. Antidepressants are commonly prescribed, and they are safe. They do not create an artificial "high," and they are not habit-forming.

If you are given an antidepressant, it may take a number of weeks, or even several months, before you and your doctor know whether the drug is helping you. It is important for you to take the medicine exactly as it is prescribed. If the antidepressant drug helps you feel better, you may need to take this medicine for several years. In other words, continue to take the antidepressant drug until your doctor tells you to stop, even though you begin to feel better. If you stop taking the medicine, you may get depressed again.

Will I have to see a psychiatrist or psychotherapist?

You may not have to see a psychiatrist or psychotherapist unless medication is not working or you have problems taking the drugs that are usually prescribed for depression. Sometimes, in addition to taking an antidepressant medicine, patients are referred for psychotherapy to help them deal with specific problems. This type of therapy can be very helpful for some people. In most cases, the treatment of dysthymic disorder is specifically planned for each person.

What can I do to help myself feel better?

Talking to your doctor about how you're feeling and getting treatment for dysthymic disorder are the first steps to feeling better. The following are other ways to make yourself feel better:

- Get involved in activities that make you feel good or make you feel like you've accomplished something. For example, go to a movie, take a drive on a pleasant day, go to a ball game or work in the garden.

- Eat well-balanced, healthy meals.

- Don't use drugs or alcohol. Both can make depression worse.

- Exercise as much as you can. Exercising 4 to 6 times a week for 30 to 60 minutes each time is a good goal. Exercise can help lift your mood.

Chapter 7

Bipolar Disorder (Manic Depression)

Bipolar disorder, also known as manic-depressive illness, is a brain disorder that causes unusual shifts in a person's mood, energy, and ability to function. Different from the normal ups and downs that everyone goes through, the symptoms of bipolar disorder are severe. They can result in damaged relationships, poor job or school performance, and even suicide. But there is good news: bipolar disorder can be treated, and people with this illness can lead full and productive lives.

More than 2 million American adults,[1] or about one percent of the population age 18 and older in any given year,[2] have bipolar disorder. Bipolar disorder typically develops in late adolescence or early adulthood. However, some people have their first symptoms during childhood, and some develop them late in life. It is often not recognized as an illness, and people may suffer for years before it is properly diagnosed and treated. Like diabetes or heart disease, bipolar disorder is a long-term illness that must be carefully managed throughout a person's life.

What Are the Symptoms of Bipolar Disorder?

Bipolar disorder causes dramatic mood swings—from overly "high" and/or irritable to sad and hopeless, and then back again, often with periods of normal mood in between. Severe changes in energy and

"Bipolar Disorder," by Melissa Spearing, National Institute of Mental Health (NIMH), NIH Publication No. 01-3679, 2001.

behavior go along with these changes in mood. The periods of highs and lows are called episodes of mania and depression.

Manic Episode

Signs and symptoms of mania (or a manic episode) include:

- Increased energy, activity, and restlessness
- Excessively "high," overly good, euphoric mood
- Extreme irritability
- Racing thoughts and talking very fast, jumping from one idea to another
- Distractibility, can't concentrate well
- Little sleep needed
- Unrealistic beliefs in one's abilities and powers
- Poor judgment
- Spending sprees
- A lasting period of behavior that is different from usual
- Increased sexual drive
- Abuse of drugs, particularly cocaine, alcohol, and sleeping medications
- Provocative, intrusive, or aggressive behavior
- Denial that anything is wrong

A manic episode is diagnosed if elevated mood occurs with three or more of the other symptoms most of the day, nearly every day, for one week or longer. If the mood is irritable, four additional symptoms must be present.

Depressive Episode

Signs and symptoms of depression (or a depressive episode) include:

- Lasting sad, anxious, or empty mood
- Feelings of hopelessness or pessimism
- Feelings of guilt, worthlessness, or helplessness

- Loss of interest or pleasure in activities once enjoyed, including sex
- Decreased energy, a feeling of fatigue or of being "slowed down"
- Difficulty concentrating, remembering, making decisions
- Restlessness or irritability
- Sleeping too much, or can't sleep
- Change in appetite and/or unintended weight loss or gain
- Chronic pain or other persistent bodily symptoms that are not caused by physical illness or injury
- Thoughts of death or suicide, or suicide attempts

A depressive episode is diagnosed if five or more of these symptoms last most of the day, nearly every day, for a period of two weeks or longer.

A Range of Mood States

A mild to moderate level of mania is called hypomania. Hypomania may feel good to the person who experiences it and may even be associated with good functioning and enhanced productivity. Thus even when family and friends learn to recognize the mood swings as possible bipolar disorder, the person may deny that anything is wrong. Without proper treatment, however, hypomania can become severe mania in some people or can switch into depression.

Sometimes, severe episodes of mania or depression include symptoms of psychosis (or psychotic symptoms). Common psychotic symptoms are hallucinations (hearing, seeing, or otherwise sensing the presence of things not actually there) and delusions (false, strongly held beliefs not influenced by logical reasoning or explained by a person's usual cultural concepts). Psychotic symptoms in bipolar disorder tend to reflect the extreme mood state at the time. For example, delusions of grandiosity, such as believing one is the President or has special powers or wealth, may occur during mania; delusions of guilt or worthlessness, such as believing that one is ruined and penniless or has committed some terrible crime, may appear during depression. People with bipolar disorder who have these symptoms are sometimes incorrectly diagnosed as having schizophrenia, another severe mental illness.

It may be helpful to think of the various mood states in bipolar disorder as a spectrum or continuous range. At one end is severe depression, above which is moderate depression and then mild low mood, which many people call "the blues" when it is short-lived, but is termed "dysthymia" when it is chronic. Then there is normal or balanced mood, above which comes hypomania (mild to moderate mania), and then severe mania.

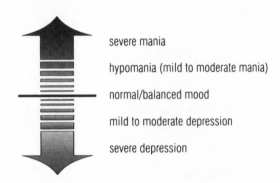

severe mania

hypomania (mild to moderate mania)

normal/balanced mood

mild to moderate depression

severe depression

Figure 7.1. The various mood states in bipolar disorder.

In some people, however, symptoms of mania and depression may occur together in what is called a mixed bipolar state. Symptoms of a mixed state often include agitation, trouble sleeping, significant change in appetite, psychosis, and suicidal thinking. A person may have a very sad, hopeless mood while at the same time feeling extremely energized.

Bipolar disorder may appear to be a problem other than mental illness—for instance, alcohol or drug abuse, poor school or work performance, or strained interpersonal relationships. Such problems in fact may be signs of an underlying mood disorder.

Mood Experiences

Descriptions offered by people with bipolar disorder give valuable insights into the various mood states associated with the illness:

Depression: I doubt completely my ability to do anything well. It seems as though my mind has slowed down and burned out to the point of being virtually useless.... [I am] haunt[ed]... with the total, the desperate hopelessness of it all.... Others say, "It's only temporary, it will pass, you will get over it," but of course they haven't any idea of how I feel, although they are certain they do. If I can't feel, move, think, or care, then what on earth is the point?

Hypomania: At first when I'm high, it's tremendous... ideas are fast... like shooting stars you follow until brighter ones appear.... All shyness disappears, the right words and gestures are suddenly there... uninteresting people, things become intensely interesting. Sensuality is pervasive, the desire to seduce and be seduced is irresistible. Your marrow is infused with unbelievable feelings of ease, power, well-being, omnipotence, euphoria... you can do anything... but, somewhere this changes.

Mania: The fast ideas become too fast and there are far too many... overwhelming confusion replaces clarity... you stop keeping up with it—memory goes. Infectious humor ceases to amuse. Your friends become frightened.... everything is now against the grain... you are irritable, angry, frightened, uncontrollable, and trapped.

Suicide

Some people with bipolar disorder become suicidal. Anyone who is thinking about committing suicide needs immediate attention, preferably from a mental health professional or a physician. Anyone who talks about suicide should be taken seriously. Risk for suicide appears to be higher earlier in the course of the illness. Therefore, recognizing bipolar disorder early and learning how best to manage it may decrease the risk of death by suicide.

Signs and Symptoms of Suicidal Feelings

Signs and symptoms that may accompany suicidal feelings include:

- talking about feeling suicidal or wanting to die
- feeling hopeless, that nothing will ever change or get better
- feeling helpless, that nothing one does makes any difference
- feeling like a burden to family and friends
- abusing alcohol or drugs
- putting affairs in order (for example, organizing finances or giving away possessions to prepare for one's death)

- writing a suicide note

- putting oneself in harm's way, or in situations where there is a danger of being killed

If you are feeling suicidal or know someone who is:

- call a doctor, emergency room, or 911 right away to get immediate help

- make sure you, or the suicidal person, are not left alone

- make sure that access is prevented to large amounts of medication, weapons, or other items that could be used for self-harm

While some suicide attempts are carefully planned over time, others are impulsive acts that have not been well thought out; thus, the final point above may be a valuable long-term strategy for people with bipolar disorder. Either way, it is important to understand that suicidal feelings and actions are symptoms of an illness that can be treated. With proper treatment, suicidal feelings can be overcome.

What Is the Course of Bipolar Disorder?

Episodes of mania and depression typically recur across the life span. Between episodes, most people with bipolar disorder are free of symptoms, but as many as one-third of people have some residual symptoms. A small percentage of people experience chronic unremitting symptoms despite treatment.[4]

The classic form of the illness, which involves recurrent episodes of mania and depression, is called bipolar I disorder. Some people, however, never develop severe mania but instead experience milder episodes of hypomania that alternate with depression; this form of the illness is called bipolar II disorder. When four or more episodes of illness occur within a 12-month period, a person is said to have rapid-cycling bipolar disorder. Some people experience multiple episodes within a single week, or even within a single day. Rapid cycling tends to develop later in the course of illness and is more common among women than among men.

People with bipolar disorder can lead healthy and productive lives when the illness is effectively treated (see below—"How Is Bipolar Disorder Treated?"). Without treatment, however, the natural course of bipolar disorder tends to worsen. Over time a person may suffer more frequent (more rapid-cycling) and more severe manic and depressive episodes than those experienced when the illness first appeared.[5] But in most cases, proper treatment can help reduce the frequency and severity of episodes and can help people with bipolar disorder maintain good quality of life.

Can Children and Adolescents Have Bipolar Disorder?

Both children and adolescents can develop bipolar disorder. It is more likely to affect the children of parents who have the illness.

Unlike many adults with bipolar disorder, whose episodes tend to be more clearly defined, children and young adolescents with the illness often experience very fast mood swings between depression and mania many times within a day.[6] Children with mania are more likely to be irritable and prone to destructive tantrums than to be overly happy and elated. Mixed symptoms also are common in youths with bipolar disorder. Older adolescents who develop the illness may have more classic, adult-type episodes and symptoms.

Bipolar disorder in children and adolescents can be hard to tell apart from other problems that may occur in these age groups. For example, while irritability and aggressiveness can indicate bipolar disorder, they also can be symptoms of attention deficit hyperactivity disorder, conduct disorder, oppositional defiant disorder, or other types of mental disorders more common among adults such as major depression or schizophrenia. Drug abuse also may lead to such symptoms.

For any illness, however, effective treatment depends on appropriate diagnosis. Children or adolescents with emotional and behavioral symptoms should be carefully evaluated by a mental health professional. Any child or adolescent who has suicidal feelings, talks about suicide, or attempts suicide should be taken seriously and should receive immediate help from a mental health specialist.

What Causes Bipolar Disorder?

Scientists are learning about the possible causes of bipolar disorder through several kinds of studies. Most scientists now agree that there is no single cause for bipolar disorder—rather, many factors act together to produce the illness.

Because bipolar disorder tends to run in families, researchers have been searching for specific genes—the microscopic "building blocks" of DNA inside all cells that influence how the body and mind work and grow—passed down through generations that may increase a person's chance of developing the illness. But genes are not the whole story. Studies of identical twins, who share all the same genes, indicate that both genes and other factors play a role in bipolar disorder. If bipolar disorder were caused entirely by genes, then the identical twin of someone with the illness would always develop the illness, and research has shown that this is not the case. But if one twin has bipolar disorder, the other twin is more likely to develop the illness than is another sibling.[7]

In addition, findings from gene research suggest that bipolar disorder, like other mental illnesses, does not occur because of a single gene.[8] It appears likely that many different genes act together, and in combination with other factors of the person or the person's environment, to cause bipolar disorder. Finding these genes, each of which contributes only a small amount toward the vulnerability to bipolar disorder, has been extremely difficult. But scientists expect that the advanced research tools now being used will lead to these discoveries and to new and better treatments for bipolar disorder.

Brain-imaging studies are helping scientists learn what goes wrong in the brain to produce bipolar disorder and other mental illnesses.[9,10] New brain-imaging techniques allow researchers to take pictures of the living brain at work, to examine its structure and activity, without the need for surgery or other invasive procedures. These techniques include magnetic resonance imaging (MRI), positron emission tomography (PET), and functional magnetic resonance imaging (fMRI). There is evidence from imaging studies that the brains of people with bipolar disorder may differ from the brains of healthy individuals. As the differences are more clearly identified and defined through research, scientists will gain a better understanding of the underlying causes of the illness, and eventually may be able to predict which types of treatment will work most effectively.

How Is Bipolar Disorder Treated?

Most people with bipolar disorder—even those with the most severe forms—can achieve substantial stabilization of their mood swings and related symptoms with proper treatment.[11,12,13] Because bipolar disorder is a recurrent illness, long-term preventive treatment is strongly recommended and almost always indicated. A strategy that combines medication and psychosocial treatment is optimal for managing the disorder over time.

In most cases, bipolar disorder is much better controlled if treatment is continuous than if it is on and off. But even when there are no breaks in treatment, mood changes can occur and should be reported immediately to your doctor. The doctor may be able to prevent a full-blown episode by making adjustments to the treatment plan. Working closely with the doctor and communicating openly about treatment concerns and options can make a difference in treatment effectiveness.

In addition, keeping a chart of daily mood symptoms, treatments, sleep patterns, and life events may help people with bipolar disorder and their families to better understand the illness. This chart also can help the doctor track and treat the illness most effectively.

Medications

Medications for bipolar disorder are prescribed by psychiatrists— medical doctors (M.D.s) with expertise in the diagnosis and treatment of mental disorders. While primary care physicians who do not specialize in psychiatry also may prescribe these medications, it is recommended that people with bipolar disorder see a psychiatrist for treatment.

Medications known as "mood stabilizers" usually are prescribed to help control bipolar disorder.[11] Several different types of mood stabilizers are available. In general, people with bipolar disorder continue treatment with mood stabilizers for extended periods of time (years). Other medications are added when necessary, typically for shorter periods, to treat episodes of mania or depression that break through despite the mood stabilizer.

- Lithium, the first mood-stabilizing medication approved by the U.S. Food and Drug Administration (FDA) for treatment of mania, is often very effective in controlling mania and preventing the recurrence of both manic and depressive episodes.

- Anticonvulsant medications, such as valproate (Depakote®) or carbamazepine (Tegretol®), also can have mood-stabilizing effects and may be especially useful for difficult-to-treat bipolar episodes. Valproate was FDA-approved in 1995 for treatment of mania.

- Newer anticonvulsant medications, including lamotrigine (Lamictal®), gabapentin (Neurontin®), and topiramate (Topamax®), are being studied to determine how well they work in stabilizing mood cycles.

- Anticonvulsant medications may be combined with lithium, or with each other, for maximum effect.

- Children and adolescents with bipolar disorder generally are treated with lithium, but valproate and carbamazepine also are used. Researchers are evaluating the safety and efficacy of these and other psychotropic medications in children and adolescents. There is some evidence that valproate may lead to adverse hormone changes in teenage girls and polycystic ovary syndrome in women who began taking the medication before age 20.[14] Therefore, young female patients taking valproate should be monitored carefully by a physician.

- Women with bipolar disorder who wish to conceive, or who become pregnant, face special challenges due to the possible harmful effects of existing mood stabilizing medications on the developing fetus and the nursing infant.[15] Therefore, the benefits and risks of all available treatment options should be discussed with a clinician skilled in this area. New treatments with reduced risks during pregnancy and lactation are under study.

- Atypical antipsychotic medications, including clozapine (Clozaril®), olanzapine (Zyprexa®), risperidone (Risperdal®), and ziprasidone (Zeldox®), are being studied as possible treatments for bipolar disorder. Evidence suggests clozapine may be helpful as a mood stabilizer for people who do not respond to lithium or anticonvulsants.[17] Other research has supported the efficacy of olanzapine for acute mania, an indication that has recently received FDA approval.[18] Olanzapine may also help relieve psychotic depression.[19]

- If insomnia is a problem, a high-potency benzodiazepine medication such as clonazepam (Klonopin®) or lorazepam (Ativan®) may be helpful to promote better sleep. However, since these medications may be habit-forming, they are best prescribed on a short-term basis. Other types of sedative medications, such as zolpidem (Ambien®), are sometimes used instead.

- Changes to the treatment plan may be needed at various times during the course of bipolar disorder to manage the illness most effectively. A psychiatrist should guide any changes in type or dose of medication.

- Be sure to tell the psychiatrist about all other prescription drugs, over-the-counter medications, or natural supplements you may be taking. This is important because certain medications and supplements taken together may cause adverse reactions.

- To reduce the chance of relapse or of developing a new episode, it is important to stick to the treatment plan. Talk to your doctor if you have any concerns about the medications.

Other Notes Regarding Medications for Bipolar Disorder

- Research has shown that people with bipolar disorder are at risk of switching into mania or hypomania, or of developing rapid cycling, during treatment with antidepressant medication.[16] Therefore, "mood-stabilizing" medications generally are required, alone or in combination with antidepressants, to protect people with bipolar disorder from this switch. Lithium and valproate are the most commonly used mood-stabilizing drugs today. However, research studies continue to evaluate the potential mood-stabilizing effects of newer medications.

- People with bipolar disorder often have abnormal thyroid gland function.[5] Because too much or too little thyroid hormone alone can lead to mood and energy changes, it is important that thyroid levels are carefully monitored by a physician. People with rapid cycling tend to have co-occurring thyroid problems and may need to take thyroid pills in addition to their medications for bipolar disorder. Also, lithium treatment may cause low thyroid levels in some people, resulting in the need for thyroid supplementation.

- Before starting a new medication for bipolar disorder, always talk with your psychiatrist and/or pharmacist about possible side effects. Depending on the medication, side effects may include weight gain, nausea, tremor, reduced sexual drive or performance, anxiety, hair loss, movement problems, or dry mouth. Be sure to tell the doctor about all side effects you notice during treatment. He or she may be able to change the dose or offer a different medication to relieve them. Your medication should not be changed or stopped without the psychiatrist's guidance.

Psychosocial Treatments

As an addition to medication, psychosocial treatments—including certain forms of psychotherapy (or "talk" therapy)—are helpful in providing support, education, and guidance to people with bipolar disorder and their families. Studies have shown that psychosocial interventions can lead to increased mood stability, fewer hospitalizations, and improved functioning in several areas.[13] A licensed psychologist, social worker, or counselor typically provides these therapies and often works together with the psychiatrist to monitor a patient's progress. The number, frequency, and type of sessions should be based on the treatment needs of each person.

Psychosocial interventions commonly used for bipolar disorder are cognitive behavioral therapy, psychoeducation, family therapy, and a newer technique, interpersonal and social rhythm therapy. NIMH researchers are studying how these interventions compare to one another when added to medication treatment for bipolar disorder.

- Cognitive behavioral therapy helps people with bipolar disorder learn to change inappropriate or negative thought patterns and behaviors associated with the illness.

- Psychoeducation involves teaching people with bipolar disorder about the illness and its treatment, and how to recognize signs of relapse so that early intervention can be sought before a full-blown illness episode occurs. Psychoeducation also may be helpful for family members.

- Family therapy uses strategies to reduce the level of distress within the family that may either contribute to or result from the ill person's symptoms.

- Interpersonal and social rhythm therapy helps people with bipolar disorder both to improve interpersonal relationships and to regularize their daily routines. Regular daily routines and sleep schedules may help protect against manic episodes.

- As with medication, it is important to follow the treatment plan for any psychosocial intervention to achieve the greatest benefit.

Other Treatments

In situations where medication, psychosocial treatment, and the combination of these interventions prove ineffective, or work too slowly to relieve severe symptoms such as psychosis or suicidality, electroconvulsive therapy (ECT) may be considered. ECT may also be considered to treat acute episodes when medical conditions, including pregnancy, make the use of medications too risky. ECT is a highly effective treatment for severe depressive, manic, and/or mixed episodes. The possibility of long-lasting memory problems, although a concern in the past, has been significantly reduced with modern ECT techniques. However, the potential benefits and risks of ECT, and of available alternative interventions, should be carefully reviewed and discussed with individuals considering this treatment and, where appropriate, with family or friends.[20]

Herbal or natural supplements, such as St. John's wort (*Hypericum perforatum*), have not been well studied, and little is known about their effects on bipolar disorder. Because the FDA does not regulate their production, different brands of these supplements can contain different amounts of active ingredient. Before trying herbal or natural supplements, it is important to discuss them with your doctor. There is evidence that St. John's wort can reduce the effectiveness of certain medications (see http://www.nimh.nih.gov/events/stjohnwort .cfm).[21] In addition, like prescription antidepressants, St. John's wort may cause a switch into mania in some individuals with bipolar disorder, especially if no mood stabilizer is being taken.[22]

Omega-3 fatty acids found in fish oil are being studied to determine their usefulness, alone and when added to conventional medications, for long-term treatment of bipolar disorder.[23]

A Long-Term Illness That Can Be Effectively Treated

Even though episodes of mania and depression naturally come and go, it is important to understand that bipolar disorder is a long-term illness that currently has no cure. Staying on treatment, even during well times, can help keep the disease under control and reduce the chance of having recurrent, worsening episodes.

Do Other Illnesses Co-occur with Bipolar Disorder?

Alcohol and drug abuse are very common among people with bipolar disorder. Research findings suggest that many factors may contribute to these substance abuse problems, including self-medication of symptoms, mood symptoms either brought on or perpetuated by substance abuse, and risk factors that may influence the occurrence of both bipolar disorder and substance use disorders.[24] Treatment for co-occurring substance abuse, when present, is an important part of the overall treatment plan.

Anxiety disorders, such as post-traumatic stress disorder and obsessive-compulsive disorder, also may be common in people with bipolar disorder.[25,26] Co-occurring anxiety disorders may respond to the treatments used for bipolar disorder, or they may require separate treatment. For more information on anxiety disorders, contact the National Institute of Mental Health (NIMH).

How Can Individuals and Families Get Help for Bipolar Disorder?

Anyone with bipolar disorder should be under the care of a psychiatrist skilled in the diagnosis and treatment of this disease. Other mental health professionals, such as psychologists, psychiatric social workers, and psychiatric nurses, can assist in providing the person and family with additional approaches to treatment.

Help can be found at:

- University—or medical school—affiliated programs
- Hospital departments of psychiatry
- Private psychiatric offices and clinics
- Health maintenance organizations (HMOs)
- Offices of family physicians, internists, and pediatricians
- Public community mental health centers

People with bipolar disorder may need help to get help.

- Often people with bipolar disorder do not realize how impaired they are, or they blame their problems on some cause other than mental illness.

- A person with bipolar disorder may need strong encouragement from family and friends to seek treatment. Family physicians can play an important role in providing referral to a mental health professional.

- Sometimes a family member or friend may need to take the person with bipolar disorder for proper mental health evaluation and treatment.

- A person who is in the midst of a severe episode may need to be hospitalized for his or her own protection and for much-needed treatment. There may be times when the person must be hospitalized against his or her wishes.

- Ongoing encouragement and support are needed after a person obtains treatment, because it may take a while to find the best treatment plan for each individual.

- In some cases individuals with bipolar disorder may, when the disorder is under good control, agree to a preferred course of action in the event of a future manic or depressive relapse.

- Like other serious illnesses, bipolar disorder is also hard on spouses, family members, friends, and employers.

- Family members of someone with bipolar disorder often have to cope with the person's serious behavioral problems, such as wild spending sprees during mania or extreme withdrawal from others during depression, and the lasting consequences of these behaviors.

- Many people with bipolar disorder benefit from joining support groups such as those sponsored by the National Depressive and Manic Depressive Association (NDMDA), the National Alliance for the Mentally Ill (NAMI), and the National Mental Health Association (NMHA). Families and friends can also benefit from support groups offered by these organizations. For contact information, see the end section of this book.

What about Clinical Studies for Bipolar Disorder?

Some people with bipolar disorder receive medication and/or psychosocial therapy by volunteering to participate in clinical studies (clinical trials). Clinical studies involve the scientific investigation of illness and treatment of illness in humans. Clinical studies in mental health can yield information about the efficacy of a medication or a combination of treatments, the usefulness of a behavioral intervention or type of psychotherapy, the reliability of a diagnostic procedure, or the success of a prevention method. Clinical studies also guide scientists in learning how illness develops, progresses, lessens, and affects both mind and body. Millions of Americans diagnosed with mental illness lead healthy, productive lives because of information discovered through clinical studies. These studies are not always right for everyone, however. It is important for each individual to consider carefully the possible risks and benefits of a clinical study before making a decision to participate.

In recent years, NIMH has introduced a new generation of "real-world" clinical studies. They are called "real-world" studies for several reasons. Unlike traditional clinical trials, they offer multiple different treatments and treatment combinations. In addition, they aim to include large numbers of people with mental disorders living in communities throughout the U.S. and receiving treatment across a wide variety of settings. Individuals with more than one mental disorder, as well as those with co-occurring physical illnesses, are encouraged to consider participating in these new studies. The main goal of the real-world studies is to improve treatment strategies and outcomes for all people with these disorders. In addition to measuring improvement in illness symptoms, the studies will evaluate how treatments influence other important, real-world issues such as quality of life, ability to work, and social functioning. They also will assess the cost-effectiveness of different treatments and factors that affect how well people stay on their treatment plans.

The Systematic Treatment Enhancement Program for Bipolar Disorder (STEP-BD) is seeking participants for the largest-ever, "real-world" study of treatments for bipolar disorder. To learn more about STEP-BD or other clinical studies, see the Clinical Trials page on the NIMH web site http://www.nimh.nih.gov, visit the National Library of Medicine's clinical trials database http://www.clinicaltrials.gov, or contact NIMH.

References

1. Narrow WE. One-year prevalence of depressive disorders among adults 18 and over in the U.S.: NIMH ECA prospective data. Population estimates based on U.S. Census estimated residential population age 18 and over on July 1, 1998. Unpublished.

2. Regier DA, Narrow WE, Rae DS, et al. The de facto mental and addictive disorders service system. Epidemiologic Catchment Area prospective 1-year prevalence rates of disorders and services. *Archives of General Psychiatry*, 1993; 50(2): 85-94.

3. American Psychiatric Association. *Diagnostic and Statistical Manual for Mental Disorders, fourth edition (DSM-IV)*. Washington, DC: American Psychiatric Press, 1994.

4. Hyman SE, Rudorfer MV. Depressive and bipolar mood disorders. In: Dale DC, Federman DD, eds. *Scientific American®; Medicine. Vol. 3*. New York: Healtheon/WebMD Corp., 2000; Sect. 13, Subsect. II, p. 1.

5. Goodwin FK, Jamison KR. *Manic-depressive illness*. New York: Oxford University Press, 1990.

6. Geller B, Luby J. Child and adolescent bipolar disorder: a review of the past 10 years. *Journal of the American Academy of Child and Adolescent Psychiatry*, 1997; 36(9): 1168-76.

7. NIMH Genetics Workgroup. *Genetics and mental disorders.* NIH Publication No. 98-4268. Rockville, MD: National Institute of Mental Health, 1998.

8. Hyman SE. Introduction to the complex genetics of mental disorders. *Biological Psychiatry*, 1999; 45(5): 518-21.

9. Soares JC, Mann JJ. The anatomy of mood disorders—review of structural neuroimaging studies. *Biological Psychiatry*, 1997; 41(1): 86-106.

10. Soares JC, Mann JJ. The functional neuroanatomy of mood disorders. *Journal of Psychiatric Research*, 1997; 31(4): 393-432.

11. Sachs GS, Printz DJ, Kahn DA, Carpenter D, Docherty JP. The expert consensus guideline series: medication treatment of bipolar disorder 2000. *Postgraduate Medicine*, 2000; Spec No:1-104.

12. Sachs GS, Thase ME. Bipolar disorder therapeutics: maintenance treatment. *Biological Psychiatry*, 2000; 48(6): 573-81.

13. Huxley NA, Parikh SV, Baldessarini RJ. Effectiveness of psychosocial treatments in bipolar disorder: state of the evidence. *Harvard Review of Psychiatry*, 2000; 8(3): 126-40.

14. Vainionpaa LK, Rattya J, Knip M, Tapanainen JS, Pakarinen AJ, Lanning P, Tekay A, Myllyla VV, Isojarvi JI. Valproate-induced hyperandrogenism during pubertal maturation in girls with epilepsy. *Annals of Neurology*, 1999; 45(4): 444-50.

15. Llewellyn A, Stowe ZN, Strader JR Jr. The use of lithium and management of women with bipolar disorder during pregnancy and lactation. *Journal of Clinical Psychiatry*, 1998; 59(Suppl 6): 57-64; discussion 65.

16. Thase ME, Sachs GS. Bipolar depression: pharmacotherapy and related therapeutic strategies. *Biological Psychiatry*, 2000; 48(6): 558-72.

17. Suppes T, Webb A, Paul B, Carmody T, Kraemer H, Rush AJ. Clinical outcome in a randomized 1-year trial of clozapine versus treatment as usual for patients with treatment-resistant illness and a history of mania. *American Journal of Psychiatry*, 1999; 156(8): 1164-9.

18. Tohen M, Sanger TM, McElroy SL, Tollefson GD, Chengappa KN, Daniel DG, Petty F, Centorrino F, Wang R, Grundy SL, Greaney MG, Jacobs TG, David SR, Toma V. Olanzapine versus placebo in the treatment of acute mania. Olanzapine HGEH Study Group. *American Journal of Psychiatry*, 1999; 156(5): 702-9.

19. Rothschild AJ, Bates KS, Boehringer KL, Syed A. Olanzapine response in psychotic depression. *Journal of Clinical Psychiatry*, 1999; 60(2): 116-8.

20. U.S. Department of Health and Human Services. *Mental health: a report of the Surgeon General*. Rockville, MD: U.S. Department of Health and Human Services, Substance Abuse and Mental Health Services Administration, Center for Mental Health Services, National Institutes of Health, National Institute of Mental Health, 1999.

21. Henney JE. Risk of drug interactions with St. John's wort. From the Food and Drug Administration. *Journal of the American Medical Association*, 2000; 283(13): 1679.

22. Nierenberg AA, Burt T, Matthews J, Weiss AP. Mania associated with St. John's wort. *Biological Psychiatry*, 1999; 46(12): 1707-8.

23. Stoll AL, Severus WE, Freeman MP, Rueter S, Zboyan HA, Diamond E, Cress KK, Marangell LB. Omega 3 fatty acids in bipolar disorder: a preliminary double-blind, placebo-controlled trial. *Archives of General Psychiatry*, 1999; 56(5): 407-12.

24. Strakowski SM, DelBello MP. The co-occurrence of bipolar and substance use disorders. *Clinical Psychology Review*, 2000; 20(2): 191-206.

25. Mueser KT, Goodman LB, Trumbetta SL, Rosenberg SD, Osher FC, Vidaver R, Auciello P, Foy DW. Trauma and post-traumatic stress disorder in severe mental illness. *Journal of Consulting and Clinical Psychology*, 1998; 66(3): 493-9.

26. Strakowski SM, Sax KW, McElroy SL, Keck PE Jr, Hawkins JM, West SA. Course of psychiatric and substance abuse syndromes co-occurring with bipolar disorder after a first psychiatric hospitalization. *Journal of Clinical Psychiatry*, 1998; 59(9): 465-71.

Chapter 8

Child and Adolescent Bipolar Disorder

Research findings, clinical experience, and family accounts provide substantial evidence that bipolar disorder, also called manic-depressive illness, can occur in children and adolescents. Bipolar disorder is difficult to recognize and diagnose in youth, however, because it does not fit precisely the symptom criteria established for adults, and because its symptoms can resemble or co-occur with those of other common childhood-onset mental disorders. In addition, symptoms of bipolar disorder may be initially mistaken for normal emotions and behaviors of children and adolescents. But unlike normal mood changes, bipolar disorder significantly impairs functioning in school, with peers, and at home with family. Better understanding of the diagnosis and treatment of bipolar disorder in youth is urgently needed. In pursuit of this goal, the National Institute of Mental Health (NIMH) is conducting and supporting research on child and adolescent bipolar disorder.

A Cautionary Note

Effective treatment depends on appropriate diagnosis of bipolar disorder in children and adolescents. There is some evidence that using antidepressant medication to treat depression in a person who has bipolar disorder may induce manic symptoms if it is taken without a mood stabilizer. In addition, using stimulant medications to treat attention deficit hyperactivity disorder (ADHD) or ADHD-like symptoms

"Child and Adolescent Bipolar Disorder: An Update from the National Institute of Mental Health," NIH Pub. No. 00-4778, updated October 2001.

in a child with bipolar disorder may worsen manic symptoms. While it can be hard to determine which young patients will become manic, there is a greater likelihood among children and adolescents who have a family history of bipolar disorder. If manic symptoms develop or markedly worsen during antidepressant or stimulant use, a physician should be consulted immediately, and diagnosis and treatment for bipolar disorder should be considered.

Symptoms and Diagnosis

Bipolar disorder is a serious mental illness characterized by recurrent episodes of depression, mania, and/or mixed symptom states. These episodes cause unusual and extreme shifts in mood, energy, and behavior that interfere significantly with normal, healthy functioning.

Manic symptoms include:

- Severe changes in mood—either extremely irritable or overly silly and elated
- Overly-inflated self-esteem; grandiosity
- Increased energy
- Decreased need for sleep—ability to go with very little or no sleep for days without tiring
- Increased talking—talks too much, too fast; changes topics too quickly; cannot be interrupted
- Distractibility—attention moves constantly from one thing to the next
- Hypersexuality—increased sexual thoughts, feelings, or behaviors; use of explicit sexual language
- Increased goal-directed activity or physical agitation
- Disregard of risk—excessive involvement in risky behaviors or activities

Depressive symptoms include:

- Persistent sad or irritable mood
- Loss of interest in activities once enjoyed
- Significant change in appetite or body weight
- Difficulty sleeping or oversleeping

- Physical agitation or slowing
- Loss of energy
- Feelings of worthlessness or inappropriate guilt
- Difficulty concentrating
- Recurrent thoughts of death or suicide

Symptoms of mania and depression in children and adolescents may manifest themselves through a variety of different behaviors.[1,2] When manic, children and adolescents, in contrast to adults, are more likely to be irritable and prone to destructive outbursts than to be elated or euphoric. When depressed, there may be many physical complaints such as headaches, muscle aches, stomachaches or tiredness, frequent absences from school or poor performance in school, talk of or efforts to run away from home, irritability, complaining, unexplained crying, social isolation, poor communication, and extreme sensitivity to rejection or failure. Other manifestations of manic and depressive states may include alcohol or substance abuse and difficulty with relationships.

Existing evidence indicates that bipolar disorder beginning in childhood or early adolescence may be a different, possibly more severe form of the illness than older adolescent- and adult-onset bipolar disorder.[1,2] When the illness begins before or soon after puberty, it is often characterized by a continuous, rapid-cycling, irritable, and mixed symptom state that may co-occur with disruptive behavior disorders, particularly attention deficit hyperactivity disorder (ADHD) or conduct disorder (CD), or may have features of these disorders as initial symptoms. In contrast, later adolescent- or adult-onset bipolar disorder tends to begin suddenly, often with a classic manic episode, and to have a more episodic pattern with relatively stable periods between episodes. There is also less co-occurring ADHD or CD among those with later onset illness.

A child or adolescent who appears to be depressed and exhibits ADHD-like symptoms that are very severe, with excessive temper outbursts and mood changes, should be evaluated by a psychiatrist or psychologist with experience in bipolar disorder, particularly if there is a family history of the illness. This evaluation is especially important since psychostimulant medications, often prescribed for ADHD, may worsen manic symptoms. There is also limited evidence suggesting that some of the symptoms of ADHD may be a forerunner of full-blown mania.

Findings from an NIMH-supported study suggest that the illness may be at least as common among youth as among adults. In this study, one percent of adolescents ages 14 to 18 were found to have met criteria for bipolar disorder or cyclothymia, a similar but milder illness, in their lifetime.[3] In addition, close to six percent of adolescents in the study had experienced a distinct period of abnormally and persistently elevated, expansive, or irritable mood even though they never met full criteria for bipolar disorder or cyclothymia. Compared to adolescents with a history of major depressive disorder and to a never-mentally-ill group, both the teens with bipolar disorder and those with subclinical symptoms had greater functional impairment and higher rates of co-occurring illnesses (especially anxiety and disruptive behavior disorders), suicide attempts, and mental health services utilization. The study highlights the need for improved recognition, treatment, and prevention of even the milder and subclinical cases of bipolar disorder in adolescence.

Treatment

Once the diagnosis of bipolar disorder is made, the treatment of children and adolescents is based mainly on experience with adults, since as yet there is very limited data on the efficacy and safety of mood stabilizing medications in youth.[4] The essential treatment for this disorder in adults involves the use of appropriate doses of mood stabilizers, most typically lithium and/or valproate, which are often very effective for controlling mania and preventing recurrences of manic and depressive episodes. Research on the effectiveness of these and other medications in children and adolescents with bipolar disorder is ongoing. In addition, studies are investigating various forms of psychotherapy, including cognitive-behavioral therapy, to complement medication treatment for this illness in young people.

NIMH is attempting to fill the current gaps in treatment knowledge with carefully designed studies involving children and adolescents with bipolar disorder. Data from adults do not necessarily apply to younger patients, because the differences in development may have implications for treatment efficacy and safety.[4] Current multi-site studies funded by NIMH are investigating the value of long-term treatment with lithium and other mood stabilizers in preventing recurrence of bipolar disorder in adolescents. Specifically, these studies aim to determine how well lithium and other mood stabilizers prevent recurrences of mania or depression and control subclinical symptoms in adolescents; to identify factors that predict outcome; and to assess side effects and overall adherence to treatment. Another NIMH-funded study is evaluating the safety and efficacy of valproate for treatment of acute mania in children and adolescents, and also is investigating the biological correlates of treatment response. Other NIMH-supported investigators are studying the effects of antidepressant medications added to mood stabilizers in the treatment of the depressive phase of bipolar disorder in adolescents.

Valproate Use

According to studies conducted in Finland in patients with epilepsy, valproate may increase testosterone levels in teenage girls and produce polycystic ovary syndrome in women who began taking the medication before age 20.[5] Increased testosterone can lead to polycystic ovary syndrome with irregular or absent menses, obesity, and abnormal growth of hair. Therefore, young female patients taking valproate should be monitored carefully by a physician.

For More Information

Office of Communications and Public Liaison, NIMH
Information Resources and Inquiries Branch
6001 Executive Blvd., Room 8184, MSC 9663
Bethesda, MD 20892-9663
Phone: 301-443-4513
TTY: 301-443-8431
Fax: 301-443-4279
Mental Health FAX4U: 301-443-5158
Website; http://www.nimh.nih.gov
E-mail: nimhinfo@nih.gov

References

1. Carlson GA, Jensen PS, Nottelmann ED, eds. Special issue: current issues in childhood bipolarity. *Journal of Affective Disorders*, 1998; 51: entire issue.

2. Geller B, Luby J. Child and adolescent bipolar disorder: a review of the past 10 years. *Journal of the American Academy of Child and Adolescent Psychiatry*, 1997; 36(9): 1168-76.

3. Lewinsohn PM, Klein DN, Seely JR. Bipolar disorders in a community sample of older adolescents: prevalence, phenomenology,

comorbidity, and course. *Journal of the American Academy of Child and Adolescent Psychiatry*, 1995; 34(4): 454-63.

4. McClellan J, Werry J. Practice parameters for the assessment and treatment of adolescents with bipolar disorder. *Journal of the American Academy of Child and Adolescent Psychiatry*, 1997; 36(Suppl 10): 157S-76S.

5. Vainionpaa LK, Rattya J, Knip M, et al. Valproate-induced hyperandrogenism during pubertal maturation in girls with epilepsy. *Annals of Neurology*, 1999; 45(4): 444-50.

Chapter 9

Schizoaffective Disorder

Schizoaffective disorder symptoms look like a mixture of two kinds of major mental illnesses that are usually thought to run in different families, involve different brain mechanisms, develop in different ways, and respond to different treatments: mood (affective) disorders and schizophrenia.

Symptoms of Schizoaffective Disorder

The two major mood disorders are unipolar depression and bipolar or manic-depressive illness. Seriously depressed people:

- feel constantly sad and fatigued
- have lost interest in everyday activities
- are indecisive and unable to concentrate
- sleep and eat too little or too much
- complain of various physical symptoms
- may have recurrent thoughts of death and suicide

People experiencing a manic\mood are:

- suffering from sleeplessness

- compulsively talkative
- agitated and distractible
- convinced of their own inflated importance
- susceptible to buying sprees; indiscreet sexual advances, and foolish investments
- prone to cheerfulness turning to irritability, paranoia, and rage

People with chronic schizophrenia:

- appear apathetic
- are emotionally unresponsive
- have limited speech
- have confused thinking
- may suffer from hallucinations and delusions
- perplex others with their strange behavior and inappropriate emotional reactions

Difficulty In Distinguishing Illnesses

People with:

- **affective disorders** usually appear normal between episodes of illness and do not become more seriously disabled with time.
- **schizophrenia** rarely seem normal, and their condition tends to deteriorate, at least in the early years of the illness.

This distinction is not always as obvious as the description suggests. Emotion and behavior are more fluid and less easy to classify than physical symptoms. Seriously depressed and manic people often have hallucinations and delusions. Mania can be impossible to distinguish from an acute schizophrenic reaction, and psychotic or delusional depression is important enough to rate its own classification by some psychiatrists. Mood changes occur both as symptoms of schizophrenia and as reactions to its devastating effects; for example, depression after a schizophrenic episode (post-psychotic depression) is common and often severe, and it is during this time that a person suffering from schizophrenia is most likely to commit suicide.

Schizophrenic apathy and an incapacity for pleasure can also be mistaken for depression. Often a diagnosis has to be changed from one kind of major mental disorder to the other. In a recent study of more than 936 people with a severe psychiatric disorder who were hospitalized at least four times in a seven-year period, investigators found that a significant percentage of those originally given other diagnoses (including bipolar disorder) had a final diagnosis of schizophrenia.

Signs That May Help Define Schizoaffective as the Diagnosis

- The illness usually begins in early adulthood.
- It is more common in women.
- A person has difficulty in following a moving object with their eyes.
- A person's rapid eye movement (dreaming) begins unusually early in the night.

However, the research is inadequate and the results have been confused by varying definitions.

Choice of Therapies

If a person is in a psychotic state, a neuroleptic (antipsychotic) drug is most often used, since antidepressants and lithium (used for bipolar disorder) take several weeks to start working. Antipsychotic drugs may cause tardive dyskinesia, a serious and sometimes irreversible disorder of body movement, so people are asked to take them for long periods only when there is no other alternative.

After the psychosis has ended, the mood symptoms may be treated with antidepressants, lithium, anticonvulsants, or electroconvulsive therapy (ECT). Sometimes a neuroleptic is combined with lithium or an antidepressant and then gradually withdrawn, to be restored if necessary. The few studies on drug treatment of this disorder suggest that antipsychotic drugs are most effective. The greater effectiveness of these new drugs may be partly due to their activity at receptors for the neurotransmitter serotonin, which is not influenced as strongly by standard antipsychotic drugs.

For More Information

Please contact your local Mental Health Association or:

National Mental Health Association
1021 Prince Street
Alexandria, VA 22314
Phone: (800) 969-NMHA
TTY: (800) 433-5959
http://www.nmha.org

Other resources for further help and information are listed in the end section of this book.

Chapter 10

Dual Diagnosis: Substance Abuse

What Is Dual Diagnosis?

A person who has both an alcohol or drug problem and an emotional/psychiatric problem is said to have a dual diagnosis. To recover fully, the person needs treatment for both problems.

How Common Is Dual Diagnosis?

Dual diagnosis is more common than you might imagine. According to a report published by the *Journal of the American Medical Association*:

- Thirty-seven percent of alcohol abusers and fifty-three percent of drug abusers also have at least one serious mental illness.

- Of all people diagnosed as mentally ill, 29 percent abuse either alcohol or drugs.

What Kind of Mental or Emotional Problems are Seen in People with Dual Diagnosis?

The following psychiatric problems are common to occur in dual diagnosis, that is, in tandem with alcohol or drug dependency.

- Depressive disorders, such as depression and bipolar disorder.

- Anxiety disorders, including generalized anxiety disorder, panic disorder, obsessive-compulsive disorder, and phobias.

- Other psychiatric disorders, such as schizophrenia and personality disorders.

Someone suffering from schizophrenia is at a 10.1 percent higher-than-average risk of being an alcoholic or drug abuser. Someone who is having an episode of major depression is at a 4.1 percent higher-than-average risk of being an alcohol or drug abuser...and so on. Table 10.1, based on a National Institute of Mental Health study, lists seven major psychiatric disorders and shows how much each one increases an individual's risk for substance abuse.

Table 10.1. Psychiatric Disorders and Substance Abuse Risk

Psychiatric Disorder	Increased Risk For Substance Abuse
Antisocial personality disorder	15.5%
Manic episode	14.5
Schizophrenia	10.1
Panic disorder	4.3
Major depressive episode	4.1
Obsessive-compulsive disorder	3.4
Phobias	2.4

Which Develops First—Substance Abuse or the Emotional Problem?

It depends. Often the psychiatric problem develops first. In an attempt to feel calmer, more peppy, or more cheerful, a person with emotional symptoms may drink or use drugs; doctors call this "self-medication." Frequent self-medication may eventually lead to physical or psychological dependency on alcohol or drugs. If it does, the person then suffers from not just one problem, but two. In adolescents, however, drug or alcohol abuse may merge and continue into adulthood, which may contribute to the development of emotional difficulties or psychiatric disorders.

In other cases, alcohol or drug dependency is the primary condition. A person whose substance abuse problem has become severe may develop symptoms of a psychiatric disorder: perhaps episodes of depression, fits of rage, hallucinations, or suicide attempts.

How Can a Physician Tell Whether the Person's Primary Problem Is Substance Abuse or an Emotional Disorder?

At the initial examination, it may be difficult to tell. Since many symptoms of severe substance abuse mimic other psychiatric conditions, the person must go through a withdrawal from alcohol and/or drugs before the physician can accurately assess whether there's an underlying psychiatric problem also.

If a Person Does Have Both an Alcohol/Drug Problem and an Emotional Problem, Which Should Be Treated First?

Ideally, both problems should be treated simultaneously. For any substance abuser, however, the first step in treatment must be detoxification—a period of time during which the body is allowed to cleanse itself of alcohol or drugs. Ideally, detoxification should take place under medical supervision. It can take a few days to a week or more, depending on what substances the person abused and for how long.

Until recently, alcoholics and drug addicts dreaded detoxification because it meant a painful and sometimes life-threatening "cold turkey" withdrawal. Now, doctors are able to give hospitalized substance abusers carefully chosen medications which can substantially ease withdrawal symptoms. Thus, when detoxification is done under medical supervision, it's safer and less traumatic.

What Is Next after Detoxification?

Once detoxification is completed, it's time for dual treatment; rehabilitation for the alcohol or drug problem and treatment for the psychiatric problem.

Rehabilitation for a substance abuse problem usually involves individual and group psychotherapy, education about alcohol and drugs, exercise, proper nutrition, and participation in a 12-step recovery program such as Alcoholics Anonymous. The idea is not just to stay off booze and drugs, but to learn to enjoy life without these "crutches."

Treatment for a psychiatric problem depends upon the diagnosis. For most disorders, individual and group therapy as well as medications are recommended. Expressive therapies and education about the particular psychiatric condition are often useful adjuncts. A support group of other people who are recovering from the same condition may also prove highly beneficial. Adjunct treatment, such as occupational or expressive therapy, can help individuals better understand and communicate their feelings or develop better problem-solving or decision-making skills.

Must a Dual Diagnosis Patient Be Treated in a Hospital?

Not necessarily. The nature and severity of the illness, the associated risks or complications, and the person's treatment history are some of the facts considered in determining the appropriate level of care. There are several different levels or intensities of care including full hospitalization or inpatient treatment, partial hospitalization, and outpatient treatment.

What Is the Role of the Patient's Family in Treatment?

With both rehabilitation for substance abuse and treatment for a psychiatric problem, education, counseling sessions, and support groups for the patient's family are important aspects of overall care. The greater the family's understanding of the problems, the higher the chances the patient will have a lasting recovery.

How Can Family and Friends Help with Recovery from the Substance Abuse?

They need to learn to stop enabling. Enabling is acting in ways that essentially help or encourage the person to maintain their habit of drinking or getting high. For instance, a woman whose husband routinely drinks too much, might call in sick for him when he is too drunk to go to work. That's enabling. Likewise, family members or friends might give an addict money which is used to buy drugs, because they're either sorry for him or afraid of him. That's enabling also.

When family and friends participate in the recovery program, they learn how to stop enabling. If they act on what they've learned, the recovering substance abuser is much less likely to relapse into drinking or taking drugs.

How Can Family and Friends Help with Recovery from a Psychiatric Condition?

They should be calm and understanding, rather than frightened or critical. They should be warm and open, rather than cool or cautious. Although it is fine to ask the person matter-of-factly about the psychiatric treatment, that shouldn't be the only focus of conversation.

If Someone I Know Appears to Have a Substance Abuse Problem and the Symptoms of a Psychiatric Disorder, How Can I Help?

Encourage the person to acknowledge the problems and seek help for themselves. Suggest a professional evaluation with a licensed physician, preferably at a medical center that's equipped to treat addiction problems and psychiatric conditions. If the person is reluctant, do the legwork yourself—find the facility, make the appointment, offer to go with the person. A little encouragement may be all it takes. If you talk to the physician first, be honest and candid about the troubling behavior. Your input may give the doctor valuable diagnostic clues.

There Is Hope

As a relative or friend, you can play an important role in encouraging a person to seek professional diagnosis and treatment. By learning about dual diagnosis, you can help this person find and stick with an effective recovery program.

The more you know about dual diagnosis, the more you will see how substance abuse can go hand-in-hand with another psychiatric condition. As with any illness, a person with dual diagnosis can improve once proper care is given. By seeking out information, you can learn to recognize the signs and symptoms of dual diagnosis—and help someone live a healthier or more fulfilling life.

For More Information

Contact your local Mental Health Association, community mental health center, or:

National Mental Health Association
1021 Prince Street
Alexandria, VA 22314
Phone: 800-969-6642
Stigma Watch Line: 800-969-NMHA
TTY: 800-433-5959
Website: http://www.nmha.org

Other resources for further help and information are listed in the end section of this book.

Chapter 11

Alcohol and Depression

Introduction

Alcohol is our favorite drug. More than 90% of the population drink and only a minority come to any harm as a consequence. Socially we may use it to help us relax and alter the way we feel. Taken in moderation it presents few problems and has some benefits.

Sensible Drinking

Drinking less than 21 units a week for a man or 14 for a woman, is unlikely to cause problems as long as it is spread out sensibly throughout the week. A recent government report has suggested that it is sensible to limit consumption to 4 units in any one day for a man and 3 for a woman. A unit of alcohol is the amount contained in a standard measure of spirits: a half pint of normal strength beer or lager, or a small glass of wine or sherry. Remember that measures served at home are commonly much larger than those in bars, and some lagers and fortified wines are much stronger than average. (See the guide to units in Table 11.1).

We often underestimate the amount we drink and one way of keeping a check on this is to record our consumption in units in a diary

---

"Alcohol and Depression," © 2001 The Royal College of Psychiatrists; reprinted with permission. This text has been revised to conform to American spelling conventions. Text of the original document is available online at www.rcpsych.ac.uk/help/alcohol/index.htm.

(see illustration in Table 11.2) over the course of a week. Doing this from time to time helps us see if our drinking is excessive or potentially harmful. A glance at the diary will also highlight any occasions or regular times of the week when we seem more likely to drink a lot than others. A few useful tips about developing sensible drinking habits are given at the end of this chapter.

Link between Depression and Alcohol

Sometimes we may drink to relieve a depressed mood; to 'drown our sorrows.' Occasionally, drinking excessively is a symptom of severe clinical depression. More often it is the other way around and depression is a consequence of excessive drinking. It is important to be clear about the extent to which the depression is causing the excessive drinking or the drinking causing depression.

Alcohol is a depressant of the brain, reducing your ability to face up to problems and releasing inhibitions. This is why it plays such an important part in overcoming social fears; for instance, helping conversation flow at a party. For some, alcohol releases powerful feelings of self hatred and disgust, producing angry, aggressive, or suicidal behavior. We all know people who have become gloomy and

Table 11.1. How many units of alcohol are in your drink?

Drink	Units
1 pub measure of spirits (whisky, gin, vodka)	1
1 glass of fortified wine (sherry, martini, port)	1
1 average sized glass of table wine	1.5
1 pint of beer	2
1 can of beer	1.5
1 bottle of 'super' or 'special' lager	2.5
1 liter bottle of table wine	12
1 bottle of table wine	9
1 bottle of fortified wine (sherry, martini, port)	14
1 bottle of spirits (whisky, gin, vodka)	30

These guidelines are approximate and may vary depending on brand chosen and size of measure.

embittered when drunk and yet have little recollection of this mood the following day.

Some individuals drink alcohol as a means of bolstering self confidence or obtaining relief from anxiety and distress, including of course, depression. If dissolving tensions and grief in this way is so common, it is understandable that excessive drinking and depression are so closely linked.

Some people who are very depressed and lacking in energy may use alcohol to help them keep going and cope with life. This is a very short-lived solution because any benefits of alcohol soon wear off and the drinking becomes part of a routine and therefore difficult to change. Alcohol is like other drugs acting on the brain, such as tranquilizers; it produces tolerance so that we need a larger and larger dose to get the desired effect. In consequence, the drinker finds that he or she can take large quantities but feel very little benefit. This tolerance or habituation is a step toward dependence.

The down side of the emotional release associated with drunkenness is that it often leaves us tired, depressed, and hung over as the blood alcohol level falls. There is evidence that changes in the chemistry of the brain itself may be produced by alcohol and that these changes increase the likelihood of a depressed mood.

Hangovers and Depression

Hangovers are in themselves depressing experiences. The drinker wakes feeling ill, anxious, and jittery. The day may be spent ruminating

Table 11.2. Drinking Diary

Day	How Much?	When/Where/Who With?	Units	Total
Monday				
Tuesday				
Wednesday				
Thursday				
Friday				
Saturday				
Sunday				
Total for Week				

over the guilt associated with the events of the previous evening. As drinking bouts become habitual, there may well be troubles at home, conflicts with partners and family, quality of work deteriorates, and the drinker will often feel that he or she is being unjustly criticized by colleagues. Failing memory, sexual impotence, and declining physical health add to the sense of despair.

Given these circumstances, it is hardly surprising that depression and even thoughts of suicide are common events in the life of someone who has become seriously dependent on alcohol. Self harm and suicide are much commoner in people with alcohol problems.

Taking Action

As a first step, it is usually best to tackle the drinking habit and then consider dealing with depression if that does not lift of its own accord.

If drinking seems to be getting out of hand, or is causing problems to yourself or others, there are a number of self help measures which will help you to analyze the problem and deal with it, or if necessary seek help.

Taking stock of current drinking habits is a good starting point. Keeping a careful diary of one week's drinking is a useful way of doing this. The diary will also provide an opportunity for working out the relationship between events in the week and times when you drink more. If the diary shows that drinking is outside sensible limits or causing problems, a good first plan is to set yourself a target to reduce your intake or stop completely. Identify the risky situations and factors when you will be tempted to drink: these may include the people you drink with, the time of day when you drink, and the feelings that trigger drinking. Take steps to avoid or deal with these situations. It is often a great help to involve a partner or friend in agreeing the goal and discussing progress.

It is of course often very hard to give up drinking totally, even for a short time. Try this and see how you feel without it. At first you may feel a craving or a sense of loss, and even some shakiness and restlessness. If these symptoms are severe, it is wise to consult your family doctor for help and advice about coming off alcohol and receiving help with what are withdrawal symptoms.

If the dependence on alcohol is very severe, it may be that you will benefit from seeking help with the problem, either from a self help group such as Alcoholics Anonymous.

A few weeks abstinence from alcohol will often produce an improved sense of well-being, fitness, and much less depression. Friends and family may well start treating you better because they can talk to the real person rather than through a haze of drink. If the depression which was so prominent before has lifted, this strongly suggests that the mood was caused by the drinking rather than the other way round. If this is what you find, keep on monitoring your drinking using the diary every four weeks and keep to the target you have set yourself.

Dealing with Persistent Depression

If the depression is still with you after two or three weeks of not drinking and still seems very severe, then it is time to talk to your family doctor about further help. An opportunity to talk about your feelings can be very helpful, particularly when the depression seems linked to some crisis in your life such as a relationship problem, bereavement, or other loss.

If the depression does not lift and is particularly severe, your doctor may suggest antidepressants. In most cases you will be advised not to drink alcohol while taking these. Remember these antidepressants will take two or three weeks to work. Do not expect immediate changes, but persevere in taking them.

Treatment for both alcohol problems and depression can be very successful. It often requires continued contact with someone you can trust, either your own doctor, counselor, or a specialist psychiatrist. It is also advisable to continue to keep a regular record of your drinking habits, using the diary to ensure that you are keeping to your plan. Remember also that many antidepressants need to be continued for a long time. Do not stop them too soon and discuss any planned reduction with your family doctor or specialists. Changing habits and style of life is always a challenge and takes time to achieve.

There may be setbacks but the evidence is that, with appropriate help, even the most severe depression and drinking problems can be overcome.

A Sensible Approach to Alcohol

- Remember not to use alcohol as a means of drowning your sorrows or improving the way you feel.

- If hangovers are more than an occasional event, take careful stock of your drinking habits, and review these by means of a diary.

- Sip your drink slowly and do not gulp. Space your drinks with a non-alcoholic drink in between.

- Do not drink on an empty stomach.

- Do not get into the habit of drinking every day. Have two or three drink-free days in the week.

- Do not suggest a drink to someone who is emotionally upset.

- As a host, make sure you offer non-alcoholic drinks as well as alcohol on social occasions.

- Do ask your doctor or pharmacist if it is safe to drink with any medicine that you have been prescribed.

- Remember that alcohol is a drug. Use it with care and do not rely on it to lift depression.

Chapter 12

Medicines That Can Cause Mood Disorders

Mood Disorders

The term "mood disorders" refers to a group of illnesses that cause persistent changes in mood and behavior serious enough to impair functioning. Common mood disorders include depression and bipolar disorder (manic-depressive disorder).

Depression is an illness that consists of depressed mood, fatigue, and a loss of interest in activities that usually are pleasurable. Depression can rob a person of the joys of life, disrupt relationships, and interfere with work and daily activities.

Mania may be loosely thought of as the opposite of depression. It is characterized by very happy or irritable moods and increased energy. A related condition called hypomania is a mild form of mania. It is characterized by emotional highs, scattered thoughts, and over-activity in the absence of dangerous, reckless or destructive behavior.

Bipolar disorder is a mental illness that causes people to have episodes of serious mania and depression. The person's moods swing from overly "high" and irritable (mania) to sad and hopeless (depression), with periods of normal mood in between.

Certain drugs prescribed for various medical conditions have been found to cause depression or mania in some people. But not all people who take these drugs will experience mania or depression.

If you do experience these or other disturbing side effects, call your doctor immediately. Do not stop taking the medicine unless directed to do so by your doctor. In all cases, the risk of side effects must be balanced against the risk and discomfort of not treating the disease.

Drugs that Can Cause Mania

Mania can occur as the result of drug treatment for many medical problems, especially in people already susceptible to mood disorders. The drugs that can cause mania include:

Amphetamines: Central nervous system stimulants used to treat childhood hyperactivity, obesity, and narcolepsy. Examples include Dexedrine, Ritalin, Adderall and their longer-acting counterparts, Concerta and Meta Date.

Anticholinergics: A group of medicines used to relieve cramps or spasms of the stomach, intestines, and bladder. Examples include Anaspaz, Bentyl, Gastrosed, Levbid and Symax.

Baclofen: A muscle relaxant and antispastic agent often used to treat multiple sclerosis and spinal cord injuries.

Benztropine: A medicine used to treat Parkinson's disease.

Bromocriptine: A drug used to treat Parkinson's disease.

Bupropion: A medicine used to treat depression.

Captopril: A medicine used to treat high blood pressure.

Cimetidine (Tagamet): One of the histamine H2-receptor antagonists, a group of medicines used to prevent and treat duodenal ulcers. These medicines also are used to prevent and relieve heartburn, acid indigestion, and sour stomach.

Corticosteroids: A group of medicines that decrease inflammation (swelling) and reduce the activity of the immune system. Corticosteroids may be topical (rubbed on the skin), oral (swallowed), or inhaled through the nose or mouth. Topical steroids are used to treat various skin problems such as poison ivy, and include Hydrocortisone, Clobetasol, and Triamcinolone. Oral steroids are used to treat a variety of inflammation-based diseases, including asthma and lupus, as well as to help prevent transplant rejection. Examples include Prednisone and Methylprednisolone. Inhaled steroids are used to reduce inflammation associated with asthma and nasal allergies. Examples include Flonase, Nasacort, Nasonex, Flovent, and Azmacort.

Cyclosporine: A drug used to suppress the immune system to prevent the rejection of transplanted organs.

Disulfiram (Antabuse): A medicine that produces sensitivity to alcohol and results in a highly unpleasant reaction when the person taking it drinks alcohol. It is used to treat alcoholism.

Hydralazine: A medicine used to treat high blood pressure.

Isoniazid: A drug used to treat tuberculosis (TB).

Levodopa (Dopar, Sinemet): A medicine used to treat Parkinson's disease.

Levothyroxine (Synthroid): A drug commonly prescribed as a thyroid hormone replacement. It is used to treat patients whose thyroid glands are not producing enough hormones on their own.

MAOIs: A group of medicines used to treat depression. Examples include Nardil and Parnate.

Methylphenidate (Ritalin): A mild central nervous system stimulant used to treat attention-deficit hyperactivity disorder (ADHD).

Metrizamide (Amipaque): A special medical dye used in certain radiology tests. These dyes help doctors visualize blood vessels and organs.

Opioids: A class of narcotics used to relieve moderate to severe pain. These drugs have a high potential for abuse and addiction. Examples include codeine, Demerol, Darvocet, morphine, and Percodan.

Procarbazine: An anticancer drug commonly used to treat Hodgkin's disease and lymphomas.

Procyclidine: A medicine used to treat Parkinson's disease and adverse effects of anti-psychotics.

Trihexyphenidyl (Artane): A medicine used to treat Parkinson's disease.

Yohimbine: A drug used to treat male impotence.

Drugs that Can Cause Depression

The following drugs have been reported to cause depression in some patients. Elderly people are particularly at risk.

Acyclovir (Zovirax): An antiviral drug used to treat shingles and herpes.

Alcohol: Alcohol is a drug.

Anticonvulsants: A drug used to control epileptic seizures. Examples include Celontin and Zarontin.

Asparaginase (Elspar): An anticancer drug.

Baclofen (Lioresal): A muscle relaxant and antispastic agent often used to treat multiple sclerosis and spinal cord injuries.

Barbiturates: A group of central nervous system depressants that slow down brain function. These medicines have been used to treat anxiety and to prevent epileptic seizures. They are commonly abused. Examples are phenobarbital and secobarbital.

Benzodiazepines: A group of central nervous system depressants often used to treat anxiety and insomnia, and relax muscles. Examples include Ativan, Dalmane, Halcion, Klonopin, Librium, Valium, Xanax, and Restoril.

Beta-adrenergic blockers: Also known as beta-blockers, these medicines are used in the treatment of various heart problems, including high blood pressure, chest pain caused by angina, and certain abnormal heart rhythms. They may also be used to treat migraine headaches. Examples include acebutolol, atenolol, propanolol, bisoprolol, metoprolol, nadolol, and timolol.

Bromocriptine (Parlodel): A medicine used to treat Parkinson's disease.

Calcium-channel blockers: A group of medicines that slow the heart rate and relax blood vessels. Calcium channel blockers are used to treat high blood pressure, chest pain, congestive heart failure, and certain abnormal heart rhythms. Examples include verapamil, diltiazem, and nifedipine.

Corticosteroids: A group of medicines that decrease inflammation (swelling) and reduce the activity of the immune system. Corticosteroids may be topical (rubbed on the skin), oral (swallowed), or inhaled through the nose or mouth. Topical steroids are used to treat various skin disorders, including poison ivy, and include Hydrocortisone, Clobetasol, and Triamcinolone. Oral steroids are used to treat a variety of inflammation-based diseases, including asthma and lupus, as well as to help prevent transplant rejection. Examples include Prednisone and Methylprednisolone. Inhaled steroids are used to reduce inflammation associated with asthma and nasal allergies. Examples include Flonase, Nasacort, Nasonex, Flovent, and Azmacort.

Cycloserine (Seromycin): An antibiotic used primarily to treat tuberculosis (TB).

Dapsone: An antibacterial/anti-infection medicine used to prevent and treat a type of pneumonia called PCP pneumonia. Dapsone also is used to treat leprosy and a skin problem called dermatitis herpetiformis.

Disopyramide (Norpace): A drug used to treat abnormal heart rhythms, or arrhythmias.

Disulfiram (Antabuse): A medicine that produces sensitivity to alcohol and results in a highly unpleasant reaction when the person taking it drinks alcohol. It is used to treat alcoholism.

Estrogens: A class of female hormones often used in hormone replacement therapy (HRT) to treat menopause symptoms and to prevent or treat osteoporosis. Examples include Premarin and Prempro.

Fluoroquinolone antibiotics: A class of antibiotics used to treat respiratory tract infections, including chronic bronchitis, pneumonia, and bacterial sinusitis. Levaquin is one example of fluoroquinolone antibiotics.

Histamine H2-receptor antagonists: Medicines used to prevent and treat duodenal ulcers. These medicines also are used to prevent and relieve heartburn, acid indigestion, and sour stomach. Examples include Axid, Mylanta, Pepcid, Tagamet, and Zantac.

HMG-CoA reductase inhibitors (statins): A group of medicines used to lower cholesterol, protect against damage from coronary artery disease and prevent heart attacks. Examples include Mevacor, Zocor, Pravachol, Lescol, and Lipitor.

Interferon alfa (Roferon-A): A highly purified protein used to treat certain cancers and chronic, active hepatitis B.

Isotretinoin (Accutane): A drug used to treat severe acne.

Mefloquine (Lariam): A medicine used to prevent or treat malaria.

Methyldopa (Aldomet): A drug used to treat high blood pressure.

Metoclopramide (Reglan): A medicine that increases the contractions of the stomach. It is used to help diagnose certain disorders of the stomach and/or intestines. It also is used to prevent nausea and vomiting that may occur after treatment with anticancer drugs.

Metrizamide (Amipaque): A special medical dye used in certain radiology tests. These dyes help doctors visualize blood vessels and organs.

Metronidazole (Flagyl): An antibacterial agent used to treat infections.

Narcotics: A group of drugs used to relieve intense pain and suppress coughs. These drugs have a high potential for abuse and addiction. Examples include codeine, Demerol, Darvocet, morphine, and Percodan.

Progestins, implanted (Norplant): Medicines used for birth control.

Sulfonamides: A group of drugs used to prevent and treat infections.

What to Do

When a medicine produces symptoms of depression, mania, or both, your doctor may recommend discontinuing the drug or reducing the dosage (if possible). If this is not possible, your doctor may treat the manic or depressive symptoms with other drugs.

Chapter 13

Depression:
What Else Could It Be?

Adjustment

People who have suffered a life event, such as the break-up of a relationship or the loss of a job, go through a period of adjustment. During this time, their emotions may be upset, with periods of depression, anxiety, irritability, and poor sleep. Usually this settles down over a period of days or weeks without the need for treatment such as antidepressants. However, if the symptoms persist for more than a few weeks, or are severe, it is possible that a depressive illness is present.

Anxiety

Anxiety disorders are illnesses in which the main symptom is worry about a real or imagined threat. Often anxiety disorders exist alone, without depression. However, often they are present with depression. This is because anxiety and its effects on people's lives can lead to depression, and because depression can lead to anxiety. For these reasons, it can be difficult to distinguish between a depressive illness and anxiety. The Hospital Anxiety and Depression (HAD) scale is a questionnaire which can help to distinguish between the two.

Bipolar Affective Disorder

This is also called 'manic depression'. In this illness, people suffer not only episodes of depression but also episodes of elation (increased mood) and over-activity. Such periods of mania are more extreme than the lifted mood which we all experience when we have received good news, such as getting a job, passing an exam, or being with good friends. Episodes of mania often lead onto episodes of depression.

Chronic Fatigue Syndrome (CFS)

This illness is often called ME (myalgic encephalomyelitis). People with CFS suffer mainly from fatigue, in that they feel much more tired than is usual after mental or physical activity, such as studying or gardening. CFS can severely limit what people can do in their daily life. Unfortunately, there is no agreement over what causes CFS, and treatment is therefore often poorly directed or unavailable. Understandably, people with CFS often feel low. Some people with CFS develop a depressive illness. Therefore, it is important to make sure that people who are both fatigued and depressed are not suffering from a depressive illness. If they are, this needs treatment separately to the CFS.

Dementia

People with dementia have poor memory, which can progress to involve other brain functions, such as speech, writing, and spatial functions. The diagnosis needs to be made by a doctor, as many people who believe that they have poor memory or worsened memory do not have dementia. One common reason for the experience of poor memory is poor concentration due to depression. In an extreme form, this is called 'pseudodementia', in which the depression, poor concentration, and resulting apparent (but not actual) poor memory are sufficiently severe to give the appearance of early dementia. Sometimes, depression and dementia occur together.

Depressive Personality

Some people have what is termed a depressive personality or dysthymia. These people are persistently slightly gloomy and despondent, as though they are seeing their life and the world through grey-colored spectacles. This attitude will have been present since early adulthood. However, this is not usually sufficiently to cause problems with their daily life. Unsurprisingly, people with a depressive personality are more at risk of developing a depressive illness than people without this personality.

Obsessive-Compulsive Disorder (OCD)

This is an illness which is characterized by repetitive, intrusive thoughts or actions, which are recognized as senseless, but which are carried out anyway. Cleaning, counting and checking are common compulsive actions. In patients with depression, obsessional features, such as difficulty making decisions, and checking, may be prominent. Equally, depression is common in patients with OCD. As with anxiety, a distinction between the two can often be made by determining which set of symptoms started first or which are more severe.

Physical Illness and Side Effects of Medicines

Many physical illnesses can cause depression. These include, for example, heart attack, hypothyroidism, and cancer. If these physical illnesses are treated effectively, the depressive symptoms may resolve. Sometimes, medicines themselves can cause depression. These include the oral contraceptive pill ('the pill'), drugs used to treat high blood pressure, and corticosteroids.

Schizophrenia

Schizophrenia affects about 1% of the population. It is a mental illness in which several aspects of mental state can be affected. The way in which sufferers think, and the thoughts that they have, are often abnormal. Also, their behavior, perceptions, and mood, can be affected. Understandably, difficulties thinking, unusual perceptual experiences, and unusual behavior can lead to depression. However, depression is much more common than schizophrenia, and some people with depression can experience similar difficulties to those with schizophrenia.

Seasonal Affective Disorder (SAD)

This is an illness in which the symptoms of depression are present only in the winter months of the year, when the days are short. In the summer, when the days are longer, the symptoms are not present, or are much diminished.

97

Part Two

Understanding the Experience of Depression

Chapter 14

Depression Checklist

- I feel sad.
- I feel like crying a lot.
- I'm bored.
- I feel so alone.
- I don't really feel sad, just empty.
- I don't have any confidence in myself.
- I don't like myself.
- I feel scared a lot of the time, but I don't know why.
- I feel mad, like I could just explode.
- I feel guilty.
- I can't concentrate.
- I have a hard time remembering.
- I don't want to make decisions—it's too much work.
- I feel like I'm in a fog.

- I'm so tired, no matter how much sleep I get.
- I'm frustrated with everything and everybody.
- I don't have fun anymore.
- I feel so helpless.
- I'm always getting into trouble.
- I'm so restless and jittery. I just can't sit still.
- I feel nervous.
- I feel disorganized, like my head is spinning.
- I feel so self-conscious.
- I can't think straight. My brain doesn't seem to work.
- I feel ugly.
- I don't feel like talking anymore—I just don't have anything to say.
- I feel my life has no direction.
- I feel life isn't worth living.
- I consume alcohol/take drugs regularly.
- My whole body feels slowed down—my speech, my walk, my movements.
- I don't want to go out with friends anymore.
- I don't feel like taking care of my appearance.
- Occasionally, my heart will pound very hard, I can't catch my breath, and I feel tingly, my vision feels strange, and I feel I might pass out. The feeling passes in seconds, but I'm afraid it will happen again. (panic attack/anxiety attack)
- Sometimes I feel like I'm losing it.
- I feel different from everyone else.
- I smile, but inside I'm miserable.
- I have difficulty falling asleep or I awaken between 1 a.m. and 5 a.m. and then I can't get back to sleep.
- My appetite has diminished—food tastes so bland.
- My appetite has increased—I feel I could eat all the time.
- My weight has increased/decreased.
- I have headaches.

- I have stomachaches.
- My arms and legs hurt.
- I feel nauseous.
- I'm dizzy.
- My vision seems blurred or slow at times.
- I'm clumsy.
- My neck hurts.

We're all going to feel these things from time to time—that's normal. But, if you've checked several of the symptoms listed, and they have been present for 2–3 weeks or longer, you should see your doctor or psychiatrist to be evaluated for clinical depression. Clinical depression is a chemical imbalance in the brain. It can be treated with antidepressant medication, psychotherapy or a combination of both. You don't have to feel this way. You can feel good again.

Please note, however, that there are other illnesses and certain medications that can mimic the symptoms of depression. A complete medical examination should be performed to rule out other possibilities.

Chapter 15

The Depressed Child

Not only adults become depressed. Children and teenagers also may have depression, which is a treatable illness. Depression is defined as an illness when the feelings of depression persist and interfere with a child or adolescent's ability to function.

About five percent of children and adolescents in the general population suffer from depression at any given point in time. Children under stress, who experience loss, or who have attentional, learning, conduct or anxiety disorders are at a higher risk for depression. Depression also tends to run in families.

The behavior of depressed children and teenagers may differ from the behavior of depressed adults. Child and adolescent psychiatrists advise parents to be aware of signs of depression in their youngsters.

If one or more of these signs of depression persist, parents should seek help:

- Frequent sadness, tearfulness, crying

- Hopelessness

- Decreased interest in activities; or inability to enjoy previously favorite activities

- Persistent boredom; low energy

- Social isolation, poor communication

- Low self esteem and guilt
- Extreme sensitivity to rejection or failure
- Increased irritability, anger, or hostility
- Difficulty with relationships
- Frequent complaints of physical illnesses such as headaches and stomachaches
- Frequent absences from school or poor performance in school
- Poor concentration
- A major change in eating and/or sleeping patterns
- Talk of or efforts to run away from home
- Thoughts or expressions of suicide or self destructive behavior

A child who used to play often with friends may now spend most of the time alone and without interests. Things that were once fun now bring little joy to the depressed child. Children and adolescents who are depressed may say they want to be dead or may talk about suicide. Depressed children and adolescents are at increased risk for committing suicide. Depressed adolescents may abuse alcohol or other drugs as a way to feel better.

Children and adolescents who cause trouble at home or at school may actually be depressed but not know it. Because the youngster may not always seem sad, parents and teachers may not realize that troublesome behavior is a sign of depression. When asked directly, these children can sometimes state they are unhappy or sad.

Early diagnosis and medical treatment are essential for depressed children. This is a real illness that requires professional help. Comprehensive treatment often includes both individual and family therapy. It may also include the use of antidepressant medication. For help, parents should ask their physician to refer them to a child and adolescent psychiatrist, who can diagnose and treat depression in children and teenagers.

Chapter 16

Depression on the College Campus

What Do These Students Have in Common?

When I took a part-time job and started living off-campus, my course work fell apart. I couldn't concentrate or sleep, and I was always **irritable** and angry.—Leah, sophomore year

After two years of straight A's, I couldn't finish assignments anymore. I felt exhausted but couldn't sleep, and drank **a lot**. I couldn't enjoy life like my friends did anymore.—John, junior year

I've always been anxious and never had much confidence. College was harder than I expected, and then my parents divorced, which was traumatic for me. After a while, all I did was cry, sleep, and feel waves of panic.—Marta, freshman year

They are college students who got depressed...got treatment...and got better.

College offers new experiences and challenges. This can be exciting—it can also be stressful and make you, or someone you know, feel sad. But when "the blues" last for weeks, or interfere with academic or social functioning, it may be clinical depression. Clinical depression is a common, frequently unrecognized illness that can be effectively treated.

"What do These Students Have in Common?" National Institute of Mental Health (NIMH), National Institutes of Health (NIH), NIH Publication No. 97-4266, updated June 1, 1999.

What Is Clinical Depression?

Clinical depression can affect your body, mood, thoughts, and behavior. It can change your eating habits, how you feel and think about things, your ability to work and study, and how you interact with people.

Clinical depression is *not* a passing mood, a sign of personal weakness or a condition that can be willed away. Clinically depressed people cannot "pull themselves together" and get better.

Depression *can* be successfully treated by a mental health professional or certain health care providers. With the right treatment, 80 percent of those who seek help get better. And many people begin to feel better in just a few weeks.

Types of Depressive Illness

Depressive illnesses come in different forms. The following are general descriptions of the three most prevalent, though for an individual, the number, severity, and duration of symptoms will vary.

Major depression. Major depression is manifested by a combination of symptoms that interfere with your ability to work, sleep, eat, and enjoy once pleasurable activities. These impairing episodes of depression can occur once, twice, or several times in a lifetime.

Symptoms of major depression:

- Sadness, anxiety, or "empty" feelings
- Decreased energy, fatigue, being "slowed down"
- Loss of interest or pleasure in usual activities
- Sleep disturbances (insomnia, oversleeping, or waking much earlier than usual)
- Appetite and weight changes (either loss or gain)
- Feelings of hopelessness, guilt, and worthlessness
- Thoughts of death or suicide, or suicide attempts
- Difficulty concentrating, making decisions, or remembering
- Irritability or excessive crying
- Chronic aches and pains not explained by another physical condition

Dysthymia. A less intense type of depression, dysthymia, involves long-term, chronic symptoms that are less severe, but keep you from functioning at your full ability and from feeling well.

Bipolar illness. In bipolar illness (also known as manic-depressive illness), cycles of depression alternate with cycles of elation and increased activity, known as mania.

How to Recognize Depression

The first step in defeating depression is recognizing it. It's normal to have some signs of depression some of the time. But five or more symptoms for two weeks or longer, or noticeable changes in usual functioning, are all factors that should be evaluated by a health or mental health professional. And remember, people who are depressed may not be thinking clearly and may need help to get help.

> I kept asking myself, "How could I be depressed? I'd had a normal family life, had been getting good grades, and hadn't experienced any big trauma—where did my depression come from?"—John

What Causes Depression?

The causes of depression are complex. Very often a combination of genetic, psychological and environmental factors is involved in the onset of clinical depression. At times, however, depression occurs for no apparent reason. Regardless of the cause, depression is almost always treatable.

Family History. Depression often runs in families, which usually means that some, but not all, family members have a tendency to develop the illness. On the other hand, sometimes people who have no family history also develop depression.

Stress. Psychological and environmental stressors can contribute to a depressive episode, though individuals react differently to life events and experiences.

In coping with stress, some people find writing in a journal, exercising, or talking with friends helpful. But in clinical depression you need some form of treatment (usually medication and short-term psychotherapy) to start feeling better soon.

I had a period of nearly constant turmoil when I wanted to "come out" to my friends about being gay but didn't want to be treated like an outsider. A good friend made jokes about homosexuals and I was afraid of what he'd say about me. That stress played a big part in my becoming depressed.—Josh

My family wanted me home every other weekend and I didn't fit in there anymore. I'd argue constantly with my father, who still treated me like a child. My sister thought I was 'uppity.' Everyone was miserable and I felt guilty.—Kim

College and Stress

Common stressors in college life include:

- Greater academic demands
- Being on your own in a new environment
- Changes in family relations
- Financial responsibilities
- Changes in your social life
- Exposure to new people, ideas, and temptations
- Awareness of your sexual identity and orientation
- Preparing for life after graduation

Psychological make-up can also play a role in vulnerability to depression. People who have low self-esteem, who consistently view themselves and the world with pessimism, or are readily overwhelmed by stress may be especially prone to depression.

For Marta, her feelings of being "not good enough" were worsened by the stress of the academic demands of college and the emotional conflict caused by her parents' divorce, which combined to trigger her episode of major depression.

Bipolar Disorder (Manic Depression)

As mentioned earlier, bipolar disorder is a type of depressive illness that involves mood swings that go from periods of depression to periods of being overly "up" and irritable. Sometimes the mood swings are dramatic or rapid, but most often they occur gradually, over several weeks. The "up" or manic phase can include increased energy and

110

activity, insomnia, grandiose notions and impulsive or reckless behavior, including sexual promiscuity.

Medication usually is effective in controlling manic symptoms and preventing the recurrence of both manic and depressive episodes.

> During a manic episode, I stayed awake for five days straight, but had a lot of energy. I spent my tuition on a major shopping spree and long distance phone calls. I also had sex with several guys that I hardly knew. At the time, I felt so great that I couldn't see that there were serious problems with what I was doing.—Teresa

Suicide

Thoughts of death or suicide are usually signs of severe depression. "If you're feeling like you can't cope anymore, or that life isn't worth living, get help," advised Darrel, a student who tried to kill himself during his freshman year. "Talking to a professional can get you past those intense feelings and save your life."

Suicidal feelings, thoughts, impulses, or behaviors **always** should be taken seriously. If you are thinking about hurting or killing yourself, **seek help immediately**. Contact someone you trust to help you: a good friend, academic or resident advisor, or:

- Staff at the student health or counseling center

- A professor, coach, or advisor

- A local suicide or emergency hotline (get the phone number from the information operator or directory)

- A hospital emergency room
- Call 911

If someone you know has thoughts about suicide, the best thing to do is help him or her get professional help.

"I'm back from the edge," Darrel continued. "Now that I've gotten some treatment, I know how to keep from being out there again."

Depression and Alcohol and Other Drugs

A lot of depressed people, especially teenagers, also have problems with alcohol or other drugs. (Alcohol is a drug, too.) Sometimes the depression comes first and people try drugs as a way to escape it. (In the long run, drugs or alcohol just make things worse.) Other times, the alcohol or other drug use comes first, and depression is caused by:

- the drug itself, or
- withdrawal from it, or
- the problems that substance use causes.

And sometimes you can't tell which came first... the important point is that when you have both of these problems, the sooner you get treatment, the better.

Getting Help—Treatment Works

If you think you might be depressed, discuss this with a qualified health care or mental health professional who can evaluate your concerns. Bring along an understanding friend for support if you are hesitant or anxious about the appointment.

Several effective treatments for depression are available and can provide relief from symptoms in just a few weeks. The most commonly used treatments are psychotherapy, antidepressant medication, or a combination of the two. Which is the best treatment for an individual depends on the nature and severity of the depression.

Sharing your preferences and concerns with your treatment provider helps determine the course of treatment. Certain types of psychotherapy, particularly cognitive behavioral therapy, can help resolve the psychological or interpersonal problems that contribute to, or result from, the illness. Antidepressant medications relieve the physical and mood symptoms of depression and are not habit-forming. In severe depression, medication is usually required.

Individuals respond differently to treatment. If you don't start feeling better after several weeks, talk to the professional you are seeing about trying other treatments or getting a second opinion.

Making a Decision

Don't let fear of what others might say or think stop you from doing what's best for you. Parents and friends may understand more than you think they might, and they certainly want you to feel better.

Taking the First Step

I knew I was depressed but thought I could pull out of it by my-self. Unfortunately, friends reinforced this attitude by telling me to just toughen up. When that didn't work, I felt even worse be-cause I had 'failed' again. When a friend suggested I talk to his counselor, I resisted at first. In my mind, professional help was for weak, messed up people. But then, I hit a bottom so low that I was willing to try anything. —John

I decided to try treatment when my friends got fed up with me. They didn't want to talk about my problems any more, but my problems were the major focus of my life. I needed someone who could help me understand what was happening to me. I'd seen ads for the counseling center and decided to give it a try. —Kim

When I began considering suicide, I knew I needed serious help. My resident advisor helped me call a local hotline where I got some good referrals. It was just a phone call, but it was the start-ing point that got me to the professional help I needed. —Leah

Help Yourself: Be an Informed Consumer

Don't give in to negative thinking. Depression can make you feel exhausted, worthless, helpless and hopeless, making some people want to give up. Remember, these negative views are part of the de-pression, and will fade as treatment takes effect.

Take an active role in getting better. Make the most of the help available by being actively involved in your treatment and by work-ing with a qualified therapist or doctor. Once in treatment, don't hesi-tate to ask questions in order to understand your illness and the way treatment works. And, if you don't start feeling better in a few weeks, speak with the professional you are seeing about new approaches.

Be good to yourself while you're getting well. Along with pro-fessional help, there are some other simple things you can do to help yourself get better, for example: participating in a support group, spending time with other people, or taking part in activities, exercise, or hobbies. Just don't overdo it and don't set big goals for yourself. The health care professional you are seeing may suggest useful books to read and other self-help strategies.

Helping a Depressed Friend

The best thing you can do for a depressed friend is to help him or her get treatment. This may involve encouraging the person to seek professional help or to stay in treatment once it is begun. The next best thing is to offer emotional support. This involves understanding, patience, affection, and encouragement. Engage the depressed person in conversation or activities and be gently insistent if you meet with resistance. Remind that person that with time and help, he or she will feel better.

Helpful Resources

The professionals at a student health center or counseling service, the Resident Advisor in your dorm, your family health care provider, and your clergy can be helpful resources for getting treatment. You also might contact any of the following organizations in your area for mental health services or referrals:

- A community mental health agency
- A hospital psychiatric outpatient department or clinic
- A private or nonprofit counseling center
- Your local Mental Health Association

The telephone directory or information operator at your school or in your community, or a local hotline, should have telephone numbers for these and other mental health services.

Finding Affordable Treatment

People are sometimes reluctant to seek help because they are concerned about the cost of treatment. Services at college counseling centers are often low-cost or free. Also city or county mental health services are often offered on a "sliding scale" (the fee is based on your financial resources). Check out any health insurance you may have and see if it pays for private mental health services.

Is It Worth It?..........Yes!!

Actually, while the depression was painful, working to get better has taught me a lot about who I am and how to stay healthy.—Marta

Getting treatment definitely changed my life for the better and helped me avoid flunking a semester.—John

For Additional Information about Depression

National Mental Health Institute
6001 Executive Boulevard, Room 8184, MSC 9663
Bethesda, MD 20892-9663
Website: http://www.nimh.nih.gov

For free brochures on depression and its treatment, call: 1-800-421-4211.

Chapter 17

Depression: What Every Woman Should Know

Life is full of emotional ups and downs. But when the "down" times are long lasting or interfere with your ability to function, you may be suffering from a common, serious illness—depression. Clinical depression affects mood, mind, body, and behavior. Research has shown that in the United States about 19 million people—one in ten adults—experience depression each year, and nearly two-thirds do not get the help they need.[9] Treatment can alleviate the symptoms in over 80 percent of the cases. Yet, because it often goes unrecognized, depression continues to cause unnecessary suffering.

Depression is a pervasive and impairing illness that affects both women and men, but women experience depression at roughly twice the rate of men.[1] Researchers continue to explore how special issues unique to women—biological, life cycle, and psychosocial—may be associated with women's higher rate of depression.

No two people become depressed in exactly the same way. Many people have only some of the symptoms, varying in severity and duration. For some, symptoms occur in time-limited episodes; for others, symptoms can be present for long periods if no treatment is sought. Having some depressive symptoms does not mean a person is clinically depressed. For example, it is not unusual for those who have lost a loved one to feel sad, helpless, and disinterested in regular activities. Only when these symptoms persist for an unusually long time is there reason to suspect that grief has become depressive illness.

National Institute of Mental Health (NIMH), NIH Publication No. 00-4779, August 2000, updated September 13, 2001.

Similarly, living with the stress of potential layoffs, heavy workloads, or financial or family problems may cause irritability and "the blues." Up to a point, such feelings are simply a part of human experience. But when these feelings increase in duration and intensity and an individual is unable to function as usual, what seemed a temporary mood may have become a clinical illness.

The Types of Depressive Illness

1. In **major depression**, sometimes referred to as unipolar or clinical depression, people have some or all of the symptoms listed below for at least two weeks but frequently for several months or longer. Episodes of the illness can occur once, twice, or several times in a lifetime.

2. In **dysthymia**, the same symptoms are present though milder and last at least two years. People with dysthymia are frequently lacking in zest and enthusiasm for life, living a joyless and fatigued existence that seems almost a natural outgrowth of their personalities. They also can experience major depressive episodes.

3. **Manic-depression**, or bipolar disorder, is not nearly as common as other forms of depressive illness and involves disruptive cycles of depressive symptoms that alternate with mania. During manic episodes, people may become overly active, talkative, euphoric, irritable, spend money irresponsibly, and get involved in sexual misadventures. In some people, a milder form of mania, called hypomania, alternates with depressive episodes. Unlike other mood disorders, women and men are equally vulnerable to bipolar disorder; however, women with bipolar disorder tend to have more episodes of depression and fewer episodes of mania or hypomania.[5]

Symptoms of Depression and Mania

A thorough diagnostic evaluation is needed if three to five or more of the following symptoms persist for more than two weeks (one week in the case of mania), or if they interfere with work or family life. An evaluation involves a complete physical checkup and information gathering on family health history. Not everyone with depression experiences each of these symptoms. The severity of the symptoms also varies from person to person.

118

Depression

- Persistent sad, anxious, or "empty" mood
- Loss of interest or pleasure in activities, including sex
- Restlessness, irritability, or excessive crying
- Feelings of guilt, worthlessness, helplessness, hopelessness, pessimism
- Sleeping too much or too little, early-morning awakening
- Appetite and/or weight loss or overeating and weight gain
- Decreased energy, fatigue, feeling "slowed down"
- Thoughts of death or suicide, or suicide attempts
- Difficulty concentrating, remembering, or making decisions
- Persistent physical symptoms that do not respond to treatment, such as headaches, digestive disorders, and chronic pain

Mania

- Abnormally elevated mood
- Irritability
- Decreased need for sleep
- Grandiose notions
- Increased talking
- Racing thoughts
- Increased activity, including sexual activity
- Markedly increased energy
- Poor judgment that leads to risk-taking behavior
- Inappropriate social behavior

Causes of Depression

Genetic Factors

There is a risk for developing depression when there is a family history of the illness, indicating that a biological vulnerability may be inherited. The risk is somewhat higher for those with bipolar disorder. However, not everybody with a family history develops the illness. In addition, major depression can occur in people who have had no family members with the illness. This suggests that additional factors, possibly biochemistry, environmental stressors, and other psychosocial factors, are involved in the onset of depression.

Biochemical Factors

Evidence indicates that brain biochemistry is a significant factor in depressive disorders. It is known, for example, that individuals with major depressive illness typically have dysregulation of certain brain chemicals, called neurotransmitters. Additionally, sleep patterns, which are biochemically influenced, are typically different in people with depressive disorders. Depression can be induced or alleviated with certain medications, and some hormones have mood-altering properties. What is not yet known is whether the "biochemical disturbances" of depression are of genetic origin, or are secondary to stress, trauma, physical illness, or some other environmental condition.

Environmental and Other Stressors

Significant loss, a difficult relationship, financial problems, or a major change in life pattern have all been cited as contributors to depressive illness. Sometimes the onset of depression is associated with acute or chronic physical illness. In addition, some form of substance abuse disorder occurs in about one-third of people with any type of depressive disorder.[7]

Other Psychological and Social Factors

Persons with certain characteristics—pessimistic thinking, low self-esteem, a sense of having little control over life events, and a tendency to worry excessively—are more likely to develop depression. These attributes may heighten the effect of stressful events or interfere with taking action to cope with them or with getting well. Upbringing or sex role expectations may contribute to the development of these traits. It appears that negative thinking patterns typically develop in childhood or adolescence. Some experts have suggested that the traditional upbringing of girls might foster these traits and may be a factor in women's higher rate of depression.

Women Are at Greater Risk for Depression Than Men

Major depression and dysthymia affect twice as many women as men. This two-to-one ratio exists regardless of racial and ethnic background or economic status. The same ratio has been reported in ten other countries all over the world.[12] Men and women have about the same rate of bipolar disorder (manic-depression), though its course in women typically has more depressive and fewer manic episodes. Also, a greater number of women have the rapid cycling form of bipolar disorder, which may be more resistant to standard treatments.[5]

A variety of factors unique to women's lives are suspected to play a role in developing depression. Research is focused on understanding these, including: reproductive, hormonal, genetic or other biological factors; abuse and oppression; interpersonal factors; and certain psychological and personality characteristics. And yet, the specific causes of depression in women remain unclear; many women exposed to these factors do not develop depression. What is clear is that regardless of the contributing factors, depression is a highly treatable illness.

The Many Dimensions of Depression in Women

Investigators are focusing on the following areas in their study of depression in women:

The Issues of Adolescence

Before adolescence, there is little difference in the rate of depression in boys and girls. But between the ages of 11 and 13 there is a precipitous rise in depression rates for girls. By the age of 15, females are twice as likely to have experienced a major depressive episode as males.[2] This comes at a time in adolescence when roles and expectations change dramatically. The stresses of adolescence include forming an identity, emerging sexuality, separating from parents, and making decisions for the first time, along with other physical, intellectual, and hormonal changes. These stresses are generally different for boys and girls, and may be associated more often with depression in females. Studies show that female high school students have significantly higher rates of depression, anxiety disorders, eating disorders, and adjustment disorders than male students, who have higher rates of disruptive behavior disorders.[6]

Adulthood: Relationships and Work Roles

Stress in general can contribute to depression in persons biologically vulnerable to the illness. Some have theorized that higher incidence of depression in women is not due to greater vulnerability, but

121

to the particular stresses that many women face. These stresses include major responsibilities at home and work, single parenthood, and caring for children and aging parents. How these factors may uniquely affect women is not yet fully understood.

For both women and men, rates of major depression are highest among the separated and divorced, and lowest among the married, while remaining always higher for women than for men. The quality of a marriage, however, may contribute significantly to depression. Lack of an intimate, confiding relationship, as well as overt marital disputes, have been shown to be related to depression in women. In fact, rates of depression were shown to be highest among unhappily married women.

Reproductive Events

Women's reproductive events include the menstrual cycle, pregnancy, the postpregnancy period, infertility, menopause, and sometimes, the decision not to have children. These events bring fluctuations in mood that for some women include depression. Researchers have confirmed that hormones have an effect on the brain chemistry that controls emotions and mood; a specific biological mechanism explaining hormonal involvement is not known, however.

Many women experience certain behavioral and physical changes associated with phases of their menstrual cycles. In some women, these changes are severe, occur regularly, and include depressed feelings, irritability, and other emotional and physical changes. Called premenstrual syndrome (PMS) or premenstrual dysphoric disorder (PMDD), the changes typically begin after ovulation and become gradually worse until menstruation starts. Scientists are exploring how the cyclical rise and fall of estrogen and other hormones may affect the brain chemistry that is associated with depressive illness.[10]

Postpartum mood changes can range from transient "blues" immediately following childbirth to an episode of major depression to severe, incapacitating, psychotic depression. Studies suggest that women who experience major depression after childbirth very often have had prior depressive episodes even though they may not have been diagnosed and treated.

Pregnancy (if it is desired) seldom contributes to depression, and having an abortion does not appear to lead to a higher incidence of depression. Women with infertility problems may be subject to extreme anxiety or sadness, though it is unclear if this contributes to a higher rate of depressive illness. In addition, motherhood may be a time of heightened risk for depression because of the stress and demands it imposes.

Menopause, in general, is not associated with an increased risk of depression. In fact, while once considered a unique disorder, research has shown that depressive illness at menopause is no different than at other ages. The women more vulnerable to change-of-life depression are those with a history of past depressive episodes.

Specific Cultural Considerations

As for depression in general, the prevalence rate of depression in African American and Hispanic women remains about twice that of men. There is some indication, however, that major depression and dysthymia may be diagnosed less frequently in African American and slightly more frequently in Hispanic than in Caucasian women. Prevalence information for other racial and ethnic groups is not definitive.

Possible differences in symptom presentation may affect the way depression is recognized and diagnosed among minorities. For example, African Americans are more likely to report somatic symptoms, such as appetite change and body aches and pains. In addition, people from various cultural backgrounds may view depressive symptoms in different ways. Such factors should be considered when working with women from special populations.

Victimization

Studies show that women molested as children are more likely to have clinical depression at some time in their lives than those with no such history. In addition, several studies show a higher incidence of depression among women who have been raped as adolescents or adults. Since far more women than men were sexually abused as children, these findings are relevant. Women who experience other commonly occurring forms of abuse, such as physical abuse and sexual harassment on the job, also may experience higher rates of depression. Abuse may lead to depression by fostering low self-esteem, a sense of helplessness, self-blame, and social isolation. There may be biological and environmental risk factors for depression resulting from growing up in a dysfunctional family. At present, more research is needed to understand whether victimization is connected specifically to depression.

Poverty

Women and children represent seventy-five percent of the U.S. population considered poor. Low economic status brings with it many stresses, including isolation, uncertainty, frequent negative events, and poor access to helpful resources. Sadness and low morale are more common among persons with low incomes and those lacking social supports. But research has not yet established whether depressive illnesses are more prevalent among those facing environmental stressors such as these.

Depression in Later Adulthood

At one time, it was commonly thought that women were particularly vulnerable to depression when their children left home and they were confronted with "empty nest syndrome" and experienced a profound loss of purpose and identity. However, studies show no increase in depressive illness among women at this stage of life.

As with younger age groups, more elderly women than men suffer from depressive illness. Similarly, for all age groups, being unmarried (which includes widowhood) is also a risk factor for depression. Most important, depression should not be dismissed as a normal consequence of the physical, social, and economic problems of later life. In fact, studies show that most older people feel satisfied with their lives.

About 800,000 persons are widowed each year. Most of them are older, female, and experience varying degrees of depressive symptomatology. Most do not need formal treatment, but those who are moderately or severely sad appear to benefit from self-help groups or various psychosocial treatments. However, a third of widows/widowers do meet criteria for major depressive episode in the first month after the death, and half of these remain clinically depressed one year later. These depressions respond to standard antidepressant treatments, although research on when to start treatment or how medications should be combined with psychosocial treatments is still in its early stages.[4,8]

Depression Is a Treatable Illness

Even severe depression can be highly responsive to treatment. Indeed, believing one's condition is "incurable" is often part of the hopelessness that accompanies serious depression. Such individuals should be provided with the information about the effectiveness of modern treatments for depression in a way that acknowledges their likely skepticism about whether treatment will work for them. As with many illnesses, the earlier treatment begins, the more effective and the greater the likelihood of preventing serious recurrences. Of course, treatment will not eliminate life's inevitable stresses and ups and downs. But it can greatly enhance the ability to manage such challenges and lead to greater enjoyment of life.

The first step in treatment for depression should be a thorough examination to rule out any physical illnesses that may cause depressive symptoms. Since certain medications can cause the same symptoms as depression, the examining physician should be made aware of any medications being used. If a physical cause for the depression is not found, a psychological evaluation should be conducted by the physician or a referral made to a mental health professional.

Types of Treatment for Depression

The most commonly used treatments for depression are antidepressant medication, psychotherapy, or a combination of the two. Which of these is the right treatment for any one individual depends on the nature and severity of the depression and, to some extent, on individual preference. In mild or moderate depression, one or both of these treatments may be useful, while in severe or incapacitating depression, medication is generally recommended as a first step in the treatment.[3] In combined treatment, medication can relieve physical symptoms quickly, while psychotherapy allows the opportunity to learn more effective ways of handling problems.

Medications

There are several types of antidepressant medications used to treat depressive disorders. These include newer medications—chiefly the selective serotonin reuptake inhibitors (SSRIs)—and the tricyclics and monoamine oxidase inhibitors (MAOIs). The SSRIs—and other newer medications that affect neurotransmitters such as dopamine or norepinephrine—generally have fewer side effects than tricyclics. Each acts on different chemical pathways of the human brain related to moods. Antidepressant medications are not habit-forming. Although some individuals notice improvement in the first couple of weeks, usually antidepressant medications must be taken regularly for at least four weeks and, in some cases, as many as eight weeks, before the full therapeutic effect occurs. To be effective and to prevent a relapse of the depression, medications must be taken for about 6 to 12 months, carefully following the doctor's instructions. Medications must be monitored to ensure the most effective dosage and to minimize side effects. For those who have had several bouts of depression, long-term treatment with medication is the most effective means of preventing recurring episodes.

The prescribing doctor will provide information about possible side effects and, in the case of MAOIs, dietary and medication restrictions. In addition, other prescribed and over-the-counter medications or dietary supplements being used should be reviewed because some can interact negatively with antidepressant medication. There may be restrictions during pregnancy.

For bipolar disorder, the treatment of choice for many years has been lithium, as it can be effective in smoothing out the mood swings common to this disorder. Its use must be carefully monitored, as the range between an effective dose and a toxic one can be relatively small. However, lithium may not be recommended if a person has pre-existing thyroid, kidney, or heart disorders or epilepsy. Fortunately, other medications have been found helpful in controlling mood swings. Among these are two mood-stabilizing anticonvulsants, carbamazepine (Tegretol®) and valproate (Depakote®). Both of these medications have gained wide acceptance in clinical practice, and valproate has been approved by the Food and Drug Administration for first-line treatment of acute mania. Studies conducted in Finland in patients with epilepsy indicate that valproate may increase testosterone levels in teenage girls and produce polycystic ovary syndrome in women who began taking the medication before age 20.[11] Therefore, young female patients should be monitored carefully by a physician. Other anticonvulsants that are being used now include lamotrigine (Lamictal®) and gabapentin (Neurontin®); their role in the treatment hierarchy of bipolar disorder remains under study.

Most people who have bipolar disorder take more than one medication. Along with lithium and/or an anticonvulsant, they often take a medication for accompanying agitation, anxiety, insomnia, or depression. Some research indicates that an antidepressant, when taken without a mood stabilizing medication, can increase the risk of switching into mania or hypomania, or of developing rapid cycling, in people with bipolar disorder. Finding the best possible combination of these medications is of utmost importance to the patient and requires close monitoring by the physician.

Herbal Therapy

In the past few years, much interest has risen in the use of herbs in the treatment of both depression and anxiety. St. John's wort (*Hypericum perforatum*), an herb used extensively in the treatment of

126

mild to moderate depression in Europe, has recently aroused interest in the United States. St. John's wort, an attractive bushy, low-growing plant covered with yellow flowers in summer, has been used for centuries in many folk and herbal remedies. Today in Germany, *Hypericum* is used in the treatment of depression more than any other antidepressant. However, the scientific studies that have been conducted on its use have been short-term and have used several different doses.

Because of the widespread interest in St. John's wort, the National Institutes of Health (NIH) is conducting a 3-year study, sponsored by three NIH components—the National Institute of Mental Health, the National Institute for Complementary and Alternative Medicine, and the Office of Dietary Supplements. The study is designed to include 336 patients with major depression, randomly assigned to an 8-week trial with one-third of patients receiving a uniform dose of St. John's wort, another third an SSRI commonly prescribed for depression, and the final third a placebo (a pill that looks exactly like the SSRI and the St. John's wort, but has no active ingredients). The study participants who respond positively will be followed for an additional 18 weeks. After the 3-year study has been completed, results will be analyzed and published.

The Food and Drug Administration issued a Public Health Advisory on February 10, 2000. It stated that St. John's wort appears to affect an important metabolic pathway that is used by many drugs prescribed to treat conditions such as heart disease, depression, seizures, certain cancers, and rejection of transplants. Therefore, health care providers should alert their patients about these potential drug interactions. Any herbal supplement should be taken only after consultation with the doctor or other health care provider.

Psychotherapy

In mild to moderate cases of depression, psychotherapy is also a treatment option. Some short-term (10 to 20 week) therapies have been very effective in several types of depression. "Talking" therapies help patients gain insight into and resolve their problems through verbal give-and-take with the therapist. "Behavioral" therapies help patients learn new behaviors that lead to more satisfaction in life and "unlearn" counter-productive behaviors. Research has shown that two short-term psychotherapies, interpersonal and cognitive-behavioral, are helpful for some forms of depression. Interpersonal therapy works to change interpersonal relationships that cause or exacerbate depression.

Cognitive-behavioral therapy helps change negative styles of thinking and behaving that may contribute to the depression.

Electroconvulsive Therapy

For individuals whose depression is severe or life threatening or for those who cannot take antidepressant medication, electroconvulsive therapy (ECT) is useful.[3] This is particularly true for those with extreme suicide risk, severe agitation, psychotic thinking, severe weight loss or physical debilitation as a result of physical illness. Over the years, ECT has been much improved. A muscle relaxant is given before treatment, which is done under brief anesthesia. Electrodes are placed at precise locations on the head to deliver electrical impulses. The stimulation causes a brief (about 30 seconds) seizure within the brain. The person receiving ECT does not consciously experience the electrical stimulus. At least several sessions of ECT, usually given at the rate of three per week, are required for full therapeutic benefit.

Treating Recurrent Depression

Even when treatment is successful, depression may recur. Studies indicate that certain treatment strategies are very useful in this instance. Continuation of antidepressant medication at the same dose that successfully treated the acute episode can often prevent recurrence. Monthly interpersonal psychotherapy can lengthen the time between episodes in patients not taking medication.

The Path to Healing

Reaping the benefits of treatment begins by recognizing the signs of depression. The next step is to be evaluated by a qualified professional. Although depression can be diagnosed and treated by primary care physicians, often the physician will refer the patient to a psychiatrist, psychologist, clinical social worker, or other mental health professional. Treatment is a partnership between the patient and the health care provider. An informed consumer knows her treatment options and discusses concerns with her provider as they arise.

If there are no positive results after 2 to 3 months of treatment, or if symptoms worsen, discuss another treatment approach with the provider. Getting a second opinion from another health or mental health professional may also be in order.

Here, again, are the steps to healing:

- Check your symptoms against those listed.

- Talk to a health or mental health professional.

- Choose a treatment professional and a treatment approach with which you feel comfortable.

- Consider yourself a partner in treatment and be an informed consumer.

- If you are not comfortable or satisfied after 2 to 3 months, discuss this with your provider. Different or additional treatment may be recommended.

- If you experience a recurrence, remember what you know about coping with depression and don't shy away from seeking help again. In fact, the sooner a recurrence is treated, the shorter its duration will be.

Depressive illnesses make you feel exhausted, worthless, helpless, and hopeless. Such feelings make some people want to give up. It is important to realize that these negative feelings are part of the depression and will fade as treatment begins to take effect.

Along with professional treatment, there are other things you can do to help yourself get better. Some people find participating in support groups very helpful. It may also help to spend some time with other people and to participate in activities that make you feel better, such as mild exercise or yoga. Just don't expect too much from yourself right away. Feeling better takes time.

Where to Get Help

If unsure where to go for help, ask your family doctor, OB/GYN physician, or health clinic for assistance. You can also check the Yellow Pages under "mental health," "health," "social services," "suicide prevention," "crisis intervention services," "hotlines," "hospitals," or "physicians" for phone numbers and addresses. In times of crisis, the emergency room doctor at a hospital may be able to provide temporary help for an emotional problem and will be able to tell you where and how to get further help.

Listed below are the types of people and places that will make a referral to, or provide, diagnostic and treatment services.

- Family doctors

- Mental health specialists such as psychiatrists, psychologists, social workers, or mental health counselors
- Health maintenance organizations
- Community mental health centers
- Hospital psychiatry departments and outpatient clinics
- University- or medical school-affiliated programs
- State hospital outpatient clinics
- Family service/social agencies
- Private clinics and facilities
- Employee assistance programs
- Local medical and/or psychiatric societies

For More Information

National Institute of Mental Health
Information Resources and Inquiries Branch
6001 Executive Boulevard
Room 8184, MSC 9663
Bethesda, MD 20892-9663
Telephone: 1-301-443-4513
FAX: 1-301-443-4279
Depression brochures: 1-800-421-4211
TTY: 1-301-443-8431
FAX4U: 1-301-443-5158
Website: http://www.nimh.nih.gov/
E-mail: nimhinfo@nih.gov

Other resources can be found in the end section of this book.

References

1. Blehar MC, Oren DA. Gender differences in depression. Medscape Women's Health, 1997;2:3. Revised from: Women's increased vulnerability to mood disorders: Integrating psycho-biology and epidemiology. *Depression*, 1995;3:3-12.

2. Cyranowski JM, Frank E, Young E, Shear MK. Adolescent on-set of the gender difference in lifetime rates of major depression. *Archives of General Psychiatry*, 2000; 57:21-27.

3. Frank E, Karp JF, and Rush AJ. Efficacy of treatments for major depression. *Psychopharmacology Bulletin*, 1993;29:457-75.

4. Lebowitz BD, Pearson JL, Schneider LS, Reynolds CF, Alexopoulos GS, Bruce ML, Conwell Y, Katz IR, Meyers BS, Morrison MF, Mossey J, Niederehe G, and Parmelee P. Diagnosis and treatment of depression in late life: Consensus statement update. *Journal of the American Medical Association*, 1997;278:1186-90.

5. Leibenluft E. Issues in the treatment of women with bipolar illness. *Journal of Clinical Psychiatry* (supplement 15), 1997;58:5-11.

6. Lewisohn PM, Hyman H, Roberts RE, Seeley JR, and Andrews JA. Adolescent psychopathology: 1. Prevalence and incidence of depression and other DSM-III-R disorders in high school students. *Journal of Abnormal Psychology*, 1993;102:133-44.

7. Regier DA, Farmer ME, Rae DS, Locke BZ, Keith SJ, Judd LL, and Goodwin FK. Comorbidity of mental disorders with alcohol and other drug abuse: Results from the epidemiologic catchment area (ECA) study. *Journal of the American Medical Association*, 1993;264:2511-8.

8. Reynolds CF, Miller MD, Pasternak RE, Frank E, Perel JM, Cornes C, Houck PR, Mazumdar S, Dew MA, and Kupfer DJ. Treatment of bereavement-related major depressive episodes in later life: A controlled study of acute and continuation treatment with nortriptyline and interpersonal psychotherapy. *American Journal of Psychiatry*, 1999;156:202-8.

9. Robins LN and Regier DA (Eds). *Psychiatric Disorders in America, The Epidemiologic Catchment Area Study*. New York: The Free Press, 1990.

10. Rubinow DR, Schmidt PJ, and Roca CA. Estrogen-serotonin interactions: Implications for affective regulation. *Biological Psychiatry*, 1998;44(9):839-50.

11. Vainionpaa LK, Rattya J, Knip M, Tapanainen JS, Pakarinen AJ, Lanning P, Tekay, A, Myllyla, VV, Isojarvi JI. Valproate-induced hyperandrogenism during pubertal maturation in girls with epilepsy. *Annals of Neurology*, 1999;45(4):444-50.

12.   Weissman MM, Bland RC, Canino GJ, Faravelli C, Greenwald S, Hwu HG, Joyce PR, Karam EG, Lee CK, Lellouch J, Lepine JP, Newman SC, Rubin-Stiper M, Wells JE, Wickramaratne PJ, Wittchen H, and Yeh EK. Cross-national epidemiology of major depression and bipolar disorder. *Journal of the American Medical Association*, 1996;276:293-9.

Chapter 18

Major Depression during Conception and Pregnancy

Depression is an illness that affects up to one in four women at some point in their lives. It often begins when women are in their 20s and 30s, at the same time they may be considering having children. If you or someone you know has major depression, you may be wondering whether it is safe to become pregnant—especially if you are taking medication for your symptoms—or safe to continue medication if you are already pregnant. This guide is intended to answer some commonly asked questions about the treatment of major depression while trying to conceive and during pregnancy.

What Is Major Depression?

Major depression is a mood disorder. Mood disorders are illnesses that affect a person's ability to experience normal mood states. Research suggests that mood disorders are biological illnesses involving changes in brain chemistry. Emotional stress can sometimes trigger these changes, though some individuals may experience depression

The information in this chapter is reprinted with permission from "Major Depression during Conception and Pregnancy: A Guide for Patients and Families," by David A. Kahn, M.D., Margaret L. Moline, Ph.D., Ruth W. Ross, M.A., Lee S. Cohen, M.D., and Lori L. Altshuler, M.D. which appeared in Altshuler LL, Cohen LS, Moline ML, et al. "The expert consensus guideline series: Treatment of depression in women 2001." *Postgraduate Medicine Special Report*, pp. 110–111, March 2001, © 2001 Expert Knowledge Systems, LLC, a division of Comprehensive NeuroScience, Inc. Complete information about Comprehensive NeuroScience Inc. is included at the end of this chapter.

for no apparent external cause. The symptoms of major depression include:

- Depressed mood most of the day, nearly every day for two weeks or longer and/or

- Loss of interest or pleasure in activities that the person usually enjoys

Other symptoms can include:

- Fatigue or lack of energy
- Restlessness or feeling slowed down
- Feelings of guilt or worthlessness
- Difficulty concentrating
- Trouble sleeping or sleeping too much
- Recurrent thoughts of death or suicide

Depression during Pregnancy: Special Issues

Contrary to popular belief, pregnancy does not protect a woman from becoming depressed. About 20% of women experience some depressive symptoms during pregnancy, and about 10% of women develop major depression. Women who have had major depression in the past have a higher risk of becoming depressed in pregnancy, especially if they stopped taking antidepressant medication while trying to become pregnant.

Treating depression in a woman who wants to conceive or is pregnant is complicated. When pregnancy is not an issue, psychotherapy can help with milder symptoms, but antidepressant medication is often needed to bring relief from severe major depression. However, in pregnancy concerns arise about using medications to treat depression since they cross the placenta and may harm the fetus. At the same time, untreated major depression has serious potential risks for mother and fetus, since it may lead to poor nutrition, smoking, drinking, suicidal behavior, prolonged or premature labor, and low birth weights.

Unfortunately, research information about the safety of antidepressants in pregnancy is limited because there are important ethical concerns about conducting such research. However, many pharmaceutical companies do maintain registries of pregnant women who have taken their products, and some hospital clinics publish information on groups of women who have used antidepressants during pregnancy. These records provide helpful information about several of the most widely used antidepressants, although we lack such information about a number of other antidepressants.

In deciding whether a woman should use antidepressant medication while pregnant or trying to become pregnant, a woman and her doctor have to balance the possible risks of the medication against the severity of the depression. Because our research knowledge is limited, we surveyed leading experts in the area of women's mental health to develop recommendations based on their best judgments. This chapter summarizes the results of this survey.

Treatment while Trying to Conceive

Many women who have had depression may be taking antidepressants to prevent symptoms at the time they wish to become pregnant. Whether the medication should be stopped depends on how severe the history of depression has been. If a woman has had only one previous episode of depression and has been feeling well for at least six months, the experts recommend that she taper off medication before trying to conceive. Several weeks may be required before all traces of medication have been eliminated. The experts also suggest that continuing or beginning psychotherapy may be helpful in preventing symptoms from returning. However, if a woman has a history of severe major depression with multiple previous episodes, the experts recommend that she continue medication at full dose through conception. If she is already taking an antidepressant for which there is a fair amount of information suggesting that it is safe (these are listed later), it is fine to continue. However, if she is taking a medication for which there is little information, she should switch to a medication thought to be safer.

What about a woman who is depressed, is not receiving treatment, and wants to conceive?

If the depression is mild, the experts would recommend trying to treat her symptoms with psychotherapy alone. However, if the symptoms are severe, whether it is a first episode or one of many, a combination of medication and psychotherapy is advised.

Treatment in the First Trimester

The first trimester (12 weeks) of pregnancy is a crucial time when medication can cause malformations of the fetus. Women may be taking antidepressants at the start of pregnancy for one of the reasons discussed above or may have an unplanned pregnancy while on medication. If a woman has had only mild symptoms in the past, the experts recommend gradually stopping the medication over several weeks as soon as she knows she is pregnant. (But recall that it is a good idea to stop the medication before trying to conceive, unless a woman has had multiple episodes of severe depression.) For a woman who has had multiple past episodes of severe depression, the experts clearly prefer that she remain on medication and, if necessary, switch from her current drug to one viewed as relatively safe. For the in-between case of a woman who has had only one episode, but a severe one, the experts are divided as to whether to continue or stop the medication. Whether the woman remains on medication or not, in all these situations, the experts advise using psychotherapy to help prevent depression from coming back.

Treatment during the Second and Third Trimesters

Later in pregnancy there is not the concern about medication causing malformation of organs. However, there are still questions about whether medication might cause a miscarriage or subtle changes in the early development of the future child. If there has been a good reason to use medication during the first trimester (such as recurrent bouts of severe depression), medication should probably be continued through delivery, since women who have histories of depression before or during pregnancy are vulnerable to postpartum depression.

What if a woman who has not been taking medication becomes depressed?

The first step is to start psychotherapy, or intensify it if already underway. If there is a history of severe depression, many experts would resume medication at the first sign of symptoms coming back. If the woman has had only mild depression in the past, the experts would wait to see if the depression comes back in full force before starting medication.

What about a woman with a history of depression, who has done well off medication through the later stages of pregnancy? Should medication be restarted to prevent depression after delivery (postpartum depression)?

Experts agree that preventive treatment is a good idea for women who have had previous postpartum depression but would wait until the last month of pregnancy to resume medication.

136

Medications Used to Treat Depression

Many types of antidepressants are available with different chemical actions and side effects. For the treatment of women with depression who are trying to conceive or who are pregnant, the experts recommend a kind of antidepressant that increases brain levels of a chemical called serotonin. These medications are called selective serotonin reuptake inhibitors (SSRIs). SSRIs are currently the most widely prescribed antidepressants in the world and have been used by millions of women. There is even evidence that they work more effectively in women than other antidepressants. It is not a surprise that many women have therefore become pregnant while taking SSRIs. Records show that the rate of infants with birth defects born to women taking SSRIs is no higher than the rate seen in women who took no medication—about 2%–3%. Thus, there is no current evidence that SSRIs cause birth defects.

The SSRIs preferred by the experts for use in pregnancy are fluoxetine (Prozac), sertraline (Zoloft), and paroxetine (Paxil). A small number of research studies support these choices. Fluoxetine, the first of this group to be used in the United States (since 1987), is the treatment of choice of most experts, probably because there has been more experience with its use in pregnancy than with other medications. In addition, there is research suggesting that exposure to fluoxetine before birth does not have negative effects on later child development. Many pregnant women have also taken sertraline and paroxetine without apparent problems. After we conducted our survey, researchers reported that another SSRI, citalopram (Celexa), has a similar profile of apparent safety.

The experts also favor tricyclic antidepressants, another kind of antidepressant that affects other brain chemicals in addition to serotonin. Tricyclic antidepressants have been used for over 40 years. Like SSRIs, extensive use in pregnancy has not revealed evidence of causing birth defects. Some other antidepressants have not shown evidence of causing birth defects but have not been used widely enough in pregnancy for doctors to feel confident.

What about side effects of SSRI medications?

SSRIs may cause the following side effects: nervousness, insomnia, restlessness, nausea, diarrhea, and sexual problems. Side effects differ from one person to another. Also, what may be a side effect for one person (for example, drowsiness) may be a benefit for someone

137

else (for example, a woman with insomnia). If you are having any problems with side effects, tell your doctor right away. Don't stop the medication on your own. Your doctor may try to lower the dose or switch you to a different SSRI.

Psychotherapy to Treat Depression

Several types of psychotherapy have been proven effective in the treatment of patients with major depression in general. Some researchers have also applied these successfully in pregnancy. Interpersonal therapy focuses on reducing the strain that a mood disorder may place on relationships. Cognitive-behavioral therapy focuses on identifying and changing the pessimistic thoughts and beliefs that can lead to depression. When used alone, psychotherapy usually works more gradually than medication and may take two months or more to show its full effects. However, the benefits may be long-lasting.

A Special Word about Depression with Psychosis

A severe form of major depression may include psychotic symptoms, such as delusions or hallucinations. Depression with psychosis is a great concern because it may cause a number of behaviors that compromise the safety of the mother and her unborn child. For a psychotic depression during any trimester of pregnancy, the experts recommend combining an antidepressant with a second medication called an antipsychotic. Electroconvulsive therapy is also an important option that can be used safely in pregnancy instead of medication for this type of depression. The experts would not rely on psychotherapy alone in this situation.

Comprehensive NeuroScience, Inc.

Comprehensive NeuroScience, Inc. (CNS) provides products and services that enhance the efficiencies of knowledge development and clinical care in neuro-psychopharmacology and related areas. Comprised of three complementary divisions (Drug Development, Clinical Trials, and Medical Information Technologies), CNS supports drug development and treatment process from discovery through clinical trial evaluation to the synthesis and dissemination of clinically actionable medical information. The Company employs 250 people in 30 locations nationwide and abroad. Headquarters: 21 Bloomingdale Road, White Plains, NY 10605; Phone: (914) 997-4010; Home Page: www.cnswebsite.com.

Chapter 19

Depression in Men

Willy Loman in *Death of a Salesman* exemplifies the quintessential depressed midlife man whose inner rage at his life prompts tumultuous actions resulting in self-destruction. How many men unconsciously replicate Faust's "contract with the Devil" in their 20s, only to find that the "ole Devil" has gotten the best of them by their mid-40s? What do these characters from great literature have in common?

Scope of the Problem

Depression is one of the most common responses of men to "Male Menopause." Midlife men often do not see themselves in the mirror of major depressive responses which include persistent sad moods, diminished ability to think or concentrate, feeling worthless, sleeping too much, low energy, significant weight loss or gain, loss of pleasure in activities, and recurrent thoughts of death. Approximately 40% of men in the forty to sixty midlife age ranges will experience some degree of depression. Whereas men complete 20% of all suicides in the United States, the suicide rate triples in midlife men and increases seven times in men over age 65. Having a history of depression makes the risk of suicide 78 times greater. The proper recognition and diagnosis of depression can take up to ten years and three or more healthcare

From "Depression in Men—Its Different!" by Caroline Dott, Ph.D., L.C.S.W. and Andrew B. Dott, M.D., M.P.H., originally published in *Atlanta Medicine*, Spring, 2001. © 2001. Reprinted with permission of the authors and the Medical Association of Atlanta.

139

professionals. Even though 80–90% of people seeking help for depression obtain relief, 60–80% of depressed adults never receive available professional help (Diamond, 1998).

What Contributes to Depression in Men at Midlife?

To answer this question, the incidences of physical, emotional, and spiritual challenges either already present, or that appear at midlife, need to be addressed. Depression may be a reaction to acute or chronic illness such as cancer, heart disease, or HIV (human immunodeficiency virus) infection. There are a number of physiological imbalances—especially endocrine and metabolic disorders, that can be accompanied by depression. Suboptimal nutrition can reinforce and worsen a depressive state. The depressive effects of alcohol on the body and psyche are well known. In general, because depression negatively impacts the immune system, its unrecognized and untreated presence contributes to compromised health overall. Finally, occupational and environmental pollutants may result in compromised energy resources that can contribute to or cause depression. As an example, while changes in the functioning of the thyroid gland are far more common in midlife women than in men at midlife, the decreased hormone output of the thyroid gland, or hypothyroidism, is often accompanied by depression. Men may mask real depression connected with low thyroid functioning by presenting with, "I'm tired, exhausted and can't function the way I used to" (Arem, 1999, p. 20). Adjusting to these feelings and struggling to appear normal to avoid the cultural stigma placed on emotional conditions, men may deny and dismiss their own symptoms and inner pain, not seeking professional help. Men and doctors may miss a correct diagnosis of malfunctioning thyroid by focusing on and treating resulting physical symptoms rather than diagnosing the underlying thyroid disease.

Other hormone changes such as a decrease in testosterone, the male hormone, DHEA, or insulin may result in the neurochemically based feeling of depression. Psychologist James Dabbs (Dabbs and Dabbs, 2000) found that his own testosterone level was lower when he was depressed and higher when he was optimistic. Endocrinologists have found that low testosterone results in lowered energy and reduced sexual activity. There is some evidence (Steiger, et al, 1991) that very low levels of testosterone may be associated with clinical depression, although this is controversial. Most studies to date do not confirm this finding (Rubin et al., 1989).

Testosterone interacts with other hormones such as cortisol, serotonin, and prolactin, which moderate the effects of testosterone. Cortisol lowers testosterone in men (Cumming et al, 1983). Released in stressful situations, cortisol contributes to the body's fight-or-flight response by providing energy to help one deal with emergencies. Men who are chronically high in cortisol and low in testosterone are not particularly aggressive or likely to confront others. Instead, they tend to be less friendly and cheerful than other men with low testosterone with an increase in anxiety related to high cortisol levels.

Serotonin is a neurotransmitter that affects the brain and behavior by stimulating a pleasant outlook. Elevated levels of serotonin tend to produce calmness, confidence, lowered irritability, increased optimism, less impulsivity, and increased pleasantness. Studies show that high-serotonin male vervet monkeys are dominant and calm whereas high-testosterone male vervet monkeys are dominant and more aggressive. An uncommon spate of other physiological changes in midlife men may contribute to feelings of depression. Thus, men can optimize their own health and continuous normal functioning by seeking informed professional help immediately for distressing symptoms rather than adjusting to and doing nothing about them.

Normal Male Psychological Development

Psychological and emotional stressors are the largest contributors to depression in midlife men. In order to understand these challenges, we need to know normal male psychological development. Daniel Levinson, in his enlightening book *The Seasons of a Man's Life*, outlines male adult developmental stages. During the major life phases of adolescence and young adulthood, life structures are built, defining choices are made, and goals and values are pursued within that structure. Following each major life phase is a transition period of four to five years when a man completes existing life tasks and creates new opportunities for growth and development.

In the pre-midlife stage of adulthood, men achieve the life goal of "Becoming a Man." This formidable accomplishment includes speaking with their own voice; becoming a senior, authoritative member in their world; and carrying the burden of increasing responsibility and its accompanying stress. These achievements lead to fulfilling their "Dream." At midlife, a man must terminate Early Adulthood. Perhaps the most significant task is discovering who he really is—not the "self" of social, business/professional or family expectations.

What are the primary tasks of every transition period?

1.   Questioning and reappraising existing life structures,

2. Exploring various options for change in oneself and in one's surrounding environments,

3. Moving toward a commitment to defining choices that form the basis for a new life structure in the next major life phase.

For most men, this transition period evokes tumultuous struggles within the self and with their external world leading to moderate to severe crises. Men question every aspect of their life, often experiencing some sense of horror at what they discover. They blame themselves and others severely for their life situation. Realizing they cannot continue as before, they require time either to choose a new path or to modify the old one. A man may begin to change the unacceptable parts of his existing life structure, entering a time of confusion, experimentation and, inevitably, some mistakes. Thus, in some ways, the midlife transition mirrors the earlier stage of adolescence.

What are the common events that precipitate men entering into midlife?

These events fall into three major categories—personal, family, and occupational. In the personal realm, a man may experience some health crisis, separation or divorce, or experience erectile failure twice in a row. Family events include the death or illness of a family member or peer, children leaving or returning home, or becoming a grandparent. Occupationally, he may be the unwilling victim of involuntary retirement, non-advancement, or of being displaced by a younger male. That old culprit, stress, accumulating in midlife men who are also in their peak years of responsibility, productivity, and financial output, may stimulate panic, anxiety, or depression. Stress, vascular disease, normal aging, and/or lowered testosterone levels can lead to compromised erectile functioning. Approximately 40% of men between the ages of forty and sixty will experience some degree of difficulty in attaining and sustaining an erection. Closely associated responses include lethargy, depression, increased irritability, and mood swings. Many men may develop a reactive depression secondary to issues relating to loss of virility and sexual identity.

Each of these major events can stimulate emotional reactions involving varying degrees of personal pain. Changes in any one or all major life areas may result in feelings of loss of power and self-esteem, questioning virility and personal desirability, and performance or global anxiety and/or depression which frequently occur together.

Why don't we recognize depression in men?

The signs and symptoms of depression in men commonly are not recognized for several reasons:

1. The behavioral expression of depression in men is often quite different from the classic symptoms people in our culture define as depressed.

2. Men in our culture often are not aware when they are depressed because of the association with being weak when men are taught to be strong.

3. Men do not allow themselves to admit to themselves that they are having a problem with sexual expression and do not understand its relationship to depression.

4. The behavioral expression of male depression is not familiar to family members or healthcare providers who do not recognize it.

Depression Looks Different in Men and Women

Empirically and anecdotally, women generally turn inward when they are depressed, whereas men are more likely to act out their unrecognized and denied feelings of depression. Jed Diamond, PhD, in his book, *Male Menopause* (1998), details the differences between men's and women's expression of depression (summarized in Table 19.1).

The most striking overall difference between the ways women and men handle depression can be described best as polar opposite behaviors. For example, one common emotion that underlies depression in both men and women is anger. Women usually hold in their anger and this negative energy lodges inside the body down to the cellular level, depressing the whole system. Men, on the other hand, more often express their unrecognized inner feelings of depression by showing increasing impatience, irritability, hostility, and anger toward those with whom they are closest emotionally, and often toward others as well.

What Can Men Do about Their Depression?

Unfortunately, because most men do not recognize that they are depressed or because they deny it, there is little they do to seek help. If and when their own inner pain finally becomes unbearable, they may inadvertently and, at times, impulsively try out some new behaviors in a desperate and misdirected attempt to rid themselves of inescapable and painful situations. These often unconscious attempts at fixing an ill-defined and often-denied painful state may result in behaviors which are self-destructive and destructive to those closest to them—thus we have the full blown midlife crisis. In actuality, it is

Table 19.1. Differences between Male and Female Depression

Female Depression	Male Depression
Blame themselves	Blame others
Feel sad, apathetic, worthless	Feel angry, irritable
Feel anxious, scared	Feel suspicious, guarded
Avoid conflict at all costs	Create conflict
Always try to be nice	Overtly or covertly hostile
Withdraw when feeling hurt	Attack when feeling hurt
Have little self-respect	Demand respect from others
Feel they were born to fail	Feel the world set them up to fail
Slowed down and nervous	Restless and agitated
Chronic procrastinator	Compulsive time keeper
Sleep too much	Sleep too little
Trouble setting boundaries	Control everything, everybody
Feel guilty for everything	Feel ashamed for who they are
Uncomfortable receiving praise	Frustrated if not praised enough
Easily talk about weaknesses, doubts	Terrified to admit weaknesses, doubts
Strong fear of success	Strong fear of failure
Need to "blend in" to feel safe	Need to be "top dog" to feel safe
Use food, friends, and "love" to self-medicate	Use alcohol, TV, sports, and sex to self-medicate
Believe their problems could be solved only if they could be a better spouse, co-worker, parent, friend	Believe their problems could be solved only if their spouse, co-worker, parent, friend would treat them better
Constantly wonder, "Am I lovable enough?	Constantly think, "I'm not getting enough love"

Source: Adapted from *Male Menopause*, by Jed Diamond, PhD, Naperville, Ill: Sourcebooks, Inc., 1998.

not necessarily the stage of midlife that creates the crisis for the man but his response to his own midlife stress and confusion.

Often we receive questions on our website, www.midlife-passages .com, from distressed women who wonder what is happening to their partner. For example:

- My husband has just separated from me after 22 years of marriage. I don't know what happened but he has changed overnight. He says he loves me but he doesn't want to live with me any more. Our friends and our children are angry with him because they think he is acting crazy. I am hurt, confused and don't know what to do. I still love him. Please help!

Without further information, we cannot make a definite determination about the underlying cause of this man's distress, but this type of situation is described frequently. We can speculate that this man may be feeling depressed, may not recognize it or may deny it, and is handling it in the only way his current repertoire of coping mechanisms allows him—to escape the situation, which generally is not a viable solution. This is an example of the way in which some men are not aware of the reasons for their depression and may react impulsively rather than create thoughtful, proactive solutions. Lack of awareness is a common emotional defense in many men.

Why is this defense so common in men?

In the emotional realm, men often do not want to face the fact that they need to "fix" something about themselves that feels threatening or painful. They can avoid the whole uncomfortable fixing process by denying that they have a problem. Thus, most men seek help only when pressured to do so by significant people in their life who recognize that they are struggling and in distress.

Men can be helped or help themselves through a variety of approaches. Through loving, gentle encouragement, a partner can help a man begin to realize he needs help in identifying the major stressors in his life. The partner can take the lead in rallying support for him from family members, friends, and co-workers who can assist him to modify the situations and environments that are stress provoking. A partner can assist him in determining how to modify what he provides for family members, emphasizing his increasing need for better self-care while still addressing family members' needs.

Other time-honored and effective methods for achieving and maintaining harmony and balance in a man's life include:

145

1. Having a thorough medical evaluation

2. Exercising regularly

3. Starting an individualized nutritional program

4. Learning to love and accept themselves for whom they are

5. Recreating close social supports they have lost and/or learning to create closeness and intimacy they never had

6. Growing spiritually

7. Engaging in individual and/or group psychotherapy or support groups

8. Taking appropriate medications and/or hormones

How effective is exercise in reducing depression?

We know that people who exercise tend to be less depressed than those who do not exercise (Goleman and Gurin, 1993). What we do not know is whether the primary stimulus that differentiates more depressed from less depressed people is the exercise or the depression. By itself, exercise is unlikely to help a man with long-term depression or an acute severely depressive episode. There is evidence that exercise is an effective adjunct for moderate types of depression that still require professional help.

Two different studies (Griest et al., 1979; Schwartz et al., 1978) investigated the differential benefits of exercise, time-limited or long-term psychotherapy, and meditation training. Results indicated that exercise is similar to or better than standard medical treatment for moderate depression. Other studies show that exercise is ameliorative for mild, transient forms of depression experienced at times by most people. Mild depression may include acute feelings of sadness, discouragement, and self-deprecation. Probably, the effect of an integrated approach of both psychology and physiology determines how exercise benefits mood.

What if the man does know he is suffering, is depressed, or is in pain? What can he do to help himself?

He needs to have the courage to share his vulnerabilities with his partner, family, and close friends, asking for their understanding and support. He must do whatever he needs to do to take care of his distress, including seeking outside professional help. Hopefully in time, those closest to him will hear his distress and assist him in his recovery.

Medications

Excellent antidepressant medications are available. No one medication is perfect, and it is very important to choose and monitor therapy carefully. These medications include:

1. Tricyclic Antidepressants (TCAs)—amitriptyline (Elavil®), desipramine (Norpramin®), doxepin (Sinequan®), protriptyline (Vivactil®) etc. These are generic and cheap but have side effects including sedation, dry mouth, and urinary retention.

2. SSRIs—fluoxetine (Prozac®), sertraline (Zoloft®), citalopram (Celexa®), paroxetine (Paxil®), and fluvoxamine (Luvox®)— the drugs of choice in the 1990s. They eliminate virtually all the side effects of TCAs but they are not perfect. Each medication has a slightly different profile of side effects so it may be necessary to try several different preparations to obtain the optimal response. One of the most common side effects of this class of medications is sexual dysfunction (see Table 19.2).

3. Reported incidence of sexual problems is as high as 17%. Obviously these medications would be a poor choice for a male in mid-life crisis who is obsessing about inadequate sexual performance. These medications should be used cautiously when combined with weight reduction pills, agents used in smoking cessation such as bupropion (Zyban®), tryptophan, St. John's Wort, and other serotonin-like agents.

4. Atypical Antidepressants— bupropion (Wellbutrin®), venlafaxine (Effexor®), and nefazodone (Serzone®). These act on the brain through the inhibition of both serotonin and norepinephrine uptake. Bupropion and nefazodone, in particular, have a lower incidence of sexual side effects. At this time, there is no one best agent for the pharmacological management of the unique issues associated with male depression at midlife.

5. Amphetamines and MAO Inhibitors—tranylcypromine (Parnate®) and phenelzine (Nardil®)— these are dangerous and should be dispensed only by psychiatrists highly skilled in their use. They are rarely used today.

Table 19.2. Reported Incidence of Sexually Related Side Effects in Men with Common Anti-Depressants

Medication	Abnormal Ejaculation (Reported *vs.* Control)		Decreased Libido (Reported *vs.* Control)		Impotence (Reported *vs.* Control)	
Prozac	7%	>1%	4%	0%	2%	>1%
Zoloft	14	1	6	1	N.A.	N.A.
Paxil	13	0	3	1	10	0
Celexa	6.1	1	3.8	1	2.8	1
Wellbutrin	No data	No data	3.1	1.6	3.4	3.1
Effexor	17	1	6	2	6	1
Serzone	>1	>1	1	>1	>1	>1
Luvox	8	1	2	1	2	1

Source: Compiled from the *Physicians Desk Reference* (PDR-2001), 55th ed., Montvale, N.J.: Medical Economics, 2001.

Ultimate recovery from midlife depression is possible with the working through of relevant issues, the loving support of partner, family, and friends and appropriate professional help. The courageous man who takes on this "last great dragon" gives himself and others the gift of his full passion, well-honed powers, and mutual fulfillment.

References

Arem, Ridha, MD. *The Thyroid Solution: A Mind-Body Program for Beating Depression and Regaining Your Emotional and Physical Health*. New York: Ballantine Books, 1999.

Carruthers, Malcolm, MD. *Maximizing Manhood: Beating the Male Menopause*. Hammersmith, London: Harper/Collins, 1997.

Cumming, D.C., Quigley, M.E., and Yen, S.S.C. "Acute Suppression of circulating testosterone levels by cortisol in men," *Journal of Clinical Endocrinology and Metabolism*, Vol. 57 (1983), pp. 671-673.)

Dabbs, J.M. and Dabbs, M.G. Heroes, *Rogues, and Lovers: Testosterone and Behavior*. New York: McGraw-Hill, 2000.

Diamond, Jed, PhD. *Male Menopause*. Naperville, Ill: Sourcebooks, Inc., 1998.

Diamond, Jed, PhD. *Surviving Male Menopause: A Guide for Women and Men*. Naperville, Ill: Sourcebooks, Inc., 2000.

Dym, Barry and Glenn, M.L. *Couples — Exploring and Understanding the Cycles of Intimate Relationships*. San Francisco: Harper/Collins, 1993.

Goleman, Daniel, PhD. *Emotional Intelligence*. New York: Bantam, 1996.

Goleman, Daniel, PhD, and Gurin, Joel (Eds.). *Mind-Body Medicine: How To Use Your Mind For Better Health*. New York: Consumer Reports Books, 1993.

Griest, J.H., Klein, M.H., Eischens, R.R., Faris, J., Gurman, A.S., and Morgan, W.P. "Running as a Treatment for Depression," *Comparative Psychiatry*, 53(1979): pp. 20-41.

Hudson, F.M., PhD, and McLean, P.D., PhD. *Life Launch: A Passionate Guide to the Rest of Your Life*. Santa Barbara, CA. The Hudson Institute Press, 1995.

Levinson, Daniel. *The Seasons of a Man's Life*. New York: Knopf, 1978.

Oppenheim, Michael, MD. *The Man's Health Book*. New Jersey: Prentice-Hall, 1994.

Osherman, Samuel, PhD. *Wrestling with Love: How Men Struggle with Intimacy*. New York: Fawcett Columbine, 1992.

Osherman, Samuel, PhD. *Finding our Fathers: How a Man's Life is Shaped by His Relationship with His Father*. New York: Fawcett Columbine, 1986.

Rubin, R.T., Poland, R.E., and Lesser, I.M. "Neuroendocrine Aspects of Primary Endogenous Depression VIII. Pituitary-Gonadal Axis Activity in Male Patients and Matched Control Subjects," *Psychoneuroendocrinology*, Vol. 14 (1989), pp. 217-229.

Schwartz, G.E., Davidson, R.J., and Goleman, D.J. "Patterning of Cognitive and Somatic Processes in the Self-Regulation of Anxiety: Effects of Meditation Versus Exercise." *Psychosomatic Medicine*, 40(1978); pp. 321-328.

Sheehy, Gail. *Understanding Men's Passages: Discovering the New Map of Men's Lives*. New York: Random House, 1998.

Steiger, A., von Bardeleben, U., Wiedemann, K., and Holsboer, F. "Sleep EEG and Nocturnal Secretion of Testosterone and Cortisol in Patients with Major Endogenous Depression During Acute Phase and after Remission," *Journal of Psychiatric Research*, Vol.25 (1991), pp. 169-177.

Tatelbaum, Judy. *The Courage to Grieve: Creative Living, Recovery, and Growth Through Grief*. New York: Harper & Row, 1980.

Viorst, Judith. *Necessary Losses*. New York: Simon & Schuster, 1986.

Whitehead, E. Douglas, MD. *Viagra: The Wonder Drug for Peak Performance*. New York: Dell, 1999.

Chapter 20

Depression in the Workplace

The Effects of Depression in the Workplace

Success in the work environment depends on everyone's contribution. That's why no one in the workplace can afford to ignore depression.

Annually, an estimated 19 million American adults (9.5% of the population) will suffer from this often misunderstood disorder. It is not a passing mood. It is not a personal weakness. It is a major—but treatable—illness. No job category or professional level is immune, and even a formerly outstanding employee can be affected.

The good news is that, in more than 80% of cases, treatment is effective. It enables people with depression to return to satisfactory, functioning lives. And nearly everyone gets some degree of relief. Treatment includes medication, short-term talk therapy, or a combination of both.

Untreated depression is costly. A RAND Corporation study found that patients with depressive symptoms spend more days in bed than those with diabetes, arthritis, back problems, lung problems, or gastrointestinal disorders. Estimates of the total cost of depression to the nation in 1990 range from $30-$44 billion. Of the $44 billion figure, depression accounts for close to $12 billion in lost work days each year. Additionally, more than $11 billion in other costs accrue from decreased productivity due to symptoms that sap energy, affect work

This chapter includes text from "The Effects of Depression in the Workplace," National Institute of Mental Health (NIMH), June 1999; and "What to do When an Employee is Depressed: A Guide for Supervisors," NIMH, NIH Pub. No. 96-3919, updated November 1999.

habits, cause problems with concentration, memory, and decision-making. And costs escalate still further if a worker's untreated depression contributes to alcoholism or drug abuse.

Still more business costs result when an employee or colleague has a family member suffering from depression. The depression of a spouse or child can disrupt working hours, lead to days absent from work, effect concentration and morale, and decrease productivity.

Workers at every level in an organization can do something about depression. You can start by learning more about this common and serious illness. If you think you or a loved one may have depression, take action.

Seek consultation from an employee assistance counselor or contact your health provider. The information you share will remain confidential. You can't overcome depression by willpower, so it is important to seek professional help.

Employers and managers can play an additional role in altering the impact of depression in the workplace:

- Review corporate medical programs and employee health benefits.

- Make sure your employee assistance program staff are trained to recognize depressive disorders, make appropriate referrals, and provide other assistance consistent with policies and practices.

- Increase management awareness.

- Educate employees.

- Work with national or community organizations to obtain, display, and distribute information about depression at your workplace and provide employees with referrals to treatment.

What to Do When an Employee Is Depressed

As a supervisor, you may notice that some employees seem less productive and reliable than usual—they may often call in sick or arrive late to work, have more accidents, or just seem less interested in work. These individuals may be suffering from a very common illness called clinical depression. While it is not your job to diagnose depression, your understanding may help an employee get needed treatment. Untreated clinical depression may become a chronic condition that disrupts work, family, and personal life.

Many companies are helping employees with depression by providing training on depressive illnesses for supervisors, employee assistance, and occupational health personnel. Employers are also making appropriate treatment available through employee assistance programs and through company-sponsored health benefits. Such efforts are contributing to significant reductions in lost time and job-related accidents as well as marked increases in productivity.

Depression Is More Than the Blues

Everyone gets the blues or feels sad from time to time. However, if a person experiences these emotions intensely or for two weeks or longer, it may signal clinical depression, a condition that requires treatment.

Clinical depression affects the total person—body, feelings, thoughts, and behaviors—and comes in various forms. Some people have a single bout of depression; others suffer recurrent episodes. Still others experience the severe mood swings of bipolar disorder—sometimes called manic-depressive illness—with moods alternating between depressive lows and manic highs. In the workplace, symptoms of depression often may be recognized by:

- Decreased productivity
- Morale problems
- Lack of cooperation
- Safety risks, accidents
- Absenteeism
- Frequent statements about being tired all the time
- Complaints of unexplained aches and pains
- Alcohol and drug abuse

Depression Affects Your Employees

Depression can affect your workers' productivity, judgment, ability to work with others, and overall job performance. The inability to concentrate fully or make decisions may lead to costly mistakes or accidents. In addition, it has been shown that depressed individuals have high rates of absenteeism and are more likely to abuse alcohol and drugs, resulting in other problems on and off the job.

Unfortunately, many depressed people suffer needlessly because they feel embarrassed, fear being perceived as weak, or do not recognize depression as a treatable illness.

As many as 80% of people with depression can be treated effectively, generally without missing much time from work or needing costly hospitalization. Effective treatments for depression include medication, psychotherapy, or a combination of both. These treatments usually begin to relieve symptoms in a matter of weeks.

What Can a Supervisor Do?

As a supervisor, you can:

- A supervisor can say: "I'm concerned that recently you've been late to work often and aren't meeting your performance objectives. . . I'd like to see you get back on track. I don't know whether this is the case for you, but if personal issues are affecting your work, you can speak confidentially to one of our employee assistance counselors. The service was set up to help employees. Our conversation today and appointments with the counselor will be kept confidential. Whether or not you contact this service, you will still be expected to meet your performance goals."

- Learn about depression and the sources of help: Reading this book is a good first step. Familiarize yourself with your company's health benefits. Find out if your company has an employee assistance program (EAP) that can provide on-site consultation or refer employees to local resources.

- Recognize when an employee shows signs of a problem affecting performance which may be depression-related and refer employees appropriately: As a supervisor, you cannot diagnose depression. You can, however, note changes in work performance and listen to employee concerns. If your company does not have an EAP, ask a counselor for suggestions on how best to approach an employee who you suspect is experiencing work problems that may be related to depression. When a previously productive employee begins to be absent or tardy frequently, or is unusually forgetful and error-prone, he/she may be experiencing a significant health problem.

- Discuss changes in work performance with the employee. You may suggest that the employee seek consultation if there are personal concerns. Confidentiality of any discussion with the employee is critical. If an employee voluntarily talks with you about health problems, including feeling depressed or down all the time, keep these points in mind:

- Do not try to diagnose the problem yourself.

- Recommend that any employee experiencing symptoms of depression seek professional consultation from an EAP counselor or other health or mental health professional.

- Recognize that a depressed employee may need a flexible work schedule during treatment. Find out about your company's policy by contacting your human resources specialist.

- Remember that severe depression may be life-threatening to the employee, but rarely to others. If an employee makes comments like "life is not worth living" or "people would be better off without me," take the threats seriously. Immediately call an EAP counselor or other specialist and seek advice on how to handle the situation.

Professional Help Is Available

- Physicians
- Mental health specialists
- Employee assistance programs
- Health maintenance organizations
- Community mental health centers
- Hospital departments of psychiatry or outpatient psychiatric clinics
- University or medical school affiliated programs
- State hospital outpatient clinics
- Family service/social agencies
- Private clinics and facilities

You can also receive publications and information from the National Institute of Mental Health (NIMH).

Office of Communications and Public Liaison, NIMH
Information Resources and Inquiries Branch
6001 Executive Blvd., Room 8184, MSC 9663
Bethesda, MD 20892-9663
Toll-free: 800-421-4211 for depression-related information
(NIMH) *address continued on next page*

155

Phone: 301-443-4513
TTY: 301-443-8431
FAX: 301-443-4279
Mental Health FAX 4U: 301-443-5158
Website: http://www.nimh.nih.gov
E-mail: nimhinfo@nih.gov

Additional resources for help and further information are included in the end section of this book.

Chapter 21

Depression in Late Life: Not a Natural Part of Aging

Everyone Feels Sad or Blue Sometimes.

Sad feelings are a natural part of life. But when the sadness persists and interferes with everyday life, it may be depression. Depression is not a normal part of growing older. It is a treatable medical illness, much like heart disease or diabetes.

Depression is a serious illness affecting approximately 15 out of every 100 adults over age 65 in the United States. The disorder affects a much higher percentage of people in hospitals and nursing homes. When depression occurs in late life, it sometimes can be a relapse of an earlier depression. But when it occurs for the first time in older adults, it usually is brought on by another medical illness. When someone is already ill, depression can be both more difficult to recognize and more difficult to endure.

Depression Is Not a Passing Mood

Sadness associated with normal grief or everyday "blues" is different from depression. A sad or grieving person can continue to carry

This material is reprinted with permission from "Depression in Late Life: Not A Natural Part Of Aging," published by the American Association for Geriatric Psychiatry. © 2002. For additional information, or a copy of this brochure, contact the American Association for Geriatric Psychiatry at 7910 Woodmont Ave., Suite 1050, Bethesda, MD 20814-3004, 301-654-7850, or on the Internet at www.aagponline.org.

on with regular activities. The depressed person suffers from symptoms that interfere with his or her ability to function normally for a prolonged period of time.

Recognizing depression in the elderly is not always easy. It often is difficult for the depressed elder to describe how he or she is feeling. In addition, the current population of older Americans came of age at a time when depression was not understood to be a biological disorder and medical illness. Therefore, some elderly fear being labeled "crazy," or worry that their illness will be seen as a character weakness.

The depressed person or their family members may think that a change in mood or behavior is simply "a passing mood," and the person should just "snap out of it." But someone suffering from depression can not just "get over it." Depression is a medical illness that must be diagnosed and treated by trained professionals. Untreated, depression may last months or even years. Untreated, depression can:

- lead to disability
- worsen symptoms of other illnesses
- lead to premature death
- result in suicide

When it is properly diagnosed and treated, more than 80 percent of those suffering from depression recover and return to their normal lives.

The most common symptoms of late-life depression include:

- persistent sadness (lasting two weeks or more)
- feeling slowed down
- excessive worries about finances and health problems
- frequent tearfulness
- feeling worthless or helpless
- weight changes
- pacing and fidgeting
- difficulty sleeping
- difficulty concentrating
- physical symptoms such as pain or gastrointestinal problems

One important sign of depression is when people withdraw from their regular social activities. Rather than explaining their symptoms as a medical illness, often depressed persons will give different explanations such as:

- "It's too much trouble,"
- "I don't feel well enough," or
- "I don't have the energy."

For the same reasons, they often neglect their personal appearance, or may begin cooking and eating less. Like many illnesses, there are varying levels and types of depression. A person may not feel "sad" about anything, but may exhibit symptoms such as difficulty sleeping, weight loss, or physical pain with no apparent explanation. This person still may be clinically depressed. Those same symptoms also may be a sign of another problem—only a doctor can make the correct diagnosis.

It Can Happen to Anyone

Sometimes depression will occur for no apparent reason. In other words, nothing necessarily needs to "happen" in one's life for depression to occur. This can be because the disease often is caused by biological changes in the brain. However, in older adults, there usually are understandable reasons for the depression.

As the brain and body age, a number of natural bio-chemical changes begin to take place. Changes as the result of aging, medical illnesses or genetics may put the older adult at a greater risk for developing depression.

Life Changes

Chronic or serious illness is the most common cause of depression in the elderly. But even when someone is struggling with a chronic illness such as arthritis, it is not natural to be depressed. Depression is defined as an illness if it lasts two weeks or more and if it affects one's ability to lead a normal life.

Many factors can contribute to the development of depression. Often people describe one specific event that triggered their depression, such as the death of a partner or loved one, or the loss of a job through layoff or retirement. What seems like a normal period of sadness or grief may lead to a prolonged, intense grief that requires medical attention.

The loss of a life-long partner or a friend is a frequent occurrence in later life. It is normal to grieve after such a loss. But it may be depression rather than bereavement if the grief persists, or is accompanied by any of the following symptoms:

- guilt unconnected with the loved one's death
- thoughts of one's own death
- persistent feelings of worthlessness

Table 21.1. Geriatric Depression Scale (continued on next page)

Mood Assessment

1. Are you basically satisfied with your life?
2. Have you dropped many of your activities and interests?
3. Do you feel that your life is empty?
4. Do you often get bored?
5. Are you hopeful about the future?
6. Are you bothered by thoughts you can t get out of your head?
7. Are you in good spirits most of the time?
8. Are you afraid that something bad is going to happen to you?
9. Do you feel happy most of the time?
10. Do you often feel helpless?
11. Do you often get restless and fidgety?
12. Do you prefer to stay at home, rather than going out and doing new things?
13. Do you frequently worry about the future?
14. Do you feel you have more problems with memory than most?
15. Do you think it is wonderful to be alive now?
16. Do you often feel downhearted and blue?
17. Do you feel pretty worthless the way you are now?
18. Do you worry a lot about the past?
19. Do you find life very exciting?
20. Is it hard for you to get started on new projects?
21. Do you feel full of energy?
22. Do you feel that your situation is hopeless?
23. Do you think that most people are better off than you are?
24. Do you frequently get upset over little things?

- inability to function at one's usual level
- difficulty sleeping
- weight loss

If any of these symptoms are triggered by a loss, a physician should be consulted.

Table 21.1. Geriatric Depression Scale (continued)

Mood Assessment (Continued)

25. Do you frequently feel like crying?
26. Do you have trouble concentrating?
27. Do you enjoy getting up in the morning?
28. Do you prefer to avoid social gatherings?
29. Is it easy for you to make decisions?
30. Is your mind as clear as it used to be?

This is the original scoring for the scale: One point for each of these answers.

1. no	6. yes	11. yes	16. yes	21. no	26. yes
2. yes	7. no	12. yes	17. yes	22. yes	27. no
3. yes	8. yes	13. yes	18. yes	23. yes	28. yes
4. yes	9. no	14. yes	19. no	24. yes	29. no
5. no	10. yes	15. no	20. yes	25. yes	30. no

Number of points
    normal: 0–9
    mild depressives: 10–19
    severe depressives: 20–30

Source: Jerome Yesavage, MD, Director, Aging Clinical Research Center, Stanford University School of Medicine, 1983, available online at www.stanford.edu/~yesavage/GDS.english.long.html.

Note: Readers interested in other forms and translations of this scale can find links online at www.stanford.edu/~yesavage/GDS.html.

Changes in the older adult's sensory abilities or environment may contribute to the development of depression. Examples of such changes include:

- changes in vision and hearing
- changes in mobility
- retirement
- moving from the family home
- neighborhood changes

Other Illnesses

In the older population, medical illnesses are a common trigger for depression, and often depression will worsen the symptoms of other illnesses. The following illnesses are common causes of late-life depression:

- cancer
- Parkinson's disease
- heart disease
- stroke
- Alzheimer's disease

In addition, certain medical illnesses may hide the symptoms of depression. When a depressed person is preoccupied with physical symptoms resulting from a stroke, gastrointestinal problems, heart disease, or arthritis, he or she may attribute the depressive symptoms to an existing physical illness, or may ignore the symptoms entirely. For this reason, he or she may not report the depressive symptoms to his or her doctor, creating a barrier to becoming well.

Depression Is Treatable

Most depressed elderly people can improve dramatically from treatment. In fact, there are highly effective treatments for depression in late life. Common treatments prescribed by physicians include:

- psychotherapy
- antidepressant medications
- electroconvulsive therapy (ECT)

Psychotherapy can play an important role in the treatment of depression with, or without, medication. This type of treatment is most often used alone in mild to moderate depression. There are many forms of short-term therapy (10–20 weeks) that have proven to be effective. It is important that the depressed person find a therapist with whom he or she feels comfortable and who has experience with older patients.

Antidepressants work by increasing the level of neurotransmitters in the brain. Neurotransmitters are the brain's "messengers." Many feelings, including pain and pleasure, are a result of the neurotransmitters' function. When the supply of neurotransmitters is imbalanced, depression may result.

A frequent reason some people do not respond to antidepressant treatment is because they do not take the medication properly. Missing doses or taking more than the prescribed amount of the medication compromises the effect of the antidepressant. Similarly, stopping the medication too soon often results in a relapse of depression. In fact, most patients who stop taking their medication before four to six months after recovery will experience a relapse of depression.

Usually, antidepressant medication is taken for at least six months to a year. Typically, it takes four to 12 weeks to begin seeing results from antidepressant medication. If after this period of time the depression does not subside, the patient should consult his or her physician. Antidepressant drugs are not habit-forming or addictive. And because depression is often a recurrent illness, it usually is necessary to stay on the medication for six months after recovery to prevent new episodes of depression.

Electroconvulsive therapy (ECT) is a treatment that unnecessarily evokes fear in many people. In reality, ECT is one of the most safe, fast-acting and effective treatments for severe depression. It can be life saving. ECT often is the best choice for the person who has a life-threatening depression that is not responding to antidepressant medication or for the person who cannot tolerate the medication.

After a thorough evaluation, a physician will determine the treatment best suited for a person's depression. The treatment of depression demands patience and perseverance for the patient and the physician. Sometimes several different treatments must be tried before full recovery. Each person has individual biological and psychological characteristics that require individualized care.

Suicide

Suicide is more common in older people than in any other age group. The population over age 65 accounts for more than 25 percent of the nation's suicides. In fact, white men over age 80 are six times more likely to commit suicide than the general population, constituting the largest risk group. Suicide attempts or severe thoughts or wishes by older adults must always be taken seriously.

It is appropriate and important to ask a depressed person:

- Do they feel as though life is no longer an option for them?
- Have they had thoughts about harming themselves?
- Are they planning to do it?
- Is there a collection of pills or guns in the house?
- Are they often alone?

Most depressed people welcome care, concern, and support, but they are frightened and may resist help. In the case of a potentially suicidal elder, caring friends or family members must be more than understanding. They must actively intervene by removing pills and weapons from the home and calling the family physician, mental health professional or, if necessary, the police.

Caring for a Depressed Person

The first step in helping an elderly person who may be depressed is to make sure he or she gets a complete physical checkup. Depression may be a side effect of a pre-existing medical condition or of a medication. If the depressed older adult is confused or withdrawn, it is helpful for a caring family member or friend to accompany the person to the doctor and provide important information.

The physician may refer the older adult to a psychiatrist with geriatric training or experience. If a person is reluctant to see a psychiatrist, he or she may need assurance that an evaluation is necessary to determine if treatment is needed to reduce symptoms, improve functioning, and enhance well-being.

It is important to remember that depression is a highly treatable medical condition and is not a normal part of growing older. Therefore, it is crucial to understand and recognize the symptoms of the illness. As with any medical condition, the primary care physician should be consulted if someone has symptoms that interfere with everyday life. An older person who is diagnosed with depression also should know that there are trained professionals who specialize in treating the elderly (called "geriatric psychiatrists") who may be able to help.

How Can I Learn More about Mental Health Issues Related to the Elderly?

The American Association for Geriatric Psychiatry (AAGP) is a national professional organization of geriatric psychiatrists. AAGP's 1,400 members are the leading researchers, educators and clinical practitioners in the areas of late-life depression, dementia, schizophrenia, psychosis, anxiety, and sleep disorders and other mental health disorders affecting the elderly.

AAGP offers consumer brochures on :The Role of the Geriatric Psychiatrist," "Depression in Late-Life," and "Alzheimer's Disease" (single copies, free of charge) as well as the book *Growing Older and Wiser: Coping with Expectations, Challenges, and Change in the Later Years* (contact AAGP for current pricing information).

American Association for Geriatric Psychiatry
7910 Woodmont Avenue, Suite 1050
Bethesda, MD 20814
Phone: 301-654-7850
http://www.aagponline.org

Other resources for further help and information are included in the end section of this book.

Chapter 22

Depression and Poverty

Introduction

This chapter reports on a study that reviewed the literature on the prevalence, treatment, and consequences of depression in low-income women, highlighting the relationship of depression to welfare and employment. Depression is a debilitating illness, characterized by profound feelings of sadness, low mood, and loss of interest in usual activities, that can have severe adverse effects, not only on the individual woman but also on her job and family life.

Recent changes in welfare policy in the United States, including the five-year lifetime limit on assistance and the requirement that recipients obtain jobs after two years of continuous support, have increased concern about depression and other problems facing many women on welfare. The research findings reviewed here have a range of implications for research and for TANF (Temporary Assistance for Needy Families) and welfare-to-work policies and programs, which are outlined in this report.

From "Depression and Low Income Women: Challenges for TANF and Welfare-to-Work Policies and Programs," a report prepared for the Center for Mental Health Services (CMHS) of the Substance Abuse and Mental Health Services Administration (SAMHSA), U.S. Department of Health and Human Services, by Mary Clare Lennon, Juliana Blome, and Kevin English, March 2001. For more information contact Center for Mental Health Services, Office of Policy, Planning, and Administration, at (301) 443-000.

Prevalence of Depression Nationally

Data from large-scale national and community surveys reveal that:

- In any given year, approximately 4 percent to 10 percent of adults suffer from major depression.
- Rates of depression among women are 1.5 to 3 times that of men.
- Women from low-income groups are about twice as likely as those from higher income groups to be depressed.

These results suggest that low-income women and women on welfare are at particularly high risk for developing depressive disorder.

Prevalence of Depression in Women on Welfare

Studies of women on public assistance that have used comparable and reliable measures of Major Depressive Disorder (MDD) to evaluate high levels of depressive symptoms find:

- Twelve-month prevalence rates of MDD between 12 percent to 36 percent (median: 22 percent).
- High levels of depressive symptoms exist in 25 percent to 57 percent of women (median: 47 percent).

While variation in rates across studies may reflect differences in local caseload characteristics, in timing of the studies, or in assessment strategies, these levels of depression and its symptoms are quite high in welfare samples, as compared to community samples.

Relationship of Employment and Depression

Although considerations of depression among welfare recipients generally focus on depression as an obstacle to employment, other explanations of the association between depression and employment have empirical support in the literature. The following are possible causes and consequences of depression:

- Depression as a barrier to employment
- Depression as limiting the capacity to retain employment
- Depression as a consequence of poor-quality jobs
- Depression triggered by job loss

Because these possibilities are not mutually exclusive, it is important to better understand the conditions under which they emerge.

Consequences of Maternal Depression for Children

For mothers, major depression compromises their ability to respond to their children and places children at considerable risk for psychopathology and developmental difficulties. The problems found in children of depressed mothers include: increased rates of clinical diagnoses, impairments in psychological functioning, difficulties in meeting social and academic demands, more internalizing and externalizing behaviors, and substantial risk for psychiatric diagnoses later in life. Thus, any intervention aimed at mothers should consider strategies for reaching at risk children.

Treatment Effectiveness

A large number of studies document the effectiveness of various treatment and prevention options for depression. Research findings from experimental assignment to treatment show:

- Equal effectiveness of psychopharmacological and psychotherapeutic treatments, as compared with placebo, for mild to moderately severe depression
- Possibly greater effectiveness when drugs and psychotherapy are combined to treat recurrent severe depression

Few studies have specifically focused on low-income populations or women. While little attention has been given to rigorous evaluations of nonmedical or nonpsychotherapeutic interventions in this population, two promising approaches are:

- Incorporating attention to mental health problems in job search programs
- Offering welfare recipients financial incentives to work

Research suggests that each of these strategies may both reduce depressive symptoms and increase self-sufficiency.

Treatment Availability

Despite the availability of effective therapies, depression in the general population remains largely mistreated or altogether untreated.

Moreover, income, health insurance type, ethnicity, and gender affect treatment rates and the type of treatment received. A number of disparities are found in the literature, including:

- Individuals with low incomes are less likely to receive treatment from mental health specialists, such as psychiatrists and psychotherapists.

- Medicaid beneficiaries are less likely to receive newer forms of antidepressants, such as Prozac.

- Medicaid beneficiaries are less likely to obtain psychotherapy than are individuals with private insurance.

- Additionally, racial disparities are apparent within depressed Medicaid recipients, with nonwhite patients receiving less optimal treatment than white patients.

Care Received Once Access Has Been Achieved

Unfortunately, adequate treatment of depression is not guaranteed by access to health care. In fact, studies consistently reveal:

- High patient attrition rates

- Poor treatment adherence rates

- Subtheraputic dosing patterns in the management of depression

Many of these problems are exacerbated among individuals with low incomes.

Barriers to Treatment

Barriers to effective treatment for depression abound in the low-income population, including:

- High costs

- Lack of medical insurance

- Stigma

- Poor recognition of depression by physicians

- Patient barriers, such as language barriers or mistrust of strangers

Screening and Assessment—Implications for TANF and Welfare-to-Work Programs

Identifying and treating those in need of mental health services will require screening individuals to determine whether or not they have symptoms that warrant further (diagnostic) assessment. Currently, screening adults for depression, other mental disorders, or co-morbidity is not standard practice at welfare agencies or in welfare-to-work programs. This raises a number of issues for policymakers, including:

- What (if any) screening tools are available?

- How willing are welfare recipients to reveal information about depression?

- How can the confidentiality of results be insured?

- What system changes may be required to deliver adequate mental health services?

- Evaluate the adequacy of the current diagnostic system for depression.

- Develop longitudinal, nationally representative samples of low-income women to study the onset, causes, and consequences of depression.

- Understand the sources of disparities in treatment.

- Evaluate how treatment of depressed mothers affects their children.

- Compare the costs and benefits of treating depression, including savings for welfare systems.

To ensure that there is timely and effective treatment and preventive intervention for depression faced by low-income women, policymakers and program administrators will want to:

- Ensure access to health insurance.

- Institute adequate coverage for mental health treatment and intervention.

- Develop screening tools and procedures.

- Utilize multiple points of entry to identify at-risk women and children.

171

- Ensure adequate income support.

For more information about this study and the full report, as well as research citations, please refer to *Depression and Low-Income Women: Challenges for TANF and Welfare-to-Work Policies and Programs*. Copies of the full publication are available on the Research Forum Web site: http://www.researchforum.org or by writing to NCCP, 154 Haven Avenue, New York, NY 10032; Tel: (212) 304-7100; Fax: (212) 544-4200 or 544-4201; E-mail: info@researchforum.org.

Chapter 23

Stress: Coping with Everyday Problems

Stress is a natural part of life. The expressions are familiar to us, "I'm stressed out," "I'm under too much stress," or "Work is one big stress."

Stress is hard to define because it means different things to different people; however, it's clear that most stress is a negative feeling rather than a positive feeling.

Stress Can Be Both Physical and Mental

You may feel physical stress which is the result of too much to do, not enough sleep, a poor diet or the effects of an illness. Stress can also be mental: when you worry about money, a loved one's illness, retirement, or experience an emotionally devastating event, such as the death of a spouse or being fired from work.

However, much of our stress comes from less dramatic everyday responsibilities. Obligations and pressures which are both physical and mental are not always obvious to us. In response to these daily strains your body automatically increases blood pressure, heart rate, respiration, metabolism, and blood flow to your muscles. This response, is intended to help your body react quickly and effectively to a high-pressure situation.

However, when you are constantly reacting to stressful situations without making adjustments to counter the effects, you will feel stress which can threaten your health and well-being.

It is essential to understand that external events, no matter how you perceive those events, may cause stress. Stress often accompanies the feeling of "being out of control."

How Do I Know If I Am Suffering from Stress?

Remember, each person handles stress differently. Some people actually seek out situations which may appear stressful to others. A major life decision, such as changing careers or buying a house, might be overwhelming for some people, while others may welcome the change. Some find sitting in traffic too much to tolerate, while others take it in stride. The key is determining your personal tolerance levels for stressful situations.

Stress can cause physical, emotional and behavioral disorders which can affect your health, vitality, peace-of-mind, as well as personal and professional relationships. Too much stress can cause relatively minor illnesses like insomnia, backaches, or headaches, and can contribute to potentially life-threatening diseases like high blood pressure and heart disease.

Tips for Reducing or Controlling Stress

As you read the following suggestions, remember that success will not come from a half hearted effort, nor will it come overnight. It will take determination, persistence and time. Some suggestions may help immediately, but if your stress is chronic, it may require more attention and/or lifestyle changes. Determine *your* tolerance level for stress and try to live within these limits. Learn to accept or change stressful and tense situations whenever possible.

Be realistic. If you feel overwhelmed by some activities (yours and/ or your family's), learn to say, "No." Eliminate an activity that is not absolutely necessary. You may be taking on more responsibility than you can or should handle. If you meet resistance, give reasons why you're making the changes. Be willing to listen to other's suggestions and be ready to compromise.

Shed the "superman/superwoman" urge. No one is perfect, so don't expect perfection from yourself or others. Ask yourself, "What really needs to be done? How much can I do? Is the deadline realistic? What adjustments can I make?" Don't hesitate to ask for help if you need it.

Meditate. Just ten to twenty minutes of quiet reflection may bring relief from chronic stress as well as increase your tolerance to it. Use the time to listen to music, relax and try to think of pleasant things or nothing.

Visualize. Use your imagination and picture how you can manage a stressful situation more successfully. Whether it's a business presentation or moving to a new place, many people feel visual rehearsals boost self-confidence and enable them to take a more positive approach to a difficult task.

Take one thing at a time. For people under tension or stress, an ordinary workload can sometimes seem unbearable. The best way to cope with this feeling of being overwhelmed is to take one task at a time. Pick one urgent task and work on it. Once you accomplish that task, choose the next one. The positive feeling of "checking off" tasks is very satisfying. It will motivate you to keep going.

Exercise. Regular exercise is a popular way to relieve stress. Twenty to thirty minutes of physical activity benefits both the body and the mind.

Hobbies. Take a break from your worries by doing something you enjoy. Whether it's gardening or painting, schedule time to indulge your interest.

Healthy life style. Good nutrition makes a difference. Limit intake of caffeine and alcohol (alcohol actually disturbs regular sleep patterns), get adequate rest, exercise, and balance work and play.

Share your feelings. A conversation with a friend lets you know that you are not the only one having a bad day, caring for a sick child or working in a busy office. Stay in touch with friends and family. Let them provide love, support and guidance. Don't try to cope alone.

Give in occasionally. *Be flexible.* If you find you're meeting constant opposition in either your personal or professional life, rethink your position or strategy. Arguing only intensifies stressful feelings. If you know you are right, stand your ground, but do so calmly and rationally. Make allowances for other's opinions and be prepared to compromise. If you are willing to give in, others may meet you halfway.

Not only will you reduce your stress, you may find better solutions to your problems.

Go easy with criticism. You may expect too much of yourself and others. Try not to feel frustrated, let down, disappointed or even "trapped" when another person does not measure up. The "other person" may be a wife, a husband, or child whom you are trying to change to suit yourself. Remember, everyone is unique, and has his or her own virtues, shortcomings, and right to develop as an individual.

Where to Get Help

Help may be as close as a friend or spouse. But if you think that you or someone you know may be under more stress than just dealing with a passing difficulty, it may be helpful to talk with your doctor, spiritual advisor, or employee assistance professional. They may suggest you visit with a psychiatrist, psychologist, social worker, or other qualified counselor.

Ideas to consider when talking with a professional:

- List the things which cause stress and tension in your life.
- How does this stress and tension affect you, your family and your job?
- Can you identify the stress and tensions in your life as short or long term?
- Do you have a support system of friends/family that will help you make positive changes?
- What are your biggest obstacles to reducing stress?
- What are you willing to change or give up for a less stressful and tension-filled life?
- What have you tried already that didn't work for you?
- If you do not have control of a situation, can you accept it and get on with your life?

Other Resources

For additional resources, please call 1-800-969-NMHA.

Chapter 24

Coping with Loss: Bereavement and Grief

Coping with Loss

The loss of a loved one is life's most stressful event and can cause a major emotional crisis. After the death of someone you love, you experience bereavement, which literally means "to be deprived by death."

Knowing What to Expect

When a death takes place, you may experience a wide range of emotions, even when the death is expected. Many people report feeling an initial stage of numbness after first learning of a death, but there is no real order to the grieving process.

Some emotions you may experience include:

• Denial	• Shock	• Anger	• Guilt
• Disbelief	• Sadness	• Humiliation	
• Confusion	• Yearning	• Despair	

These feelings are normal and common reactions to loss. You may not be prepared for the intensity and duration of your emotions or how swiftly your moods may change. You may even begin to doubt the stability of your mental health. But be assured that these feelings are healthy and appropriate and will help you come to terms with your loss.

Remember: It takes time to fully absorb the impact of a major loss. You never stop missing your loved one, but the pain eases after time and allows you to go on with your life.

Mourning a Loved One

It is not easy to cope after a loved one dies. You will mourn and grieve. Mourning is the natural process you go through to accept a major loss. Mourning may include religious traditions honoring the dead or gathering with friends and family to share your loss. Mourning is personal and may last months or years.

Grieving is the outward expression of your loss. Your grief is likely to be expressed physically, emotionally, and psychologically. For instance, crying is a physical expression, while depression is a psychological expression.

It is very important to allow yourself to express these feelings. Often, death is a subject that is avoided, ignored or denied. At first it may seem helpful to separate yourself from the pain, but you cannot avoid grieving forever. Someday those feelings will need to be resolved or they may cause physical or emotional illness.

Many people report physical symptoms that accompany grief. Stomach pain, loss of appetite, intestinal upsets, sleep disturbances and loss of energy are all common symptoms of acute grief. Of all life's stresses, mourning can seriously test your natural defense systems. Existing illnesses may worsen or new conditions may develop.

Profound emotional reactions may occur. These reactions include anxiety attacks, chronic fatigue, depression and thoughts of suicide. An obsession with the deceased is also a common reaction to death.

Dealing with a Major Loss

The death of a loved one is always difficult. Your reactions are influenced by the circumstances of a death, particularly when it is sudden or accidental. Your reactions are also influenced by your relationship with the person who died.

A child's death arouses an overwhelming sense of injustice—for lost potential, unfulfilled dreams and senseless suffering. Parents may feel responsible for the child's death, no matter how irrational that may seem. Parents may also feel that they have lost a vital part of their own identity.

A spouse's death is very traumatic. In addition to the severe emotional shock, the death may cause a potential financial crisis if the spouse was the family's main income source. The death may necessitate major social adjustments requiring the surviving spouse to parent alone, adjust to single life and maybe even return to work.

Elderly people may be especially vulnerable when they lose a spouse because it means losing a lifetime of shared experiences. At this time, feelings of loneliness may be compounded by the death of close friends.

A loss due to suicide can be among the most difficult losses to bear. They may leave the survivors with a tremendous burden of guilt, anger and shame. Survivors may even feel responsible for the death. Seeking counseling during the first weeks after the suicide is particularly beneficial and advisable.

Living with Grief

Coping with death is vital to your mental health. It is only natural to experience grief when a loved one dies. The best thing you can do is allow yourself to grieve. There are many ways to cope effectively with your pain.

- Seek out caring people. Find relatives and friends who can understand your feelings of loss. Join support groups with others who are experiencing similar losses.

- Express your feelings. Tell others how you are feeling; it will help you to work through the grieving process.

- Take care of your health. Maintain regular contact with your family physician and be sure to eat well and get plenty of rest. Be aware of the danger of developing a dependence on medication or alcohol to deal with your grief.

- Accept that life is for the living. It takes effort to begin to live again in the present and not dwell on the past.

- Postpone major life changes. Try to hold off on making any major changes, such as moving, remarrying, changing jobs or having another child. You should give yourself time to adjust to your loss.

- Be patient. It can take months or even years to absorb a major loss and accept your changed life.

- Seek outside help when necessary. If your grief seems like it is too much to bear, seek professional assistance to help work through your grief. It's a sign of strength, not weakness, to seek help.

Helping Others Grieve

If someone you care about has lost a loved one, you can help them through the grieving process.

- Share the sorrow. Allow them—even encourage them—to talk about their feelings of loss and share memories of the deceased.

- Don't offer false comfort. It doesn't help the grieving person when you say "it was for the best" or "you'll get over it in time." Instead, offer a simple expression of sorrow and take time to listen.

- Offer practical help. Baby-sitting, cooking and running errands are all ways to help someone who is in the midst of grieving.

- Be patient. Remember that it can take a long time to recover from a major loss. Make yourself available to talk.

- Encourage professional help when necessary. Don't hesitate to recommend professional help when you feel someone is experiencing too much pain to cope alone.

Helping Children Grieve

Children who experience a major loss may grieve differently than adults. A parent's death can be particularly difficult for small children, affecting their sense of security or survival. Often, they are confused about the changes they see taking place around them, particularly if well-meaning adults try to protect them from the truth or from their surviving parent's display of grief.

Limited understanding and an inability to express feelings puts very young children at a special disadvantage. Young children may revert to earlier behaviors (such as bed-wetting), ask questions about the deceased that seem insensitive, invent games about dying or pretend that the death never happened.

Coping with a child's grief puts added strain on a bereaved parent. However, angry outbursts or criticism only deepen a child's anxiety and delays recovery. Instead, talk honestly with children, in terms they can understand. Take extra time to talk with them about death and the person who has died. Help them work through their feelings and remember that they are looking to adults for suitable behavior.

Looking to the Future

Remember, with support, patience and effort, you will survive grief. Some day the pain will lessen, leaving you with cherished memories of your loved one.

Other Resources

For additional resources, please call 1-800-969-NMHA.

Chapter 25

Depression and the Holidays

Preventing Holiday Blues

"Holiday blues" range from mild sadness during the holidays to severe depression. This sadness or depression can be prevented, and if it's already present, it can be eased.

The Problem

Holiday blues can affect both men and women, young and old. Factors contributing to holiday blues include increased stress and fatigue, unrealistic expectations, too much commercialization, and the inability to be with one's family. The increased demands of shopping, parties, family reunions, and house guests may also contribute to tension and sadness during the holidays. Common stress reactions during the holidays include headaches, excessive drinking, over-eating or not eating enough, and difficulty sleeping.

A post-holiday let down, resulting from emotional disappointments during the holiday months as well as the physical reactions caused

---

The first part of this chapter "Preventing Holiday Blues," is from Centers for Disease Control and Prevention, updated January 2002. Regarding the section titled "Helping Older People Cope with Holiday Depression": This material is reprinted with permission from " Coping with Depression and the Holidays," published by the American Association for Geriatric Psychiatry. © 2002. For additional information, or a copy of this brochure, contact the American Association for Geriatric Psychiatry at 7910 Woodmont Ave., Suite 1050, Bethesda, MD 20814-3004, 301-654-7850, or on the Internet at www.aagponline.org.

by excess fatigue and stress, may cause holiday blues to continue into the new year.

For some people—particularly those who live in the northern, darker regions—holiday blues may be caused by seasonal affective disorder (SAD). SAD results from fewer hours of sunlight as the days grow shorter during the winter months.

To help prevent holiday blues, follow these tips from the Centers for Disease Control and Prevention, the American Psychological Association, the National Mental Health Association, and the Mental Health Association of Colorado.

If You Are Experiencing Holiday Blues

- Establish realistic goals and expectations for the holiday season, and do not label the holiday season as a time to cure all past problems. The holidays do not prevent sadness or loneliness.

- Limit your drinking.

- Do not feel obliged to feel festive. Accept your inner experience and do not force yourself to express specific feelings. If you have recently experienced a tragedy, death, or romantic break-up, tell people about your needs.

- To relieve holiday stress, know your spending limit and stick to it. Enjoy holiday activities that are free, such as driving around to look at holiday decorations. Go window shopping without buying anything.

- Express your feelings to those around you in a constructive, honest, and open way. If you need to confront someone with a problem, begin your sentences with "I feel."

If Someone You Know Is Experiencing Holiday Blues

- Try to involve that person in holiday activities, but don't be forceful.

- Be a good listener. If people express suicidal thoughts or feel depressed, hopeless, or worthless, be supportive. Let them know you are there for them and are willing to help them seek professional help. Never issue challenges or dares.

- Familiarize yourself with resources such as mental health centers, counseling centers, and hotlines.

- If the depressed person is chronically ill, express that you understand that the holidays do not cure the illness.

- Be aware that holidays can be difficult for people, especially when reality doesn't measure up to their expectations. Help them establish what is realistic and what is not.

Helping Older People Cope with Holiday Depression

For most of us, the holidays are a time to gather with friends and family, celebrate, reflect on the past and plan for the future. However, for some, especially older individuals, the holidays can be a difficult time. During the holidays, older adults may feel more acutely the passing of time, the absence of parents, siblings and friends who have died, and the distance of loved ones who have moved away. Traditional reunions and rituals that were observed in the past may not be possible and in their absence, the holidays may seem devoid of meaning. This holiday season may be particularly difficult as we adjust to a world forever changed by terrorism.

It is normal to feel subdued, reflective and sad in the face of these losses and changes. But family members or friends may notice that a senior is experiencing the "blues" for a long time and that what they may have thought was simple sadness is actually a serious case of depression.

Some major factors contributing to holiday depression in the elderly are:

- Financial limitations

- Loss of independence

- Being alone or separated from loved ones

- Failing eyesight (and lessening of the ability to write or read holiday correspondence)

- Loss of mobility and/or the inability to get to religious services

Depression Is Not a Natural Part of Aging

Everyone feels sad or blue sometimes, and the stress associated with holidays may stir feelings of loss or separation. However, a person who is sad or anxious around the holidays, can, in most cases, continue to carry on with regular activities. Such feelings are generally temporary and the individual eventually returns to his or her normal mood state. However, a clinically depressed person suffers from symptoms that interfere with his or her ability to function in every day life. These symptoms include much more than feeling blue.

When clinically depressed, the affected older person may lose the will to live. These persons begin to question the value of life and may think of suicide. There are often feelings of diminished self-esteem or excessive feelings of guilt. As these symptoms develop, the older person may take to bed or not bother getting dressed in the morning.

Appetite and sleep may suffer while lethargy sets in. The person may show little interest in his or her own welfare and little interest in doing things that in the past brought pleasure.

Recognizing depression in older individuals is not always easy. It often is difficult for a depressed older person to describe how he or she is feeling. In addition, the current population of older Americans came of age at a time when depression was not understood to be a biological illness. Those who are depressed may fear being labeled "difficult" or worse, or may worry that their illness will be seen as a character weakness.

Those who are depressed, their families and friends may think that a change in temperament or behavior is simply "a passing mood," and that the person will just "snap out of it." Unfortunately, a person suffering from depression cannot just "get over it." Depression is a medical illness that should be diagnosed and treated by trained professionals. Left untreated, depression may last months or even years.

Talking to Someone Who Is Depressed

Sometimes the hardest part in helping someone who is depressed or blue is finding an approach that does not contribute to him or her feeling defensive, sad, or helpless. If you are at a loss for words, you may want to consider some of the following ways to begin:

- Discuss your own varied feelings or a time in your life when you were depressed or blue. Knowing that you understand may give them the means to talk about their feelings.

- Acknowledge that the holidays can be difficult. Many people don't want to admit that life is not always as cheerful as portrayed in the media or in advertisements.

- If the older individual is not eating or has lost weight, you might start by gently asking about their appetite or why they do not seem interested in food.

- Once you have gotten past the initial awkwardness, you may be surprised to learn that your loved one will talk to you. At that point, it is up to you to listen and offer support. Too often, younger friends or family members do not want to hear some of the less than pleasant aspects—emotional and physical—of growing older. But one of the most important things you can do is listen.

- Offer specific suggestions for help and be willing to assist in implementing them. You may want to suggest that your relative or friend visit the family doctor or make an appointment with a psychiatrist. You may want to be involved in helping them select a doctor if they don't have one in mind. They may wish to make the decision on their own, but, if not, it will be a comfort to have help.

- It may take more than one conversation and it may take more than one day or one week to get the individual to agree to get help. If they are struggling with depression, they may not want to hear what you have to say and may resist your suggestions. Be persistent. This is a difficult process for you and the older individual, but knowing that depression is treatable makes it easier to address.

Remember, for many older family members and friends there may be a stigma attached to asking for help and to having any discussion of depression or mental illness. Part of your role is letting them know that depression is treatable, that their lives can be better and that depression is not an inevitable part of growing old.

The Holidays and World Events

Today's senior citizens are a resilient and resourceful group, and the vast majority manage the stress of current events very well. However, during the holidays, the elderly and their families should be sensitive to possible delayed responses to the events of September 11, 2001 and the subsequent threats to our nation's sense of security.

Over the holidays, how might older individuals respond to terrorism?

In addition to feeling depressed, seniors may find themselves irritable and uninterested in previously cherished rituals or loved ones. Those traumatized by earlier life experiences may become preoccupied with unwelcome images from the past. Older émigrés who fled political terror or religious persecution in their homelands may be particularly vulnerable. Near phobic dread of travel or unwarranted worries over traveling family members can lead to isolation. These are all symptoms of anxiety and depressive disorders as well as acute and post-traumatic stress disorders.

Why might these responses be delayed?

During the holidays, we let our emotional guard down. Our psychological defenses are loosened in anticipation of the warm, secure feelings associated with the holidays. Seniors who have busied themselves and kept the terror out of mind may find that the change of pace leaves them vulnerable. The delayed response may also be triggered by seeing family members in distress. Reactions to stress are emotionally infectious.

What are signs that an older person may need help from a mental health professional?

- Suicidal thoughts are not the norm even in very old persons and their presence indicates the need for professional help.

- An escalation in the use of alcohol, pain relievers (analgesics) or sleeping pills may indicate depression.

- Seniors who seem confused, cannot concentrate or seem lost in the midst of family events may benefit from a professional assessment.

- Shedding a tear of two during the holidays is a sign of sentiment. But when crying becomes disruptive or disabling it may be a sign of depression.

- Seniors who suddenly isolate themselves are clearly having problems.

What can friends, family members and caregivers do to help?

The simple answer is to openly communicate one's concerns. Offer to call the individual's doctor and accompany the senior to an appointment. A conversation with the senior's clergy can also facilitate referral to a mental health professional. Do not ask the older person to follow through without giving your support.

Holidays and Nursing Home Residents

Many families rely on nursing homes to provide the consistent care their older relative needs. Holiday depression can arise—for many of the reasons previously mentioned—when individuals are in nursing homes or other long-term care situations. The holidays may be especially hard on these individuals because of the loss of their own mobility.

What kind of care can a patient receive for depression in a nursing home?

If your older family member is in a nursing home and you suspect he or she is depressed, you may want to talk with the nursing home administrator or director of nursing about the symptoms you notice. You may want to request a consultation with a physician or psychiatrist. If the individual is in frail health, you need to be especially certain that the doctor is trained in caring for the mental health of the frail elderly whose ability to tolerate treatments may be different from other elderly patients.

Remember that all patients should have access to the care they need—physical and mental—regardless of the setting. If the individual is in a nursing home and you suspect he or she is suffering from depression, insist that the nursing home help provide appropriate treatment.

What questions should I ask about mental health care in the nursing home?

- Ask whether the facility provides physical and social activities for the residents. Like all of us, elderly family members need to get exercise if they can and need to have positive interaction with friends and peers.

- Ask about the qualifications of staff professionals monitoring care, especially regarding the careful dispensing of all medications.

- Ask specifically about mental health care, including access to group therapy.

- Ask about the availability of psychiatric care through a staff or affiliated psychiatrist.

For More Information about Mental Health in the Elderly

The American Association for Geriatric Psychiatry (AAGP) offers consumer brochures on "The Role of the Geriatric Psychiatrist," "Depression in Late-Life," and "Alzheimer's Disease" (single copies, free of charge) as well as the book *Growing Older and Wiser: Coping with Expectations, Challenges, and Change in the Later Years* (contact AAGP for current pricing information). AAGP can also provide the names of board-certified geriatric psychiatrists practicing in your area.

American Association for Geriatric Psychiatry
7910 Woodmont Avenue, Suite 1050
Bethesda, MD 20814
Phone: 301-654-7850
http://www.aagponline.org

Other resources for further help and information are included in the end section of this book.

Chapter 26

Depression and Sexual Desire

Symptomatic loss of libido is a common problem in the United States. In a national survey conducted in 1994, 33 percent of women and 17 percent of men reported sexual disinterest.[1] In another survey, one third of women 18 to 59 years of age reported feeling a lack of sexual desire within the previous year.[2] Patients with major depressive disorder or bipolar disorder have an even higher prevalence of sexual dysfunction, including lowered libido, than the general population.[3]

In one study it was found that more than 70 percent of depressed patients had a loss of sexual interest when not taking medication, and they reported that the severity of this loss of interest was worse than the other symptoms of depression.[4] In this same study, libido declined with increasing severity of psychologic illness. The complex association between depression and lowered libido is further illustrated in a case control study in which increased lifetime prevalence rates of affective disorder were found among patients with inhibited sexual desire.[5]

Regardless of the cause-and-effect relationship, depression and decreased libido are associated, and the treatment of one condition may improve the other. This chapter focuses on decreased libido associated with depression, the effects of treatment of depression on libido, and the effects of changes in libido and sexual functioning on compliance.

Discussing Libido

Patients have difficulty discussing sexual dysfunction (decreased libido, erectile dysfunction, and anorgasmia) and acknowledging decreased libido may be particularly difficult. Patients under-report sexual problems caused by medications.[6,7] They may acknowledge a decline in libido only if their partner complains. Even when a declining interest in sex is recognized, it may be rationalized on the basis of social values and practices, especially among aging women.[8] Discovery of sexual problems is further limited by the frequent failure of physicians to ask about such problems.[9] The latter point is critical: in one study it was found that patients taking selective serotonin reuptake inhibitors (SSRIs) were four times more likely to reveal sexual dysfunction if asked directly by their physician.[7]

It is important to get baseline information about sexual dysfunction, including lowered libido, to accurately assess the effects of treatment. The authors have found that placing libidinal effects in the context of the patient's general interests and activities avoids suggestion and excessive preoccupation, but allows adequate assessment before and after treatment is initiated.

Other Issues Affecting Libido

Patients whose depression improves with treatment but who continue to experience a lowered libido should be asked about their use of other medications. Several antipsychotic agents, including haloperidol (Haldol), thioridazine (Mellaril) and risperidone (Risperdal) can decrease libido.[9,10] Cimetidine (Tagamet), in contrast to ranitidine (Zantac), has been found to lower libido and cause erectile dysfunction.[11]

Women in their late reproductive years who take oral contraceptives and postmenopausal women who are given estrogen replacement therapy may experience an improvement of depressive symptoms but a lowering of libido.[12] Libido lowering is attributed to estrogen-induced deficiency of free testosterone.[12,13] Testosterone testing and supplementation should be considered in women who experience a decline in libido after starting estrogen therapy.[14] Testosterone testing should also be considered in men who have a gradual loss of libido and no improvement despite adequate treatment for depression.[15]

It is important to assess the patient for psychologic and interpersonal factors that commonly affect depression and sexual desire. These factors include stressful life events (loss of job or family trauma), life milestones (children leaving home) and ongoing relationship problems.[16]

Alcohol and narcotics are known to decrease libido, arousal, and orgasm.[17] Because the use of alcohol and other drugs is more common in patients with psychologic disorders, alcohol and drug abuse should be considered when investigating libido problems in patients with depression.

Lowered Libido after Treatment

Consistent evidence shows that, with the exception of bupropion (Wellbutrin), trazodone (Desyrel) and nefazodone (Serzone), antidepressant medications may cause a decline in libido or sexual functioning despite improvement of depression.[18] Up to one half of patients surveyed before and after starting therapy with the SSRIs fluoxetine (Prozac), paroxetine (Paxil), fluvoxamine (Luvox), citalopram (Celexa) and sertraline (Zoloft) reported a decline in libido with medication use.[7] SSRIs also cause other sexual dysfunction that can affect libido and compliance.[19,20]

In a double-blind clinical trial of treatment with imipramine (Tofranil), phenelzine (Nardil) or placebo, it was found that 30 to 40 percent of patients taking either antidepressant reported a decline in sexual desire, while six percent of those taking placebo experienced the same effect.[21] Although the use of monoamine oxidase inhibitors (MAOIs) and tricyclic antidepressants to treat depression is on the decline, tricyclic agents are increasingly being prescribed for control of pain. When tricyclics are prescribed for pain, it is not uncommon for them to be used in conjunction with SSRIs. SSRIs increase serum levels of tricyclics, so this combination may affect libido more than either alone. Table 26.1 summarizes the effects of various antidepressants and antipsychotics on libido.

Management

When libido remains low after depression has been treated, the other issues discussed above should be considered. When decreased libido begins or worsens after a patient starts taking antidepressant medications, it is important to address the problem without compromising the treatment of the depression. Failure to deal with the sexual problem may result in treatment noncompliance.[22]

In patients with decreased libido secondary to SSRI therapy, decreasing the dosage may increase libido without changing medication effectiveness.

Several options exist for managing medication-induced sexual dysfunction. Decreasing the dosage of the antidepressant may improve libido while maintaining adequate treatment of depression. In one study, 73 percent of patients whose SSRI dosage was halved reported improved sexual function while antidepressant effectiveness continued.[7] This dosage effect has also been found for SSRIs and imipramine in other studies.[21,23,24] The only evidence about drug holidays comes from a small, open study in which findings suggest that one- to two-day holidays from the shorter half-life SSRIs (sertraline, paroxetine) may be helpful. This effect did not apply to fluoxetine.[25]

If a reduction in the antidepressant dosage does not maintain adequate treatment of depression, other options are to add a medication and change the medication. In studies comparing bupropion with sertraline and placebo, patients treated with bupropion experienced improvement in libido.[26] There is good evidence that treatment with bupropion raises libido above predepression levels.[27] In less rigorous

Table 26.1. Effects on Libido of Various Antidepressants and Other Medications

Medication	Libido effect	Other sexual effects
SSRIs		
fluoxetine (Prozac), paroxetine (Paxil), fluvoxamine (Luvox), citalopram (Celexa), sertraline (Zoloft)	Decrease	Anorgasmia, delayed ejaculation, erectile dysfunction
imipramine (Tofranil), phenelzine (Nardil)	Decrease	Erectile dysfunction
bupropion (Wellbutrin)	Increase	None
trazodone (Desyrel)	Increase	Priapism (rare)
nefazodone (Serzone)	No change	None
Antipsychotics		
haloperidol (Haldol), thioridazine (Mellaril), risperidone (Risperdal)	Decrease	Anorgasmia, erectile dysfunction, painful ejaculation

SSRIs = selective serotonin reuptake inhibitors.

Information from references 7, 9, 10, and 18 through 21.

studies, improvement of libido with a change to bupropion or the addition of bupropion to existing medications was found.[28,29] Patients who switched from sertraline to nefazodone in a double-blind clinical trial reported that their libido returned to baseline levels.[30]

Psychiatric Therapy for Disorders of Sexual Desire

Psychotherapy has variable effects for depression-related problems of sexual desire.[31] Better outcomes are associated with the absence of life-long or global desire disorders and with strong relationships.[16] In a review of published studies regarding psychotherapy for sexual dysfunction, it was found that in nearly 80 percent of the published reports the research was of poor quality and that no treatment was consistently useful.[32]

Final Comment

Decreased libido affects many patients but disproportionately affects patients with depression. There is evidence that the decline in libido is related to the depth of depression. It is important to get baseline information regarding libido and sexual function before initiating treatment for depression. It is also important to assess patients' libido and sexual functioning after starting antidepressant therapy, as patients may be reluctant to report difficulties.

If treating the depression does not improve libido, other causes of sexual dysfunction should be considered, such as hormone deficiencies, chronic disease, drug and alcohol abuse, or use of other medications. Evidence supports several treatment options in patients who experience sexual dysfunction or decreased libido as a consequence of antidepressant use. These include decreasing the dosage of an SSRI or tricyclic antidepressant, instigating medication holidays, adding or switching to bupropion, and using nefazodone as an alternative agent. Cause and effect may not be clear, but addressing sexual desire when treating depression may improve compliance and overall outcome.

References

1. Michael RT. *Sex in America: A Definitive Survey*. Boston: Little, Brown, 1994.

2. Laumann EO. *The Social Organization of Sexuality: Sexual Practices in the United States*. Chicago: University of Chicago Press, 1994.

3. Segraves RT, "Psychiatric illness and sexual function," *Int J Impot Res* 1998;10(suppl 2):S131-3,S138-40.

4. Casper RC, Redmond DE, Katz MM, Schaffer CB, Davis JM, Koslow SH. "Somatic symptoms in primary affective disorder. Presence and relationship to the classification of depression," *Arch Gen Psychiatry* 1985;42:1098-104.

5. Schreiner-Engel P, Schiavi RC. "Lifetime psychopathology in individuals with low sexual desire," *J Nerv Ment Dis* 1986; 174:646-51.

6. Monteiro WO, Noshirvani HF, Marks IM, Lelliott PT. "Anorgasmia from clomipramine in obsessive-compulsive disorder. A controlled trial," *Br J Psychiatry* 1987;151:107-12.

7. Montejo-Gonzalez AL, Llorca G, Izquierdo JA, Ledesma A, Bousono M, Calcedo A, et al. "SSRI-induced sexual dysfunction: fluoxetine, paroxetine, sertraline, and fluvoxamine in a prospective, multicenter, and descriptive clinical study of 344 patients," *J Sex Marital Ther* 1997;23:176-94.

8. Kingsberg SA. "Postmenopausal sexual functioning: A case study," *Int J Fertil Womens Med* 1998; 43:122-8.

9. Peuskens J, Sienaert P, De Hert M. "Sexual dysfunction: the unspoken side effect of antipsychotics," *European Psychiatry* 1998;13(suppl 1):23s-30s.

10. Hummer M, Kemmler G, Kurz M, Kurzthaler I, Oberbauer H, Fleischhacker WW. "Sexual disturbances during clozapine and haloperidol treatment for schizophrenia," *Am J Psychiatry* 1999;156:631-3.

11. Zimmerman TW. "Problems associated with medical treatment of peptic ulcer disease," *Am J Med* 1984;77:51-6.

12. Nathorst-Boos J, von Schoultz B, Carlstrom K. "Elective ovarian removal and estrogen replacement therapy—effects on sexual life, psychological well-being and androgen status," *J Psychosom Obstet Gynaecol* 1993;14:283-93.

13. Davis SR, Burger HG. "Use of androgens in postmenopausal women," *Curr Opin Obstet Gynecol* 1997;9:177-80.

14. Sherwin BB, Gelfand MM, Brender W. "Androgen enhances sexual motivation in females: A prospective, crossover study of sex steroid administration in the surgical menopause," *Psychosom Med* 1985; 47:339-51.

15. Bagatell CJ, Bremner WJ. "Androgens in men—uses and abuses," *N Engl J Med* 1996;334:707-14.

16. Heiman JR, Meston CM. "Evaluating sexual dysfunction in women," *Clin Obstet Gynecol* 1997; 40:616-29.

17. Miller NS, Gold MS. "The human sexual response and alcohol and drugs," *J Subst Abuse Treat* 1988; 5:171-7.

18. Lane RM. "A critical review of selective serotonin reuptake inhibitor-related sexual dysfunction; incidence, possible aetiology and implications for management," *J Psychopharmacol* 1997;11:72-82.

19. Segraves RT. "Antidepressant-induced sexual dysfunction," *J Clin Psychiatry* 1998;59(suppl 4):48-54.

20. Michael A, Herrod JJ. "Citalopram-induced decreased libido [Letter]," *Br J Psychiatry* 1997;171:90.

21. Harrison WM, Rabkin JG, Ehrhardt AA, Stewart JW, McGrath PJ, Ross D, et al. "Effects of antidepressant medication on sexual function: A controlled study." *J Clin Psychopharmacol* 1986;6:144-9.

22. Harvey KV, Balon R. "Clinical implications of antidepressant drug effects on sexual function," *Ann Clin Psychiatry* 1995;7:189-201.

23. Benazzi F, Mazzoli M. "Fluoxetine-induced sexual dysfunction: A dose-dependent effect?" *Pharmacopsychiatry* 1994;27:246.

24. *Clinical management of depression: Bupropion—an update*, 1993. Monograph series, vol. 1, no. 1. Proceedings of a closed symposium, "Antidepressant Drug Therapy: Bupropion—An Update Meeting," held in Boca Raton, Fla., October 30-31, 1992.

25. Rothschild AJ. "Selective serotonin reuptake inhibitor-induced sexual dysfunction: Efficacy of a drug holiday," *Am J Psychiatry* 1995;152:1514-6.

26. Crenshaw TL, Goldberg JP, Stern WC. "Pharmacologic modification of psychosexual dysfunction," *J Sex Marital Ther* 1987;13:239-52.

27. Gardner EA, Johnston JA. "Bupropion—an antidepressant without sexual pathophysiological action," *J Clin Psychopharmacol* 1985;5:24-9.

28. Walker PW, Cole JO, Gardner EA, Hughes AR, Johnston JA, Batey, SR, et al. "Improvement in fluoxetine-associated sexual dysfunction in patients switched to bupropion," *J Clin Psychiatry* 1993;54:459-65.

29. Ashton AK, Rosen RC. "Bupropion as an antidote for serotonin reuptake inhibitor-induced sexual dysfunction," *J Clin Psychiatry* 1998;59:112-5.

30. Ferguson JM, Shrivastava RK, Stahl SM. "Effects of double-blind treatment with nefazodone or sertraline on re-emergence of sexual dysfunction in depressed patients," *New research program and abstracts of the 149th annual meeting of the American Psychiatric Association*, New York: American Psychiatric Association, 1996.

31. Leiblum SR. *Sexual desire disorders*. New York: Guilford; 1988.

32. O'Donohue W, Dopke CA, Swingen DN. "Psychotherapy for female sexual dysfunction: A review." *Clin Psychol Rev* 1997;17:537-66.

Chapter 27

What to Do If a Friend Has Depression

Educate Yourself on Depression

What is clinical depression?

Depression is a medical illness, just like cancer or diabetes. It is not the blues. The blues are normal feelings that eventually pass. The feelings associated with depression last longer than a couple of weeks. If your friend has depression, he can't talk himself out of it. Your friend isn't weak and doesn't have a character flaw. Having depression isn't his fault. Depression affects the whole body—thoughts, feelings, behavior, physical health, appearance, and all areas of a person's life—home, work, school and social life. Depression can be treated successfully just like other illnesses.

What causes depression?

Depression is triggered by a complex combination of genetic, psychological, and environmental factors. Genetic means that in some families, depression is inherited, passed down through genes. Psychological makeup has to do with personality traits and environmental factors means life circumstances. The brain is an organ of the body just like the heart, liver, and kidneys. If the chemicals in the brain (neurotransmitters) that regulate how a person thinks, feels and acts, get out of balance, the brain can get sick and the result can be clinical depression. A bad or stressful life event could trigger depression, however, a person can also be born with depression. It can also appear out of nowhere, when everything is going fine, at a time when there is no reason to get depression. Depression is nothing to be ashamed of.

Who can get depression?

Anyone. People of all ages can get depression—even children. Boys and girls and men and women can get depression. It doesn't matter what race, ethnicity, or economic group a person comes from. Depression affects more than 19 million people living in the United States each year.

Why is it important for friends to recognize the signs and symptoms of depression?

Your friend may not know she has a treatable illness. Depression affects thinking—she may not be able to think clearly or rationally, or may believe that she can't be helped. When depression is severe, it can cause thoughts of hopelessness and helplessness. The number one cause of suicide is untreated depression. Early recognition and treatment of depression can save lives.

Know the Symptoms of Depression

Your friend might have only a few of the symptoms of depression listed below or he might have many symptoms. Everyone is different. There is no set number of symptoms that, once checked, signal depression for sure. If any of the following are particularly bothersome or interfere with life, a person should get help. Can you hear your friend saying these things?

- I feel sad.
- I feel like crying a lot.
- I feel so alone.
- I don't really feel sad, just empty.
- I don't have any confidence in myself.

- I don't like myself.
- I feel scared a lot of the time, but I don't know why.
- I feel mad a lot, like I could just explode.
- I feel guilty.
- I can't concentrate.
- I have a hard time remembering.
- I don't want to make decisions—it's too much work.
- I feel like I'm in a fog.
- I'm so tired, no matter how much sleep I get.
- I'm frustrated with everything and everybody.
- I don't have fun anymore.
- I feel so helpless.
- I'm always getting into trouble.
- I'm so restless and jittery. I just can't sit still.
- I feel so disorganized, like my head is spinning.
- I feel so self-conscious.
- I can't think straight. My brain doesn't seem to work.
- I don't feel like talking—I just don't have anything to say.
- Sometimes I feel I can't go on living.
- I use alcohol or drugs to escape or to mask feelings.
- Sometimes I do things that are dangerous or that could hurt me.
- My whole body feels slowed down; my speech, my walk, my movements.
- I don't want to go out with friends anymore.
- I don't feel like taking care of my appearance or myself.
- I feel my life has no direction.
- Occasionally, my heart will pound very hard, I can't catch my breath, I feel tingly, my vision seems strange, and I feel like I might pass out. It passes in seconds, but I'm afraid it will happen again. (panic attack)
- I feel different from everyone else.

- I smile, but inside I'm miserable.
- I have trouble falling asleep or wake up in the middle of the night and can't get back to sleep.
- I don't feel like eating anymore.
- I feel I could eat all the time.
- I've gained or lost a significant amount of weight.
- I have headaches, stomachaches, backaches, and/or pain in my arms and legs.
- I feel dizzy a lot.
- My vision seems blurred or slow at times.
- Nothing I do makes me feel better.

In 90% or more of cases, a combination of antidepressant medication and therapy works to treat depression. People with depression can be helped. Your friend can feel good again. A physical exam from a doctor is important to rule out any other illnesses that may have the same symptoms as depression.

Know the Danger Signs of Suicide

Your friend may have symptoms of depression, but not be suicidal. It is always important to watch for danger signs of suicide though, just in case your friend might be having suicidal thoughts. Have you noticed any of these warning signs of suicide in your friend?

- Talking, reading, or writing about suicide or death.
- Talking about feeling worthless or helpless.
- Saying things like, "I'm going to kill myself," "I wish I were dead," or "I shouldn't have been born."
- Visiting or calling people to say goodbye.
- Giving things away or returning borrowed items.
- Organizing or cleaning bedroom "for the last time."
- Self-destructive behavior like self-cutting, or other risk-taking behaviors.
- Obsessed with death, violence, and guns or knives.
- Previous suicidal thoughts or suicide attempts.

If you see any of these danger signs in your friend, get help immediately.

Know What To Do

There is a direct link between depression and suicide. Every year in the United States, over 2,000 teenagers die by suicide.

Take Suicide Seriously

- The statement, "People who talk about suicide, won't really do it," is false.

- If your friend makes comments like, "I wish I were dead," or "It doesn't matter, I won't be around much longer," or "Everyone

Table 27.1. Tell Fact from Fiction

If you are concerned about depression in a friend, talk to someone about it. If you don't know where to turn, the telephone directory or information operator should have phone numbers for local hotline or mental health services referrals. Depression can affect people of any age, race, ethnic, or economic group. Some common myths are:

Myth: It's normal for teenagers to be moody; teens don't suffer from "real" depression.

Fact: Depression is more than just being moody, and it can affect people at any age, including teenagers.

Myth: Telling someone that a friend might be depressed is betraying a trust. If someone wants help, he or she will get it.

Fact: Depression, which saps energy and self-esteem, interferes with a person's ability or wish to get help. It is an act of true friendship to share your concerns with someone who can help.

Myth: Talking about depression only makes it worse.

Fact: Talking through feelings with a good friend is often a helpful first step. Friendship, concern, and support can provide the encouragement to talk about getting evaluated for depression.

Source: Excerpted from "Let's Talk about Depression," National Institute of Mental Health, NIH Pub. No. 00-4162, 2000.

would be better off without me," it may signal that he is thinking about suicide.

Never Keep Suicide a Secret

- It's okay to ask your friend, "Have you ever felt so badly that you've thought of suicide?" Asking the question won't plant the idea in a person's mind.

- If you suspect a friend has been thinking of suicide, tell a responsible adult, someone who will listen, take you seriously, and take action to get your friend help.

- If the first adult you go to doesn't feel there is cause for concern, keep going until you find someone who takes you seriously. This is an act of true friendship. A suicidal threat, even if said jokingly, should always be taken seriously.

Offer to Help

- Listen carefully, don't judge, and focus on the behaviors that concern you.

- Reassure your friend that there is help and that suicidal thoughts are only temporary.

- Offer to go with your friend to his or her parents, counselor or doctor.

- You can say things like, "I can tell you're really hurting," or "I care about you and will do my best to help." Tell him or her, "It's okay, it isn't your fault." A supportive friend can mean so much to someone who is in pain.

- Explain to your friend why you are concerned.

Find Someone Who Can Help

- Parent(s), guardian, or other family member
- School psychologist, social worker, counselor or nurse
- Teacher
- Personal physician or nurse
- Personal clergy
- Your local hospital

Many people can help you help a friend who is depressed or suicidal. But sometimes people don't understand depression and suicide. Ask for help until you find it.

For Emergency

- Call 1-800-SUICIDE

Information about other resources for mental health crisis help is included in the end section of this book.

For Educational Information

- Call 1-888-511-SAVE, or
- Visit WWW.SAVE.ORG on the internet

Information about other resources for information about depression and related topics is included in the end section of this book.

Part Three

Treating Depression

Chapter 28

Psychotherapy

According to the National Institute of Mental Health, an estimated 17 million adult Americans suffer from depression during any one-year period. Depression is a real illness and carries with it a high cost in terms of relationship problems, family suffering, and lost work productivity. Yet, depression is a highly treatable illness.

How does depression differ from occasional sadness?

Everyone feels sad or "blue" on occasion. It is also perfectly normal to grieve over upsetting life experiences, such as a major illness, a death in the family, a loss of a job, or a divorce. But, for most people, these feelings of grief and sadness tend to lessen with the passing of time.

However, if a person's feelings of sadness last for two weeks or longer, and if they interfere with daily life activities, something more serious than "feeling blue" may be going on.

Depressed individuals tend to feel helpless and hopeless and to blame themselves for having these feelings. People who are depressed may become overwhelmed and exhausted and may stop participating in their routine activities. They may withdraw from family and friends. Some may even have thoughts of death or suicide.

What causes depression?

There is no single answer to this question. Some depression is caused by changes in the body's chemistry that influence mood and thought processes. Biological factors can also cause depression. In other cases, depression is a sign that certain mental and emotional aspects of a person's life are out of balance. For example, significant life transitions and life stresses, such as the death of a loved one, can bring about a depressive episode.

Can depression be successfully treated?

Yes, it can. A person's depression is highly treatable when he or she receives competent care. It is critical for people who suspect that they or a family member may be suffering from depression seek care from a licensed mental health professional who has training and experience in helping people recover from depression. Simply put, people with depression who do not seek help suffer needlessly. Unexpressed feelings and concerns accompanied by a sense of isolation can worsen a depression; therefore, the importance of getting appropriate help cannot be overemphasized.

How does psychotherapy help people recover from depression?

Several approaches to psychotherapy—including cognitive-behavioral, interpersonal, and psychodynamic—help depressed people recover. Psychotherapy offers people the opportunity to identify the factors that contribute to their depression and to deal effectively with the psychological, behavioral, interpersonal, and situational causes. Skilled therapists can work with depressed individuals to:

- Pinpoint the life problems that contribute to their depression and help them understand which aspects of those problems they may be able to solve or improve. A trained therapist can help depressed patients identify options for the future and set realistic goals that enable them to enhance their mental and emotional well-being. Therapists also help individuals identify how they have successfully dealt with similar feelings if they have been depressed in the past.

- Identify negative or distorted thinking patterns that contribute to feelings of hopelessness and helplessness that accompany depression. For example, depressed individuals may tend to over

210

generalize, that is, to think of circumstances in terms of "always" or "never." They may also take events personally. A trained and competent therapist can help nurture a more positive outlook on life.

- Explore other learned thoughts and behaviors that create problems and contribute to depression. For example, therapists can help depressed individuals understand and improve patterns of interacting with other people that contribute to their depression.

- Help people regain a sense of control and pleasure in life. Psychotherapy helps people see choices as well as gradually incorporate enjoyable, fulfilling activities back into their lives.

Having one episode of depression greatly increases the risk of having another episode. There is some evidence that ongoing psychotherapy may lessen the chance of future episodes or reduce their intensity. Through therapy, people can learn skills to avoid unnecessary suffering from later bouts of depression.

In what other ways do therapists help depressed individuals and their loved ones?

The support and involvement of family and friends can play a crucial role in helping someone who is depressed. Individuals in the "support system" can help by encouraging a depressed loved one to stick with treatment and practice the coping techniques and problem-solving skills he or she is learning through psychotherapy.

Living with a depressed person can be very difficult and stressful on family members and friends. The pain of watching a loved one suffer from depression can bring about feelings of helplessness and loss. Family or marital therapy may be beneficial in bringing together all the individuals affected by depression and helping them learn effective ways to cope together. This type of psychotherapy can also provide a good opportunity for individuals who have never experienced depression themselves to learn more about it and identify constructive ways of supporting a loved one who is suffering from depression.

Are medications useful for treating depression?

Medications can be very helpful for reducing the symptoms of depression in some people, particularly in cases of moderate to severe depression. Often a combination of psychotherapy and medications is the best course of treatment. However, given the potential side effects, any use of medication requires close monitoring by the physician who prescribes the drugs.

Some depressed individuals may prefer psychotherapy to the use of medications, especially if their depression is not severe. By conducting a thorough assessment, a licensed and trained mental health professional can help make recommendations about an effective course of treatment for an individual's depression.

In Summary

Depression can seriously impair a person's ability to function in everyday situations. But the prospects for recovery for depressed individuals who seek professional care are very good. By working with a qualified and experienced therapist, people suffering from depression can help regain control of their lives.

Chapter 29

How Psychotherapy Works

How to Find Help through Psychotherapy

Millions of Americans have found relief from depression and other emotional difficulties through psychotherapy. Even so, some people find it hard to get started or stay in psychotherapy. This brief question-and-answer guide provides some basic information to help individuals take advantage of outpatient (non-hospital) psychotherapy.

Why do people consider using psychotherapy?

Psychotherapy is a partnership between an individual and a professional such as a psychologist who is licensed and trained to help people understand their feelings and assist them with changing their behavior. According to the National Institute of Mental Health, one-third of adults in the United States experience an emotional or substance abuse problem. Nearly 25 percent of the adult population suffers at some point from depression or anxiety.

People often consider psychotherapy, also known as therapy, under the following circumstances:

- They feel an overwhelming and prolonged sense of sadness and helplessness, and they lack hope in their lives.

"How Therapy Helps: How to Find Help Through Psychotherapy," October 1998, APA HelpCenter, American Psychological Association, 750 First Street, NE, Washington, DC 20002-4242; Phone 800-347-2721, available online at http://www.helping.apa.org/therapy/psychotherapy.html. Copyright © 1998 by the American Psychological Association. Reprinted with permission.

- Their emotional difficulties make it hard for them to function from day to day. For example, they are unable to concentrate on assignments and their job performance suffers as a result.

- Their actions are harmful to themselves or to others. For instance, they drink too much alcohol and become overly aggressive.

- They are troubled by emotional difficulties facing family members or close friends.

What does research show about the effectiveness of psychotherapy?

Research suggests that therapy effectively decreases patients' depression and anxiety and related symptoms—such as pain, fatigue and nausea. Psychotherapy has also been found to increase survival time for heart surgery and cancer patients, and it can have a positive effect on the body's immune system. Research increasingly supports the idea that emotional and physical health are very closely linked and that therapy can improve a person's overall health status.

There is convincing evidence that most people who have at least several sessions of psychotherapy are far better off than untreated individuals with emotional difficulties. One major study showed that 50 percent of patients noticeably improved after eight sessions while 75 percent of individuals in psychotherapy improved by the end of six months. Psychotherapy with children is similar in effectiveness to psychotherapy with adults.

How do I find a qualified therapist?

Selecting a therapist is a highly personal matter.

A professional who works very well with one individual may not be a good choice for another person. There are several ways to get referrals to qualified therapists such as licensed psychologists, including the following:

- Talk to close family members and friends for their recommendations, especially if they have had a good experience with psychotherapy.

- Many state psychological associations operate referral services which put individuals in touch with licensed and competent mental health providers. (Call the American Psychological

Association's Practice Directorate at 202-336-5800 for the name and phone number of the appropriate state organization.)

- Ask your primary care physician (or other health professional) for a referral. Tell the doctor what's important to you in choosing a therapist so he or she can make appropriate suggestions.

- Inquire at your church or synagogue.

- Look in the phone book for the listing of a local mental health association or community mental health center and check these sources for possible referrals.

Ideally, you will end up with more than one lead. Call and request the opportunity, either by phone or in person, to ask the therapist some questions. You might want to inquire about his or her licensure and level of training, approach to psychotherapy, participation in insurance plans and fees. Such a discussion should help you sort through your options and choose someone with whom you believe you might interact well.

If I begin psychotherapy, how should I try to gain the most from it?

There are many approaches to outpatient psychotherapy and various formats in which it may occur—including individual, group and family psychotherapy. Despite the variations, all psychotherapy is a two-way process that works especially well when patients and their therapists communicate openly. Research has shown that the outcome of psychotherapy is improved when the therapist and patient agree early about what the major problems are and how psychotherapy can help.

You and your therapist both have responsibilities in establishing and maintaining a good working relationship. Be clear with your therapist about your expectations and share any concerns that may arise. Psychotherapy works best when you attend all scheduled sessions and give some forethought to what you want to discuss during each one.

How can I evaluate whether therapy is working well?

As you begin psychotherapy, you should establish clear goals with your therapist. Perhaps you want to overcome feelings of hopelessness associated with depression. Or maybe you would like to control a fear that disrupts your daily life. Keep in mind that certain tasks require more time to accomplish than others. You may need to adjust your goals depending on how long you plan to be in psychotherapy.

After a few sessions, it's a good sign if you feel the experience truly is a joint effort and that you and the therapist enjoy a good rapport. On the other hand, you should be open with your therapist if you find yourself feeling 'stuck' or lacking direction once you've been in psychotherapy awhile.

There may be times when a therapist appears cold and disinterested or doesn't seem to regard you positively. Tell your therapist if this is the situation, or if you question other aspects of his or her approach. If you find yourself thinking about discontinuing psychotherapy, talk with your therapist. It might be helpful to consult another professional, provided you let your therapist know you are seeking a second opinion.

Patients often feel a wide range of emotions during psychotherapy. Some qualms about psychotherapy that people may have result from the difficulty of discussing painful and troubling experiences. When this happens, it can actually be a positive sign indicating that you are starting to explore your thoughts and behaviors.

You should spend time with your therapist periodically reviewing your progress (or your concern that you are not making sufficient headway). Although there are other considerations affecting the duration of psychotherapy, success in reaching your primary goals should be a major factor in deciding when your psychotherapy should end.

Psychotherapy isn't easy. But patients who are willing to work in close partnership with their therapist often find relief from their emotional distress and begin to lead more productive and fulfilling lives.

Chapter 30

Antidepressants and Other Medications Used in Treating People with Depression

This information is designed to help people understand how and why drugs can be used as part of the treatment of mental health problems. It is important for persons who use mental health services to be well informed about medications for mental illnesses, but this chapter is not a "do-it-yourself" manual. Self-medication can be dangerous. Interpretation of both signs and symptoms of the illness and side effects are jobs for the professional. The prescription and management of medication, in all cases, must be done by a responsible physician working closely with the patient and sometimes the patient's family or other mental health professionals. This is the only way to ensure that the most effective use of medication is achieved with minimum risk of side effects or complications.

Oftentimes an individual is taking more than one medication and at different times of the day. It is essential to take the correct dosage

Text is this chapter is excerpted from "Medications," National Institute of Mental Health, NIH Pub. No. 95-3929, updated December 2001; the section titled "Questions and Answers about Antidepressants," is from "Fact Sheet: Antidepressant Medicines," available from Ask NOAH About: Mental Health at http://www.noah-health.org/english/illness/mentalhealth/cornell/medications/ antidepres.html, © 1996 New York-Presbyterian Hospital, Behavioral Health Nursing Service Line, revised 2001; reprinted with permission. The section titled "Questions and Answers about MAOI Antidepressants" is from "Fact Sheet: MAOI Antidepressants," available from Ask NOAH About: Mental Health at http://www.noah-health.org/english/illness/mentalhealth/cornell/medications/ maoiantideprs.html © 1996 New York-Presbyterian Hospital, Behavioral Health Nursing Service Line, revised February 2000; reprinted with permission.

217

of each medication. An easy way to ensure this is to use a 7-day pill box, available at the prescription counter in any pharmacy, and to fill the box with the proper medications at the beginning of each week.

Introduction

Anyone can develop a mental illness you, a family member, a friend, or the fellow down the block. Some disorders are mild, while others are serious and long-lasting. These conditions can be helped. One way an important way is with psychotherapeutic medications. Compared to other types of treatment, these medications are relative newcomers in the fight against mental illness. It was only 41 years ago that the first one, chlorpromazine, was introduced. But considering the short time they've been around, psychotherapeutic medications have made dramatic changes in the treatment of mental disorders. People who, years ago, might have spent many years in mental hospitals because of crippling mental illness may now only go in for brief treatment, or might receive all their treatment at an outpatient clinic.

Psychotherapeutic medications also may make other kinds of treatment more effective. Someone who is too depressed to talk, for instance, can't get much benefit from psychotherapy or counseling; but often, the right medication will improve symptoms so that the person can respond better.

Another benefit from these medications is an increased understanding of the causes of mental illness. Scientists have learned a great deal more about the workings of the brain as a result of their investigations into how psychotherapeutic medications relieve disorders such as psychosis, depression, anxiety, obsessive compulsive disorder, and panic disorder.

Symptom Relief, Not Cure

Just as aspirin can reduce a fever without clearing up the infection that causes it, psychotherapeutic medications act by controlling symptoms. Like most drugs used in medicine, they correct or compensate for some malfunction in the body. Psychotherapeutic medications do not cure mental illness, but they do lessen its burden. In many cases, these medications can help a person get on with life despite some continuing mental pain and difficulty coping with problems. For example, drugs like chlorpromazine can turn off the "voices" heard by some people with schizophrenia and help them to perceive reality more accurately. And antidepressants can lift the dark, heavy moods

218

of depression. The degree of response ranging from little relief of symptoms to complete remission depends on a variety of factors related to the individual and the particular disorder being treated.

How long someone must take a psychotherapeutic medication depends on the disorder. Many depressed and anxious people may need medication for a single period—perhaps for several months—and then never have to take it again. For some conditions, such as schizophrenia or manic-depressive illness, medication may have to be take indefinitely or, perhaps, intermittently.

Like any medication, psychotherapeutic medications do not produce the same effect in everyone. Some people may respond better to one medication than another. Some may need larger dosages than others do. Some experience annoying side effects, while others do not. Age, sex, body size, body chemistry, physical illnesses and their treatments, diet, and habits such as smoking, are some of the factors that can influence a medication's effect.

Questions for Your Doctor

To increase the likelihood that a medication will work well, patients and their families must actively participate with the doctor prescribing it. They must tell the doctor about the patient's past medical history, other medications being taken, anticipated life changes such as planning to have a baby and, after some experience with a medication, whether it is causing side effects. When a medication is prescribed, the patient or family member should ask the following questions recommended by the U.S. Food and Drug Administration (FDA) and professional organizations:

- What is the name of the medication, and what is it supposed to do?

- How and when do I take it, and when do I stop taking it?

- What foods, drinks, other medications, or activities should I avoid while taking the prescribed medication?

- What are the side effects, and what should I do if they occur?

- Is there any written information available about the medication?

About the Medications Discussed in This Chapter

In this chapter, medications are described by their generic (chemical) names and by their trade names (brand names used by drug companies).

Treatment evaluation studies have established the efficacy of the medications described here; however, much remains to be learned about these medications. The National Institute of Mental Health, other federal agencies, and private research groups are sponsoring studies of these medications. Scientists are hoping to improve their understanding of how and why these medications work, how to control or eliminate unwanted side effects, and how to make the medications more effective.

Antidepressant Medications

The kind of depression that will most likely benefit from treatment with medications is more than just "the blues." It's a condition that's prolonged, lasting 2 weeks or more, and interferes with a person's ability to carry on daily tasks and to enjoy activities that previously brought pleasure.

The depressed person will seem sad, or "down," or may show a lack of interest in his surroundings. He may have trouble eating and lose weight (although some people eat more and gain weight when depressed). He may sleep too much or too little, have difficulty going to sleep, sleep restlessly, or awaken very early in the morning. He may speak of feeling guilty, worthless, or hopeless. He may complain that his thinking is slowed down. He may lack energy, feeling "everything's too much," or he might be agitated and jumpy. A person who is depressed may cry. He may think and talk about killing himself and may even make a suicide attempt. Some people who are depressed have psychotic symptoms, such as delusions (false ideas) that are related to their depression. For instance, a psychotically depressed person might imagine that he is already dead, or "in hell," being punished.

Not everyone who is depressed has all these symptoms, but everyone who is depressed has at least some of them. A depression can range in intensity from mild to severe.

Antidepressants are used most widely for serious depressions, but they can also be helpful for some milder depressions. Antidepressants, although they are not "uppers" or stimulants, take away or reduce the symptoms of depression and help the depressed person feel the way he did before he became depressed.

Antidepressants are also used for disorders characterized principally by anxiety. They can block the symptoms of panic, including rapid heartbeat, terror, dizziness, chest pains, nausea, and breathing problems. They can also be used to treat some phobias.

The physician chooses the particular antidepressant to prescribe based on the individual patient's symptoms. When someone begins taking an antidepressant, improvement generally will not begin to show immediately. With most of these medications, it will take from one to three weeks before changes begin to occur. Some symptoms diminish early in treatment; others, later. For instance, a person's energy level or sleeping or eating patterns may improve before his depressed mood lifts. If there is little or no change in symptoms after five to six weeks, a different medication may be tried. Some people will respond better to one than another. Since there is no certain way of determining beforehand which medication will be effective, the doctor may have to prescribe first one, then another, until an effective one is found. Treatment is continued for a minimum of several months and may last up to a year or more.

While some people have one episode of depression and then never have another, or remain symptom-free for years, others have more frequent episodes or very long-lasting depressions that may go on for years. Some people find that their depressions become more frequent and severe as they get older. For these people, continuing (maintenance) treatment with antidepressants can be an effective way of reducing the frequency and severity of depressions. Those that are commonly used have no known long-term side effects and may be continued indefinitely. The prescribed dosage of the medication may be lowered if side effects become troublesome. Lithium can also be used for maintenance treatment of repeated depressions whether or not there is evidence of a manic or manic-like episode in the past.

Dosage of antidepressants varies, depending on the type of drug, the person's body chemistry, age, and, sometimes, body weight. Dosages are generally started low and raised gradually over time until the desired effect is reached without the appearance of troublesome side effects.

There are a number of antidepressant medications available. They differ in their side effects and, to some extent, in their level of effectiveness. Tricyclic antidepressants (named for their chemical structure) are more commonly used for treatment of major depressions than are monoamine oxidase inhibitors (MAOIs); but MAOIs are often helpful in so-called "atypical" depressions in which there are symptoms like oversleeping, anxiety, panic attacks, and phobias.

The last few years have seen the introduction of a number of new antidepressants. Several of them are called "selective serotonin reuptake inhibitors" (SSRIs). Those available at the present time in the United States are fluoxetine (Prozac), fluvoxamine (Luvox), paroxetine (Paxil), and sertraline (Zoloft). (Luvox has been approved for obsessive-compulsive disorder, and Paxil has been approved for panic disorder.) Though structurally different from each other, all the SSRIs' antidepressant effects are due to their action on one specific neurotransmitter, serotonin. Two other antidepressants that affect two neurotransmitters serotonin and norepinephrine have also been approved by the FDA. They are venlafaxine (Effexor) and nefazodone (Serzone). All of these newer antidepressants seem to have less bothersome side effects than the older tricyclic antidepressants.

The tricyclic antidepressant clomipramine (Anafranil) affects serotonin but is not as selective as the SSRIs. It was the first medication specifically approved for use in the treatment of obsessive-compulsive disorder (OCD). Prozac and Luvox have now been approved for use with OCD.

Another of the newer antidepressants, bupropion (Wellbutrin), is chemically unrelated to the other antidepressants. It has more effect on norepinephrine and dopamine than on serotonin. Wellbutrin has not been associated with weight gain or sexual dysfunction. It is contraindicated for individuals with, or at risk for, a seizure disorder or who have been diagnosed with bulimia or anorexia nervosa.

Questions and Answers about Antidepressants

What are the names of the antidepressant medicines?

In the United States, the antidepressants in use are imipramine (Tofranil), amitriptyline (Elavil), desipramine (Norpramin), nortriptyline (Pamelor), doxepin (Sinequan), protriptyline (Vivactil), trimipramine (Surmontil), maprotiline (Ludiomil), amoxapine (Asendin), trazodone (Desyrel), fluoxetine* (Prozac)*, bupropion (Wellbutrin), clomipramine* (Anafranil)*, sertraline* (Zoloft)*, paroxetine* (Paxil)*, venlafaxine (Effexor), nefazodone (Serzone), fluvoxamine* (Luvox)*, mirtazapine (Remeron), and citalopram* (Celexa)* For each of these medicines, the generic name is followed by the most common brand name in parentheses. An asterisk next to a name indicates an SSRI (Selective Serotonin Reuptake Inhibitor) antidepressant.

Which illnesses or problems are helped by these medicines?

Antidepressants are used to treat depression, panic attacks, agoraphobia, eating disorders, obsessive-compulsive disorder, social phobia and posttraumatic stress disorder.

When these medicines are used to treat depression, what symptoms do they treat?

Antidepressants are used to treat sad mood, loss of appetite, sleep problems, hopelessness, helplessness, guilt, loss of energy, loss of sex drive, lack of pleasure, trouble concentrating, feeling slowed down, agitation, and preoccupation with death or suicide.

What are some of the facts about antidepressant medicines?

- They are not addictive.
- You may have to take them for as long as eight weeks before they start working.
- They work best when you take them every day exactly as prescribed.
- The dose that works can be very different from person to person.
- Antidepressants are usually only a part of treatment. Therapy, skills training, and lifestyle are important too.
- There are no known long-term risks.

What are the most common side effects of the antidepressants?

Any of the following side effects may occur: sleepiness, dry mouth, blurred vision, constipation, delay in urinating, sweating, dizziness, agitation, trouble sleeping at night, anxiety, nausea, headache, tremors, weight gain, delayed orgasm, or reduced sexual desire.

What is the usual course of treatment with antidepressants?

- You're given a small test dose to start.
- The dose is gradually increased to a standard range.
- Your doctor will wait for it to work on getting rid of your symptoms.
- You continue to take the antidepressant for a minimum of 6–12 months after recovery. For some people, lifetime medicine is the best treatment.

What do I need to do to manage these medicines on my own?

- Ask your doctor or nurse questions about anything you don't understand.
- Use some kind of reminder system so you don't forget to take any doses.

- Take your medicine exactly as prescribed.
- Carry a list of all the medications you take regularly.
- Report any side effects.
- Use no other medications, prescription or non-prescription, without first consulting your prescriber. If another doctor or nurse prescribes something for you, tell him or her what you are already taking.
- Don't take old, outdated medicine.
- Don't lend or borrow your medicines.
- Keep all medicines out of the reach of children.
- Whether or not you drink alcohol is a personal decision you should make together with your prescriber.
- If the medicine makes you sleepy, don't drive a car or operate other dangerous machinery.

Questions and Answers about MAOI Antidepressants

What are MAOI antidepressants?

MAOI antidepressants are a small group of antidepressants that require a special diet and avoidance of certain other medicines. The most common ones are phenelzine (Nardil), tranylcypromine (Parnate) and isocarboxazid (Marplan).

What are These Medicines Used for?

MAOI antidepressants are used mostly to treat depression, panic attacks, eating disorders or agoraphobia.

What symptoms do they treat?

When MAOIs are used to treat depression, they help best with:

- sadness
- insomnia or oversleeping
- hopelessness
- under-eating or overeating
- anxiety
- loss of energy, sex drive or pleasure

- helplessness
- trouble concentrating
- worthlessness
- slow thinking
- guilt
- preoccupation with death or suicide

What are some of the basic facts about MAOI antidepressants?

- They are not addictive.
- They may begin to work almost immediately, or they may take as long as eight weeks to start working.
- You need to take them exactly as prescribed whether you feel very good, very bad, or in between.
- The dose prescribed is very different from person to person.
- Antidepressants are usually only a part of treatment. Therapy, skills training, and lifestyle are important too.
- There are no known long-term risks.
- You must carefully avoid certain foods and medicines while you are taking an MAOI antidepressant and for two weeks after stopping it.

How was this specific antidepressant chosen?

- Past response in yourself or a close family member. Good and bad responses run in families.
- Certain kinds of depression respond better to MAOIs.
- If other antidepressants don't work, this kind might.
- You must be able to follow the food and medication restrictions.

What is the usual course of treatment?

- You learn the food and medications to avoid.
- You start the special diet.
- You begin taking a low starting dose.
- The dose is gradually increased to a standard level.

- After a few weeks, you take the whole dose at bedtime or twice a day.

- You wait for it to work.

- You continue to take the antidepressant for at least 6–12 months after recovery from depression. Some people continue the medicine for the rest of their lives.

What are the most common side effects?

The most common side effects of the MAOI antidepressants are low blood pressure, feeling light-headed, trouble sleeping, sleepiness, dry mouth, weight gain and reduced tolerance for alcohol.

A less common side effect is high blood pressure if you eat prohibited foods or medications. Symptoms of rising blood pressure may include stiff neck, headache, palpitations, chest pain, nausea or vomiting, flushing or chills, fear, pallor or sweating. The blood pressure may rise so high that it is life threatening. This is called a hypertensive crisis.

What do I have to do to take an MAOI antidepressant safely?

- Ask your doctor or nurse questions about anything you don't understand.

- Use some kind of reminder system so you don't forget to take any doses.

- Take your medicine exactly as prescribed.

- Carry a list of all the medicines you take regularly.

- Report any side effects to your prescriber.

- Use no other medicines, prescription or non-prescription, without first talking to your prescriber. If another doctor or nurse prescribes something for you, tell him or her what you are already taking.

- Don't take old, outdated medication.

- Don't lend or borrow this medicine.

- Keep all medicines out of the reach of children.

- Whether or not you drink alcohol is a personal decision you should make with your prescriber.

- If this medication makes you sleepy, don't drive a car or operate other dangerous machinery.

- Carry a copy of the list of food and medicines to avoid with you at all times.

Side Effects of Antidepressant Medications

Tricyclic Antidepressants

There are a number of possible side effects with tricyclic antidepressants that vary, depending on the medication. For example, amitriptyline (Elavil) may make people feel drowsy, while protriptyline (Vivactil) hardly does this at all and, in some people, may have an opposite effect, producing feelings of anxiety and restlessness. Because of this kind of variation in side effects, one antidepressant might be highly desirable for one person and not recommended for another. Tricyclics on occasion may complicate specific heart problems, and for this reason the physician should be aware of all such difficulties. Other side effects with tricyclics may include blurred vision, dry mouth, constipation, weight gain, dizziness when changing position, increased sweating, difficulty urinating, changes in sexual desire, decrease in sexual ability, muscle twitches, fatigue, and weakness. Not all these medications produce all side effects, and not everybody gets them. Some will disappear quickly, while others may remain for the length of treatment. Some side effects are similar to symptoms of depression (for instance, fatigue and constipation). For this reason, the patient or family should discuss all symptoms with the doctor, who may change the medication or dosage.

Tricyclics also may interact with thyroid hormone, antihypertensive medications, oral contraceptives, some blood coagulants, some sleeping medications, antipsychotic medications, diuretics, antihistamines, aspirin, bicarbonate of soda, vitamin C, alcohol, and tobacco.

An overdose of antidepressants is serious and potentially lethal. It requires immediate medical attention. Symptoms of an overdose of tricyclic antidepressant medication develop within an hour and may start with rapid heartbeat, dilated pupils, flushed face, and agitation, and progress to confusion, loss of consciousness, seizures, irregular heart beats, cardiorespiratory collapse, and death.

The Newer Antidepressants

The most common side effects of these antidepressants are gastrointestinal problems and headache. Others are insomnia, anxiety, and agitation. Because of potentially serious interaction between these medications and monoamine oxidase inhibitors, it is advisable to stop taking one medication from two to four or five weeks before starting the other, depending on the specific medications involved. In addition, some SSRIs have been found to affect metabolism of certain other medications in the liver, creating possible drug interactions.

Monoamine Oxidase Inhibitors (MAOIs)

MAOIs may cause some side effects similar to those of the other antidepressants. Dizziness when changing position and rapid heartbeat are common. MAOIs also react with certain foods and alcoholic beverages (such as aged cheeses, foods containing monosodium glutamate (MSG), Chianti and other red wines), and other medications (such as over-the-counter cold and allergy preparations, local anesthetics, amphetamines, insulin, some narcotics, and antiparkinsonian medications). These reactions often do not appear for several hours. Signs may include severe high blood pressure, headache, nausea, vomiting, rapid heartbeat, possible confusion, psychotic symptoms, seizures, stroke, and coma. For this reason, people taking MAOIs must stay away from restricted foods, drinks, and medications. They should be sure that they are furnished, by their doctor or pharmacist, a list of all foods, beverages, and other medications that should be avoided.

Precautions to be Observed when Taking Antidepressants

When taking antidepressants, it is important to tell all doctors (and dentists) being seen not just the one who is treating the depression about all medications being used, including over-the-counter preparations and alcohol. Antidepressants should be taken only in the amount prescribed and should be kept in a secure place away from children. When used with proper care, following doctors' instructions, antidepressants are extremely useful medications that can reverse the misery of a depression and help a person feel like himself again.

Antimanic Medications

Bipolar disorder (manic-depressive illness) is characterized by cycling mood changes: severe highs (mania) and lows (depression). Cycles may be predominantly manic or depressive with normal mood between cycles. Mood swings may follow each other very closely, within hours or days, or may be separated by months to years. These "highs" and "lows" may vary in intensity and severity.

When someone is in a manic "high," he may be overactive, overtalkative, and have a great deal of energy. He will switch quickly from one topic to another, as if he cannot get his thoughts out fast enough; his attention span is often short, and he can easily be distracted. Sometimes, the "high" person is irritable or angry and has false or inflated ideas about his position or importance in the world. He may be very elated, full of grand schemes which might range from business deals to romantic sprees. Often, he shows poor judgment in these ventures. Mania, untreated, may worsen to a psychotic state.

Depression will show in a "low" mood, lack of energy, changes in eating and sleeping patterns, feelings of hopelessness, helplessness, sadness, worthlessness, and guilt, and sometimes thoughts of suicide.

Lithium

The medication used most often to combat a manic "high" is lithium. It is unusual to find mania without a subsequent or preceding period of depression. Lithium evens out mood swings in both directions, so that it is used not just for acute manic attacks or flare-ups of the illness, but also as an ongoing treatment of bipolar disorder.

Lithium will diminish severe manic symptoms in about five to 14 days, but it may be anywhere from days to several months until the condition is fully controlled. Antipsychotic medications are sometimes used in the first several days of treatment to control manic symptoms until the lithium begins to take effect. Likewise, antidepressants may be needed in addition to lithium during the depressive phase of bipolar disorder.

Someone may have one episode of bipolar disorder and never have another, or be free of illness for several years. However, for those who have more than one episode, continuing (maintenance) treatment on lithium is usually given serious consideration.

Some people respond well to maintenance treatment and have no further episodes, while others may have moderate mood swings that lessen as treatment continues. Some people may continue to have episodes that are diminished in frequency and severity. Unfortunately, some manic-depressive patients may not be helped at all. Response to treatment with lithium varies, and it cannot be determined beforehand who will or will not respond to treatment.

Regular blood tests are an important part of treatment with lithium. A lithium level must be checked periodically to measure the amount of the drug in the body. If too little is taken, lithium will not be effective. If too much is taken, a variety of side effects may occur. The range between an effective dose and a toxic one is small. A lithium level is routinely checked at the beginning of treatment to determine the best lithium dosage for the patient. Once a person is stable and on a maintenance dosage, a lithium level should be checked every few months. How much lithium a person needs to take may vary over time, depending on how ill he is, his body chemistry, and his physical condition.

Anything that lowers the level of sodium (table salt is sodium chloride) in the body may cause a lithium buildup and lead to toxicity. Reduced salt intake, heavy sweating, fever, vomiting, or diarrhea may do this. An unusual amount of exercise or a switch to a low-salt diet are examples. It's important to be aware of conditions that lower sodium and to share this information with the doctor. The lithium dosage may have to be adjusted.

When a person first takes lithium, he may experience side effects, such as drowsiness, weakness, nausea, vomiting, fatigue, hand tremor, or increased thirst and urination. These usually disappear or subside quickly, although hand tremor may persist. Weight gain may also occur. Dieting will help, but crash diets should be avoided because they may affect the lithium level. Drinking low-calorie or no-calorie beverages will help keep weight down. Kidney changes, accompanied by increased thirst and urination, may develop during treatment. These conditions that may occur are generally manageable and are reduced by lowering the dosage. Because lithium may cause the thyroid gland to become underactive (hypothyroidism) or sometimes enlarged (goiter), thyroid function monitoring is a part of the therapy. To restore normal thyroid function, thyroid hormone is given along with lithium.

Because of possible complications, lithium may either not be recommended or may be given with caution when a person has existing thyroid, kidney, or heart disorders, epilepsy, or brain damage. Women of child-bearing age should be aware that lithium increases the risk of congenital malformations in babies born to women taking lithium. Special caution should be taken during the first three months of pregnancy.

Lithium, when combined with certain other medications, can have unwanted effects. Some diuretics substances that remove water from the body increase the level of lithium and can cause toxicity. Other diuretics, like coffee and tea, can lower the level of lithium. Signs of lithium toxicity may include nausea, vomiting, drowsiness, mental dullness, slurred speech, confusion, dizziness, muscle twitching, irregular heart beat, and blurred vision. A serious lithium overdose can be life-threatening. Someone who is taking lithium should tell all the doctors including dentists he sees about all other medications he is taking.

With regular monitoring, lithium is a safe and effective drug that enables many people, who otherwise would suffer from incapacitating mood swings, to lead normal lives.

Anticonvulsants

Not all patients with symptoms of mania benefit from lithium. Some have been found to respond to another type of medication, the anticonvulsant medications that are usually used to treat epilepsy. Carbamazepine (Tegretol) is the anticonvulsant that has been most widely used. Manic-depressive patients who cycle rapidly that is, they change from mania to depression and back again over the course of hours or days, rather than months seem to respond particularly well to carbamazepine.

Early side effects of carbamazepine, although generally mild, include drowsiness, dizziness, confusion, disturbed vision, perceptual distortions, memory impairment, and nausea. They are usually transient and often respond to temporary dosage reduction. Another common but generally mild adverse effect is the lowering of the white blood cell count which requires periodic blood tests to monitor against the rare possibility of more serious, even life-threatening, bone marrow depression. Also serious are the skin rashes that can occur in 15 to 20 percent of patients. These rashes are sometimes severe enough to require discontinuation of the medication.

In 1995, the anticonvulsant divalproex sodium (Depakote) was approved by the Food and Drug Administration for manic-depressive illness. Clinical trials have shown it to have an effectiveness in controlling manic symptoms equivalent to that of lithium; it is effective in both rapid-cycling and non-rapid-cycling bipolar.

Though divalproex can cause gastrointestinal side effects, the incidence is low. Other adverse effects occasionally reported are headache, double vision, dizziness, anxiety, or confusion. Because in some cases divalproex has caused liver disfunction, liver function tests should be performed prior to therapy and at frequent intervals thereafter, particularly during the first six months of therapy.

Antianxiety Medications

Everyone experiences anxiety at one time or another "butterflies in the stomach" before giving a speech or sweaty palms during a job interview are common symptoms. Other symptoms of anxiety include irritability, uneasiness, jumpiness, feelings of apprehension, rapid or irregular heartbeat, stomach ache, nausea, faintness, and breathing problems.

Anxiety is often manageable and mild. But sometimes it can present serious problems. A high level or prolonged state of anxiety can be incapacitating, making the activities of daily life difficult or impossible. Besides generalized anxiety, other anxiety disorders are panic, phobia, obsessive-compulsive disorder (OCD), and posttraumatic stress disorder.

Phobias, which are persistent, irrational fears and are characterized by avoidance of certain objects, places, and things, sometimes accompany anxiety. A panic attack is a severe form of anxiety that may occur suddenly and is marked with symptoms of nervousness, breathlessness, pounding heart, and sweating. Sometimes the fear that one may die is present.

Antianxiety medications help to calm and relax the anxious person and remove the troubling symptoms. There are a number of antianxiety medications currently available. The preferred medications for most anxiety disorders are the benzodiazepines. In addition to the benzodiazepines, a non-benzodiazepine, buspirone (BuSpar), is used for generalized anxiety disorders. Antidepressants are also effective for panic attacks and some phobias and are often prescribed for these conditions. They are also sometimes used for more generalized forms of anxiety, especially when it is accompanied by depression. The medications approved by the FDA for use in OCD are all antidepressants, clomipramine, fluoxetine, and fluvoxamine.

The most commonly used benzodiazepines are alprazolam (Xanax) and diazepam (Valium), followed by chlordiazepoxide (Librium, Librax, Libritabs). Benzodiazepines are relatively fast-acting medications; in contrast, buspirone must be taken daily for two or three weeks prior to exerting its antianxiety effect. Most benzodiazepines will begin to take effect within hours, some in even less time. Benzodiazepines differ in duration of action in different individuals; they may be taken two or three times a day, or sometimes only once a day. Dosage is generally started at a low level and gradually raised until symptoms are diminished or removed. The dosage will vary a great deal depending on the symptoms and the individual's body chemistry.

Benzodiazepines have few side effects. Drowsiness and loss of coordination are most common; fatigue and mental slowing or confusion can also occur. These effects make it dangerous to drive or operate some machinery when taking benzodiazepines especially when the patient is just beginning treatment. Other side effects are rare.

Benzodiazepines combined with other medications can present a problem, notably when taken together with commonly used substances such as alcohol. It is wise to abstain from alcohol when taking benzodiazepines, as the interaction between benzodiazepines and alcohol can lead to serious and possibly life-threatening complications. Following the doctor's instructions is important. The doctor should be informed of all other medications the patient is taking, including over-the-counter preparations. Benzodiazepines increase central nervous system depression when combined with alcohol, anesthetics, antihistamines, sedatives, muscle relaxants, and some prescription pain medications. Particular benzodiazepines may influence the action of some anticonvulsant and cardiac medications. Benzodiazepines have also been associated with abnormalities in babies born to mothers who were taking these medications during pregnancy.

With benzodiazepines, there is a potential for the development of tolerance and dependence as well as the possibility of abuse and withdrawal reactions. For these reasons, the medications are generally prescribed for brief periods of time, days or weeks, and sometimes intermittently, for stressful situations or anxiety attacks. For the same reason, ongoing or continuous treatment with benzodiazepines is not recommended for most people. Some patients may, however, need long-term treatment.

Consult with the doctor before discontinuing a benzodiazepine. A withdrawal reaction may occur if the treatment is abruptly stopped. Symptoms may include anxiety, shakiness, headache, dizziness, sleeplessness, loss of appetite, and, in more severe cases, fever, seizures, and psychosis. A withdrawal reaction may be mistaken for a return of the anxiety, since many of the symptoms are similar. Thus, after benzodiazepines are taken for an extended period, the dosage is gradually tapered off before being completely stopped.

Although benzodiazepines, buspirone, tricyclic antidepressants, or SSRIs are the preferred medications for most anxiety disorders, occasionally, for specific reasons, one of the following medications may be prescribed: antipsychotic medications; antihistamines (such as Atarax, Vistaril, and others); barbiturates such as phenobarbital; and beta-blockers such as propranolol (Inderal, Inderide). Propanediols such as meprobamate (Equanil) were commonly prescribed prior to the introduction of the benzodiazepines, but today rarely are used.

Antipsychotic Medications

A person who is psychotic is out of touch with reality. He may "hear voices" or have strange and untrue ideas (for example, thinking that others can hear his thoughts, or are trying to harm him, or that he is the President of the United States or some other famous person). He may get excited or angry for no apparent reason, or spend a lot of time off by himself, or in bed, sleeping during the day and staying awake at night. He may neglect his appearance, not bathing or changing clothes, and may become difficult to communicate with saying things that make no sense, or barely talking at all.

These kinds of behaviors are symptoms of psychotic illness, the principal form of which is schizophrenia. All of the symptoms may not be present when someone is psychotic, but some of them always are. Antipsychotic medications, as their name suggests, act against these symptoms. These medications cannot "cure" the illness, but they can take away many of the symptoms or make them milder. In some cases, they can shorten the course of the illness as well.

There are a number of antipsychotic (neuroleptic) medications available. They all work; the main differences are in the potency—that is, the dosage (amount) prescribed to produce therapeutic effects—and the side effects. Some people might think that the higher the dose of medication, the more serious the illness, but this is not always true.

A doctor will consider several factors when prescribing an antipsychotic medication, besides how "ill" someone is. These include the patient's age, body weight, and type of medication. Past history is important, too. If a person took a particular medication before and it worked, the doctor is likely to prescribe the same one again. Some less potent drugs, like chlorpromazine (Thorazine), are prescribed in higher numbers of milligrams than others of high potency, like haloperidol (Haldol).

If a person has to take a large amount of a "high-dose" antipsychotic medication, such as chlorpromazine, to get the same effect as a small amount of a "low-dose" medication, such as haloperidol, why doesn't the doctor just prescribe "low-dose" medications? The main reason is the difference in their side effects (actions of the medication other than the one intended for the illness). These medications vary in their side effects, and some people have more trouble with certain side effects than others. A side effect may sometimes be desirable. For instance, the sedative effect of some antipsychotic medications is useful for patients who have trouble sleeping or who become agitated during the day.

Unlike some prescription drugs, which must be taken several times during the day, antipsychotic medications can usually be taken just once a day. Thus, patients can reduce daytime side effects by taking the medications once, before bed. Some antipsychotic medications are available in forms that can be injected once or twice a month, thus assuring that the medicine is being taken reliably.

Most side effects of antipsychotic medications are mild. Many common ones disappear after the first few weeks of treatment. These include drowsiness, rapid heartbeat, and dizziness when changing position.

Some people gain weight while taking antipsychotic medications and may have to change their diet to control their weight. Other side effects that may be caused by some antipsychotic medications include decrease in sexual ability or interest, problems with menstrual periods, sunburn, or skin rashes. If a side effect is especially troublesome, it should be discussed with the doctor who may prescribe a different medication, change the dosage level or schedule, or prescribe an additional medication to control the side effects.

Movement difficulties may occur with the use of antipsychotic medications, although most of them can be controlled with an anticholinergic medication. These movement problems include muscle spasms of the neck, eye, back, or other muscles; restlessness and pacing; a general slowing-down of movement and speech; and a shuffling walk. Some of these side effects may look like psychotic or neurologic (Parkinson's disease) symptoms, but aren't. If they are severe, or persist with continued treatment with an antipsychotic, it is important to notify the doctor, who might either change the medication or prescribe an additional one to control the side effects.

Just as people vary in their responses to antipsychotic medications, they also vary in their speed of improvement. Some symptoms diminish in days, while others take weeks or months. For many patients, substantial improvement is seen by the sixth week of treatment, although this is not true in every case. If someone does not seem to be improving, a different type of medication may be tried.

Even if a person is feeling better or completely well, he should not just stop taking the medication. Continuing to see the doctor while tapering off medication is important. Some people may need to take medication for an extended period of time, or even indefinitely. These people usually have chronic (long-term, continuous) schizophrenic disorders, or have a history of repeated schizophrenic episodes, and are likely to become ill again. Also, in some cases a person who has experienced one or two severe episodes may need medication indefinitely. In these cases, medication may be continued in as low a dosage as possible to maintain control of symptoms. This approach, called maintenance treatment, prevents relapse in many people and removes or reduces symptoms for others.

While maintenance treatment is helpful for many people, a drawback for some is the possibility of developing long-term side effects, particularly a condition called tardive dyskinesia. This condition is characterized by involuntary movements. These abnormal movements most often occur around the mouth, but are sometimes seen in other muscle areas such as the trunk, pelvis, or diaphragm. The disorder may range from mild to severe. For some people, it cannot be reversed, while others recover partially or completely. Tardive dyskinesia is seen most often after long-term treatment with antipsychotic medications. There is a higher incidence in women, with the risk rising with age. There is no way to determine whether someone will develop this condition, and if it develops, whether the patient will recover. At present, there is no effective treatment for tardive dyskinesia. The possible risks of long-term treatment with antipsychotic medications must be weighed against the benefits in each individual case by patient, family, and doctor.

Antipsychotic medications can produce unwanted effects when taken in combination with other medications. Therefore, the doctor should be told about all medicine being taken, including over-the-counter preparations, and the extent of the use of alcohol. Some antipsychotic medications interfere with the action of antihypertensive medications (taken for high blood pressure), anticonvulsants (taken for epilepsy), and medications used for Parkinson's disease. Some antipsychotic medications add to the effects of alcohol and other central nervous system depressants, such as antihistamines, antidepressants, barbiturates, some sleeping and pain medications, and narcotics.

Atypical Neuroleptics

In 1990, clozapine (Clozaril), an "atypical neuroleptic," was introduced in the United States. In clinical trials, this medication was found to be more effective than traditional antipsychotic medications in individuals with treatment-resistant schizophrenia, and the risk of tardive dyskinesia is lower. However, because of the potential side effect of a serious blood disorder, agranulocytosis, patients who are on clozapine must have a blood test each week. The expense involved in this monitoring, together with the cost of the medication, has made maintenance on clozapine difficult for many persons with schizophrenia. However, five years after its introduction in the United States, approximately 58,000 persons were being treated with clozapine.

Since clozapine's approval in the United States, other atypical neuroleptics (also called atypical antipsychotics) have been introduced.

Risperidone (Risperdal) was released in 1994, olanzapine (Zyprexa) in 1996, and quetiapine (Seroquel) in 1997. Several other atypical neuroleptics are in development. While they have some side effects, these newer medications are generally better tolerated than either clozapine or the traditional antipsychotics, and they do not cause agranulocytosis. Like clozapine, they have shown little tendency to give rise to tardive dyskinesia or other movement difficulties. Their main disadvantages compared to the older medications are a greater tendency to produce weight gain, and much higher cost.

Children, the Elderly, and Pregnant, Nursing, or Childbearing Age Women: Special Considerations

Children, the elderly, and pregnant and nursing women have special concerns and needs when taking psychotherapeutic medications. Some effects of medications on the growing body, the aging body, and the childbearing body are known, but much remains to be learned. Research in these areas is ongoing.

While, in general, what has been said in this chapter applies to these groups, below are a few special points to bear in mind.

Children

Studies consistently show that about 15 percent of the U.S. population below age 18, or over 9 million children, suffer from a psychiatric disorder that compromises their ability to function. It is easy to overlook the seriousness of childhood mental disorders. In children, these disorders may present symptoms that are different or less clearcut than the same disorders in adults. Younger children, especially, may not talk about what's bothering them, but this is sometimes a problem with older children as well. For this reason, having a doctor, other mental health professional, or psychiatric team examine the child is especially important.

There is an array of treatments that can help these children. These include medications and psychotherapy behavioral therapy, treatment of impaired social skills, parental and family therapy, and group therapy. The therapy used for an individual child is based on the child's diagnosis and individual needs.

When the decision is reached that a child should take medication, active monitoring by all caretakers (parents, teachers, others who have charge of the child) is essential. Children should be watched and questioned for side effects (many children, especially younger ones, do not

237

volunteer information). They should also be monitored to see that they are actually taking the medication and taking the proper dosage.

The Elderly

Persons over the age of 65 make up 12 percent of the population of the United States, yet they receive 30 percent of prescriptions filled. The elderly generally have more medical problems and often are taking medications for more than one of these problems. In addition, they tend to be more sensitive to medications. Even healthy older people eliminate some medications from the body more slowly than younger persons and therefore require a lower or less frequent dosage to maintain an effective level of medication.

The elderly may sometimes accidentally take too much of a medication because they forget that they have taken a dose and take another dose. The use of a 7-day pill box is especially helpful to an elderly person.

The elderly and those close to them friends, relatives, caretakers need to pay special attention and watch for adverse (negative) physical and psychological responses to medication. Because they often take more medications—not only those prescribed but also over-the-counter preparations and home or folk remedies—the possibility of negative drug interactions is higher.

Pregnant, Nursing, or Childbearing-Age Women

In general, during pregnancy, all medications (including psychotherapeutic medications) should be avoided where possible, and other methods of treatment should be tried.

A woman who is taking a psychotherapeutic medication and plans to become pregnant should discuss her plans with her doctor; if she discovers that she is pregnant, she should contact her doctor immediately. During early pregnancy, there is a possible risk of birth defects with some of these medications, and for this reason:

1. Lithium is not recommended during the first 3 months of pregnancy.

2. Benzodiazepines are not recommended during the first 3 months of pregnancy.

The decision to use a psychotherapeutic medication should be made only after a careful discussion with the doctor concerning the risks and benefits to the woman and her baby.

Small amounts of medication pass into the breast milk; this is a consideration for mothers who are planning to breast-feed.

A woman who is taking birth-control pills should be sure that her doctor is aware of this. The estrogen in these pills may alter the breakdown of medications by the body, for example increasing side effects of some antianxiety medications and/or reducing their efficacy to relieve symptoms of anxiety.

For more detailed information, talk to your doctor or mental health professional, consult your local public library, or write to the pharmaceutical company that produces the medication or the U.S. Food and Drug Administration, 5600 Fishers Lane, Rockville, MD 20857.

References

AHFS Drug Information, 91. Gerald K. McEvoy, Editor. Bethesda, Maryland: American Society of Hospital Pharmacists, Inc., 1991.

Bohn J. and Jefferson J.W., *Lithium and Manic Depression: A Guide*. Madison, Wisconsin: Lithium Information Center, rev. ed. 1990.

Goodwin F.K. and Jamison K.R. *Manic-Depressive Illness*. New York: Oxford University Press, 1990.

Jensen P.S., Vitiello B., Leonard H., and Laughren T.P. Child and adolescent psychopharmacology: expanding the research base. *Psychopharmacology Bulletin*, Vol. 30, No. 1, 1994.

Johnston H.F. *Stimulants and Hyperactive Children: A Guide*. Madison, Wisconsin: Lithium Information Center, 1990.

Medenwald J.R., Greist J.H., and Jefferson J.W. *Carbamazepine and Manic Depression: A Guide*. Madison, Wisconsin: Lithium Information Center, rev. ed., 1990.

Physicians' Desk Reference, 48th edition. Montvale, New Jersey: Medical Economics Data Production Company, 1994.

New Developments in Pharmacologic Treatment of Schizophrenia. Rockville, Maryland: National Institute of Mental Health, 1992.

Chapter 31

Treatment of Depression: Newer Medications

Newer Antidepressant Drugs Are Equally as Effective as Older-generation Drug Treatments

Overview of Study Results

Newer categories of antidepressant drugs are equally as effective as older-generation antidepressants and roughly equal numbers of patients drop out of clinical trials because of side effects, according to a new evidence report comparing drug treatments for depression. The evidence report was conducted by the San Antonio Evidence-based Practice Center on behalf of the Agency for Health Care Policy and Research (now Agency for Healthcare Policy and Research). It found that selective serotonin reuptake inhibitors (SSRIs) are equally as effective in treating depression as older generation antidepressants, such as tricyclics.

"SSRIs are therapies of choice for many practitioners, but there are a lot of options out there and no particular class of drugs is routinely

This chapter includes text excerpted from "Newer Antidepressant Drugs Are Equally as Effective as Older-generation Drug Treatments, Research Shows," Press Release, March 18, 1999, Agency for Healthcare Research and Quality (formerly Agency for Health Care Policy and Research), Rockville, MD, available online at http://www.ahrq.gov/news/press/pr1999/deprespr.htm; and, "Treatment of Depression—Newer Pharmacotherapies," Summary, Evidence Report/Technology Assessment: Number 7, March 1999, Agency for Healthcare Research and Quality (formerly Agency for Health Care Policy and Research), Rockville, MD, available online at http://www.ahrq.gov/clinic/epcsums/deprsumm.htm.

more effective than others," said Cynthia D. Mulrow, M.D., MSc, the study's lead investigator and a professor of medicine and geriatrics at The University of Texas Health Science Center at San Antonio (UTHSCSA).

The study found that both newer- and older-generation antidepressants have side effects. Patients taking the newer antidepressants were more likely to have higher rates of diarrhea, nausea, insomnia, and headache. The older drugs were likely to cause adverse effects on the heart and blood pressure, and result in dry mouth, constipation, dizziness, blurred vision, and tremors. While anecdotal reports suggest high rates of difficulty in sexual functioning, this report found little data that directly addressed this problem.

"The good news for the many people suffering from depression is that this rigorous analysis of the scientific literature has endorsed the effectiveness of a wide array of medication options, however the risks and benefits of these options must be carefully weighed," said co-author John W. Williams, Jr., M.D. "In the studies we analyzed, people dropped out of clinical trials for both older and newer antidepressants at similar rates because of drug side effects."

The study did not compare drug costs for the nine categories of antidepressants, the dosing schedules, nor the risk of various drug-to-drug interactions. The report was designed to provide a comprehensive evaluation of the efficacy of newer pharmacotherapies and herbal medications, such as St. John's wort, kava kava, and valeriana, for depressive disorders.

The literature review found no evidence of effectiveness of kava kava and valeriana, and concluded the that the evidence about the effectiveness of St. John's wort is unclear. However, compared to a placebo, the literature suggests that St. John's wort shows promise for mild to moderate depression, and may have fewer adverse effects reported than older generation antidepressants.

Treatment of Depression—Newer Pharmacotherapies

Study Overview

Depressive disorders, including major depression and dysthymia, are serious, disabling illnesses. It is estimated that one in five individuals is affected by a mood disorder in his or her lifetime. The economic costs to society and personal costs to individuals and families are enormous. In the U.S. alone, the estimated monetary costs for depression exceeded $44 billion in 1990. The personal costs are reflected by higher mortality and impairment in multiple areas of functioning. The World Health Organization estimates that major depression is the fourth most important cause worldwide of loss in disability-adjusted life years, and will be the second most important cause by 2020.

In the late 80s, the U.S. Department of Health and Human Services sponsored the development of standard treatment guidelines for major depression. The guidelines advanced knowledge substantially, but available evidence was insufficient to address many clinically important questions. Since publication of the guidelines, a widely publicized emphasis on recognizing and treating depression as well as the development of many new antidepressants have contributed to explosive growth in antidepressant prescribing and increasing pharmacy costs for health plans. Newer antidepressants and readily available herbal remedies have led to wider but sometimes confusing choices for clinicians.

Reporting the Evidence

The ultimate purpose of this report is to help clinicians make informed choices about newer antidepressant drugs and herbal therapies, and to aid organizations developing clinical guidelines for the treatment of depression. The report provides a comprehensive evaluation of the benefits and adverse effects of newer pharmacotherapies and herbal treatments for depressive disorders in adults and children. The report focuses on 29 newer antidepressant drugs and three herbal remedies. Older antidepressants and psychosocial therapies are considered only when they are compared directly to a newer antidepressant.

An expert multidisciplinary panel formulated 24 specific questions, guided by two key principles: the potential to summarize new information not addressed in previous literature synthesis, and relevance to clinicians making treatment decisions and policymakers developing guidelines.

Questions address the efficacy of newer pharmacotherapies for the most prevalent forms of depression and for individuals with recurrent or refractory depression. Additional questions involve the relative efficacy of newer agents compared to psychosocial therapies and the efficacy of herbal remedies. The primary outcomes of interest for these questions were depressive symptoms as assessed by a rating scale or a clinical diagnosis, total dropouts, and dropouts due to adverse effects. Secondary outcomes were health-related quality of life, functional status, and suicides. The report also focuses on specific patient populations (for example, children and adolescents) and specific settings (for example, primary care). Issues involving combination treatments with other psychotropics, psychosocial therapies, and augmenting agents are addressed. The important question of long-term efficacy is examined through relapse prevention studies. Finally, the report addresses a group of questions related to adherence, common adverse effects, and rare but serious adverse effects.

Findings

More than 300 randomized trials evaluated newer pharmacotherapies for depression. For most of these (more than 90 percent), the focus was major depression. Nine studies focused on dysthymia and three studies each examined subsyndromal and mixed anxiety depression. The largest number of comparisons (n=206) were between newer and older antidepressants. Over 100 studies compared the efficacy of newer antidepressants to placebo.

More than 90 percent of the included trials were short duration (six to eight weeks) and used double-blind methodology. Trial reporting was often incomplete. Less than one-third of studies described study settings, few studies described the nature and content of clinical interactions between providers and patients, and fewer than 10 percent described ethnic background or socioeconomic status of the participants. Secondary outcomes (health-related quality of life, functional status, suicides) were reported too infrequently for analysis.

Summary results follow for specific disorders and groups. Key findings are presented first. They are followed by gaps in knowledge which could not be answered by the available evidence.

Major Depression

More than 80 studies prove newer antidepressant drugs are more efficacious than placebo for treating adults with major depression. Response rates were 50 percent for active treatment compared to 32 percent for placebo.

Newer antidepressants are equally efficacious compared to first and second generation tricyclic antidepressants. The number of studies comparing different classes of newer antidepressants is relatively small but the studies show no difference in overall efficacy. For patients who have recovered from major depression, continued treatment with a newer antidepressant for at least six months decreases the risk of relapse by 70 percent. The large protective effect is best established for patients recruited from mental health settings or who have recurrent depression.

Gaps in Knowledge

A number of important questions could not be answered with available evidence. No studies compared combinations of newer antidepressants or newer antidepressants plus another psychotropic (for example, an anxiolytic) to a single antidepressant. Data were insufficient to determine if the combination of newer antidepressants with psychosocial therapies is more effective than antidepressants alone. Data also were insufficient to determine if augmenting agents (for example, pindolol, lithium) in combination with a newer antidepressant quicken or improve response rates in patients with resistant depression. Whether particular antidepressant agents are more effective than others could not be determined for patients with resistant or refractory depression. Finally, the need for and efficacy of long-term antidepressant therapy needs to be evaluated in more representative populations.

Other Depressive Disorders

Two selective serotonin reuptake inhibitors (fluoxetine, sertraline) and amisulpride are efficacious for treating adults with dysthymia. Response rates for active treatment were 59 percent compared to 37 percent for placebo. There is no evidence suggesting that particular agents are more effective than others, including first generation tricyclic antidepressants.

Gaps in Knowledge

There is insufficient evidence to establish whether newer antidepressants are effective for subsyndromal (minor) depression or mixed anxiety depression.

Herbal Remedies

Hypericum (St. John's wort) appears more effective than placebo for the short-term treatment of mild to moderately severe depressive disorders. Adverse effects occur significantly less frequently with *Hypericum* compared to first generation tricyclic antidepressants. These findings are tempered by the relatively small number of trials and evidence of publication bias favoring positive trials.

245

Gaps in Knowledge

It is not clear if *Hypericum* (St. John's wort) is as effective as standard antidepressive agents. No trial data for two other herbal remedies (valeriana and kava kava) were found.

Newer Antidepressants Compared to Psychosocial Therapies

Gaps in Knowledge

There were no trials comparing newer agents to educational or supportive counseling. Only one small trial compared psychotherapy directly to a newer agent in adults. These data were too limited to determine if newer antidepressants are more or less effective than psychosocial therapies.

Newer Antidepressants in Children, Older Adults, and Other Special Populations

Multiple antidepressants proved to be better than placebo in treating major depression in older adults. Antidepressants appear equally effective. Dropouts overall and due to adverse effects do not differ significantly between older and newer antidepressants.

Gaps in Knowledge

Gaps in knowledge for selected populations of special interest are substantial. Only two small studies evaluated newer agents in children or adolescents; data are insufficient to guide management of depression in children and adolescents. A small number of studies evaluated newer antidepressants in patients with depression and either alcoholism, chronic fatigue syndrome, HIV disease, ischemic heart disease, renal failure, or stroke. The results are conflicting and insufficient to reliably determine the efficacy of newer agents compared to placebo or older agents. Since fewer than 10 percent of trials reported data about participants' ethnic background, data are insufficient to determine whether efficacy differs across ethnic groups.

Treatment in Primary Care and Postpartum Settings

Newer antidepressants are better than placebo in treating depressive disorders in adults in primary care settings. Response rates were 60 percent for active treatment compared to 35 percent for placebo. There is no evidence that particular agents are more effective than others.

Gaps in Knowledge

Only one small study with a high dropout rate evaluated newer pharmacotherapy in women with major or subsyndromal depression after childbirth. These data are insufficient to determine the efficacy of newer antidepressants in the postpartum setting.

Treatment Adherence and Adverse Effects

In general, participants discontinued treatment at similar rates for newer and older antidepressants due to lack of effect, adverse effects, or other reasons. However, fewer patients taking selective serotonin reuptake inhibitors or reversible inhibitors of monoamine oxidase A discontinued treatment due to adverse effects compared to patients taking first generation tricyclic antidepressants (rate differences 4 percent and 5 percent, respectively).

Compared to first generation tricyclic antidepressants, selective serotonin reuptake inhibitors had significantly higher rates of diarrhea (rate difference (RD) 10 percent), nausea (RD 10 percent), insomnia (RD 7 percent), and headache (RD 3 percent). Tricyclic antidepressants had significantly higher rates of dry mouth (RD 30 percent), constipation (RD 12 percent), dizziness (RD 11 percent), blurred vision (RD 4 percent), and tremors (RD 4 percent). Nine uncommon (less than one percent) but serious adverse effects were definitely associated with the selective serotonin reuptake inhibitors. They were: bradycardia, bleeding, granulocytopenia, seizures, hyponatremia, hepatotoxicity, serotonin syndrome, extrapyramidal effects, and mania in unipolar depression. Bupropion was associated with seizures. *Hypericum* (St. John's wort) was not associated with serious adverse effects.

Gaps in Knowledge

Marked variability in methods of ascertainment and reporting of common adverse effects makes interpretation difficult. Some adverse effects, such as sexual dysfunction and changes in weight, were reported too infrequently for reliable interpretation.

Summary Implications

This evidence report clearly shows newer antidepressants are effective treatments for major depression and dysthymia. They are efficacious in treating depressive disorders in mental health as well as primary care settings. Newer antidepressants have similar efficacy and total dropout rates compared to older antidepressants. Because of similar efficacy, both newer and older antidepressants should be considered when making treatment decisions. When selecting anti-depressants, clinicians should consider costs, the small but statistically significant differences in dropouts due to adverse effects, the lack of information about relative benefits compared to alternative therapies (for example, psychosocial and herbal), and the individual patient's preferences and tolerance for particular adverse effects. Health policy planners should consider these factors and advocate for cost-effectiveness studies to better guide the allocation of health care dollars.

For patients with other forms of depression, such as subsyndromal or mixed anxiety depression, and for special populations, such as children and adolescents, data on newer pharmacotherapies are insufficient to guide treatment decisions. Clinicians who choose to generalize efficacy data from adult patients with major depression to such patients should do so with care.

Availability of Full Report

The full evidence report from which this summary was taken was prepared for the Agency for Health Care Policy and Research (now Agency for Healthcare Research and Quality) by the San Antonio Evidence-based Practice Center based at The University of Texas Health Science Center at San Antonio under contract No. 290-97-0012. Printed copies may be obtained free of charge from the AHRQ Clearinghouse by calling 1-800-358-9295. Requesters should ask for Evidence Report/Technology Assessment No. 7, Treatment of Depression—Newer Pharmacotherapies (AHCPR Publication No. 99-E014). The Evidence Report is also available online at: http://text.nlm.nih.gov/ftrs/dbaccess/dep.

Chapter 32

Managing Common Side Effects of Antidepressant Medications

Antidepressant Side Effects

For each antidepressant, we've listed the most common side effects people have. Whether or not you will have these or any other side effects cannot be known ahead of time. We each have a different response to medicine. If you have side effects, tell your prescriber so your medicine can be adjusted in a way that will make you more comfortable.

- **Amitriptyline (Elavil):** Sleepiness, dry mouth, blurred vision, constipation, a delay in urinating, weight gain, sweating, worsening of heart disease, dizziness when you first stand up

- **Amoxapine (Asendin):** Worsening of heart disease, sleepiness, agitation, trouble sleeping, anxiety

- **Bupropion (Wellbutrin):** Agitation, dry mouth, trouble sleeping, headache, nausea, vomiting, constipation, tremor

---

This chapter includes text from "Antidepressant Side Effects," available from Ask NOAH About: Mental Health at http://www.noah-health.org/english/illness/mentalhealth/cornell/medications/antidepsideff.html, © 1996 New York-Presbyterian Hospital, Behavioral Health Nursing Service Line, revised 1999; reprinted with permission; and, "A Consumer's Reference Guide to Managing the Most Common Side Effects of Psychiatric Medicines," available from Ask NOAH About: Mental Health at http://www.noah-health.org/english/illness/mentalhealth/cornell/medications/side_effects.html, © 1996 New York-Presbyterian Hospital, Behavioral Health Nursing Service Line, revised 1999; reprinted with permission.

- **Citalopram (Celexa):** Anxiety, sleepiness, nausea, headache, trouble sleeping

- **Clomipramine (Anafranil):** Dry mouth, sleepiness, tremor, weight gain, sweating, dizziness when you first stand up, blurred vision, constipation, delayed orgasm, delay in urinating, nausea

- **Desipramine (Norpramin):** Dry mouth, blurred vision, constipation, a delay in urinating, weight gain, sweating, dizziness when you first stand up

- **Doxepin (Sinequan):** Sleepiness, sweating, dry mouth, blurred vision, constipation, a delay in urinating, worsening of heart disease, weight gain, dizziness when you first stand up

- **Fluoxetine (Prozac):** Agitation, anxiety, trouble sleeping, sleepiness, tremor, loss of appetite, nausea, diarrhea, headache, dizziness, delayed orgasm

- **Fluvoxamine (Luvox):** Sleepiness, trouble sleeping, anxiety, tremor, nausea, loss of appetite, vomiting, sweating, delayed orgasm, diarrhea

- **Imipramine (Tofranil):** Sleepiness, dry mouth, blurred vision, constipation, a delay in urinating, dizziness when you first stand up, worsening of heart disease, weight gain, sweating

- **Maprotiline (Ludiomil):** Sleepiness, dry mouth, blurred vision, constipation, a delay in urinating, worsening of heart disease, dizziness when you first stand up, weight gain

- **Mirtazapine (Remeron):** Sleepiness, increased appetite, weight gain, dizziness

- **Nefazodone (Serzone):** Sleepiness, dizziness when you first stand up, nausea, headache

- **Nortriptyline (Pamelor):** Sleepiness, dry mouth, a delay in urinating, constipation, blurred vision, weight gain

- **Paroxetine (Paxil):** Nausea, sleepiness, fatigue, dizziness, trouble sleeping, sweating, tremor, loss of appetite, anxiety, delayed orgasm

- **Protriptyline (Vivactil):** Dry mouth, blurred vision, constipation, a delay in urinating, worsening of heart disease, dizziness when you first stand up, trouble sleeping, anxiety

- **Sertraline (Zoloft):** Nausea, diarrhea, tremor, dizziness, trouble sleeping, sleepiness, sweating, dry mouth, delayed orgasm

- **Trazodone (Desyrel):** Sleepiness, worsening of heart disease, dizziness when you first stand up, nausea, vomiting

- **Trimipramine (Surmontil):** Sleepiness, dry mouth, blurred vision, constipation, a delay in urinating, dizziness when you first stand up, worsening of heart disease, weight gain, sweating

- **Venlafaxine (Effexor):** Sedation, nausea, sweating, dry mouth, dizziness, weakness, constipation, decreased appetite, vomiting, anxiety, tremor, blurred vision, delayed orgasm, headache

Managing Common Side Effects

Many people who take psychiatric medicines have side effects, especially during the first few weeks of treatment. Almost all of the side effects listed below are temporary; the body adjusts to the side effects so well that they disappear on their own after a few days or weeks. A few are more persistent. Some people who take psychiatric medicines never have any side effects of any kind.

Listed below are the most common side effects of psychiatric medicines and ways to manage them. Of course, whenever you have side effects from any medicine, you should report them at your next visit to the person who is prescribing your medication. This may be a doctor or a nurse. If the side effect is severe, call right away. It's a good idea to get into the habit of reminding your doctor or nurse at every visit about the side effects that are still causing you trouble. He or she may be able to adjust your dose or your dosage schedule in a way that will make you more comfortable. On the other hand, your doctor or nurse may ask you to put up with the side effects because many of them go away on their own. Either way, some of the hints we offer here may help.

When you have side effects, they can make you very uncomfortable. Sometimes people even feel like giving up on their medication when the side effects are strong. It's extremely important for you to know that most of the time, even the most uncomfortable side effects are short-lived. If you stop your medication or take less of it than prescribed, you will be at risk for becoming ill again. Instead of stopping your medication on your own or taking it less often, talk to your doctor or nurse about the problems you are having so adjustments can be made that will make the medication more comfortable for you.

251

- **Addiction:** This is a potential problem only with one kind of psychiatric medicine—the minor tranquilizer (Valium, Librium, Xanax, Ativan, Klonopin and others in that group). Antidepressants, antipsychotics and mood stabilizers are not addictive. If you are worried about addiction to a minor tranquilizer, discuss ways to reduce the risk with your prescriber. If you have a history of addiction, minor tranquilizers should probably be avoided.

- **Blurred Vision:** Blurred vision is a common problem in the beginning of treatment with many psychiatric medicines. It is almost always a temporary problem that improves on its own. If it doesn't improve after a few weeks, let your doctor or nurse know.

- **Confusion and Memory Problems:** If these problems occur, it is usually during the first few weeks of treatment. If the problem lasts beyond that time, or is severe, let your doctor or nurse know and a change in dose may solve the problem.

- **Constipation:** This can be a chronic problem for people who take psychiatric medicines, but there are many things you can do to help. Make sure you drink at least eight cups or glasses of liquids every day. Eat fresh fruits, vegetables, and whole grain breads and cereals every day. Get some exercise every day, whether it's walking, bike riding, jogging, playing sports—any physical exercise will help prevent constipation. If you're following all these suggestions, and you still have problems with constipation, your doctor or nurse may prescribe a stool softener (a tablet or liquid taken by mouth) for you to take every day, or may suggest that you regularly take a medicine made of natural psyllium fibers, like Metamucil or other similar brands.

- **Dry Mouth:** This is a common side effect that usually disappears after the first few weeks. In the meantime, it helps to have a cup or bottle of water with you during the day to sip if your mouth feels dry. Some people find it helps to occasionally chew gum or suck on hard candies. Your mouth may also feel better if you brush your teeth at least twice a day.

- **Headache:** A persistent dull headache is most likely to result from the use of the SSRI antidepressants and a few of the other newer antidepressants. It usually goes away on its own after the first few weeks, and in the meantime, aspirin or Tylenol may help. Be sure to let your doctor or nurse know at your next visit.

- **Heat Intolerance:** Most psychiatric medicines make it hard for your body to maintain a normal temperature in hot, humid conditions. When the weather is hot and humid, it's best to avoid strenuous activities and to stay as cool as you can. Wearing loose, lightweight, light-colored clothing and staying near a fan or air conditioner may help. Drink extra liquids to prevent dehydration. If you're outdoors on a very hot and humid day, stay out of direct sunlight and avoid strenuous activity of any kind.

- **High Blood Pressure (Hypertension):** This is a problem that you probably would not be able to detect on your own. Your doctor or nurse or the staff of your program will check your blood pressure a few times when you first begin taking your medicine to make sure your blood pressure is normal.

- **Increased Urination and Resulting Thirst:** These two related problems are common in people who take lithium. In most people they are annoying but not dangerous. If you find you have to urinate so often that it interferes with your life at home, school or at work, let your doctor or nurse know and some tests can be done to see if the addition of another medicine would help. The increased urination is a direct result of taking lithium, and will not slow down even if you stop drinking liquids altogether. In fact, if you cut back on drinking liquids, there's a danger of your body becoming dangerously dried out. So even if you're urinating large amounts, make sure you drink at least 8 cups of liquid every day. If you're still thirsty, drink more. Thirst is an important sign that your body needs more liquids.

- **Low Blood Pressure (Orthostatic Hypotension):** You may notice this problem as a feeling of dizziness or lightheadedness. It may be strongest when you first stand up from sitting or lying down. If you have this problem, it will help to get up slowly from a sitting or lying position (especially first thing in the morning when you're just getting out of bed). If you feel dizzy or lightheaded, sit down or hold on to something sturdy until the feeling passes. It will also help to increase the amount of liquids you drink to at least eight glasses or cups per day.

- **Muscle Jerks (Myoclonus):** If you notice that your muscles are jumpy or twitchy, or that you have involuntary jerking in

253

any part of your body, let your doctor or nurse know. A change in dose or the addition of another medicine usually helps.

- **Nausea or Vomiting:** If you have this problem, it may help to avoid taking your medicine on an empty stomach. Eating food or drinking water or juice before you take your medicine is usually helpful. If it is a severe problem, your doctor or nurse may be able to relieve it with another medicine, or with a dose adjustment.

- **Problems in Sexual Desire or Performance:** Many people who take psychiatric medicines develop one or more of the following sexual problems: lack of interest in sex, trouble having orgasm, a change in the quality of orgasm, or delay in orgasm. Sometimes it's hard to tell if these sexual problems are being caused by the illness or by the medicine, since stress, depression, and anxiety can also cause problems with sexual desire and performance. If you have either a decrease in sexual interest, or trouble with sexual performance, let your doctor or nurse know. A decrease in dose or the addition of another medicine will usually solve the problem. Sometimes it's necessary to stop the medicine and change to another.

- **Rapid Heartbeat (Tachycardia):** "Rapid" heartbeat means faster than 120 beats per minute. You may be unaware of this problem, or you may feel a rapid heartbeat as palpitations or fluttering in your chest. Rapid heartbeat is a fairly common problem that occurs in the beginning of treatment with many medicines. Most people adjust to it, and the heart gradually slows down to a normal rate. Deep breathing and other relaxation techniques may help. If this problem persists, your doctor or nurse may give you another medicine to slow your heartbeat.

- **Rash:** A rash is usually not a dangerous or uncomfortable problem. Still, if you notice a rash on any part of your body, let your doctor or nurse know. If you are taking carbamazepine (Tegretol), a rash may be a more serious problem, and should be reported to your doctor or nurse right away.

- **Restlessness or Agitation (Akathisia):** Several psychiatric medicines can cause this problem. Many people say that this intense feeling of physical restlessness is the most uncomfortable of all side effects. The restlessness can be visible to others, or it may not be. When this side effect is strong, it makes it hard to sit still or lie quietly. Because it is so hard to tolerate, be sure to persist in complaining about it. There is more than one way to get rid of this problem, so insist that your medicine be adjusted in a way that will give you relief.

- **Seizures:** Many psychiatric medicines slightly increase the risk of having a seizure, so if you have a history of seizures or head injury, you may need to increase your dose of anti-seizure medicine.

- **Sensitivity to Sunburn:** You may find that your skin is more sensitive to sunburn, so make sure to put on sunblocking lotion if you plan to be in the sun for any length of time (This is a good idea whether you are taking medicines or not).

- **Sleepiness:** It is common to feel sleepy during the first week or two (sometimes longer) when you're taking a new medicine. You may find yourself dozing off during the day. Report this problem to your doctor or nurse, but in the meantime, try to adjust your schedule to allow for short rest periods or naps during the day. For the first few weeks of treatment, you may need to limit your goals for yourself because the sleepiness may get in the way with carrying out your usual activities. Avoid driving or operating any other machinery until the sleepiness passes. Along with this sleepiness, you may notice some problems with coordination. This will pass as the sleepiness passes.

- **Stiffness (Akinesia):** Muscle stiffness can be a problem with some of the antipsychotic medicines. If you let your doctor or nurse know about it, you can usually get relief quickly with a dose adjustment or by adding another medicine.

- **Sweating (Diaphoresis):** Increased sweating occurs in some people. If you have this problem, you'll probably need to change clothing more often than usual. Wearing lighter and more loose-fitting clothes may help you feel better. Make sure to drink at least 8 glasses of liquids a day to replace the liquids lost through sweating.

- **Tremors:** If you have tremors (shaking) from your medicine, let your doctor or nurse know. A dosage adjustment usually makes the problem milder or gets rid of it altogether. In the meantime, tremors may be less of a problem if you cut down on the amount of caffeine you drink in coffee, tea and sodas.

- **Trouble Sleeping (Insomnia):** Some of the antidepressants and stimulants can make it hard to get to sleep or stay asleep. Changing the time of day you take the medicine (morning instead of evening, or vice-versa) may help. You will also probably sleep better if you reduce your caffeine intake and avoid exercise in the late afternoon and evening. A relaxing bedtime routine also helps many people.

- **Trouble Urinating (Urinary Hesitance or Retention):** You may feel your bladder is full and have the urge to urinate, but have trouble getting the urine to start flowing. Once the urine starts to flow, it may come out more slowly than usual, as though there is no force behind it. As a result, it may take longer than usual to empty your bladder. Fortunately, this is usually a temporary problem that goes away on its own in a week or two. If you have this problem, report it to your doctor or nurse. And in the meantime, let water run in the sink while you're trying to urinate, or put your hand in a cup or sink full of warm water. Either trick may help the urine start flowing. If you cannot pass urine at all (this is rare, but it does happen), let your doctor or nurse know right away.

- **Weight Gain:** With some of the psychiatric medicines, people gain weight. We're not sure what causes weight gain, but it could be any of the following: fluid retention; increased appetite from direct stimulation of the appetite center of the brain by the medicine; lack of physical activity; or a change in the metabolism of carbohydrates. In the years before we had modern psychiatric medicines, it was well known that a good appetite and weight gain were signs of recovery. So in some people, weight gain may simply be a sign of recovery. If you have an increase in appetite or notice that you're eating more than usual or putting on weight, it helps to act quickly before the problem worsens. The best ways to deal with weight gain are to decrease your food intake slightly and at the same time increase your level of physical activity. Substitute lower calorie and lower fat foods for ones that are high in fat or calories. Make sure you have several kinds of low calorie, low fat snacks around for when you have the urge to eat between meals.

- **Weight Loss:** Occasionally, people have the opposite problem and lose weight because of psychiatric medicines. If this is a problem for you, make sure you let your doctor or nurse know.

Summary

Medicines are designed to speed your recovery and prevent relapse so you can return to a productive and satisfying life. If your medicine causes any discomfort from side effects, report the problem(s) to your nurse or doctor at your next visit (or right away if it's severe) so the proper adjustments can be made. If there are changes in your health, even if they are not obvious side effects of the medicine, let your prescriber know that too. In fact, if you have any questions about your medicines, ask your nurse or doctor. That way, you can get the most benefit from the medicine with the least discomfort.

Chapter 33

Drug Interactions: What You Should Know

Drug Interactions

There are more opportunities today than ever before to learn about your health and to take better care of yourself. It is also more important than ever to know about the medicines you take. If you take several different medicines, see more than one doctor, or have certain health conditions, you and your doctors need to be aware of all the medicines you take. Doing so will help you to avoid potential problems such as drug interactions.

Drug interactions may make your drug less effective, cause unexpected side effects, or increase the action of a particular drug. Some drug interactions can even be harmful to you. Reading the label every time you use a nonprescription or prescription drug and taking the time to learn about drug interactions may be critical to your health. You can reduce the risk of potentially harmful drug interactions and side effects with a little bit of knowledge and common sense. Drug interactions fall into three broad categories:

- Drug-drug interactions occur when two or more drugs react with each other. This drug-drug interaction may cause you to experience an unexpected side effect. For example, mixing a

Excerpted from "Drug Interactions: What You Should Know," Center for Drug Evaluation and Research, U.S. Food and Drug Administration (FDA), dated August 20, 2001. The full text of this document is available online at http://www.fda.gov/cder/consumerinfo/druginteractions.htm

drug you take to help you sleep (a sedative) and a drug you take for allergies (an antihistamine) can slow your reactions and make driving a car or operating machinery dangerous.

- Drug-food/beverage interactions result from drugs reacting with foods or beverages. For example, mixing alcohol with some drugs may cause you to feel tired or slow your reactions.

- Drug-condition interactions may occur when an existing medical condition makes certain drugs potentially harmful. For example, if you have high blood pressure you could experience an unwanted reaction if you take a nasal decongestant.

Drug Interactions and Over-the-Counter Medicines

Over-the-counter (OTC) drug labels contain information about ingredients, uses, warnings and directions that is important to read and understand. The label also includes important information about possible drug interactions. Further, drug labels may change as new information becomes known. That's why it's especially important to read the label every time you use a drug.

- The "Active Ingredients" and "Purpose" sections list:
  - the name and amount of each active ingredient
  - the purpose of each active ingredient

- The "Uses" section of the label:
  - tells you what the drug is used for
  - helps you find the best drug for your specific symptoms

- The "Warnings" section of the label provides important drug interaction and precaution information such as:
  - when to talk to a doctor or pharmacist before use
  - the medical conditions that may make the drug less effective or not safe
  - under what circumstances the drug should not be used
  - when to stop taking the drug

- The "Directions" section of the label tells you:
  - the length of time and the amount of the product that you may safely use
  - any special instructions on how to use the product

- The "Other Information" section of the label tells you:
  - required information about certain ingredients, such as sodium content, for people with dietary restrictions or allergies
- The "Inactive Ingredients" section of the label tells you:
  - the name of each inactive ingredient (such as colorings, binders, etc.)
- The "Questions?" or "Questions or Comments?" section of the label (if included):
  - provides telephone numbers of a source to answer questions about the product

Learning More about Drug Interactions

Talk to your doctor or pharmacist about the drugs you take. When your doctor prescribes a new drug, discuss all OTC and prescription drugs, dietary supplements, vitamins, botanicals, minerals and herbals you take, as well as the foods you eat. Ask your pharmacist for the package insert for each prescription drug you take. The package insert provides more information about potential drug interactions.

Before taking a drug, ask your doctor or pharmacist the following questions:

- Can I take it with other drugs?
- Should I avoid certain foods, beverages or other products?
- What are possible drug interaction signs I should know about?
- How will the drug work in my body?
- Is there more information available about the drug or my condition (on the Internet or in health and medical literature)?

Know how to take drugs safely and responsibly. Remember, the drug label will tell you:

- what the drug is used for
- how to take the drug
- how to reduce the risk of drug interactions and unwanted side effects

If you still have questions after reading the drug product label, ask your doctor or pharmacist for more information.

Remember that different OTC drugs may contain the same active ingredient. If you are taking more than one OTC drug, pay attention to the active ingredients used in the products to avoid taking too much of a particular ingredient. Under certain circumstances—such as if you are pregnant or breast-feeding—you should talk to your doctor before you take any medicine. Also, make sure you know what ingredients are contained in the medicines you take. Doing so will help you to avoid possible allergic reactions.

Examples of Drug Interaction Warnings

- The following are examples of drug interaction warnings that you may see on certain OTC drug products. These examples do not include all of the warnings for the listed types of products and should not take the place of reading the actual product label.

Antiemetics
drugs for prevention or treatment of nausea, vomiting, or dizziness associated with motion sickness

Ask a doctor or pharmacist before use if you are:

- taking sedatives or tranquilizers

Ask a doctor before use if you have:

- a breathing problem, such as emphysema or chronic bronchitis
- glaucoma
- difficulty in urination due to an enlarged prostate gland

When using this product:

- avoid alcoholic beverages

Antihistamines
drugs that temporarily relieve runny nose or reduce sneezing, itching of the nose or throat, and itchy watery eyes due to hay fever or other upper respiratory problems

Ask a doctor or pharmacist before use if you are taking:

- sedatives or tranquilizers
- a prescription drug for high blood pressure or depression

Ask a doctor before use if you have:

- glaucoma or difficulty in urination due to an enlarged prostate gland
- breathing problems, such as emphysema, chronic bronchitis, or asthma

When using this product:

- alcohol, sedatives, and tranquilizers may increase drowsiness
- avoid alcoholic beverages

Antitussives (Cough Medicine)
drugs that temporarily reduce cough due to minor throat and bronchial irritation as may occur with a cold

Ask a doctor or pharmacist before use if you are:

- taking sedatives or tranquilizers

Ask a doctor before use if you have:

- glaucoma or difficulty in urination due to an enlarged prostate gland

Nicotine Replacement Products
drugs that reduce withdrawal symptoms associated with quitting smoking, including nicotine craving

Ask a doctor before use if you:

- have high blood pressure not controlled by medication
- have heart disease or have had a recent heart attack or irregular heartbeat, since nicotine can increase your heart rate

Ask a doctor or pharmacist before use if you are:

- taking a prescription drug for depression or asthma (your dose may need to be adjusted)
- using a prescription non-nicotine stop smoking drug

Do not use:

- if you continue to smoke, chew tobacco, use snuff, or use other nicotine-containing products

263

Nighttime Sleep Aids
drugs for relief of occasional sleeplessness

Ask a doctor or pharmacist before use if you are:

• taking sedatives or tranquilizers

Ask a doctor before use if you have:

• a breathing problem such as emphysema or chronic bronchitis
• glaucoma
• difficulty in urination due to an enlarged prostate gland

When using this product:

• avoid alcoholic beverages

Pain Relievers
drugs for the temporary relief of minor body aches, pains, and head-aches

Ask a doctor before taking if you:

• consume three or more alcohol-containing drinks per day

The following ingredients are found in different OTC pain relievers: acetaminophen, aspirin, ibuprofen, ketoprofen, magnesium salicylate, and naproxen. It is important to read the label of pain reliever products to learn about different drug interaction warnings for each ingredient.

Stimulants
drugs that help restore mental alertness or wakefulness during fatigue or drowsiness

When using this product:

• limit the use of foods, beverages, and other drugs that have caffeine. Too much caffeine can cause nervousness, irritability, sleeplessness, and occasional rapid heart beat
• be aware that the recommended dose of this product contains about as much caffeine as a cup of coffee

264

Chapter 34

Treating Mood Disorders in Drug Abuse Patients Improves Both Conditions

For many drug abuse patients, mood disorders are a constant companion. Among cocaine abusers, for example, depressive disorders are the most commonly diagnosed coexisting, or comorbid, conditions. The relationship between mood disorders and drug abuse in these patients is often complex and interconnected: Drug abuse patients may develop depression as a result of the physical and psychological suffering associated with their drug use, and patients suffering from mood disorders may become drug dependent in attempts to self-medicate. For patients suffering from both drug abuse and mood disorders, the conditions once seemed impossible to untangle, but recent National Institute on Drug Abuse (NIDA) research suggests that treatment for the mood disorder alone also can have a positive effect on drug abuse treatment.

One NIDA-supported study found that drug use declined among teenage drug dependence patients being treated with a medication for bipolar disorder, which is characterized by alternating periods of depression and mania. In a related study, chronic opiate-dependent adults reported less drug abuse when they were treated with the antidepressant imipramine for comorbid depression.

Reducing Substance Dependence in Bipolar Teens

Lithium has proven effective in treating adult bipolar disorder patients and research with adult patients suggests that lithium also

"Treating Mood Disorders in Drug Abuse Patients Yields Improvement in Both Conditions," by Patrick Zickler, *NIDA NOTES*, Volume 13, Number 6, March 1999.

may be an effective treatment for comorbid substance dependence. However, no double-blind, placebo-controlled studies have tested the therapy in adolescents. Now, at Washington University in St. Louis, Dr. Barbara Geller and her colleagues have found that, in adolescent patients, lithium treatment for the manic phase of bipolar disorder also reduces drug and alcohol dependence.

The researchers' double-blind, placebo-controlled study involved 25 teenage patients who had been diagnosed with bipolar disorder and secondary substance abuse disorder involving marijuana, alcohol, inhalants, or multiple drugs. "Most of these kids have had bipolar disorder since the age of nine," Dr. Geller says. "They have been severely ill for a long time, and most are from families with a history of bipolar disorder."

More than half of the patients also came from families with a history of substance abuse, sometimes reaching back several generations. All had begun using drugs in the year prior to being enrolled in the study. "Secondary substance dependence disorders are the most common and most severe comorbidity in bipolar patients," Dr. Geller says. "We wanted to get to them within the first year, when they were newly addicted."

All participants in the study received packets of capsules to be taken twice each day during the six-week study. For half the teenagers, the capsules contained lithium dosages that have proven effective in treating adult bipolar patients. The other patients received placebo only. All participants, who were treated as outpatients, also received weekly therapy sessions. Blood levels of lithium were checked twice each week—once randomly—to make sure the participants were taking the pills. Urine samples were collected twice weekly—once randomly—to monitor drug use.

The percentage of drug-positive urine samples for participants receiving placebo remained essentially unchanged, at roughly 40 percent, throughout the study. But for the group receiving lithium, drug-positive urine samples dropped from 40 percent to approximately 10 percent. "We tested randomly six times during the study and the urine samples confirmed the patients' self-reports. There was a significant decrease in drug use," Dr. Geller says.

In addition, patients in the lithium group showed significantly greater improvement in symptoms of bipolar disorder—such as their ability to function in family, school, and social settings—than did those receiving a placebo.

"Lithium treatment of bipolar disorder in adolescents with secondary substance dependence disorders was an efficacious treatment for both disorders," Dr. Geller concludes.

Reducing Craving in Methadone Patients

Dr. Edward Nunes and his colleagues at the New York State Psychiatric Institute and Columbia University College of Physicians and Surgeons in New York City found that antidepressants used to treat comorbid depressive disorders in adult methadone treatment patients not only can improve their mood but also reduce their craving for drugs.

"We were able to identify and treat primary or secondary depression in chronically drug-dependent adults," Dr. Nunes says. "In some respects, treating depression as a separable disorder represents a sea change in the way we look at comorbidity in these patients."

In Dr. Nunes' study, patients receiving imipramine to treat depression showed substantial drops in depressive symptoms, and many patients whose depressive symptoms improved also reported decreased craving and use of drugs, including opiates, cocaine, and marijuana.

"There is evidence that treating the depression helps some patients take advantage of therapy and could be successful as one part of treatment," Dr. Nunes says.

The 12-week study involved 137 patients recruited from two community-based methadone maintenance programs. Patients also were diagnosed with primary depression that predated their drug use or secondary depression that emerged or persisted through a period of abstinence or had lasted for at least three months during a current period of drug use. Patients were randomly assigned to either imipramine or placebo. Eighty-four patients completed at least six weeks of the trial. Fifty-seven percent of patients receiving imipramine were rated as having substantial improvement in both mood and drug use compared with only seven percent among the patients receiving placebo. Fourteen percent of patients receiving imipramine achieved abstinence, confirmed by urinalysis, for four weeks compared with two percent of patients who received placebo.

"Imipramine had a very robust and positive effect on mood. This improved mood was associated with less intense and less frequent drug craving and, to a lesser extent, with reduced drug use," Dr. Nunes says.

Sources

Geller, B., et al. Double-blind and placebo-controlled study of lithium for adolescent bipolar disorders with secondary substance dependency.

Journal of the American Academy of Child and Adolescent Psychiatry 37(2):171-178, 1998.

Nunes, E.V., et al. Imipramine treatment of opiate-dependent patients with depressive disorders. *Archives of General Psychiatry* 55:153-160, 1998.

Chapter 35

Treating Depression in Patients with a History of Alcohol Dependency

Comorbidity[1]

The term "comorbidity" refers to the presence of any two or more illnesses in the same person. These illnesses can be medical or psychiatric conditions, as well as drug use disorders, including alcoholism. Comorbid illnesses may occur simultaneously or sequentially. The fact that two illnesses are comorbid, however, does not necessarily imply that one is the cause of the other, even if one occurs first.

Alcoholism and other disorders might be related in a number of ways, including the following:

1. Alcoholism and a second disorder can co-occur, either sequentially or simultaneously, by coincidence.

2. Alcoholism can cause various medical and psychiatric conditions or increase their severity.

3. Comorbid disorders might cause alcoholism or increase its severity.

4. Both alcoholism and the comorbid disorder may be caused, separately, by some third condition.

This chapter includes excerpts from documents produced by the National Institute on Alcohol Abuse and Alcoholism and the National Clearinghouse for Alcohol and Drug Information. Section headings include numbered references to documents from which excerpts are taken; citations are provided in the end notes to this chapter.

5. Alcohol use or alcohol withdrawal can produce symptoms that mimic those of an independent psychiatric disorder.

Treatment for co-occurring illnesses in persons with alcoholism should be a standard part of every alcoholism treatment program. Unfortunately, many patients with such illnesses fall through the cracks; for example, alcoholic patients with psychiatric problems who may be rejected by both alcoholism programs and mental health programs.

Alcohol and Depression: Which Comes First?[2]

The relationship between alcohol-use disorders and psychiatric symptoms is both clinically important and very complex. As a typical depressant, alcohol affects the brain in many ways, and it is likely that high doses will cause feelings of sadness (depression) during intoxication that evolve into feelings of nervousness (anxiety) during the subsequent hangover and withdrawal. The greater the amounts of alcohol consumed and the more regular the intake, the more likely a person will be to develop temporary anxiety and depressive symptoms. As consumption increases even more, these symptoms also are likely to intensify.

It is, therefore, not surprising that more than one out of every three alcoholics has experienced episodes of intense depression and/or severe anxiety. These psychological conditions are often intense enough to interfere with life functioning, and the symptoms are often recognized by physicians and other health care providers as serious enough to require treatment. When depressed or anxious alcohol-dependent people are asked their opinions about cause and effect, they often reply that they believe they drink in order to cope with their symptoms of sadness or nervousness.

Two reviews, however, indicate that research does not unanimously support the prior existence of severe depressive or anxiety disorders as a usual cause of alcoholism. Of course, when an alcohol-dependent person complains of severe depressive or anxiety symptoms (which might or might not indicate a long-term disorder), those conditions must be acknowledged and steps must be taken to help decrease them. If the psychiatric symptoms occur, however, as a consequence of the person's consumption of high doses of alcohol (that is, the complaints are alcohol induced), then the symptoms are likely to improve fairly quickly with abstinence. In this case, it is uncertain whether the longer term treatment of alcoholism requires additional aggressive therapies aimed at treating underlying depressive or anxiety disorders.

What are the immediate clinical implications of coexisting depressive and anxiety states among alcoholics?

As many as 80 percent of alcoholics report periods of sadness in their medical histories, with approximately one out of three alcohol-dependent men and women having experienced a severe depression that lasted for at least several weeks and interfered with his or her functioning. Similarly, the majority of alcoholics admit to experiencing periods of nervousness, including at least 40 percent who have had one or more intense panic attacks characterized by a brief episode of palpitations and shortness of breath.

An alcohol-dependent person who demonstrates such psychological symptoms needs more intense intervention and support than may otherwise be provided; and if not appropriately treated, the symptoms may carry a worse prognosis for alcohol-related problems. High levels of depression are especially worthy of concern, because the risk of death by suicide among alcoholics, estimated to be 10 percent or higher, may be most acute during these depressed states.

Once a person becomes deeply depressed, regardless of the cause, he or she may need to be hospitalized and provided with the appropriate precautions against suicide. These steps should be considered even if the patient's depressive disorder is a relatively short-lived alcohol-induced state. Practitioners can counteract their patients' depressive symptoms by providing education and counseling as well as by reassuring the patients of the high likelihood that they will recover from their depressions.

What are the treatment implications of the studies regarding the relationship between alcohol abuse and depression?

The first conclusion to be drawn is that many alcohol-dependent people are likely to present with depressive or anxiety symptoms that must be recognized and addressed. These problems contribute to an increased risk for suicide attempts, may be associated with more intense withdrawal symptoms, and may contribute to alcoholism relapse. Appropriate interventions for these psychiatric symptoms include forms of supportive psychotherapy, such as counseling or crisis intervention, and behavioral treatment, such as relaxation techniques and desensitization.

Second, the possibility that a longer term anxiety or depressive disorder exists in an alcoholic must always be considered. Perhaps 10 percent of men and 10 to 20 percent of women in the general population

271

develop severe anxiety or depressive disorders; therefore, it would be logical to expect that at least this proportion of alcoholics also would have similar syndromes. Identifying when an alcohol-dependent person has an independent or long-term major anxiety or depressive disorder requires gathering a careful patient history that searches for evidence of severe psychiatric symptoms either before the onset of severe alcohol-related problems or during a subsequent period of extended abstinence. Similarly, all alcoholics evidencing symptoms of severe depression or anxiety should be followed for approximately one month after abstinence to be certain that the depressive and anxiety symptoms are improving, because it is likely that severe symptoms remaining after abstinence for such a length of time may indicate a true independent depressive or anxiety disorder that requires longer term treatment.

The Relationship between Alcoholism and Depression[3]

The presence of comorbid psychiatric disorders in alcoholic patients has clinical and prognostic implications. For instance, alcoholics with comorbid depression may be at greater risk of psychosocial and interpersonal problems, treatment noncompliance, alcoholic relapse, and attempted and completed suicide. Additionally, heavy drinking may produce or worsen depressive symptoms.

Alcoholics often report that they drink to relieve a dysphoric mood, which has been termed "self-medication." This hypothesis embodies a view of alcoholism in which psychiatric symptoms are primary, with drinking occurring in response to those symptoms. It has been shown, however, that both chronic heavy drinking and alcohol withdrawal can exacerbate negative mood states. This intensification of symptoms may result from the effects of alcohol or from psychosocial problems (for example, family, work, or legal problems) that can stem from chronic heavy drinking. Because depressive symptoms have been shown to be both a cause and a consequence of heavy drinking, a careful history is required to guide treatment decisions.

Treatment of Patients with Comorbid Alcoholism and Psychiatric Disorders

Initial treatment for alcohol dependence consists primarily of detoxification (treatment of acute physical withdrawal symptoms) and psychosocial strategies aimed at maintaining abstinence. The added presence of a comorbid psychiatric disorder can substantially complicate this approach. For instance, depressive symptoms (such as decreased energy and interest) can interfere with a person's attendance at Alcoholics Anonymous (AA) meetings or group psychotherapy sessions, two widely used psychosocial interventions for alcoholism.

The diversity of alcoholics with comorbid disorders means that individualized treatment approaches may more effectively address the comorbidity. However, with the exception of studies of antidepressant therapy for depressed alcoholics, little research exists on how best to treat alcoholics with comorbid psychiatric disorders. Although cognitive behavioral therapy (CBT) has been shown to be useful in treating patients with alcohol dependence, as well as those with certain depressive and anxiety disorders, limited research exists on the utility of integrated psychotherapeutic interventions that address the particular needs of alcoholics with comorbid disorders.

Despite the lack of systematic study, some basic principles may be helpful in approaching patients with comorbid alcohol use and mood or anxiety disorders. The clinician's first objective is to establish both an alliance with the patient and a common goal for treatment. The goal in treating a patient with major depression is to reduce the depressive symptoms and return the individual to a normal level of function. Similarly, in treating a patient with alcohol dependence, the goal is usually abstinence, in order to restore normal function.

Although it may be obvious that the appropriate treatment goal for patients with dual diagnosis is to address both the substance use and the psychiatric symptoms, this simple fact is often overlooked. Thus, it is important to emphasize that treatment of such patients requires dual goals: namely, abstinence from alcohol and stabilization of comorbid symptoms, both of which can be expected (and may be required) to improve the person's health and psychosocial functioning.

Insofar as these goals can be achieved using psychosocial or pharmacological treatments, or a combination of the two, clinicians must consider the optimal sequence of interventions. Efforts to enhance motivation for recovery can be initiated during the first contact with the patient, which for some patients may be during detoxification. This can be accomplished by providing nonjudgmental feedback to the patient concerning the specific medical, social, interpersonal, or psychiatric effects of that person's drinking on his or her life. Relapse prevention strategies can be added after detoxification is complete, assuming that the patient is adequately motivated for such treatment.

The focus of CBT is on the acquisition of skills, which may be used to manage high-risk drinking situations, or to reduce anxiety or depressive symptoms. Consequently, it makes conceptual sense to mix and match CBT techniques that are used both for relapse prevention and to treat anxiety or depressive disorders. The varying combinations make it possible to tailor a program according to the specific needs of the patient. For instance, since dysphoria is often a cue for drinking, teaching patients to avoid high-risk drinking situations can go hand in hand with teaching patients how to manage their depressed moods.

Because many psychiatric symptoms subside with abstinence, the use of medications to alleviate such symptoms should generally be postponed until at least 1 or 2 weeks of abstinence have been achieved. However, under certain clinical circumstances (for example, severe symptoms and a clear history of a primary psychiatric disorder that was medication responsive), more immediate action may be required. In other cases, the assessment of symptoms at regular intervals throughout treatment will help to determine whether medications are indicated. Meanwhile, the patient can begin to learn skills to handle high-risk situations and craving along with techniques for managing anxiety or depression, as indicated.

Although alcoholics with comorbid disorders may find AA useful, these alcoholics often require extra encouragement to initiate and continue to attend fellowship meetings. For example, a person may need to attend several AA groups before choosing the one with which he or she feels most comfortable. Dual-diagnosis patients also may have difficulty relating to other AA members whose lives may improve more rapidly than theirs as a consequence of abstinence from alcohol. Patient education, an important aspect of treatment, should include a discussion of how psychiatric symptoms and drinking may affect one another. For instance, chronic heavy drinking may produce depressive symptoms. On the other hand, untreated depression can precipitate relapse, which in turn can augment feelings of worthlessness, hopelessness, and guilt.

Frequently, recovering alcoholics believe that recovery requires a medication-free state. Although this view is not a formal position of AA, some members hold this view. Unfortunately, this belief may reduce medication compliance in alcoholic patients with comorbid psychiatric disorders.

After treatment is initiated, the clinician must monitor both drinking behavior and psychiatric symptoms. Particular attention should be given to the risk for suicide, as it may be particularly high in depressed alcoholics. In addition, any pharmacotherapy targeting either alcohol dependence or a comorbid psychiatric disorder should be monitored regularly. In so doing, it is important to consider how biochemical changes in the liver and medical disorders associated with long-term alcohol misuse may influence medication effects.

In summary, interventions aimed at alcoholics with comorbid psychiatric disorders should address both the alcohol dependence and the comorbid psychiatric disorder. Specifically, an effort should be made to assess and enhance motivation, engage and retain patients in treatment, and educate the patient on the relationship between alcohol use and psychiatric symptoms. The judicious use of medications for persistent anxiety or depressive states can augment the psychosocial and educational efforts.

Alcohol Withdrawal and Depression[4]

Withdrawing alcoholics exhibit psychiatric difficulties that may be related to the process of withdrawal itself or to co-occurring conditions. The major psychiatric problems associated with acute and protracted withdrawal are anxiety, depression, and sleep disturbance. Less frequently, psychotic symptoms, including delusions and hallucinations, may be associated with withdrawal.

Depressive symptoms often are observed in patients who are intoxicated or undergoing alcohol detoxification. As many as 15 percent of alcoholics are at risk for death by suicide, and recent consumption of alcohol appears to increase the danger of a fatal outcome from self-harm. This finding may be attributable to the release of behavioral inhibition associated with alcohol intoxication or with the depressive feeling states that accompany the decline from peak intoxication. Depressive disorders commonly emerge during alcohol withdrawal; in addition to the depressive feeling states associated with alcohol consumption and withdrawal, the social, psychological, and physical problems associated with alcoholism may contribute to the development of depressive disorders.

Treatment of Alcohol Dependence with Medications in Patients with Depression[5]

People with alcohol dependence often experience symptoms of depression when they stop drinking. For most individuals, these symptoms disappear or wane during the first 1 or 2 weeks of abstinence. Patients who continue to report serious depressed feelings after the first week of abstinence, however, are likely to have a depressive disorder that coexists with their alcohol dependence. If the depression is left untreated, many of these patients will relapse. Thus, accurate

275

diagnosis and swift treatment of depression are critical in the care of alcohol-dependent patients.

Investigators have examined different types of antidepressant agents for dually diagnosed patients, including the older tricyclic antidepressants (for example, imipramine and desipramine) that have been available since the 1960s, and the newer SSRIs, such as sertraline and fluoxetine. Regardless of the type of antidepressant used, depressed, alcohol-dependent patients who take antidepressants have better outcomes than do those who take a placebo. Some participants in these antidepressant trials, however, continued to drink even though their depression lifted, demonstrating the need for additional interventions specific to drinking.

In making decisions about diagnosis and treatment of depressed alcohol-dependent patients, some clinicians distinguish between primary depression, which occurs before the onset of alcoholism, and secondary depression, which occurs afterwards. Studies have shown that antidepressant medications can improve mood and reduce drinking regardless of whether the patients' depression is primary or secondary.

Risks Associated with Using Medications in the Treatment of Depression in Alcohol-Dependent Patients[6]

Pharmacologic effects (consequences related to the actions of drugs) can be therapeutic or detrimental. Medication often produces both effects. Therapeutic pharmacologic effects include the indicated purposes and desired outcomes of taking prescribed medications, such as a decrease in the frequency and severity of episodes of depression produced by antidepressants.

Detrimental pharmacologic effects include unwanted side effects, such as dry mouth or constipation resulting from antidepressant use. Side effects perceived as noxious by patients may decrease their compliance with taking the medications as directed.

Some detrimental pharmacologic effects relate to abuse and addiction potential. For example, some medications may be stimulating, sedating, or euphorigenic and may promote physical dependence and tolerance. These effects can promote the use of medication for longer periods and at higher doses than prescribed.

Thus, prescribing medication involves striking a balance between therapeutic and detrimental pharmacologic effects. Side effects of prescription medications vary greatly and include detrimental pharmacologic effects that may promote abuse or addiction. With regard to patients with dual disorders, special attention should be given to detrimental effects, in terms of 1) medication compliance, 2) abuse and addiction potential, 3) alcohol or other drug use disorder relapse, and 4) psychiatric disorder relapse.

Psychoactive Potential

Not all psychiatric medications are psychoactive. The term psychoactive describes the ability of certain medications, drugs, and other substances to cause acute psychomotor effects and a relatively rapid change in mood or thought. Changes in mood include stimulation, sedation, and euphoria. Thought changes can include a disordering of thought such as delusions, hallucinations, and illusions. Behavioral changes can include an acceleration or retardation of motor activity. All drugs of abuse are by definition psychoactive.

Some antidepressant and antipsychotic medications have pharmacologic side effects such as mild sedation or mild stimulation. Indeed, the side effects of these medications can be used clinically. Physicians can use a mildly sedating antidepressant medication for patients with depression and insomnia, or a mildly stimulating antipsychotic medication for patients with psychosis and hypersomnia or lethargy. While the side effects of these drugs include a mild effect on mood, they are not euphorigenic. Nevertheless, case reports of misuse of nonpsychoactive medications have been noted, and use should be monitored carefully in patients with dual disorders.

Reinforcement Potential

Some drugs promote reinforcement, or the increased likelihood of repeated use. Reinforcement can occur by either the removal of negative symptoms or conditions or the amplification of positive symptoms or states. For example, self-medication that delays or prevents an unpleasant event (such as withdrawal) from occurring becomes reinforcing. Thus, using a benzodiazepine to avoid alcohol withdrawal can increase the likelihood of continued use. Positive reinforcement involves strengthening the possibility that a certain behavior will be repeated through reward and satisfaction, as with drug-induced euphoria or drug-induced feelings of well-being. A classic example is the pleasure derived from moderate to high doses of opiates or stimulants. Drugs that are immediately reinforcing are more likely to lead to psychiatric or alcohol or other drug use problems.

Tolerance and Withdrawal Potential

Long-term or chronic use of certain medications can cause tolerance to the subjective and therapeutic effects and prompt dosage increases to recreate the desired effects. In addition, many drugs cause a well-defined withdrawal phenomenon after the cessation of chronic use. Patients' attempts to avoid withdrawal syndromes often lead them to additional drug use. Thus, drugs that promote tolerance and withdrawal generally have higher risks for abuse and addiction.

Treatment Decisions

As can be seen, there are pharmacologic as well as hereditary and environmental factors that influence the development of alcohol and other drug use problems. All of these factors should be considered prior to prescribing medication, especially when the patient is at high risk for developing an alcohol or other drug use disorder. Decisions about whether and when to prescribe medication to a high-risk patient should include a risk-benefit analysis that considers the risk of medication abuse, the risk of undertreating a psychiatric problem, the type and severity of the psychiatric problem, the relationship between the psychiatric disorder and the alcohol and other drug use disorder for the individual patient, and the therapeutic benefits of resolving the psychiatric and alcohol and other drug problems.

Glossary[2]

Alcohol-induced disorders: A group of psychiatric symptoms that develop in the course of intoxication or withdrawal from alcohol. These symptoms, including depression and anxiety, tend to be temporary and disappear within days or weeks of abstinence. Because they are short lived, the symptoms rarely require long-term counseling or psychotherapy, and little evidence indicates that they benefit from medications.

Anxiety disorders: A group of long-term, often lifelong, psychiatric disorders, the central feature of which is some form of nervousness or anxiety. These disorders include panic disorder, social phobia, and other long-term anxiety conditions. Often they require active treatment that can involve education and counseling, behavioral treatments (for example, teaching relaxation techniques or ways of approaching feared situations), and, occasionally, long-term medications.

Anxiety symptoms: Signs include feelings of nervousness, tension, or anxiety. They can include temporary symptoms that involve panic attacks, fears, or other nervous behaviors. Sometimes these symptoms occur as a reaction to a life situation; at other times, they are related to the effects of alcohol or other drugs. The symptoms may represent long-term psychiatric disorders that are outside the context of intoxication or stress.

Depressive disorders: Psychiatric conditions characterized by intense sadness and symptoms that include interference with sleep, appetite, and daily life functioning. Unless treated, such symptoms are likely to remain for many months and even years.

Depressive symptoms: General and frequently observed feelings of sadness apparent during periods of grief, reactions to difficult situations, or as consequences of medical conditions or side effects of medications or drugs. The sadness resembles the symptoms seen in depressive disorders but usually is short lived and disappears with time.

Dysthymia: A disorder characterized by at least two years of depressed mood.

Major depressive episode: A period of at least two weeks during which there is either depressed mood or the loss of interest or pleasure in nearly all activities.

Mania: An episode of intense hyperactivity, rapid thoughts, and poor judgment that is likely to last weeks to months unless actively treated. A person who experiences an independent major manic episode usually is diagnosed as demonstrating bipolar, or manic-depressive, disorder.

Manic-depressive disorder: A psychiatric disorder characterized by episodes of both manic and depressive disorders. This condition also is referred to as bipolar disorder.

Panic attacks: The abrupt onset of an episode (usually lasting about 10 to 20 minutes) of feelings of intense anxiety or nervousness accompanied by rapid heartbeats (palpitations) and a feeling of shortness of breath. Panic attacks can occur as a reaction to severe stress, as a complication of some medications (for example, diet pills), during intoxication with stimulant drugs (for example, amphetamines or cocaine), or during withdrawal from depressant drugs (for example, alcohol).

Panic disorder: A long-term, frequently lifelong, anxiety disorder characterized by panic attacks that occur frequently (multiple times per month) and develop unrelated to stress, side effects of medications, or effects of alcohol or other drugs. This disorder often responds to education and some behavioral treatments, including relaxation, but may require medications (for example, antidepressants) in certain cases.

End Notes

1. "Alcoholism and Co-occurring Disorders," *Alcohol Alert*, National Institute on Alcohol Abuse and Alcoholism, No. 14, Ph 302, October 1991; full text available online at www.niaaa.nih.gov/publications/aa14.htm.

2. Schuckit, MA. "Alcohol, Anxiety, and Depressive Disorders," *Alcohol Health and Research World*, Vol. 20, No. 2, Spring 1996, pp. 81–85.

3. Modesto-Lowe, V. and Kranzler, HR. "Diagnosis and Treatment of Alcohol-Dependent Patients with Comorbid Psychiatric Disorders," *Alcohol Research and Health*, Vol. 23, No. 2, Spring 1999. pp. 144–149.

4. Trevisan, LA; Boutros, N; Petrakis, IL; and Krystal, JH. "Complications of Alcohol Withdrawal: Pathophysiological Insights," *Alcohol Research and Health*, Vol. 22, No. 1, Winter 1998, pp. 61–66.

5. "Research Refines Alcoholism Treatment Options," *Alcohol Research and Health*, Vol. 24, No. 1, Winter 2000, 99. pp. 53–61.

6. "Chapter 9: Pharmacologic Management," *Assessment and Treatment of Patients with Coexisting Mental Illness and Alcohol and Other Drug Abuse*, Treatment Improvement Protocol (TIP) Series 9, Center for Substance Abuse Treatment, Substance Abuse and Mental Health Services Administration, DHHS Publication No. (SMA) 95-3061, 1995; full text available online at www.health.org/govpubs/bkd134/.

Additional Reading

McGrath, PJ; Nunes, EV; and Quitkin, FM. "Current Concepts in the Treatment of Depression in Alcohol-Dependent Patients," *Psychiatric Clinics of North America*, Vol. 23, No. 4, December 2000.

Chapter 36

Electroconvulsive Therapy (ECT)

What conditions does electroconvulsive therapy treat?

Electroconvulsive therapy (also called ECT) may help people who have the following conditions:

- Severe depression with insomnia (trouble sleeping), weight change, feelings of hopelessness or guilt, and thoughts of suicide (hurting or killing yourself) or homicide (hurting or killing someone else).

- Severe depression that does not respond to antidepressants (medicines used to treat depression) or counseling.

- Severe depression in patients who can't take antidepressants.

- Severe mania that does not respond to medicines. Symptoms of severe mania may include talking too much, insomnia, weight loss or impulsive behavior.

How does ECT work?

It is believed that ECT works by causing a seizure (a short period of irregular brain activity) with an electrical shock. This seizure releases

"Depresion: Electroconvulsive Therapy," reprinted with permission from http://www.familydoctor.org/handouts/058.html. Copyright © 2002 American Academy of Family Physicians. All Rights Reserved. For more information from the AAFP visit their website at http://www.familydoctor.org.

many chemicals in the brain. These chemicals, called neurotransmitters, deliver messages from one brain cell to another. The release of these chemicals makes the brain cells work better. A patient's mood will improve when these brain cells and chemical messengers work better.

What steps are taken to prepare for ECT treatment?

First, a doctor will do a physical exam to make sure you're physically able to have the treatment. If you are, you will meet with an anesthesiologist (a doctor who specializes in giving anesthesia). The anesthesiologist will examine your heart and lungs to see if it is safe for you to have anesthesia. You may need to have some blood tests and an electrocardiogram (a test showing the rhythm of your heart) before your first ECT treatment.

How are the ECT treatments given?

ECT may be given during a hospital stay, or a person can go to a hospital just for the treatment and then go home. ECT is given up to three times a week. Usually no more than 12 treatments are needed. Treatment is given by a psychiatrist.

Before each treatment, an intravenous (IV) line will be started so medicine can be put directly into your blood. You will be given an anesthetic (medicine to put you into a sleep-like state) and a medicine to relax your muscles. Your heart rate, blood pressure and breathing will be watched closely. After you are asleep, an electrical shock will be applied to your head. The shock will last only one or two seconds and will make your brain have a seizure. This seizure is controlled by medicines so your body doesn't move when you have the seizure.

You will wake up within five minutes and will be taken to a recovery room to be watched. When you are fully awake, you can eat and drink, get dressed, and return to your hospital room or go home.

What are some side effects of ECT?

Side effects may result from the anesthesia, the ECT treatment or both. Common side effects include temporary short-term memory loss, nausea, muscle aches and headache. Some people may have longer-lasting problems with memory after ECT. Sometimes a person's blood pressure or heart rhythm changes. If these changes occur, they are carefully watched during the ECT treatments and are immediately treated.

What happens after the ECT treatments are done?

After you have finished all of your ECT treatments, you will probably be started on an antidepressant medicine. It is important for you to keep taking this medicine as your doctor tells you to so that you won't become depressed again.

Chapter 37

Alternative Therapies for Depression

The effectiveness and side effects of selective serotonin reuptake inhibitors (SSRIs) and tricyclic antidepressants (TCAs) are well documented. Relatively new potential additions to the armamentarium against depression include St. John's wort and S-adenosylmethionine (SAMe).

St. John's Wort

St. John's wort (*Hypericum perforatum*) appears to act as a weak SSRI and may have an affinity for sigma receptors as well. Its clinical effectiveness may be attributable to a combination of mechanisms because each mechanism by itself is too weak to provide the overall effect.[4,5]

Studies have compared TCAs (for example, imipramine [Tofranil], amitriptyline [Elavil]) with St. John's wort in cases of mild to moderate depression and found no statistical differences between groups as evaluated by the Hamilton Depression Scale. One-third fewer side effects were noted in the subjects taking St. John's wort, compared with the subjects taking amitriptyline.[6]

Initially, it was thought that this botanical supplement rarely, if ever, led to any drug interactions.[7] However, recent evidence[8,9] indicates

---

Excerpted and reprinted with permission from "Alternative Therapies: Part I. Depression, Diabetes, Obesity," by Vincent Morelli, M.D. and Roger J. Zoorob, M.D., M.P.H. in *American Family Physician*, September 1, 2000, Vol. 62, pp. 1051-60. Copyright © 2000 by the American Academy of Family Physicians. All Rights Reserved.

interactions with digoxin, theophylline (decreased bioavailability), protease inhibitors (lowering the level of indinavir [Crixivan]), and drugs used to combat transplant rejection (increasing the metabolism of cyclosporine [Sandimmune]) via induction of cytochrome P450 enzymes. It also may cause serotonin syndrome if used with other antidepressants.

Results of 29 clinical trials[10,11] have demonstrated that St. John's wort is more effective than placebo in the treatment of mild to moderate depression. As yet, there is insufficient evidence comparing the efficacy of St. John's wort with conventional, modern antidepressants. We could find no studies that used St. John's wort in combination with other modalities to treat severe depression or treatment-resistant depression, and it should not be used in these patients.

S-Adenosylmethionine (SAMe)

Another potential antidepressant is SAMe, which is a molecule found naturally in all human cells. It plays a role in the many methylation reactions of the body, including gene expression, cell membrane homeostasis, and hormone and neurotransmitter synthesis.

The rationale for the use of SAMe in depression stems from its role in the metabolism of serotonin, dopamine, and melatonin. Oral and intravenous SAMe supplementation has been shown to significantly increase SAMe levels in cerebrospinal fluid, indicating SAMe's crossover through the blood-brain barrier. This has been associated with increased levels of serotonin metabolites in cerebrospinal fluid. Some depressed patients may have low serotonin levels associated with low levels of SAMe.[12,13]

A 1994 meta-analysis[14] performed in Italy found SAMe more efficacious than placebo in the treatment of depression and equally as effective as TCAs, with a much lower incidence of side effects. In a double-blind trial conducted that same year,[15] 26 patients received SAMe or desipramine for four weeks. At the end of the study period, 62 percent of the patients taking SAMe had significant improvement in symptoms, while only 50 percent of the patients taking desipramine had significant improvement. The study did not extend beyond this short observational period, leaving unanswered questions about the long-term side effects of SAMe and whether the antidepressant effects of SAMe persist beyond four weeks. The study did not take into account the usual four- to eight-week time period needed for TCAs to become maximally effective. The investigators did note, however, that all patients who showed a 50 percent decrease in their Hamilton

Depression Scale scoring also showed a significant increase in plasma SAMe concentration.[15]

In 1995, an open multicenter study[16] of 163 patients given 400 mg of SAMe per day showed a reduction in depressive symptoms at seven

Table 37.1. Summary of Natural Products Used in the Treatment of Depression

St. John's Wort

> **Other names:** *Hypericum perforatum*, hardhay, amber, goatweed, Klamath weed, Tipton weed
>
> **Efficacy:** Works as well as TCAs for mild or moderate depression
>
> **Mechanism of action:** Acts as weak SSRI, dopaminergic, MAOI and norepinephrine uptake inhibitor
>
> **Formulation:** Dried seeds, leaves and flowers; capsule
>
> **Dosage:*** 300 mg 3 times daily
>
> **Side effects:** Rare photo-sensitivity rash
>
> **Drug interactions:** May lower digoxin level 25%; may contribute to serotonin syndrome if used with SSRIs/TCAs/MAOIs/dopamine agonists; may lower blood levels of protease inhibitors; may interfere with drugs used in organ transplantation

SAMe

> **Other names:** S-adenosylmethionine; AdoMet
>
> **Efficacy:** Possibly efficacious; poorly studied; cost prohibitive
>
> **Mechanism of action:** Methyl donor important in neurotransmitter synthesis
>
> **Formulation:** Synthetic form of a natural metabolite of the amino acid methionine; tablet
>
> **Dosage:*** 400 to 1,200 mg per day
>
> **Side effects:** None recorded
>
> **Drug interactions:** None recorded

TCA = tricyclic antidepressant; SSRI = selective serotonergic reuptake inhibitor; MAOI = monoamine oxidase inhibitor.

* Dosages in products may vary considerably.

and 15 days. No serious side effects were observed. In their conclusion, the authors recommended that further double-blind trials be undertaken. Again, no documentation of long-term effectiveness or side effects has been reported. Finally, another review[17] concluded that SAMe seemed to have enough of an antidepressant effect to warrant further research.

In conclusion, because no studies have yet validated the long-term safety or efficacy of SAMe, further large long-term studies should be conducted before it receives widespread recommendation.

Internet Resources for Information about Alternative Therapies

Alternative Medicine Foundation
http://www.amfoundation.org

American Botanical Council
http://www.herbalgram.org

Complementary and Alternative Medicine Program at Stanford (CAMPS)
http://camps.stanford.edu

National Center for Complementary and Alternative Medicine
http://www.nccam.nih.gov

References

1. "Herbal Rx: The promises and the pitfalls," *Consum Rep* 1999;64:44-8.

2. Cupp MJ. "Herbal remedies: Adverse effects and drug interactions," *Am Fam Physician* 1999;59:1239-45.

3. Zink T, Chaffin J. "Herbal 'health' products: What family physicians need to know," *Am Fam Physician* 1998;58:1133-40 [published erratum appears in *Am Fam Physician* 1999;59:540].

4. Bennett DA Jr, Phun L, Polk JF, Voglino SA, Zlotnik V, Raffa RB. "Neuropharmacology of St. John's wort (hypericum)," *Ann Pharmacother* 1998;32:1201-8.

5. Vorbach EU, Hubner WD, Arnoldt KH. "Effectiveness and tolerance of the hypericum extract LI 160 in comparison with imipramine: Randomized double-blind study with 135 outpatients," *J Geriatr Psychiatry Neurol* 1994;7(suppl 1):S19-23.

6. Wheatley D. "LI 160, an extract of St. John's wort, versus amitriptyline in mildly to moderately depressed outpatients—a controlled 6-week clinical trial," *Pharmacopsychiatry* 1997;30(suppl 2):77-80.

7. Nordfors M, Hartvig P. "St John's wort against depression in favour again," *Lakartidningen* 1997; 94:2365-7.

8. Piscitelli SC, Burstein AH, Chai HD, Alfaro RM, Falloon J. "Indinavir concentrations and St. John's wort," *Lancet* 2000;355:547-8.

9. Fugh-Berman A. "Herb-drug interactions," *Lancet* 2000;355:134-8.

10. Stevinson C, Ernst E. "Hypericum for depression. An update of the clinical evidence," *Eur Neuropsychopharmacol* 1999;9:501-5.

11. Linde K, Ramirez G, Mulrow CD, Pauls A, Weidenhammer W, Melchart D. "St. John's wort for depression—an overview and meta-analysis of randomised clinical trials," *BMJ* 1996;313:253-8.

12. Fava M, Rosenbaum JF, MacLaughlin R, Falk WE, Pollack MH, Cohen LS, et al. "Neuroendocrine effects of S-adenosyl-L-methionine, a novel putative antidepressant," *J Psychiatr Res* 1990;24:177-84.

13. Young SN. "The use of diet and dietary components in the study of factors controlling affect in humans: A review," *J Psychiatry Neurosci* 1993;18:235-44.

14. Bressa GM. "S-adenosyl-l-methionine (SAMe) as antidepressant: Meta-analysis of clinical studies," *Acta Neurol Scand Suppl* 1994;154:7-14.

15. Bell KM, Potkin SG, Carreon D, Plon L. "S-adenosyl-L-methionine blood levels in major depression: Changes with drug treatment," *Acta Neurol Scand Suppl* 1994;154:15-8.

16. Fava M, Giannelli A, Rapisarda V, Patralia A, Guaraldi GP. "Rapidity of onset of the antidepressant effect of parenteral S-adenosyl-L-methionine," *Psychiatry Res* 1995;56:295-7.

17. Fugh-Berman A, Cott JM. "Dietary supplements and natural products as psychotherapeutic agents," *Psychosom Med* 1999;61:712-28.

Chapter 38

St. John's Wort

Introduction

St. John's wort (*Hypericum perforatum*) is a long-living, wild-growing herb with yellow flowers that has been used for centuries to treat mental disorders as well as nerve pain. In ancient times, doctors and herbalists (herb specialists) wrote about its use as a sedative and antimalarial agent as well as a balm for wounds, burns, and insect bites. Today, the herb is a popular treatment for mild to moderate depression; it also is used to treat anxiety, seasonal affective disorder, and sleep disorders.[1]

St. John's wort is most widely used in Germany, where doctors prescribed almost 66 million daily doses in 1994 for psychological complaints.[2] In fact, German doctors prescribe St. John's wort about 20 times more often than Prozac, one of the most widely prescribed antidepressants in the United States.[3]

The use of St. John's wort is growing in the United States, and several brands now are available. Extracts of the plant are sold as a nutritional supplement after being prepared with a powder or an oil; the herb is available in capsule, tea, or tincture forms. St. John's wort was among the top-selling botanical products in the United States in 1997, with industry-estimated sales of $400 million in 1998.[4]

A fact sheet produced by the National Center for Complementary and Alternative Medicine (NCCAM), available online at http://nccam.nih.gov/fcp/factsheets/stjohnswort/stjohnswort.htm, updated July 25, 2001.

FDA's Role

The FDA does not subject dietary supplements to a premarket approval process as it does new drugs.[5] However, the Dietary Supplement Health and Education Act of 1994 permits the FDA to remove a supplement from the market if it determines the supplement is unsafe. Herbal products such as St. John's wort can be marketed without stating standards for dosage or evidence of safety. Often, information on specific products may be misleading or even inaccurate. For instance, when the *Los Angeles Times*, a newspaper in California, commissioned laboratory tests on 10 St. John's wort products, researchers found that the potency of the products varied dramatically from what their labels claimed.[6]

At the same time, a St. John's wort product stating the words "standardized extract" in its label may be more likely to contain the exact amount of the specific active ingredient needed to be effective. Standardized products generally are considered the highest-quality herbal products that a consumer can buy.[7]

Treating Depression

Depression is a common illness that strikes perhaps 1 in 15 Americans each year. A person's mood, thoughts, physical health, and behavior all may be affected. Symptoms can include a persistent sad, anxious, or "empty" feeling; loss of energy, appetite, or sexual drive; and lack of interest in socializing, work, or hobbies.

Depression can be mild, moderate, or severe. Mild depression is characterized by difficulty in functioning normally, while moderate depression may involve impaired functioning at work or in social activities. Severe depression, which may involve delusions or hallucinations, markedly interferes with a person's ability to work or otherwise function and may lead to suicide. Genetic factors may put a person at risk for developing depression, and alcohol or drug use can make the problem worse.[8] While the public misperception persists that depression is voluntary or a "character flaw," depression is a real condition that can be treated effectively by qualified professionals.[9]

Specific psychotherapies (such as interpersonal and cognitive-behavioral therapy) and antidepressant medications both have been found to be effective for patients with major depression. Major depression includes mild, moderate, or severe depression that is not characterized by manic-depressive mood swings or induced by a substance such as alcohol. Several antidepressant drugs have become more widely used in the past several years and been found to be effective.

However, patients sometimes report unpleasant side effects such as a dry mouth, nausea, headache, diarrhea, or impaired sexual function or sleep.[10]

In part because of these types of drug side effects, many patients with depression are turning to herbal treatments such as St. John's wort. Researchers are studying it for possibly having fewer and less severe side effects than antidepressant drugs. St. John's wort also costs far less than antidepressant medication. In addition, St. John's wort does not require a prescription.[11]

St. John's wort is not completely free of side effects, however. Some users have complained of a dry mouth, dizziness, gastrointestinal symptoms, increased sensitivity to sunlight, and fatigue.[12] In addition, herbal treatments often are not as potent or as quick to act as conventional treatments. Furthermore, herbal treatments may not produce the desired results and may not be as effective as conventional medicine. Still, some people turn to herbs because they prefer to use "natural" products.

Clinical depression is a serious medical disorder that, in many cases, can be treated. However, St. John's wort is not a proven therapy for clinical depression. Therefore, there is some risk in taking it to treat clinical depression.[5]

In any case, St. John's wort should not be mixed with other standard antidepressants because side effects may result. This is one reason why it is important to tell your doctor about all medications you are taking. Check with your doctor before taking St. John's wort or any other herb or medication. Your doctor can help you weigh the risks and benefits of a particular treatment so you can make informed health care decisions.

How St. John's Wort Works

The major components in extracts of St. John's wort include flavonoids, kaempferol, luteolin, biapigenin, hyperforin, polycyclic phenols, hypericin, and pseudohypericin. Researchers believe the last three substances are the active ingredients.[5] New research suggests that hyperforin also may play a large role in the herb's antidepressant effects. Some German manufacturers of St. John's wort have begun standardizing, not only to hypericin as most U.S. manufacturers do, but to hyperforin as well.[13] Standardizing means that the manufacturer ensures that each individual supplement contains a uniform amount of a certain compound, in this case hypericin and hyperforin.

Recent research suggests a possible application of St. John's wort for alcoholism. Researchers from the University of North Carolina at Chapel Hill found that St. John's wort reduced alcohol intake in laboratory animals.[14]

Several mechanisms of action of St. John's wort have been proposed, including the following:

- **Inhibition of monoamine (serotonin, dopamine, and norepinephrine) re-uptake:** St. John's wort appears to reduce the rate at which brain cells reabsorb serotonin (an important neurotransmitter or chemical that aids communication between nerve cells). Low levels of serotonin in the body are associated with depression.[15,16]

- **Modulation of interleukin-6 (IL-6) activity:** Raised levels of IL-6, a protein involved in the communication between cells in the body's immune (disease-fighting) system, may lead to increases in adrenal regulatory hormones, a hallmark of depression. St. John's wort may reduce levels of IL-6, and thus help treat depression.[17]

More research is needed to determine precisely the active ingredients in St. John's wort and to learn how the herb works.

Clinical Trials

Clinical trials (studies of a treatment's safety and effectiveness in humans) have found a similar rate of response with St. John's wort as with standard, conventional antidepressants in treating mild to moderate depression.[18,19] However, it is hard to interpret these studies as definite proof of the efficacy of St. John's wort because low doses of standard antidepressants were used and there was no placebo (a pharmacologically inactive substance) control. An analysis of 23 European clinical studies of St. John's wort that was published in the *British Medical Journal* in 1996 concluded that the herb has antidepressive effects in cases of mild to moderate depression (the dosage varied considerably among the studies).[2] However, no studies of its long-term use have been conducted. More research is needed to explore the long-term effects and optimum safe dosage of the extract.

A new study funded by the National Institutes of Health's National Center for Complementary and Alternative Medicine (NCCAM), Office of Dietary Supplements, and the National Institute of Mental Health will provide more information about St. John's wort. This study, which is in progress, is the first large-scale controlled clinical trial in the United States to assess whether the herb has a significant therapeutic effect in patients with clinical depression.

The $4.3 million study will involve 336 patients with major depression. The Duke University Medical Center in Durham, North Carolina, is coordinating the three-year study, which has 13 clinical sites around the country.

There are three different treatment groups in the trial. One group will receive an initial dose of 900 mg per day of St. John's wort; a second will receive a placebo; and the third will receive Zoloft (a commonly used antidepressant). Patients who respond positively to their randomly assigned treatment will be continued on it for another 4 months.

Drug Interaction Advisory

NIH Clinical Center research shows that St. John's wort may reduce the effectiveness of several drugs by speeding up activity in a key pathway responsible for their breakdown. The end result is that blood levels of these drugs decrease because the body breaks them down faster. St. John's wort especially affects Crixivan (indinavir) and other protease inhibitors used to treat HIV infection. It also may affect cyclosporine, a drug used to help prevent organ transplant rejection, and other immunosuppressant drugs; and other medications that work through the same pathway, including birth control pills, cholesterol-lowering medications such as Mevacor (lovastatin), cancer medications, seizure drugs, and blood thinners such as Coumadin (warfarin). Doctors and patients should be aware of these negative drug interactions that could interfere with the proper functioning of these drugs. For more information, visit NCCAM's Web site http://nccam.nih.gov/; or the Food and Drug Administration (FDA) Center for Drug Evaluation and Research's Web site http://www.fda.gov/cder/drug/advisory/stjwort.htm; or call the FDA Center for Food Safety and Applied Nutrition at 201-800-332-4010.

For More Information

For more information about depression, contact the National Institute of Mental Health toll-free at 1-800-421-4211. For more information about St. John's wort, contact the American Botanical Council at 512-926-4900 or the Herb Research Foundation at 303-449-2265. For more information about complementary and alternative medicine, contact the NCCAM Clearinghouse at 1-888-644-6226.

References

1. American Herbal Pharmacopoeia and Therapeutic Compendium. "St. John's Wort *(Hypericum perforatum)* Monograph." *Herbalgram. The Journal of the American Botanical Council and the Herb Research Foundation.* 1997. (40):1-16.

2. Linde, K., Ramirez, G., Mulrow, C.D., Weidenhammer, W., and Melchart, D. "St. John's Wort for Depression—An Overview and Metaanalysis of Randomized Clinical Trials." *British Medical Journal.* 1996. 313(7052):253-8.

3. Murray, M. "Common Questions about St. John's Wort Extract." *American Journal of Natural Medicine.* 1997. 4(7):14-9.

4. *Nutrition Business Journal.* San Diego, CA: Nutrition Business International, 1998.

5. National Institute of Mental Health. *Questions and Answers about St. John's Wort.* Bethesda, MD: National Institute of Mental Health, 1997.

6. Monmaney, T. "Remedy's U.S. Sales Zoom, but Quality Control Lags. St. John's Wort: Regulatory Vacuum Leaves Doubt about Potency, Effects of Herb Used for Depression." Los Angeles, CA: *Los Angeles Times,* August 31, 1998.

7. Duke, J. *The Green Pharmacy.* Emmaus, PA: Rodale Press, 1997.

8. American Psychiatric Association. *Diagnostic and Statistical Manual of Mental Disorders. 4th ed.* Washington, DC: American Psychiatric Association, 1995.

9. National Institute of Mental Health. *General Facts about Depression.* Bethesda, MD: National Institute of Mental Health, 1997.

10, Medical Economics Company. *Physician's Desk Reference 1998. 52nd ed.* Montvale, NJ: Medical Economics Company, 1997.

11. Kincheloe, L. "Herbal Medicines Can Reduce Costs in HMO." *Herbalgram. The Journal of the American Botanical Council and the Herb Research Foundation.* 1997. (41):49-53.

12. Woelk, H., Burkard, G., and Grunwald, J. "Benefits and Risks of the Hypericum Extract LI 160: Drug Monitoring Study with 3,250 Patients." *Journal of Geriatric Psychiatry and Neurology*. 1994. 7(Supplement 1):S34-8.

13. Laakmann, G., Schule, C., Baghai, T., and Kieser, M. "St. John's Wort in Mild to Moderate Depression: The Relevance of Hyperforin for the Clinical Efficacy." *Pharmacopsychiatry*. June 1998. 31(Supplement):54-9.

14. Rezvani, A.H. 1998 *Annual Meeting of the Research Society on Alcoholism*. Hilton Head, SC: Research Society on Alcoholism, June 23, 1998.

15. Andrews, E. "In Germany, Humble Herb Is Rival to Prozac." New York, NY: *New York Times*, September 9, 1997.

16. Perovic, S. and Muller, W.E.G. "Pharmacological Profile of Hypericum Extract. Effect of Serotonin Uptake by Postsynaptic Receptors." *Arzneimittel-Forschuns*. 1995. 45:1145-8.

17. Thiele, B., Brink, I., and Ploch, M. "Modulation of Cytokine Expression by Hypericum Extract." *Journal of Geriatric Psychiatry and Neurology*. 1994. 7(Supplement 1):S60-2.

18. Harrer, G., Hubner, W.D., and Podzuweit, H. "Effectiveness and Tolerance of the Hypericum Extract LI 160 Compared to Maprotiline: A Multicenter Double-Blind Study." *Journal of Geriatric Psychiatry and Neurology*. 1994. 7(Supplement 1):S24-8.

19. Harrer, G. and Sommer, H. "Treatment of Mild/Moderate Depressions with Hypericum." *Phytomedicine*. 1994. 1:3-8.

Chapter 39

Exercise Against Depression

In Brief

Physical activity is a useful tool for preventing and easing depression symptoms. When prescribing exercise as an adjunct to medication and psychotherapy, the complexity and the individual circumstances of each patient must be considered. Hopelessness and fatigue can make physical exertion difficult, and some patients are vulnerable to guilt and self-blame if they fail to carry out a regimen. A feasible, flexible, and pleasurable program has the best chance for success. Walking—alone or in a group—is often a good option.

Primary care physicians frequently see depressed patients, varying from those who have transient symptoms that may be a normal reaction to the setbacks of everyday life to those who are clinically depressed and experience functional impairments that affect relationships, quality of life, ability to work, and physical health.

Fortunately, depression is one of the most treatable mental disorders. Used judiciously, psychotherapy and antidepressant medication alleviate symptoms, effect remissions, and may prevent relapse in most patients. Exercise also has a significant role to play: It can complement traditional treatments in those who are clinically depressed and help prevent depression in those who do not have the illness (see "Exercise as a Depression-Prevention Tactic," below).

From Artal M, Sherman C. Exercise against depression. *Phys Sportsmed* 1998; 26(10): 55-70 including sidebar by Lisa Schnirring. Reproduced with permission of McGraw-Hill, Inc.

A Vital Primary Care Role

Depression is the most common mental disorder[1] and is further classified as major depressive disorder, bipolar disorder, dysthymic disorder, or depressive disorder not otherwise specified.[2] Major depression is twice as common in women as in men.[3,4]

The somatic symptoms of depression (for example, fatigue, sleeplessness, decreased appetite, decreased sexual interest, weight change, and constipation) bring many people to their primary care physicians. Depressed individuals are more likely than others to develop cardiovascular disease and to die of all causes.[5] An estimated 15% of those with severe depression will commit suicide.

Research has consistently shown that 6% to 8% of all outpatients in primary care settings suffer from major depression.[6] According to the National Ambulatory Medical Care Survey,[7] more than 7 million primary care visits were made annually in the early 1990s for the treatment of depression, double the number 10 years earlier. Half are treated by primary care physicians and half by psychiatrists.[1]

Despite the large numbers of patients diagnosed as having depression, the disease remains underdiagnosed,[8] and, according to one study,[1] only one third of those having the diagnosis were receiving treatment.

The Exercise-Depression Link

Research on physical activity and depression goes back to the 19th century. In recent decades, many studies have documented the benefits of exercise on mood in healthy and clinically depressed individuals.

Methodologic problems in many of the studies make interpretation and application of the findings difficult.[1,9,10] Some studies used heterogeneous patient populations, mixed samples of healthy and clinically depressed subjects, or used different clinical instruments to measure depression and its alleviation. Many studies refer to depression as a homogeneous entity rather than a spectrum of disorders that vary in severity, etiology, and biologic and psychosociologic complexity.

Several studies did not differentiate the types of therapeutic interventions with which exercise was compared, while asserting that exercise was equal to or more beneficial than other treatments.[11-13] In particular, these studies did not differentiate between the different types of psychotherapy (individual, group, hospital-based milieu, brief, or long-term).

Despite methodologic problems, most studies have found exercise to have psychological and physiologic benefits for participants, with 90% of studies reporting antidepressant and anxiolytic effects.[9] Taken as a whole, the research strongly suggests that benefits are greatest in individuals who have greater psychological impairment and in those who are clinically depressed,[10] but both clinical and nonclinical populations benefit.

Clinical Populations

Studies in clinically depressed populations have included both hospitalized and ambulatory patients. One study[14] of hospitalized depressed patients found significant reductions in depression among patients who were prescribed an aerobic exercise program, but not in a control group who participated in occupational therapy. Another study[15] randomly assigned patients to 8 weeks of walking and jogging, recreational therapy, or a waiting list. Depression scores decreased only in the walking and jogging group.

There is no evidence that any one kind of exercise has a greater impact on depression than others, though many studies have used running or other aerobic activities. In one trial,[16] 40 depressed women were randomly assigned to 8 weeks of running, a weight-lifting program, or a waiting list. Members of both exercise groups were less depressed than the control group at the end of the trial and at later follow-ups; results between the exercise groups were similar. The authors concluded that a positive outcome did not depend on achieving physical fitness. Other studies reached the same conclusion. In a study[11] of hospitalized depressed patients, mood and fitness improved after a walking or jogging program, but there was no correlation between changes in the two parameters.

Nonclinical Populations

Exercise benefits have also been seen in people who are not clinically depressed but are at high risk for depression or have some depressive symptoms.[17-20]

One study[21] examined 55 college students who had had a high number of stressful life events in the previous year. The students were assigned to aerobic exercise training, relaxation training, or no treatment; after the 11-week program, the exercisers scored lower on a standard depression inventory than the other two groups. Another trial[22] involved 43 college women who manifested substantial mood symptoms that fell short of actual depression. They were randomized to participate in 10 weeks of regular aerobic exercise (1 hour, twice a week), relaxation training, or no exercise. Reductions in depression scores were significantly and consistently greater in the aerobics group.

In nonclinical populations, as in clinically depressed patients, most studies found that aerobic and nonaerobic exercise were equally beneficial.[23]

Why Does Exercise Help?

How exercise alleviates depression remains unclear. Psychological and physiologic effects have been suggested.

Psychologically, exercise may enhance one's sense of mastery, which is important for both healthy and depressed individuals who feel a loss of control over their lives. A meta-analysis of 51 studies[24] linked exercise to a small but significant increase in self-esteem. Exercise may provide a therapeutic distraction that diverts a patient's attention from areas of worry, concern, and guilt[25]

In addition, improving one's health, physique, flexibility, and weight may all enhance mood. Many exercisers report that their ability to eat more freely without worries about gaining weight also increases pleasure, satisfaction, and a sense of self-control.

Another benefit is that large-muscle activity may help discharge feelings of pent-up frustration, anger, and hostility.

Researchers continue to study the effects of exercise on the neurochemistry of mood regulation. They are focusing on metabolism and turnover of monoamines and other central neurotransmitters at presynaptic and postsynaptic sites and their role in the mediation of depression. Antidepressant medications, including the selective serotonin reuptake inhibitors (SSRIs), are believed to exert an antidepressant effect by increasing the availability of neurotransmitters at receptor sites. Exercise may exert its beneficial effect on mood by influencing the metabolism and availability of central neurotransmitters.[26-28] A recent study[29] reports that acute exercise increases brain serotonin.

The role of beta-endorphins in mood regulation has received considerable attention. These endogenous chemicals, which reduce pain and can induce euphoria, have been linked to the "runner's high" experienced by intensive exercisers. The ability of exercise to produce enough beta-endorphins to affect depression remains questionable.[30] Several authors[31,32] report elevated levels of beta-endorphins after acute exercise; however, the elevations in fit individuals are lower than in those who are not fit.

One study [33] compared 11 elite runners with a matched group of meditators. After each group engaged in running or meditation, researchers compared them by mood and circulating levels of beta-endorphin and corticotropin-releasing hormone (CRH). Mood and CRH were elevated after both activities, but beta-endorphin was elevated only in the runners, which suggests that an increase in beta-endorphins is not necessary for mood elevation.

Because disturbed sleep is both a symptom of depression and an aggravating factor, the beneficial effects of exercise on sleep may be very important. A recent controlled clinical trial [34] involving 32 older adults (ages 60 to 84) who had major depression or dysthymia demonstrated that a 10-week program of weight training exercise (three times per week) significantly improved all subjective sleep quality and depression measures. Another controlled study [35] of 43 men and women (ages 50 to 76) reported improvement in sleep disturbances after 16 weeks of moderate-intensity exercise. Investigators, however, noted the potential confounding effects of uncontrolled variables such as outdoor light, time of day, and their effects on circadian rhythms; environmental heat; and fitness of the subjects. [36]

The Exercise Prescription

When designing an exercise prescription for patients who have depression, several caveats apply.

Anticipate Barriers

Common symptoms of depression—fatigue, lack of energy, and psychomotor retardation—may pose formidable barriers to physical activity. Feelings of hopelessness and worthlessness may also interfere with motivation to exercise.

Keep Expectations Realistic

Exercise recommendations should be made cautiously. Many depressed patients have a tendency toward self-blame and may see exercise as another occasion for failure. Suggest that physical activity may be quite useful, but do not raise false expectations that can arouse anxiety and guilt. Explain that exercise may be an adjunct to, not a substitute for, primary treatment. A patient eager to escape the stigma and shame surrounding emotional illness (feelings that tend to increase during depression) may want to minimize the condition by viewing exercise as a way to avoid antidepressants and psychotherapy.

Introduce a Feasible Plan

An exercise prescription should be realistic and practical, not an additional burden that may compound the patient's sense of futility. Consider the individual's background and history. For patients who are severely depressed, exercise may need to be postponed until medication and psychotherapy begin to alleviate symptoms. Patients who have been sedentary should start with a light exercise schedule: for example, just a few minutes of walking each day.

When patients find it difficult to start exercising, one might communicate that time is on their side. With treatment, symptoms will yield, and what seems impossible today may become easier two or three weeks later.

Accentuate Pleasurable Aspects

The specific choice of exercise should be guided by the patient's preferences and circumstances. The activity must be pleasurable and easily added to the patient's schedule. Exercise enjoyment has been shown to facilitate adherence.[33]

When appropriate, group activities (for example, exercise classes, walking groups) should be encouraged. Depressed patients who are isolated and withdrawn are likely to benefit from increased social involvement. The stimulation of being outdoors and in a pleasant setting may enhance mood, and exposure to light has been shown to be therapeutic in seasonal depression.

State Specifics

Walking is almost universally acceptable, carries minimal risk of injury, and has been shown to be beneficial for mood enhancement. In keeping with recent American College of Sports Medicine (ACSM) recommendations for healthy adults,[37] a goal of 20 to 60 minutes of walking or other aerobic exercise, three to five times a week, is reasonable. The ACSM also recommends resistance training 2 to 3 days per week and flexibility training 2 to 3 days per week.

Encourage Compliance

More—more intense, more frequent—is not necessarily better. Improved fitness may be a valuable consequence of exercise but is not necessary for an antidepressant effect; however, greater antidepressant effects are seen when training continues beyond 16 weeks.[13] Compliance is likely to be better when the exercise prescribed is less demanding, and one study[38] has linked more intensive programs with increased tension and anxiety. In fact, the "staleness" that some athletes experience with overtraining resembles depression.[39]

Integrating Exercise with Other Treatments

The primary treatments for depression should not present exercise obstacles. Antidepressant medication is frequently prescribed when depression impairs a patient's ability to function. Older tricyclic antidepressants, such as imipramine hydrochloride and amitriptyline hydrochloride, often cause orthostatic hypotension and sedation, which can impair aerobic activity. Tricyclics may cause dangerous arrhythmias in athletes.[39]

The newer antidepressants (for example, fluoxetine hydrochloride, sertraline hydrochloride, paroxetine hydrochloride, nefazodone hydrochloride, and venlafaxine hydrochloride) have better side-effect and safety profiles. Frequently, they are first-choice agents and appear to be compatible with exercise.

The spectrum of brief and long-term psychotherapies is widely used for depression, either alone or with antidepressant medication. An exercise prescription makes a useful contribution to psychotherapy when the goal is to increase patients' overall activity level and add pleasurable, satisfying experiences. The patient's difficulties with exercise, such as motivational problems, fear of interpersonal situations, and/or a tendency to transform exercise into a burdensome chore, may shed light on dysfunctional attitudes that can be explored in psychotherapy.

Maintain Vigilance

Though exercise has few if any adverse effects, some patients may misuse exercise. Those who have anorexia nervosa may undertake extreme physical activity, driven by a disturbed body image. Individuals who are compulsive in other areas of their lives may become compulsive about exercise at the expense of personal relationships and increased injury risk.

These dangers may be obviated somewhat by stressing that exercise, like a prescribed drug, should be "taken as directed" and that more is not necessarily better. If dysfunctional attitudes are significant, they can be addressed in psychotherapy.

References

1. Martinsen EW: Physical activity and depression: clinical experience. *Acta Psychiatr Scand* 1994;377(suppl):23-27

2. American Psychiatric Association: *Diagnostic and Statistical Manual of Mental Disorders: DSM-IV, ed 4.* Washington, DC, American Psychiatric Association, 1994

3. Blazer DG, Kessler RC, McGonagle KA, et al: The prevalence and distribution of major depression in a national community sample: the National Comorbidity Survey. *Am J Psychiatry* 1994;151(7):979-986

4. Weissman MM, Bland R, Joyce PR, et al: Sex differences in rates of depression: cross-national perspectives. *J Affect Disord* 1993;29(2-3):77-84

5. Barefoot JC, Schroll M: Symptoms of depression, acute myocardial infarction, and total mortality in a community sample. *Circulation* 1996;93(11):1976-1980

6. *Depression in Primary Care: Detection, Diagnosis and Treatment. Quick Reference Guide for Clinicians, No. 5.* Rockville, MD, U.S. Dept of Health and Human Services, Public Health Service, Agency for Healthcare Policy and Research; April 1993. AHCPR Publication No. 93-0552

7. Pincus HA, Tanielian TL, Marcus SC, et al: Prescribing trends in psychotropic medications: primary care, psychiatry, and other medical specialties. *JAMA* 1998;279(7):526-530

8. Keller MB, Hanks DL: The natural history and heterogeneity of depressive disorders: implications for rational antidepressant therapy. *J Clin Psychiatry* 1994;55(suppl A):25-33, 98-100

9. Byrne A, Byrne DG: The effect of exercise on depression, anxiety and other mood states: a review. *J Psychosom Res* 1993; 37(6):565-574

10. LaFontaine TP, DiLorenzo TM, Frensch PA, et al: Aerobic exercise and mood: a brief review, 1985-1990. *Sports Med* 1992; 13(3):160-170

11. Sexton H, Maere A, Dahl NH: Exercise intensity and reduction in neurotic symptoms: a controlled follow-up study. *Acta Psychiatr Scand* 1989;80(3):231-235

12. Matinsen EW, Medhus A: Adherence to exercise and patients' evaluation of exercise in a comprehensive treatment programme for depression. *Nord Psykiatr Tidsk* 1989;43(5):411-415

13. North TC, McCullagh P, Tran ZV: Effect of exercise on depression. *Exerc Sport Sci Rev* 1990;18:379-415

14. Matinsen EW, Medhus A, Sandvik L: Effects of aerobic exercise on depression: a controlled study. *Br Med J* (Clin Res Ed) 1985;291(6488):109

15. Hannaford CP, Harrell EH, Ernest H, et al: Psychophysiological effects of a running program on depression and anxiety in a psychiatric population. *Psych Record* 1988;38(1):37-48

16. Doyne EJ, Ossip-Klein DJ, Bowman ED, et al: Running versus weight lifting in the treatment of depression. *J Consult Clin Psychol* 1987;55(5):748-754

17. King AC, Taylor CB, Haskell WL: Effects of differing intensities and formats of 12 months of exercise training on psychological outcomes in older adults. *Health Psychol* 1993;12(4): 292-300 [published erratum in *Health Psychol* 1993;12(5):405]

18. Berger BG, Owen DR, Man F: A brief review of literature and examination of acute mood benefits of exercise in Czechoslovakian and United States swimmers. *Int J Sport Psychol* 1993;24(2):130-150

19. Krause N, Goldenhar L, Liang J, et al: Stress and exercise among the Japanese elderly. *Soc Sci Med* 1993;36(11):1429-1441

20. Steege JF, Blumenthal JA: The effects of aerobic exercise on premenstrual symptoms in middle-aged women: a preliminary study. *J Psychosom Res* 1993;37(2):127-133

21. Roth DL, Holmes DS: Influence of aerobic exercise training and relaxation training on physical and psychological health following stressful life events. *Psychosom Med* 1987;49(4):355-365

22. McCann IL, Holmes DS: Influence of aerobic exercise on depression. *J Person Soc Psychol* 1984;46(5):1142-1147

23. Berger BG, Owen DR: Mood alteration with yoga and swimming: aerobic exercise may not be necessary. *Percept Mot Skills* 1992;75(3 pt 2):1331-1343

24. Spence JC, Poon P, Dyck P: The effect of physical-activity participation on self-concept: a meta-analysis. *J Sport Exer Psy* 1997;19:S109

25. Bahrke MS, Morgan WP: Anxiety reduction following exercise and meditation. *Cognit Ther Res* 1978;2:323-333

26. Syvalahti EK: Biological aspects of depression. *Acta Psychiatr Scand* Suppl 1994;377:11-15

27. Lechin F, van der Dijs B, Orozco B, et al: Plasma neurotransmitters, blood pressure, and heart rate during supine-resting orthostasis, and moderate exercise conditions in major depressed patients. *Biol Psychiatry* 1995;38(3):166-173

28. Dunn AL, Dishman RK: Exercise and the neurobiology of depression. *Exerc Sport Sci Rev* 1991;19:41-98

29. Chaouloff F: Effects of acute physical exercise on central serotonergic systems. *Med Sci Sports Exerc* 1997;29(1):58-62

30. Casper RC: Exercise and mood. *World Rev Nutr Diet* 1993; 71:115-143

31. Carr DB, Bullen BA, Skrinar GS, et al: Physical conditioning facilitates the exercise-induced secretion of beta-endorphin and beta-lipotropin in women. *N Engl J Med* 1981;305(10): 560-563

32. Lobstein DD, Rasmussen CL, Dunphy GE, et al: Beta-endorphin and components of depression as powerful discriminators between joggers and sedentary and middle-aged men. *J Psychosom Res* 1989;33(3):293-305

33. Wankel LM: The importance of enjoyment to adherence and psychological benefits from physical activity. *Int J Sports Psychol* 1993;24(2):151-169

34. Singh NA, Clements KM, Fiatarone MA: A randomized con-
     trolled trial of the effect of exercise on sleep. *Sleep* 1997;20(2):95-
     101

35. King AC, Oman RF, Brassington GS, et al: Moderate-intensity
     exercise and self-rated quality of sleep in older adults: a ran-
     domized controlled trial. *JAMA* 1997;227(1):32-37

36. O'Connor PJ, Youngstedt SD: Influence of exercise on human
     sleep. *Exerc Sport Sci Rev* 1995;23:105-134

37. Pollock ML, Gaesser GA, Butcher JD, et al: The recommended
     quantity and quality of exercise for developing and maintain-
     ing cardiorespiratory and muscular fitness, and flexibility in
     healthy adults. *Med Sci Sports Exerc* 1998;30(6):975-991

38. Berger DG, Owen DR: Stress reduction and mood enhance-
     ment in four exercise modes: swimming, body conditioning,
     Hatha yoga, and fencing. *Res Q Exerc Sport* 1988;59(2):148-
     159

39. Morgan WP, Brown DR, Raglin JS, et al: Psychological moni-
     toring of overtraining and staleness. *Br J Sports Med*
     1987;21(3):107-114

—Section by Michal Artal, MD, with Carl Sherman

Exercise as a Depression-Prevention Tactic

When talking to patients about exercise, physicians can share
information about its probable role in maintaining mental health.
Physical activity may play an important role in preventing depression, according to the surgeon general's report on physical activity and
health.[1]

Cross-sectional epidemiologic studies[2,3] suggest a positive association between exercise and mental health but do not prove a cause-
and-effect relationship. According to the surgeon general's report,
people who have no mental health problems may be more likely to
exercise.

Cohort studies shed light on whether physical activity prevents
mental health problems. In one study[4] of 10,201 male Harvard alumni,
low levels of activity reported during initial interviews (in 1962 or
1966) were inversely related to self-reported physician-diagnosed

depression in 1988. The relative risk of depression was 27% lower for men who reported playing 3 or more hours of sports each week than for those who reported playing no sports. The Harvard alumni study, along with another cohort study,[5] presents limited evidence for a dose-response association between levels of physical activity and depressive symptoms.

The surgeon general's report concludes that some evidence supports a protective role of exercise against depression, but more research is needed to confirm the protective effect and to determine the frequency, duration, and intensity needed to improve mental health.

References

1. U.S. Department of Health and Human Services: *Physical Activity and Health: A Report of the Surgeon General.* Atlanta, DHHS, Centers for Disease Control and Prevention, National Center for Chronic Disease Prevention and Health Promotion, 1996

2. Ross CE, Hayes D: Exercise and psychologic well-being in the community. *Am J Epidemiol* 1988;127(4):762-771

3. Stephens T: Physical activity and mental health in the United States and Canada: evidence from four population surveys. *Prev Med* 1988;17(1):35-47

4. Paffenbarger RS Jr, Lee IM, Leung R: Physical activity and personal characteristics associated with depression and suicide in American college men. *Acta Psychiatr Scand* (suppl) 1994;377:16-22

5. Camacho TC, Roberts RE, Lazarus NB, et al: Physical activity and depression: evidence from the Alameda County Study. *Am J Epidemiol* 1991;13(2):220-231

—Section by Lisa Schnirring

Chapter 40

Treatments for Depression: Study Outcomes

This chapter describes specific types of pharmacotherapies and psychosocial therapies for episodes of depression and mania. Treatment generally targets symptom patterns rather than specific disorders. Differences in the treatment strategy for unipolar and bipolar depression are described where relevant.

Treatment of Major Depressive Episodes

Pharmacotherapies

Antidepressant medications are effective across the full range of severity of major depressive episodes in major depressive disorder and bipolar disorder. The degree of effectiveness, however, varies according to the intensity of the depressive episode. With mild depressive episodes, the overall response rate is about 70 percent, including a placebo rate of about 60 percent. With severe depressive episodes, the overall response rate is much lower, as is the placebo rate. For example, with psychotic depression, the overall response rate to any one drug is only about 20 to 40 percent, including a placebo response rate of less than 10 percent. Psychotic depression is treated with either

"Specific Treatments for Episodes of Depression and Mania," excerpted from "Chapter 4: Mood Disorders," *Mental Health: A Report of the Surgeon General*, Office of the Surgeon General, 1999. The full text of this document, including references, is available online at www.surgeongeneral.gov/library/mentalhealth/.

an antidepressant/antipsychotic combination or electroconvulsive therapy (ECT).

There are four major classes of antidepressant medications. The tricyclic and heterocyclic antidepressants (TCAs and HCAs) are named for their chemical structure. The monoamine oxidase inhibitors (MAOIs) and selective serotonin reuptake inhibitors (SSRIs) are classified by their initial neurochemical effects. In general, MAOIs and SSRIs increase the level of a target neurotransmitter by two distinct mechanisms. But, as discussed below, these classes of medications have many other effects. They also have some differential effects depending on the race or ethnicity of the patient.

The mode of action of antidepressants is complex and only partly understood. Put simply, most antidepressants are designed to heighten the level of a target neurotransmitter at the neuronal synapse. This can be accomplished by one or more of the following therapeutic actions: boosting the neurotransmitter's synthesis, blocking its degradation, preventing its reuptake from the synapse into the presynaptic neuron, or mimicking its binding to postsynaptic receptors. To make matters more complicated, many antidepressant drugs affect more than one neurotransmitter. Explaining how any one drug alleviates depression probably entails multiple therapeutic actions, direct and indirect, on more than one neurotransmitter system.

Selection of a particular antidepressant for a particular patient depends upon the patient's past treatment history, the likelihood of side effects, safety in overdose, and expense. A vast majority of U.S. psychiatrists favor the SSRIs as "first-line" medications. These agents are viewed more favorably than the TCAs because of their ease of use, more manageable side effects, and safety in overdose. Perhaps the major drawback of the SSRIs is their expense: they are only available as name brands (until 2002 when they began to come off patent). At minimum, SSRI therapy costs about $80 per month, and patients taking higher doses face proportionally greater costs.

Four SSRIs have been approved by the FDA for treatment of depression: fluoxetine, sertraline, paroxetine, and citalopram. A fifth SSRI, fluvoxamine, is approved for treatment of obsessive-compulsive disorder, yet is used off-label for depression. [Technically, FDA approves drugs for a selected indication (a disorder in a certain population). However, once the drug is marketed, doctors are at liberty to prescribe it for unapproved (off-label) indications.] There are few compelling reasons to pick one SSRI over another for treatment of uncomplicated major depression, because they are more similar than different. There are, however, several distinguishing pharmacokinetic differences between SSRIs, including elimination half-life (the time it takes for the plasma level of the drug to decrease 50 percent from steady-state), propensity for drug-drug interactions (for example, via inhibition of liver enzymes), and antidepressant activity of metabolite(s). In general, SSRIs are more likely to be metabolized more slowly by African Americans and Asians, resulting in higher blood levels.

The SSRIs as a class of drugs have their own class-specific side effects, including nausea, diarrhea, headache, tremor, daytime sedation, failure to achieve orgasm, nervousness, and insomnia. Attrition from acute phase therapy because of side effects is typically 10 to 20 percent. The incidence of treatment-related suicidal thoughts for the SSRIs is low and comparable to the rate observed for other antidepressants, despite reports to the contrary.

Some concern persists that the SSRIs are less effective than the TCAs for treatment of severe depressions, including melancholic and psychotic subtypes. Yet there is no definitive answer.

Side effects and potential lethality in overdose are the major drawbacks of the TCAs. An overdose of as little as 7-day supply of a TCA can result in potentially fatal cardiac arrhythmias. TCA treatment is typically initiated at lower dosages and titrated upward with careful attention to response and side effects. Doses for African Americans and Asians should be monitored more closely, because their slower metabolism of TCAs can lead to higher blood concentrations. Similarly, studies also suggest that there may be gender differences in drug metabolism and that plasma levels may change over the course of the menstrual cycle.

In addition to the four major classes of antidepressants are bupropion, which is discussed below, and three newer FDA-approved antidepressants that have mixed or compound synaptic effects. Venlafaxine, the first of these newer antidepressants, inhibits reuptake of both serotonin and, at higher doses, norepinephrine. In contrast to the TCAs, venlafaxine has somewhat milder side effects, which are like those of the SSRIs. Venlafaxine also has a low risk of cardiotoxicity and, although experience is limited, it appears to be less toxic than the others in overdose. Venlafaxine has shown promise in treatment of severe or refractory depressive states and is superior to fluoxetine in one inpatient study. Venlafaxine also occasionally causes increased blood pressure, and this can be a particular concern at higher doses.

Nefazodone, the second newer antidepressant, is unique in terms of both structure and neurochemical effects. In contrast to the SSRIs, nefazodone improves sleep efficiency. Its side effect profile is comparable

313

to the other newer antidepressants, but it has the advantage of a lower rate of sexual side effects. The more recently FDA-approved antidepressant, mirtazapine, blocks two types of serotonin receptors, the 5-HT2 and 5-HT3 receptors. Mirtazapine is also a potent antihistamine and tends to be more sedating than most other newer antidepressants. Weight gain can be another troublesome side effect.

Table 40.1 presents summary findings on newer pharmacotherapies from a review of the treatment of depression by the Agency for Healthcare Research and Quality (AHRQ). There have been few studies of gender differences in clinical response to treatments for depression. One report found women with chronic depression to respond better to a SSRI than a tricyclic, yet the opposite for men. This effect was primarily in premenopausal women. The AHRQ report also noted

Table 40.1. Treatment of depression—newer pharmacotherapies: Summary findings (Source: Agency for Healthcare Quality and Research, 1999).

- Newer antidepressant drugs (SSRIs and all other antidepressants marketed subsequently) are effective treatments for major depression and dysthymia.

  They are efficacious in primary care and specialty mental health care settings:

  Major depression:
  > 50 percent response to active agent
  > 32 percent response to placebo

  Dysthymia (fluoxetine, sertraline, and amisulpride):
  > 59 percent response to active agent
  > 37 percent response to placebo

- Both older and newer antidepressants demonstrate similar efficacy.

- Drop-out rates due to all causes combined are similar for newer and older agents:

  > Drop-out rates due to adverse effects are slightly higher for older agents.

  > Newer agents are often easier to use because of single daily dosing and less titration.

that there were almost no data to address the efficacy of pharmacotherapies in postpartum or pregnant women.

Alternate Pharmacotherapies

Regardless of the initial choice of pharmacotherapy, about 30 to
50 percent of patients do not respond to the initial medication. It has
not been established firmly whether patients who respond poorly to
one class of antidepressants should be switched automatically to an
alternate class. Several studies have examined the efficacy of the TCAs
and SSRIs when used in sequence. Approximately 30 to 50 percent of
those not responsive to one class will respond to the other.

Among other types of antidepressants, the MAOIs and bupropion
are important alternatives for SSRI and TCA nonresponders. These
agents also may be relatively more effective than TCAs or SSRIs for
treatment of depressions characterized by atypical or reversed vegetative symptoms. Bupropion and the MAOIs also are good choices
to treat bipolar depression. Bupropion also has the advantage of a low
rate of sexual side effects.

Bupropion's efficacy and overall side effect profile might justify its
first-line use for all types of depression. Furthermore, bupropion has a
novel neurochemical profile in terms of effects on dopamine and norepinephrine. However, worries about an increased risk of seizures delayed bupropion's introduction to the U.S. market by more than 5
years. Although clearly effective for a broad range of depressions, use
of the MAOIs has been limited for decades by concerns that when taken
with certain foods containing the chemical tyramine (for example, some
aged cheeses and red wines); these medications may cause a potentially lethal hypertensive reaction. There has been continued interest in development of safer, selective and reversible MAOIs.

Hypericum (St. John's Wort). The widespread publicity and use
of the botanical product from the yellow-flowering *Hypericum
perforatum* plant with or without medical supervision is well ahead
of the science database supporting the effectiveness of this putative
antidepressant. Controlled trials, mainly in Germany, have been positive in mild-to-moderate depression, with only mild gastrointestinal
side effects reported. However, most of those studies were method-
ologically flawed, in areas including diagnosis (more similar to adjustment disorder with depressed mood than major depression), length
of trial (often an inadequate 4 weeks), and either lack of placebo control or unusually low or high placebo response rates.

Post-marketing surveillance in Germany, which found few adverse effects of *Hypericum*, depended upon spontaneous reporting of side effects by patients, an approach that would not be considered acceptable in the U.S. In clinical use, the most commonly encountered adverse effect noted appears to be sensitivity to sunlight.

Basic questions about mechanism of action and even the optimal formulation of a pharmaceutical product from the plant remain; dosage in the randomized German trials varied by sixfold. Several pharmacologically active components of St. John's wort, including hypericin, have been identified; although their long half-lives in theory should permit once daily dosing, in practice a schedule of 300 mg three times a day is most commonly used. While initial speculation about significant MAO-inhibiting properties of *Hypericum* have been largely discounted, possible serotonergic mechanisms suggest that combining this agent with an SSRI or other serotonergic antidepressant should be approached with caution. However, data regarding safety of hypericum in preclinical models or clinical samples are few. At least two placebo-controlled trials in the United States are under way to compare the efficacy of *Hypericum* with that of an SSRI.

Augmentation Strategies

The transition from one antidepressant to another is time consuming, and patients sometimes feel worse in the process. Many clinicians bypass these problems by using a second medication to augment an ineffective antidepressant. The best studied strategies of this type are lithium augmentation, thyroid augmentation, and TCA-SSRI combinations.

Increasingly, clinicians are adding a noradrenergic TCA to an ineffective SSRI or vice versa. In an earlier era, such polypharmacy (the prescription of multiple drugs at the same time) was frowned upon. Thus far, the evidence supporting TCA-SSRI combinations is not conclusive. Caution is needed when using these agents in combination because SSRIs inhibit metabolism of several TCAs, resulting in a substantial increase in blood levels and toxicity or other adverse side effects from TCAs.

Psychotherapy and Counseling

Many people prefer psychotherapy or counseling over medication for treatment of depression. Research conducted in the past two decades has helped to establish at least several newer forms of time-limited psychotherapy as being as effective as antidepressant pharmaco-therapy in mild-to-moderate depressions. The newer depression-specific therapies include cognitive-behavioral therapy and interpersonal psycho-therapy. These approaches use a time-limited approach, a present tense ("here-and-now") focus, and emphasize patient education and active collaboration. Interpersonal psychotherapy centers around four common problem areas: role disputes, role transitions, unresolved grief, and social deficits. Cognitive-behavioral therapy takes a more structured approach by emphasizing the interactive nature of thoughts, emotions, and behavior. It also helps the depressed patient to learn how to improve coping and lessen symptom distress.

There is no evidence that cognitive-behavioral therapy and inter-personal psychotherapy are differentially effective. As reported ear-lier, both therapies appear to have some relapse prevention effects, although they are much less studied than the pharmacotherapies. Other more traditional forms of counseling and psychotherapy have not been extensively studied using a randomized clinical trial design. It is important to determine if these more traditional treatments, as commonly practiced, are as effective as interpersonal psychotherapy or cognitive-behavioral therapy.

The brevity of this section reflects the succinctness of the findings on the effectiveness of these interventions as well as the lack of dif-ferential responses and "side effects." It does not reflect a preference or superiority of medication except in conditions such as psychotic depression where psychotherapies are not effective.

Bipolar Depression

Treatment of bipolar depression (this refers to episodes with symp-toms of depression in patients diagnosed with bipolar disorder) has received surprisingly little study. Most psychiatrists prescribe the same antidepressants for treatment of bipolar depression as for ma-jor depressive disorder, although evidence is lacking to support this practice. It also is not certain that the same strategies should be used for treatment of depression in bipolar II (major depression plus a his-tory of hypomania) and bipolar I (major depression with a history of at least one prior manic episode) (definitions according to the *Diag-nostic and Statistical Manual of Mental Disorders, Fourth Edition*; commonly abbreviated *DSM-IV*).

Pharmacotherapy of bipolar depression typically begins with lithium or an alternate mood stabilizer. Mood stabilizers reduce the risk of cycling and have modest antidepressant effects; response rates of 30 to 50 percent are typical. For bipolar depressions refractory to mood stabilizers, an antidepressant is typically added. Bipolar depression may be more responsive to nonsedating antidepressants, including the MAOIs, SSRIs, and bupropion. The optimal length of continuation phase pharmacotherapy of bipolar depression has not been established empirically. During the continuation phase, the risk of depressive relapse must be counterbalanced against the risk of inducing mania or rapid cycling. Although not all studies are in agreement, antidepressants may increase mood cycling in a vulnerable subgroup, such as women with bipolar II disorder. Lithium is associated with increased risk of congenital anomalies when taken during the first trimester of pregnancy, and the anticonvulsants are contraindicated. This is problematic in view of the high risk of recurrence in pregnant bipolar women.

Pharmacotherapy, Psychosocial Therapy, and Multimodal Therapy

The relative efficacy of pharmacotherapy and the newer forms of psychosocial treatment, such as interpersonal psychotherapy and the cognitive-behavioral therapies, is a controversial topic. For major depressive episodes of mild to moderate severity, meta-analyses of randomized clinical trials document the relative equivalence of these treatments. Yet for patients with bipolar and psychotic depression, who were excluded from these studies, pharmacotherapy is required; there is no evidence that these types of depressive episodes can be effectively treated with psychotherapy alone. Current standards of practice suggest that therapists who withhold somatic treatments (pharmacotherapy or ECT) from such patients risk malpractice.

For patients hospitalized with depression, somatic therapies also are considered the standard of care. Again, there is little evidence for the efficacy of psychosocial treatments alone when used instead of pharmacotherapy, although several studies suggest that carefully selected inpatients may respond to intensive cognitive-behavioral therapy. However, in an era in which inpatient stays are measured in days, rather than in weeks, this option is seldom feasible. Combined therapies emphasizing both pharmacologic and intensive psychosocial treatments hold greater promise to improve the outcome of hospitalized patients, particularly if inpatient care is followed by ambulatory treatment.

Combined therapies—also called multimodal treatments—are especially valuable for outpatients with severe forms of depression.

According to a recent meta-analysis of six studies, combined therapy (cognitive or interpersonal psychotherapy plus pharmacotherapy) was significantly more effective than psychotherapy alone for more severe recurrent depression. In milder depressions, psychotherapy alone was nearly as effective as combined therapy. This meta-analysis was unable to compare combined therapy with pharmacotherapy alone or placebo due to an insufficient number of patients.

In summary, the *DSM-IV* definition of major depressive disorder spans a heterogenous group of conditions that benefit from psychosocial and/or pharmacological therapies. People with mild to moderate depression respond to psychotherapy or pharmacotherapy alone. People with severe depression require pharmacotherapy or ECT and they may also benefit from the addition of psychosocial therapy.

Preventing Relapse of Major Depressive Episodes

Recurrent Depression. Maintenance pharmacotherapy is the best-studied means to reduce the risk of recurrent depression. The magnitude of effectiveness in prevention of recurrent depressive episodes depends on the dose of the active agent used, the inherent risk of the population (chronicity, age, and number of prior episodes), the length of time being considered, and the patient's adherence to the treatment regimen. Early studies, which tended to use lower dosages of medications, generally documented a twofold advantage relative to placebo (for example, 60 vs. 30 percent). In a more recent study of recurrent unipolar depression, the drug-placebo difference was nearly fivefold. This trial, in contrast to earlier randomized clinical trials, used a much higher dosage of imipramine, suggesting that full-dose maintenance pharmacotherapy may improve prophylaxis. Indeed, this was subsequently confirmed in a randomized clinical trial comparing full- and half-dose maintenance strategies.

There are few published studies on the prophylactic benefits of long-term pharmacotherapy with SSRIs, bupropion, nefazodone, or venlafaxine. However, available studies uniformly document 1-year efficacy rates of 80 to 90 percent in preventing recurrence of depression. Thus, maintenance therapy with the newer agents is likely to yield outcomes comparable to the TCAs.

How does maintenance pharmacotherapy compare with psychotherapy?

In one study of recurrent depression, monthly sessions of maintenance interpersonal psychotherapy had a 3-year success rate of about

35 percent (a rate falling between those for active and placebo pharmacotherapy). Subsequent studies found maintenance interpersonal psychotherapy to be either a powerful or ineffective prophylactic therapy, depending on the patient/treatment match.

Bipolar Depression. No recent randomized clinical trials have examined prophylaxis against recurrent depression in bipolar disorder. In one older, well-controlled study, recurrence rates of more than 60 percent were observed despite maintenance treatment with lithium, either alone or in combination with imipramine.

Treatment of Mania

Acute Phase Efficacy

Success rates of 80 to 90 percent were once expected with lithium for the acute phase treatment of mania; however, lithium response rates of only 40 to 50 percent are now commonplace. Most recent studies thus underscore the limitations of lithium in mania. The apparent decline in lithium responsiveness may be partly due to sampling bias (university hospitals treat more refractory patients), but could also be attributable to factors such as younger age of onset, increased drug abuse comorbidity, or shorter therapeutic trials necessitated by briefer hospital stay. The effectiveness of acute phase lithium treatment also is partially dependent on the clinical characteristics of the manic episode: dysphoric/mixed, psychotic, and rapid cycling episodes are less responsive to lithium alone.

A number of other medications initially developed for other indications are increasingly used for lithium-refractory or lithium-intolerant mania. The efficacy of two medications, the anticonvulsants carbamazepine and divalproex sodium, has been documented in randomized clinical trials. Divalproex sodium has received FDA approval for the treatment of mania. The specific mechanisms of action for these agents have not been established, although they may stabilize neuronal membrane systems, including the cyclic adenosine monophosphate second messenger system. The anticonvulsant medications under investigation for their effectiveness in mania include lamotrigine and gabapentin.

Another newer treatment, verapamil, is a calcium channel blocker initially approved by the FDA for treatment of cardiac arrhythmias and hypertension. Since the mid-1980s, clinical reports and evidence from small randomized clinical trials suggest that the calcium channel blockers may have antimanic effects. Like lithium and the anticonvulsants, the mechanism of action of verapamil has not been established. There is evidence of abnormalities of intracellular calcium levels in bipolar disorder, and calcium's role in modulating second messenger systems has spurred continued interest in this class of medication. If effective, verapamil does have the additional advantage of having a lower potential for causing birth defects than does lithium, divalproex, or carbamazepine.

Adjunctive neuroleptics and high-potency benzodiazepines are used often in combination with mood stabilizers to treat mania. The very real risk of tardive dyskinesia has led to a shift in favor of adjunctive use of benzodiazepines instead of neuroleptics for acute stabilization of mania. The novel antipsychotic clozapine has shown promise in otherwise refractory manic states, although such treatment requires careful monitoring to help protect against development of agranulocytosis, a potentially lethal bone marrow toxicity. Other newer antipsychotic medications, including risperidone and olanzapine, have safer side effect profiles than clozapine and are now being studied in mania. For manic patients who are not responsive to or tolerant of pharmacotherapy, ECT is a viable alternative.

Maintenance Treatment to Prevent Recurrences of Mania

The efficacy of lithium for prevention of mania also appears to be significantly lower now than in previous decades; recurrence rates of 40 to 60 percent are now typical despite ongoing lithium therapy. Still, more than 20 studies document the effectiveness of lithium in preventing suicide. Medication noncompliance almost certainly plays a role in the failure of longer term lithium maintenance therapy. Indeed, abrupt discontinuation of lithium has been shown to accelerate the risk of relapse. Medication "holidays" may similarly induce a lithium-refractory state, although data are conflicting. As noted earlier, antidepressant co-therapy also may accelerate cycle frequency or induce lithium-resistant rapid cycling.

With increasing recognition of the limitations of lithium prophylaxis, the anticonvulsants are used increasingly for maintenance therapy of bipolar disorder. Several randomized clinical trials have demonstrated the prophylactic efficacy of carbamazepine, whereas the value of divalproex preventive therapy is only supported by uncontrolled studies. Because of increased risk of birth defects associated with these agents, there is a need to obtain and evaluate information on alternative interventions for women with bipolar disorder of child-bearing age.

Service Delivery for Mood Disorders

The mood disorders are associated with significant suffering and high social costs. Many treatments are efficacious, yet in the case of depression, significant numbers of individuals either receive no care or inappropriate care. Limitations in insurance benefits or in the management strategies employed in managed care arrangements may make it impossible to deliver recommended treatments. In addition, treatment outcome in real-world practice is not as effective as that demonstrated in clinical trials, a problem known as the gap between efficacy and effectiveness. The gap is greatest in the primary care setting, although it also is observed in specialty mental health practice. There is a need to develop case identification approaches for women in obstetrics/gynecology settings due to the high risk of recurrence in childbearing women with bipolar disorder. Little attention also has been paid to screening and mental health services for women in obstetrics/gynecology settings despite their high risk of depression.

Primary care practice has been studied extensively, revealing low rates of both recognition and appropriate treatment of depression. Approximately one-third to one-half of patients with major depression go unrecognized in primary care settings. Poor recognition leads to unnecessary and expensive diagnostic procedures, particularly in response to patients' vague somatic complaints. Fewer than one-half receive antidepressant medication according to Agency for Healthcare Research and Quality (AHRQ) recommendations for dosage and duration. About 40 percent discontinue their medication on their own during the first 4 to 6 weeks of treatment, and fewer still continue their medication for the recommended period of 6 months. Although drug treatment is the most common strategy for treating depression in primary care practice, about one-half of primary care physicians express a preference to include counseling or therapy as a component of treatment. Few primary care practitioners, however, have formal training in psychotherapy, nor do they have the time. A variety of strategies have been developed to improve the management of depression in primary care settings.

Part Four

Depression and Common Co-Occurring Disorders

Chapter 41

Depression Co-Occurring with General Medical Disorders

Depression Co-Occurs with Medical Illnesses

Clinical depression commonly co-occurs with general medical illnesses, though it often goes undetected and untreated. In fact, while the rate of major depression among persons in the community is estimated to be between two to four percent, among primary care patients it is between five and ten percent and among medical inpatients it is between ten and fourteen percent. And an additional two to three times as many persons in these groups experience depressive symptoms. Research suggests that recognition and treatment of co-occurring depression may improve the outcome of the medical condition, enhance quality of life, and reduce the degree of pain and disability experienced by the medical patient.

What Is Depression?

Clinical depression is a common and highly treatable illness affecting over 19 million American adults—with or without a co-occurring condition—this year. Unfortunately, nearly two thirds of them do not get treatment, in part, because the effects of depression are not understood to be symptoms of an illness. With proper treatment, however, nearly 80% of those with depressive illness can feel better, and most within a matter of weeks.

"Depression Co-Occurring with General Medical Disorders: Awareness and Treatment Can Improve Overall Health and Reduce Suffering," a fact sheet produced by the National Institute of Mental Health, updated June 1999.

A Whole Body Illness

Depression affects mood, thought, body, and behavior. For some, it occurs in one or more relatively severe episodes, known as major depression. Others have ongoing, less severe but also debilitating symptoms, known as dysthymia. And still others have bipolar disorder (also known as manic depressive illness), where episodes of terrible lows alternate with excessive highs.

Symptoms of Depression

- Persistent, sad or empty mood
- Loss of interest or pleasure in ordinary activities, including sex
- Decreased energy, fatigue, being slowed down
- Sleep disturbances (insomnia, early-morning waking, or over-sleeping)
- Eating disturbances (loss of appetite and weight, or weight gain)
- Difficult concentrating, remembering, making decisions
- Feelings of guilt, worthlessness, helplessness
- Thoughts of death or suicide; suicide attempts
- Irritability
- Excessive crying
- Chronic aches and pains that don't respond to treatment

Symptoms of Mania

- Excessively high mood
- Irritability
- Decreased need for sleep
- Increased energy and activity
- Increased talking, moving, and sexual activity
- Racing thoughts
- Poor judgment or decision-making
- Grandiose notions
- Being easily distracted

If a person has five or more of these symptoms for more than two weeks, it is important that these symptoms be brought to the attention of the individual's health care provider.

Accurate Diagnosis Is Important

Since some symptoms are common to both depression and certain medical disorders, accurate diagnosis is critical to developing an effective plan for treatment. For example, symptoms of depression such as weight loss, sleep disturbances, and low energy, may also occur in diabetes, thyroid disorders, some neurologic disorders, heart disease, cancer, and stroke. Other depressive symptoms, such as loss of interest or memory, also occur early in the course of disorders such as Parkinson's and Alzheimer's disease. In addition, achiness or fatigue may be present in many other conditions. In such cases, careful assessment of an individual's emotional state, and personal and family histories can help determine if one or two illnesses are present.

Other Diagnostic Concerns

The relationship of clinical depression to a medical illness can be varied. Depression can occur as the biological result of a condition such as an underactive thyroid, or can be the side-effect of one or a combination of medications, including over-the-counter medications. In such cases, the depression may be relieved by a change in dosage or type of treatment(s). On the other hand, it is not unusual for a traumatic diagnosis, such as cancer, to trigger a period of depressive symptomatology including sadness, poor concentration, anxiety, or withdrawal. Careful monitoring of the length and severity of depressive symptoms can determine if clinical depression is an additional diagnosis.

Depression Is Treatable

When depressive illness is a co-occurring condition, it should be treated. With treatment, up to 80% of those with depression can show improvement, usually in a matter of weeks. Common interventions include a range of antidepressant medications, focused short-term psychotherapy, or a combination of the two. In addition, in special circumstances, electroconvulsive therapy (ECT), a safe and effective treatment, may be considered as an option. Which treatment is recommended depends on the severity of the depression, the type of co-occurring illness and its treatment, and, to some degree, on individual preference. In addition, maximizing the treatment of the medical disorder may also help to diminish the depressive symptoms.

Treatment of depression can improve a patient's overall quality of life in several ways. It may enhance the ability to follow the treatment regimen for the co-occurring medical condition, decreasing complications and improving the eventual outcome. In addition, effective management of depression can lessen the degree to which the patient is irritable, demanding, or experiences overall problems in functioning, any of which may contribute to slower or more difficult recovery, and greater stress and disability from the medical condition. Finally, controlling the depression will often improve the cognitive symptoms that are a part of some illnesses.

The Path to Healing

Whether or not it co-occurs with medical illness, overcoming depression requires recognition of symptoms, and evaluation and treatment by a qualified health or mental health professional. Success involves a partnership with a health care provider so that an individual's concerns can be addressed. Negative thinking is a part of the depression that will fade as symptoms resolve. Family and friends can help by encouraging the depressed person to seek or remain in treatment, and by offering emotional support. In addition, the following may be helpful adjuncts to treatment: support groups, mild exercise or hobbies, reading self-help materials.

For free brochures on depression and its treatment, call the National Institute of Mental Health: 1-800-421-4211 or visit NIMH online at www.nimh.nih.gov.

Chapter 42

Depression and Alzheimer's Disease

Do people with Alzheimer's disease become depressed?

Yes. Depression is very common among people with Alzheimer's disease. About half of these people have serious depression. In many cases, they become depressed when they realize that their memory and ability to function are getting worse.

Unfortunately, depression may make it even harder for a person with Alzheimer's disease to function, to remember things and to enjoy life.

How can I tell if my family member with Alzheimer's disease is depressed?

It may be difficult for you to know if your family member is depressed. You can look for some of the typical signs of depression:

- Not wanting to move or do things (called apathy)
- Expressing feelings of worthlessness and sadness
- Refusing to eat and losing weight
- Sleeping too much or too little

Other signs of depression include crying and being unusually emotional, being angry or agitated, and being confused. Your family member with Alzheimer's disease may refuse to help with his or her own personal care (for example, getting dressed or taking medicines). He or she may wander away from home more often.

Alzheimer's disease and depression have many symptoms that are alike. It can be hard to tell the difference between them. More than half of patients with Alzheimer's become depressed. If you think that depression is a problem for your relative with Alzheimer's disease, talk to his or her family doctor.

How can the doctor help?

Your relative's family doctor will want to check him or her. The doctor will talk with your relative. The doctor will also ask you and other family members and caregivers about whether the person has any new or changed behaviors. The doctor may wish to do some tests to rule out other medical problems. He or she may suggest medicines to help your family member feel better. The doctor may also have some advice for you and other family members and caregivers on how to cope. He or she may recommend support groups that can help you.

What medicines can help reduce depression?

Antidepressant medicines can be very helpful for people with Alzheimer's disease and depression. These medicines can improve the symptoms of sadness and depression, and may also improve appetite and sleep problems. Don't worry—these medicines are not habit-forming. The doctor may also suggest other medicines that can help reduce upsetting problems, such as hallucinations or anxiety.

What can I do to help my family member?

Try to keep a daily routine for your family member who has Alzheimer's disease. Avoid loud noises and overstimulation. A pleasant environment with familiar faces and mementos helps soothe fear and anxiety. Have a realistic expectation of what your family member can do. Expecting too much can make you both feel frustrated and upset. Let your family member help with simple, enjoyable tasks, such as preparing meals, gardening, doing crafts, and sorting photos. Most of all, be positive. Frequent praise for your family member will help him or her feel better—and it will help you as well.

As the caregiver of a person with Alzheimer's disease, you must also take care of yourself. If you become too tired and frustrated, you will be less able to help your family member. Ask for help from relatives, friends, and local community organizations. Respite care (short-term care that is given to the patient with Alzheimer's disease in order to provide relief for the caregiver) may be available from your local senior citizens' group or a social services agency. Look for caregiver support groups. Other people who are dealing with the same problems may have some good ideas on how you can cope better and on how to make caregiving easier. Adult day care centers may be helpful. They can give your family member a consistent environment and a chance to socialize.

Where can I learn more about caring for my family member with Alzheimer's disease?

A book called *The 36-Hour Day* (Johns Hopkins University Press; 410-516-6900) explains Alzheimer's disease and gives information about resources for caregivers. It gives ideas about things you can do to deal with behavior problems in an Alzheimer's patient. One chapter discusses mood disorders and depression in these patients.

You can also contact one of the following organizations for more information:

- Alzheimer's Association (800-272-3900; http://www.alz.org)
- The National Alliance for the Mentally Ill (800-950-6264; http://www.nami.org)
- The National Mental Health Association (800-969-6642; http://www.nmha.org)
- National Institute on Aging (800-222-2225; http://www.nia.nih.gov)

Chapter 43

Depression and Cancer

Introduction

This patient summary on depression and suicide is adapted from a summary written for health professionals by cancer experts. This and other credible information about cancer treatment, screening, prevention, supportive care, and ongoing clinical trials, is available from the National Cancer Institute.

Depression is a disabling illness that affects about 15% to 25% of cancer patients. This brief summary describes the causes and treatment of depression and risk factors and prevention of suicide in adults and children who have cancer.

Overview

People who face a diagnosis of cancer will experience different levels of stress and emotional upset. Fear of death, interruption of life plans, changes in body image and self-esteem, changes in the social role and lifestyle, and money and legal concerns are important issues in the life of any person with cancer, yet serious depression is not experienced by everyone who is diagnosed with cancer.

There are many misconceptions about cancer and how people cope with it, such as the following: all people with cancer are depressed;

PDQ® Cancer Information Summary. National Cancer Institute; Bethesda, MD. Depression (PDQ®): Supportive Care - Patient. Updated 01/2002. Available at: http://www.cancer.gov. Accessed March 9, 2002.

depression in a person with cancer is normal; treatment does not help the depression; and everyone with cancer faces suffering and a painful death. Sadness and grief are normal reactions to the crises faced during cancer, and will be experienced at times by all people. Since sadness is common, it is important to distinguish between normal levels of sadness and depression. An important part of cancer care is the recognition of depression that needs to be treated. Some people may have more trouble adjusting to the diagnosis of cancer than others. Major depression is not simply sadness or a blue mood. Major depression affects about 25% of patients and has common symptoms that can be diagnosed and treated.

Reactions of sadness and grief will be experienced by all people periodically throughout diagnosis, treatment, and survival of cancer. When people find out they have cancer, they often have feelings of disbelief, denial, or despair. They may also experience difficulty sleeping, loss of appetite, anxiety, and a preoccupation with worries about the future. These symptoms and fears usually lessen as a person adjusts to the diagnosis. Signs that a person has adjusted to the diagnosis include an ability to maintain active involvement in daily life activities, and an ability to continue functioning as spouse, parent, employee, or other roles by incorporating treatment into his or her schedule. A person who cannot adjust to the diagnosis after a long period of time, and who loses interest in usual activities, may be depressed. Mild symptoms of depression can be distressing and may be helped with counseling. Even patients without obvious symptoms of depression may benefit from counseling. However, when symptoms are intense and long-lasting, or when they keep coming back, more intensive treatment is important.

Diagnosis

The symptoms of major depression include having a depressed mood for most of the day and on most days; loss of pleasure and interest in most activities; changes in eating and sleeping habits; nervousness or sluggishness; tiredness; feelings of worthlessness or inappropriate guilt; poor concentration; and constant thoughts of death or suicide. To make a diagnosis of depression, these symptoms should be present for at least two weeks. The diagnosis of depression can be difficult to make in people with cancer due to the difficulty of separating the symptoms of depression from the side effects of medications or the symptoms of cancer. This is especially true in patients undergoing active cancer treatment or those with advanced disease. Symptoms of guilt, worthlessness, hopelessness, thoughts of suicide, and loss of pleasure are the most useful in diagnosing depression in people who have cancer.

Risk Factors for Depression and Suicidal Thoughts

Some people with cancer may have a higher risk for developing depression. The cause of depression is not known, but the risk of developing depression is increased by depression at the time of cancer diagnosis; a history of depression; poorly controlled pain; lack of family support; a family history of depression or suicide; previous suicide attempts; a history of alcoholism or drug abuse; an advanced stage of cancer; other life events that produce stress; increased physical impairment or pain; cancer of the pancreas; being unmarried; feelings of hopelessness, helplessness, worthlessness, and/or guilt; other illnesses that produce symptoms of depression (such as a stroke or heart attack); and treatment with some anticancer drugs.

The evaluation of depression in people with cancer should include a careful evaluation of the person's thoughts about the illness; medical history; personal or family history of depression or suicide; current mental status; physical status; side effects of treatment and the disease; other stresses in the person's life; and support available to the patient. Thinking of suicide, when it occurs, is frightening for the individual, for the health care worker, and for the family. Suicidal statements may range from an offhand comment resulting from frustration or disgust with a treatment course, "If I have to have one more bone marrow aspiration this year, I'll jump out the window," to a statement indicating deep despair and an emergency situation: "I can't stand what this disease is doing to all of us, and I am going to kill myself." Exploring the seriousness of these thoughts is important. If the thoughts of suicide seem to be serious, then the patient should be referred to a psychiatrist or psychologist, and the safety of the patient should be secured.

Reactive Depression

The most common type of depression in people with cancer is called reactive depression. This shows up as feeling moody and being unable to perform usual activities. The symptoms last longer and are more pronounced than a normal and expected reaction, but they do not meet the criteria for major depression. When these symptoms greatly interfere with a person's daily activities, such as work, school,

335

shopping, or caring for a household, they should be treated in the same way that major depression is treated (such as crisis intervention, counseling, and medication, especially with drugs that can quickly relieve distressing symptoms). Basing the diagnosis on just these symptoms can be a problem in a person with advanced disease since the illness may be causing decreased functioning. In more advanced illness, focusing on despair, guilty thoughts, and a total lack of enjoyment of life is helpful in diagnosing depression.

Medical Factors

Medical factors may also cause depression in cancer patients. Medication usually helps this type of depression more effectively than counseling, especially if the medical factors cannot be changed (for example, dosages of the medications that are causing the depression cannot be changed or stopped). Some medical causes of depression in cancer patients include uncontrolled pain; abnormal levels of calcium, sodium, or potassium in the blood; anemia; vitamin B_{12} or folate deficiency; fever; and abnormal levels of thyroid hormone or steroids in the blood.

Treatment

Major depression may be treated with a combination of counseling and medications, such as antidepressants. A primary care doctor may prescribe medications for depression and refer the patient to a psychiatrist or psychologist for the following reasons: a physician or oncologist is not comfortable treating the depression (for example, the patient has suicidal thoughts); the symptoms of depression do not improve after two to four weeks of treatment; the symptoms are getting worse; the side effects of the medication keep the patient from taking the dosage needed to control the depression; and/or the symptoms are interfering with the patient's ability to continue medical treatment.

Medications

Antidepressants are safe for cancer patients to use and are usually effective in the treatment of depression and its symptoms. Unfortunately, antidepressants are not often prescribed for cancer patients. About 25% of all cancer patients are depressed, but only about 2% receive medication for the depression. The choice of antidepressant depends on the patient's symptoms, potential side effects of the antidepressant, and the person's individual medical problems and previous response to antidepressant drugs.

St. John's wort (*Hypericum perforatum*) has been used as an over-the-counter supplement for mood enhancement. In the United States, dietary supplements are regulated as foods not drugs. Supplements are not required to be approved by the Food and Drug Administration (FDA) before being put on the market. Because there are no standards for product manufacturing consistency, dose, or purity, the safety of St. John's wort is not known. The FDA has issued a warning that there is a significant drug interaction between St. John's wort and indinavir (a drug used to treat HIV infection). When St. John's wort and indinavir are taken together, indinavir is less effective. Patients with symptoms of depression should be evaluated by a health professional and not self-treat with St. John's wort. St. John's wort is not recommended for major depression in patients who have cancer.

Most antidepressants take three to six weeks to begin working. The side effects must be considered when deciding which antidepressant to use. For example, a medication that causes sleepiness may be helpful in an anxious patient who is having problems sleeping, since the drug is both calming and sedating. Patients who cannot swallow pills may be able to take the medication as a liquid or as an injection. If the antidepressant helps the symptoms, treatment should continue for at least six months. Electroconvulsive therapy (ECT) is a useful and safe therapy when other treatments have been unsuccessful in relieving major depression.

Psychotherapies

Several psychiatric therapies have been found to be beneficial for the treatment of depression related to cancer. These therapies are often used in combination and include crisis intervention, psychotherapy, and thought/behavior techniques. These therapies usually consist of three to ten sessions and explore methods of lowering distress, improving coping and problem-solving skills; enlisting support; reshaping negative and self-defeating thoughts; and developing a close personal bond with an understanding health care provider. Talking with a clergy member may also be helpful for some people.

Specific goals of these therapies are:

- Assist people diagnosed with cancer and their families by answering questions about the illness and its treatment, explaining information, correcting misunderstandings, giving reassurance

337

about the situation, and exploring with the patient how the diagnosis relates to previous experiences with cancer.

- Assist with problem solving, improve the patient's coping skills, and help the patient and family to develop additional coping skills. Explore other areas of stress, such as family role and lifestyle changes, and encourage family members to support and share concern with each other.

Other Issues during Treatment

When the focus of treatment changes from trying to cure the cancer to relieving symptoms, the health care team will not abandon the patient and family and will maintain comfort, control pain, and maintain the dignity of the patient and his or her family members.

Cancer support groups may also be helpful in treating depression in cancer patients, especially adolescents. Support groups have been shown to improve mood, encourage the development of coping skills, improve quality of life, and improve immune response. Support groups can be found through the wellness community, the American Cancer Society, and many community resources, including the social work departments in medical centers and hospitals.

Considerations for Depression in Children

Most children cope with the emotions related to cancer and not only adjust well, but show positive emotional growth and development. However, a minority of children develop psychologic problems including depression, anxiety, sleeping problems, relationship problems, and are uncooperative about treatment. These children should be treated by a mental health specialist.

Children with severe late effects of cancer have more symptoms of depression. Anxiety usually occurs in younger patients, while depression is more common in older children. Most cancer survivors are generally able to adapt and adjust successfully to cancer and its treatment. However, a small number of cancer survivors have difficulty adjusting.

Diagnosis of Childhood Depression

The term depression refers to a symptom, a syndrome, a set of psychological responses, or an illness. The length and intensity of the response (such as sadness) distinguishes the symptoms from the disorder. For example, a child may be sad in response to trauma, and the sadness usually lasts a short time. However, depression is marked by a response that lasts a long time, and is associated with sleeplessness, irritability, changes in eating habits, and problems at school and with friends. Depression should be considered whenever any behavior problem continues. Depression does not refer to temporary moments of sadness, but rather to a disorder that affects development and interferes with the child's progress.

Some signs of depression in the school-aged child include not eating, inactivity, looking sad, aggression, crying, hyperactivity, physical complaints, fear of death, frustration, feelings of sadness or hopelessness, self criticism, frequent day dreaming, low self-esteem, refusing to go to school, learning problems, slow movements, showing anger towards parents and teachers, and loss of interest in activities that were previously enjoyed. Some of these signs can occur in response to normal developmental stages; therefore, it is important to determine whether they are related to depression or a developmental stage.

Determining a diagnosis of depression includes evaluating the child's family situation, as well as his or her level of emotional maturity and ability to cope with illness and treatment; the child's age and state of development; and the child's self esteem and prior experience with illness.

A comprehensive assessment for childhood depression is necessary for effective diagnosis and treatment. Evaluation of the child and family situation focuses on the child's health history; observations of the behavior of the child by parents, teachers, or health care workers; interviews with the child; and use of psychological tests.

Childhood depression and adult depression are different illnesses due to the developmental issues involved in childhood. The following criteria may also be used for diagnosing depression in children: a sad mood (and a sad facial expression in children younger than six) with at least four of the following signs or symptoms present every day for a period of at least two weeks: appetite changes, not sleeping or sleeping too much, being too active, or not active enough, loss of interest or pleasure in usual activities, signs of not caring about anything (in children younger than six); tiredness or loss of energy; feelings of worthlessness, self-criticism, or inappropriate guilt; inability to think or concentrate well; and constant thoughts of death or suicide.

Treatment of Childhood Depression

Individual and group counseling are usually used as the first treatment for a child with depression, and are directed at helping the child to master his or her difficulties and develop in the best way possible. Play therapy may be used as a way to explore the younger child's view of him- or herself, the disease, and treatment. From the beginning, a child needs help to understand, at his or her developmental level, the diagnosis of cancer and the treatment involved. A doctor may prescribe medications, such as antidepressants, for children. Some of the same antidepressants prescribed for adults may also be prescribed for children.

Suicide and Adolescents

Suicide is as rare among adolescents who have no other mental disorders as it is among adults. The adolescent often believes that his or her disease is outside the realm of control, and is in the hands of God or some other force. Refusing treatment is not a way of attempting suicide, but comes from his or her belief that life and death are determined by fate, luck, or God.

In the general population, about 2,000 adolescents in the United States die by suicide each year. Suicide continually ranks as the second or third leading cause of death of persons between the ages of 15 and 34 years old. Children are less prone to suicide before puberty due to immature reasoning capabilities that make planning and carrying out suicide difficult. The suicide rate in young people has more than doubled during the period between 1956 to 1993. This increasing suicide rate has been blamed on the increase of adolescent alcohol abuse. Chronic and acute illnesses were not major causes of suicide in the young. The suicide rate for male adolescents is four times as high as the rate for females. The suicide rate for white adolescents is about twice as great as the rate for African-Americans and Hispanics. Little is known about the occurrence of thoughts of suicide and attempts in children with cancer.

The risk factors for the general population of children include:

- **Biologic factors:** Family history of mental problems such as depression, schizophrenia, alcoholism, drug dependence, and conduct disorders. Genetic predisposition to low levels of serotonin are associated with depression.

- **Predisposing life events:** An early family history of abuse by a parent; negative life event such as loss of a parent; childhood grief; and disturbed, hostile relationships in the family. Many other social problems and negative life events do not seem to cause suicidal behavior.

- **Social factors:** The very nature of adolescence itself with its desire to experiment with drugs and alcohol. Conflict or confusion about sexual orientation can be a factor in adolescent suicide. Also, characteristics such as perfectionism, impulsiveness, inhibition, and isolation all can lead to thoughts of suicide.

- **Mental problems:** Ninety five percent of young people who commit suicide have a mental disorder. These are usually major depression, schizophrenia, alcoholism, drug dependence, and conduct disorder. However, most children with mental problems do not commit suicide.

- **Contagion:** An expression that describes the phenomenon of young people identifying with others who have committed suicide. Some young people who are vulnerable may copy suicidal behavior. Friends of a cancer patient who has committed suicide should be offered support and counseling.

- **Deadly weapons available:** A gun in the house can allow suicide to occur.

- **Motivating events:** The diagnosis of cancer can cause a person at risk to attempt suicide. Usually a mental disorder, other life stresses, an upsetting event such as a failure in school, or life-threatening disease such as cancer is already present.

Some adolescent cancer survivors may be overwhelmed by feelings of hopelessness. This may lead to thoughts of suicide. Suicide is treated by the careful evaluation of the child with cancer and his or her family. The multiple factors that can make a child's life unbearable need to be examined. Suicide prevention must include individual evaluation; referral to the correct health professionals; treatment with medications; and both individual counseling and family therapy.

Evaluation and Treatment of Suicidal Cancer Patients

The incidence of suicide in cancer patients may be as much as 10 times higher than the rate of suicide in the general population. Passive suicidal thoughts are fairly common in cancer patients. The relationships between suicidal tendency and the desire for hastened death, requests for physician-assisted suicide, and/or euthanasia are complicated and poorly understood. Men with cancer are at an increased risk of suicide compared with the general population, with more than twice the risk. Overdosing with pain killers and sedatives

341

is the most common method of suicide by cancer patients, with most cancer suicides occurring at home. The occurrence of suicide is higher in patients with oral, pharyngeal, and lung cancers and in HIV-positive patients with Kaposi's sarcoma. The actual incidence of suicide in cancer patients is probably underestimated, since there may be reluctance to report these deaths as suicides.

General risk factors for suicide in a person with cancer include a history of mental problems, especially those associated with impulsive behavior (such as, borderline personality disorders); a family history of suicide; a history of suicide attempts; depression; substance abuse; recent death of a friend or spouse; and having little social support.

Cancer-specific risk factors for suicide include a diagnosis of oral, pharyngeal, or lung cancer (often associated with heavy alcohol and tobacco use); advanced stage of disease and poor prognosis; confusion/delirium; poorly controlled pain; or physical impairments, such as loss of mobility, loss of bowel and bladder control, amputation, loss of eyesight or hearing, paralysis, inability to eat or swallow, tiredness, or exhaustion.

Patients who are suicidal require careful evaluation. The risk of suicide increases if the patient reports thoughts of suicide and has a plan to carry it out. Risk continues to increase if the plan is lethal, that is, the plan is likely to cause death. A lethal suicide plan is more likely to be carried out if the way chosen to cause death is available to the person, the attempt cannot be stopped once it is started, and help is unavailable. When a person with cancer reports thoughts of death, it is important to determine whether the underlying cause is depression or a desire to control unbearable symptoms. Prompt identification and treatment of major depression is important in decreasing the risk for suicide. Risk factors, especially hopelessness (which is a better predictor for suicide than depression) should be carefully determined. The assessment of hopelessness is not easy in the person who has advanced cancer with no hope of a cure. It is important to determine the basic reasons for hopelessness, which may be related to cancer symptoms, fears of painful death, or feelings of abandonment.

Talking about suicide will not cause the patient to attempt suicide; it actually shows that this is a concern and permits the patient to describe his or her feelings and fears, providing a sense of control. A crisis intervention-oriented treatment approach should be used which involves the patient's support system. Contributing symptoms, such as pain, should be aggressively controlled and depression, psychosis, anxiety, and underlying causes of delirium should be treated. These problems are usually treated in a medical hospital or at home. Although not usually necessary, a suicidal cancer patient may need to be hospitalized in a psychiatric unit.

The goal of treatment of suicidal patients is to attempt to prevent suicide that is caused by desperation due to poorly controlled symptoms. Patients close to the end of life may not be able to stay awake without a great amount of emotional or physical pain. This often leads to thoughts of suicide or requests for aid in dying. Such patients may need sedation to ease their distress.

Other treatment considerations include using medications that work quickly to alleviate distress (such as antianxiety medication or stimulants) while waiting for the antidepressant medication to work; limiting the quantities of medications that are lethal in overdose; having frequent contact with a health care professional who can closely observe the patient; avoiding long periods of time when the patient is alone; making sure the patient has available support; and determining the patient's mental and emotional response at each crisis point during the cancer experience.

Pain and symptom treatment should not be sacrificed simply to avoid the possibility that a patient will attempt suicide. Patients often have a method to commit suicide available to them. Incomplete pain and symptom treatment might actually worsen a patient's suicide risk.

Frequent contact with the health professional can help limit the amount of lethal drugs available to the patient and family. Infusion devices that limit patient access to medications can also be used at home or in the hospital. These are programmable, portable pumps with coded access and a locked cartridge containing the medication. These pumps are very useful in controlling pain and other symptoms. Some pumps can give multiple drug infusions, and some can be programmed over the phone. The devices are available through home care agencies, but are very expensive. Some of the expense may be covered by insurance.

Effects of Suicide on Family and Health Care Providers

Suicide can make the loss of a loved one especially difficult for survivors. Survivors often have reactions that include feelings of abandonment, rejection, anger, relief, guilt, responsibility, denial, identification, and shame. These reactions are affected by the type and intensity of relationship; the nature of the suicide; the age and physical condition of the deceased; the survivor's support network and coping skills; and cultural and religious beliefs. Survivors should have help during this period of grieving. Mutual support groups can lessen isolation, provide opportunities to discuss feelings, and help survivors find ways to cope.

The reactions of health care providers to the suicide are similar to those seen in family members, although caregivers often do not feel they have the right to express their feelings.

Assisted Dying, Euthanasia, and Decisions Regarding End of Life

Respecting and promoting patient control has been one of the driving forces behind the hospice movement and right-to-die issues that range from honoring living wills to promoting euthanasia (mercy killing). These issues can create a conflict between a patient's desire for control and a physician's duty to promote health. These are issues of law, ethics, medicine, and philosophy. Some physicians may favor strong pain control and approve of the right of patients to refuse life support, but do not favor euthanasia or assisted suicide. Often patients who ask for physician-assisted suicide can be treated by increasing the patient's comfort, relieving symptoms, thereby reducing the patient's need for drastic measures. Patients with the desire to die should be carefully evaluated and treated for depression.

To Learn More

Call

For more information, U.S. residents may call the Cancer Information Service toll-free at 1-800-4-CANCER (1-800-422-6237) Monday through Friday from 9:00 a.m. to 4:30 p.m. Deaf and hard-of-hearing callers with TTY equipment may call 1-800-332-8615. The call is free and a trained Cancer Information Specialist is available to answer your questions.

Publications

The National Cancer Institute (NCI) has booklets and other materials for patients, health professionals, and the public. These publications discuss types of cancer, methods of cancer treatment, coping with cancer, and clinical trials. Some publications provide information on tests for cancer, cancer causes and prevention, cancer statistics, and NCI research activities. NCI materials on these and other topics may be ordered online or printed directly from the NCI Publications Locator (at www.cancer.gov). These materials can also be ordered by telephone from the Cancer Information Service toll-free at 1-800-4-CANCER (1-800-422-6237), TTY at 1-800-332-8615.

LiveHelp

The NCI's LiveHelp (http://cancer.gov/livehelp/vp/vp_sq.html) service, a program available on several of the Institute's websites, provides internet users with the ability to chat online with a Cancer Information Specialist. The service is available from 9:00 a.m. to 5:00 p.m. Eastern time, Monday through Friday.

Organizations and Websites

There are many other places where people can get materials and information about cancer treatment and services. Local hospitals may have information on local and regional agencies that offer information about finances, getting to and from treatment, receiving care at home, and dealing with problems associated with cancer treatment. A list of organizations and websites that offer information and services for cancer patients and their families is available on from the National Cancer Institute at http://cancer.gov/support_resources.html.

Chapter 44

Chronic Pain and Depression

Which Comes First? Pain or Depression?

As early as 1684, Dr. Thomas Willis wrote of the sadness or long sorrow that accompanies many chronic illnesses.

Today, as noted by Depression.com, it is considered a two-way street. Chronic illnesses are depressing. And the depression they cause often exacerbates the illness.

Understanding Chronic Pain

Chronic pain. Intractable pain. Pain that never completely goes away. Difficult to measure. Often invisible.

Going from doctor to doctor to find the cause is exhausting and frustrating. Being told "It's all in your head."

Finding the cause, finally knowing the name of "The Intruder" as one of our readers put it (see below), still there may be no treatment that makes the pain cease and desist.

Friends and family, sympathetic at first, often tire of the burden of driving us to appointments, to surgeries, of hearing how much pain we're in today. Their love doesn't necessarily change (though it can) but they also feel a unique level of frustration.

People in chronic pain often find themselves alone in a world where only they and the pain exist, where no one else can understand. For those who live alone it can be a death curse. For others, the whole structure of the family may change. One partner may resent having to be the sole breadwinner, especially if they've always been taken care of. The one in chronic pain tries to be cheery, to be the same as before, to hang onto the love and life they've known, but chronic pain changes lives, period.

It seems that one loss piles on another and another until the burden has become so twisted and convoluted that it takes on a life of its own.

Spirits sink, gradually and almost immeasurable at first, then more and more. A spiral like water draining out a sink with a clogged pipe. Slowly but inevitably depression joins the pain.

And yet the question is begged: which came first, the pain or the depression?

Studies

Studies are showing overwhelmingly that chronic pain causes depression, not the other way around.

For example, a study recorded at Mediconsult.com used 254 chronic pain patients, whose pain had lasted at least six months.

Their statistics were:

- Average age: 40
- Employed: 33%
- Married: 66%
- Race: White 66%
- Receiving compensation: 33%
- Involved in litigation: 33%

Depression was evaluated according to the Beck Depression Inventory. Conceived by psychoanalyst Aaron Beck, this has been standard tool for 30 years. Patients rate the severity of 21 symptoms on a scale of 1 to 4.

For the 254 patients, the average score was 15.82 out of a possible 63, with the least depressed scoring 7 and the most depressed 50.

The strongest single predictor of depression was work status. Employment is heavily weighed in an adult's self-esteem and suddenly or gradually the chronic pain sufferer can no longer perform the duties the job demands.

Retirement comes early—but oh, what a retirement it is! There are no exotic vacations, no golf every morning because the person simply can't.

For those unemployed patients involved in litigation, it was a consolation which unfortunately wore off quickly once the process was confronted.

Among the employed, those pursuing litigation were most likely to be unhappy, due to the awkward position of suing their employer while still working.

Those less schooled were more vulnerable to depression.

The unmarried were less able to cope with their suffering than those who had a partner to lean on.

Ethnicity was found to bear no relation to stress.

This is perhaps the most interesting part of the test: "Comparisons of age and gender led to what are probably the most interesting results to come out of this survey. It was found that among women, depression declined with age, while among men it worsened. Thus, among those under 40, women were most affected, but among those older than this it was men who had the highest Beck scores. This is not at all a common finding in depression studies not looking at chronic pain sufferers. No obvious reason for this trend presents itself."

The degree and strength of the chronic pain, the number of surgical interventions, the number of drugs taken, and the common 1 to 10 measurement of pain—with 10 being suicidal—had no effect on level of depression.

Only the duration of the pain had an impact on the degree of depression, with the longest-suffering showing more depression.

The conclusion of the study showed that depressed chronic pain patients are less likely to respond to treatment for their pain. Since pain is harder to treat than depression, antidepressive therapy is often the best first step on the road to treating chronic pain.

Contributing to depression is the lack of adequate pain relief. More than four out of every ten people with moderate to severe chronic pain have yet to find adequate relief, saying their pain is out of control, according to a new survey by the American Pain Society, the American Academy of Pain Medicine and Janssen Pharmaceutica.

According to this survey, "Many Americans with chronic pain are suffering too much for too long and need more aggressive treatment," says Russell Portenoy, MD, president of the American Pain Society and chairman of the Department of Pain Medicine and Palliative Care at the Beth Israel Medical Center in New York City. "This survey suggests that there are millions of people living with severe uncontrolled pain. This is a great tragedy. Although not everyone can be helped, it is very likely that most of these patients could benefit if provided with state-of-the-art therapies and improved access to pain specialists when needed."

"This survey shows the stigma associated with opioid drugs. Although these drugs can clearly benefit some patients with chronic pain, patients, caregivers and physicians overestimate the risks and fail to use them appropriately," observes Dr. Portenoy. "Many patients suffer needlessly because of an inappropriate level of concern about long-term reliance on medication in general, and about addiction caused by strong pain medications such as opioids specifically. The input of pain specialists may be helpful when deciding on the best drug therapy for patients with severe chronic pain."

Depression.com also addresses the problem of depression in patients with chronic pain. Interestingly, they refer to depression specialist Arthur Rifkin, M.D., a psychiatrist at Albert Einstein Medical Center in New York, who says "the most common misconception about depression and chronic illness is that it's understandable to become depressed when faced with a chronic illness. It is understandable— but only during the initial adjustment period that should not last for more than a few months. Beyond that, persistent depression should be treated as a separate illness."

Depression.com says that any chronic condition can trigger depression, but the risk increases in direct proportion to the severity of the condition.

A broken leg that makes you miss a few ball games is a drag, but an accident that leaves you paraplegic can be severely depressing. Likewise depression increases with chronic diseases.

Chapter 45

Depression and Diabetes

Depression packs a double-punch for those with diabetes. Along with the mental anguish, blood glucose control often slips as well. But there is hope.

Having a Bad Day?

Nothing too unusual about that. We all have our ups and downs. Even a bad week or so every now and again is nothing to get too excited about. But if you find yourself wrestling with feelings of sadness, unrelieved stress, and fatigue as a matter of course, day in, day out, that's something you shouldn't shrug off. You may have a condition known as clinical depression, one that can threaten your well-being as well as your quality of life.

Clinical depression is much more common among people with diabetes than among the general population. It affects 15 to 20 percent of those with diabetes. Type 1, type 2, it doesn't matter: depression afflicts both groups equally.

That's not to say that diabetes *causes* depression. In fact, nobody knows for sure why depression is more common among those with diabetes. Its root causes—psychological, physical, and genetic—are thought to be the same across all populations. But there are both mental and physical factors that probably aggravate the situation for those with diabetes.

For example, it's possible that the extra demands of the diabetes regimen itself put some people at greater risk for depression. Adjusting to dietary restrictions, blood-testing routines, hospitalizations, and increased financial obligations can be difficult. For those whose diabetes has progressed, dealing with the loss of vision, kidney failure, or impaired sexual function is extremely stressful and can open the door to depression. Various physical changes associated with diabetes, including chemical and blood-flow changes in the brain, may also be factors.

Recent Developments

There is exciting news on the clinical trial front. Three studies published in 1997 in *Psychological Annals*, *Psychosomatic Medicine*, and *Diabetes*, have demonstrated for the first time that depression in diabetic patients can be treated effectively by either antidepressants or a specific form of psychotherapy called cognitive behavior therapy. Even more exciting, the studies found that as depression lessened, blood glucose control improved. Researchers believe that these clinical results will apply to all people with diabetes who suffer from depression. Although depression is a common and important problem, there is a solution: antidepressant medications or cognitive behavior therapy. These therapies can effectively relieve depression, and it appears likely that they will lead to better diabetes control as well.

Diagnosis

How can you tell if you are seriously depressed, or if you've just got the blues? That's a hard call, one that even medical professionals often fail to make. (More on that later.) In general, though, there are certain signs that signal serious depression.

Clinical depression is the likely diagnosis when the following three factors are present: a number of symptoms occur together, such as sadness, lethargy, and a general loss of interest in life; the symptoms are severe in nature; and the symptoms persist daily for at least two weeks. If you're constantly feeling sad or irritable, or if you are regularly having trouble sleeping, you may very well have clinical depression.

Warning Signs of Depression

- A sustained feeling of sadness, depression, or extreme irritability.

- A loss of interest or pleasure in activities you previously enjoyed. (For example, being with friends and family, sex.)

- A change in sleep patterns. (You have difficulty falling asleep, you awaken frequently during the night, or you want to sleep more than usual, including during the day.)

- You wake up early in the morning (between four and six) and aren't able to get back to sleep.

- Your appetite has increased or decreased, with corresponding weight gain or loss over a relatively short period of time.

- You have difficulty concentrating. (For example, you aren't able to watch a TV program or read an entire newspaper article because other thoughts or feelings intrude.)

- You have less energy; you feel washed out all the time.

- You feel nervous all the time and can't sit still because of anxiety.

- You feel guilty about things you've done, or feel that you're a burden to others.

- You feel like you want to die, or you're thinking about ways to hurt yourself.

If you have three or more of these symptoms and they last for two or more weeks, it's time to get help. If you have the last symptom (you feel like you want to die or hurt yourself), seek help immediately.

If you are seriously depressed, the symptoms themselves can also become a source of significant distress and have an adverse effect on the way you function in social situations or on the job.

If you recognize yourself in these symptoms, it's time to seek help. And, difficult as it may be, you may have to be the one to take the lead. That's because depression in people with diabetes often goes unrecognized; it's diagnosed in fewer than one-third of all cases. Many factors contribute to this problem.

Some health care professionals assume that depression is a natural result of living with a chronic illness such as diabetes, and therefore they are apt to dismiss it. Some are not familiar enough with the symptoms to diagnose it properly, and others are unaware of the variety of effective treatments available. The fact that most doctors are rushed—most visits now run less than 15 minutes—also shifts responsibility to the patient; the patient, not the doctor, must often bring it up first. As a result, depression in people with diabetes often remains undiagnosed.

That's bad news for people who are struggling with both diabetes and depression, because the interplay of these conditions can have devastating effects. For example, people with diabetes who are depressed tend to have poorer blood sugar control, which is the major cause of diabetes complications. Depression also contributes to obesity, physical inactivity, poor health habits (depressed people are more likely to smoke cigarettes and drink alcohol), and non-compliance with treatment. It's also related to an increased risk of retinopathy and heart disease.

To further complicate matters, depression also makes people more sensitive to, and intolerant of, physical symptoms. For example, neuropathic pain that is normally perceived as an intermittent annoyance may become unbearable during a period of depression, prompting a doctor's visit.

Treatment

The good news is that depression, once diagnosed, can usually be treated successfully. The two primary treatment methods are medication and psychotherapy. In general, both methods are equally effective. Some patients benefit from a combination of medication and therapy.

Keep in mind that the method chosen to relieve depression usually depends on whom one goes to for treatment. Primary care physicians and diabetologists are most likely to treat depression with anti-depressants, such as Prozac, Paxil, Zoloft, and Elavil, and with common-sense advice. Psychologists and social workers employ counseling and formal psychotherapy. Psychiatrists may use a combination of both of these forms of therapy, but they generally emphasize medication.

A visit to the primary care physician should be the starting point for patients who suspect they might be seriously depressed. The coverage managed care plans offer for the treatment of depression varies greatly, so patients should contact plan administrators for details. Not all doctors and therapists are equally skilled, so try to pick someone with a good reputation.

With the help of counseling or medication, the majority of patients are back to their normal, nondepressed selves within three months. If, after that time, you don't feel much better, there's still hope. Tell your doctor. Finding effective treatment may require several adjustments—adding or changing medications or therapists. Stay with treatment.

Depression is the most treatable emotional problem, and nearly all patients treated with medication and counseling are essentially free of depression within six months.

Getting Help

For general information and materials on depression and the treatment of depression, contact the following organizations:

- National Institute of Mental Health 1-800-421-4211 or http://www.nimh.nih.gov

- National Mental Health Association (can also help with referrals) 1-800-969-NMHA or http://www.nmha.org

- National Depressive and Manic-Depressive Association (can also recommend support groups in local communities) 1-800-826-3632 or http://www.ndmda.org

For emergencies only: If you are in crisis or in immediate danger of harming yourself, call Covenant House at 1-800-999-9999, or dial 911.

Chapter 46

Eating Disorders

What are eating disorders?

Each year, millions of people in the United States are affected by serious and sometimes life-threatening eating disorders. The vast majority—more than 90 percent—of those afflicted with eating disorders are adolescent and young adult women. One reason that women in this age group are particularly vulnerable to eating disorders is their tendency to go on strict diets to achieve an "ideal" figure. Researchers have found that such stringent dieting can play a key role in triggering eating disorders.

Approximately one percent of adolescent girls develop anorexia nervosa, a dangerous condition in which they can literally starve themselves to death. Another two to three percent of young women develop bulimia nervosa, a destructive pattern of excessive overeating followed by vomiting or other purging behaviors to control their weight. These eating disorders also occur in men and older women, but much less frequently.

The consequences of eating disorders can be severe. For example, one in ten cases of anorexia nervosa leads to death from starvation, cardiac arrest, other medical complications, or suicide. Fortunately, increasing awareness of the dangers of eating disorders—sparked by medical studies and extensive media coverage of the illness—has led many people to seek help. Nevertheless, some people with eating disorders

From the Office on Women's Health, Department of Health and Human Services (www.4woman.gov), 1998.

refuse to admit that they have a problem and do not get treatment. Family members and friends can help recognize the problem and encourage the person to seek treatment.

What are the medical complications of eating disorders?

Medical complications can frequently be a result of eating disorders. Individuals with eating disorders who use drugs to stimulate vomiting, bowel movements, or urination may be in considerable danger, because this practice increases the risk of heart failure.

Anorexia

In patients with anorexia, starvation can damage vital organs such as the brain and heart. To protect itself, the body shifts into "slow gear": monthly menstrual periods stop; breathing, pulse, and blood pressure rates drop; and thyroid function slows. Nails and hair become brittle; the skin dries, yellows, and becomes covered with soft hair called lanugo. Excessive thirst and frequent urination may occur. Dehydration contributes to constipation, and reduced body fat leads to lowered body temperature and the inability to withstand cold.

Mild anemia, swollen joints, reduced muscle mass, and light-headedness also commonly occur in anorexia. If the disorder becomes severe, patients may lose calcium from their bones, making them brittle and prone to breakage. They may also experience irregular heart rhythms and heart failure. In some patients, the brain shrinks, causing personality changes. Fortunately, this condition can be reversed when normal weight is reestablished.

Scientists have found that many patients with anorexia also suffer from other psychiatric illnesses. While the majority have co-occurring clinical depression, others suffer from anxiety, personality or substance abuse disorders, and many are at risk for suicide. Obsessive-compulsive disorder (OCD), an illness characterized by repetitive thoughts and behaviors, can also accompany anorexia. Individuals with anorexia are typically compliant in personality but may have sudden outbursts of hostility and anger or become socially withdrawn.

Bulimia

Bulimia nervosa patients—even those of normal weight—can severely damage their bodies by frequent binge eating and purging. In rare instances, binge eating causes the stomach to rupture; purging may result in heart failure due to loss of vital minerals such as potassium. Vomiting causes other less deadly, but serious, problems—the acid in vomit wears down the outer layer of the teeth and can cause scarring on the backs of hands when fingers are pushed down the throat to induce vomiting. Further, the esophagus becomes inflamed and glands near the cheeks become swollen. As in anorexia, bulimia may lead to irregular menstrual periods. Interest in sex may also diminish.

Some individuals with bulimia struggle with addictions including abuse of drugs and alcohol, and compulsive stealing. Like individuals with anorexia, many people with bulimia suffer from clinical depression, anxiety, OCD, and other psychiatric illnesses. These problems, combined with their impulsive tendencies, place them at higher risk for suicidal behavior.

Binge Eating Disorder

People with binge eating disorder are usually overweight so they are prone to the serious medical problems associated with obesity, such as high cholesterol, high blood pressure, and diabetes. Obese individuals also have a higher risk for gallbladder disease, heart disease, and some types of cancer.

Individuals with binge eating disorder also have high rates of co-occurring psychiatric illnesses—especially depression.

What causes eating disorders?

In trying to understand the causes of eating disorders, scientists have studied the personalities, genetics, environments, and biochemistry of people with these illnesses. As is often the case, the more that is learned, the more complex the roots of eating disorders appear.

For More Information

You can find out more about eating disorders by contacting the following organizations:

- Food and Nutrition Information Center (www.nal.usda.gov/fnic)
- Academy for Eating Disorders (www.aedweb.org)
- National Institute of Mental Health (www.nimh.nih.gov)

Additional resources for information about depression are listed in the end section of this book.

Chapter 47

Depression and Heart Disease

Awareness and Treatment Can Improve Overall Health and Reduce Suffering

Depression is a common, serious and costly illness that affects 1 in 10 adults in the U.S. each year, costs the nation between $30–$44 billion annually, and causes impairment, suffering, and disruption of personal, family, and work life.

Though 80 percent of depressed people can be effectively treated, nearly two out of three of those suffering from this illness do not seek or receive appropriate treatment. Effective treatments include both medication and psychotherapy, which are sometimes used in combination.

Depression Can Break Your Heart

Research over the past two decades has shown that depression and heart disease are common companions and, what is worse, each can lead to the other. It appears now that depression is an important risk factor for heart disease along with high blood cholesterol and high blood pressure. A study conducted in Baltimore, MD found that of 1,551 people who were free of heart disease, those who had a history of depression were four times more likely than those who did not to

This chapter includes text from "Co-Occurrence of Depression with Heart Disease," National Institute of Mental Health (NIMH), June 1999, and "Depression Can Break Your Heart," NIMH, January 2001.

suffer a heart attack in the next 14 years.[1] In addition, researchers in Montreal, Canada found that heart patients who were depressed were four times as likely to die in the next six months as those who were not depressed.[2]

Depression may make it harder to take the medications needed and to carry out the treatment for heart disease.[3] Depression also may result in chronically elevated levels of stress hormones, such as cortisol and adrenaline, and the activation of the sympathetic nervous system (part of the "fight or flight" response), which can have deleterious effects on the heart.[4]

The first studies of heart disease and depression found that people with heart disease were more likely to suffer from depression than otherwise healthy people.[4] While about one in 20 American adults experience major depression in a given year, the number goes to about one in three for people who have survived a heart attack.[5,6] Furthermore, other researchers have found that most heart patients with depression do not receive appropriate treatment. Cardiologists and primary care physicians tend to miss the diagnosis of depression;[4] and even when they do recognize it, they often do not treat it adequately.[7]

The public health impact of depression and heart disease, both separately and together, is enormous. Depression is the estimated leading cause of disability worldwide,[8] and heart disease is by far the leading cause of death in the United States.[9] Approximately one in three Americans will die of some form of heart disease.

Studies indicate that depression can appear after heart disease and/or heart disease surgery. In one investigation, nearly half of the patients studied one week after cardiopulmonary bypass surgery experienced serious cognitive problems, which may contribute to clinical depression in some individuals.[10]

There are also multiple studies indicating that heart disease can follow depression.[4] Psychological distress may cause rapid heartbeat, high blood pressure, and faster blood clotting. It can also lead to elevated insulin and cholesterol levels. These risk factors, with obesity, form a constellation of symptoms and often serve as a predictor of and a response to heart disease. People with depression may feel slowed down and still have high levels of stress hormones. This can increase the work of the heart. As high levels of stress hormones are signaling a "fight or flight" reaction, the body's metabolism is diverted away from the type of tissue repair needed in heart disease.

Regardless of cause, the combination of depression and heart disease is associated with increased sickness and death, making effective treatment of depression imperative. Pharmacological and cognitive-behavioral therapy treatments for depression are relatively well developed and play an important role in reducing the adverse impact of depression.[4] With the advent of the selective serotonin reuptake inhibitors to treat depression, more medically ill patients can be treated without the complicating cardiovascular side effects of the previous drugs available. Ongoing research is investigating whether these treatments also reduce the associated risk of a second heart attack. Furthermore, preventive interventions based on cognitive-behavior theories of depression also merit attention as approaches for avoiding adverse outcomes associated with both disorders. These interventions may help promote adherence and behavior change that may increase the impact of available pharmacological and behavioral approaches to both diseases.

Exercise is another potential pathway to reducing both depression and risk of heart disease. A recent study found that participation in an exercise training program was comparable to treatment with an antidepressant medication (a selective serotonin reuptake inhibitor) for improving depressive symptoms in older adults diagnosed with major depression.[11] Exercise, of course, is a major protective factor against heart disease as well.[12]

The National Institute of Mental Health and the National Heart, Lung and Blood Institute are invested in uncovering the complicated relationship between depression and heart disease. They support research on the basic mechanisms and processes linking co-occurring mental and medical disorders to identify potent, modifiable risk factors and protective processes amenable to medical and behavioral interventions that will reduce the adverse outcomes associated with both types of disorders.

More Facts

- Though depressed feelings can be a common reaction to heart disease, clinical depression is not the expected reaction. For this reason, when present, specific treatment should be considered for clinical depression even in the presence of heart disease

- In coronary heart disease patients with a history of myocardial infarction (heart attack), the prevalence of various forms of depression is estimated from 40 to 65 percent.

- 18-20 percent of coronary heart patients without a history of heart attack may experience depression.

- Major depression puts heart attack victims at greater risk and appears to add to the patients' disability from heart disease. Depression can contribute to a worsening of symptoms as well as poor adherence to cardiac treatment regimens.

- People who survive heart attacks but suffer from major depression have a 3-4 times greater risk of dying within six months than those who do not suffer from depression.

Take Action

Appropriate diagnosis and treatment of depression may bring substantial benefits to the patient through improved medical status, enhanced quality of life, a reduction in the degree of pain and disability, and improved treatment compliance and cooperation.

- **Don't Ignore Symptoms:** Health care professionals should always be aware of the possibility of depression co-occurring with heart disease. Patients or family members with concerns about this possibility should discuss these issues with the individual's physicians. A consultation with a psychiatrist or other mental health clinician may be recommended to clarify the diagnosis.

References

1. Pratt LA, Ford DE, Crum RM, et al. Depression, psychotropic medication, and risk of myocardial infarction. Prospective data from the Baltimore ECA follow-up. *Circulation*, 1996; 94(12): 3123-9.

2. Frasure-Smith N, Lesperance F, Talajic M. Depression and 18-month prognosis after myocardial infarction. *Circulation*, 1995; 91(4): 999-1005.

3. Ziegelstein RC, Fauerbach JA, Stevens SS, et al. Patients with depression are less likely to follow recommendations to reduce cardiac risk during recovery from a myocardial infarction. *Archives of Internal Medicine*, 2000; 160(12): 1818-23.

4. Nemeroff CB, Musselman DL, Evans DL. Depression and cardiac disease. *Depression and Anxiety*, 1998; 8(Suppl 1): 71-9.

5. Regier DA, Narrow WE, Rae DS, et al. The de facto mental and addictive disorders service system. Epidemiologic Catchment

Area prospective 1-year prevalence rates of disorders and services. *Archives of General Psychiatry*, 1993; 50(2): 85-94.

6. Lesperance F, Frasure-Smith N, Talajic M. Major depression before and after myocardial infarction: its nature and consequences. *Psychosomatic Medicine*, 1996; 58(2): 99-110.

7. Hirschfeld RM, Keller MB, Panico S, et al. The National Depressive and Manic-Depressive Association consensus statement on the undertreatment of depression. *Journal of the American Medical Association*, 1997; 277(4): 333-40.

8. Murray CJL, Lopez AD, eds. Summary: The global burden of disease: a comprehensive assessment of mortality and disability from diseases, injuries, and risk factors in 1990 and projected to 2020. Cambridge, MA: Published by the Harvard School of Public Health on behalf of the World Health Organization and the World Bank, Harvard University Press, 1996. http://www.who.int/msa/mnh/ems/dalys/intro.htm

9. Murphy SL. Deaths: final data for 1998. *National Vital Statistics Report*, 48(11). DHHS Publication No. 2000-1120. Hyattsville, MD: National Center for Health Statistics, 2000. http://www.cdc.gov/nchs/data/nvs48_11.pdf

10. Chabot RJ, Gugino LD, Aglio LS, et al. QEEG and neuropsychological profiles of patients after undergoing cardiopulmonary bypass surgical procedures. *Clinical Electroencephalography*, 1997; 28(2): 98-105.

11. Blumenthal JA, Babyak MA, Moore KA, et al. Effects of exercise training on older patients with major depression. *Archives of Internal Medicine*, 1999; 159(19): 2349-56.

12. Fletcher GF, Balady G, Blair SN, et al. Statement on exercise: benefits and recommendations for physical activity programs for all Americans. A statement for health professionals by the Committee on Exercise and Cardiac Rehabilitation of the Council on Clinical Cardiology, American Heart Association. *Circulation*, 1996; 94(4): 857-62.

Chapter 48

Depression after a Heart Attack

What does depression have to do with my heart attack?

As many as 65% of people who have a heart attack report feeling depressed. Women, people who have been depressed before, and people who feel alone and without social or emotional support are at a higher risk for feeling depressed after a heart attack.

Being depressed can make it harder for you to recover. However, depression can be treated.

What is depression?

Depression is a medical illness, like diabetes or high blood pressure. The symptoms of depression can include the following:

- Feeling sad or crying often (depressed mood)
- Losing interest in daily activities that used to be fun
- Changes in appetite and weight
- Sleeping too much or having trouble sleeping
- Feeling agitated, cranky, or sluggish
- Loss of energy

- Feeling very guilty or worthless
- Problems concentrating or making decisions
- Thoughts of death or suicide

How will I know if I am depressed?

People who are depressed have most or all of the above symptoms nearly every day, all day, for two or more weeks. One of the symptoms must be depressed mood or loss of interest in daily activities.

If you have some or all of the above symptoms, see your family doctor. Your doctor will ask you questions about your mood. He or she may have you fill out a short questionnaire about how you are feeling.

How is depression treated?

Depression can be treated by a combination of three things:

- **Medicine:** Depression can be caused by a chemical imbalance in the brain. Medicines can correct this imbalance. If your doctor prescribes an antidepressant medicine for you, follow your doctor's advice on how to take it. These medicines might take a few weeks to start working, so be patient. Also, be sure to talk to your doctor before you stop taking any medicine or if you have unusual symptoms.

- **Changing Thoughts:** How you think about yourself and your life can play a part in depression. For example, you might become more depressed when you start to think negatively. Counseling can help you identify and stop negative thoughts and replace them with more logical or positive thinking. Many people and their families benefit from counseling or "talk therapy."

- **Becoming More Active:** Many times people feel depressed because they're inactive and aren't involved in social and recreational activities. Your mood will likely improve when you begin a hobby or recreational activity. Interacting more with other people and beginning an exercise program will also help improve your mood. Many people who have had a heart attack benefit physically and mentally from a cardiac rehabilitation program. Talk to your doctor about the kinds of activities and exercise programs that are suited for you.

Does treatment for depression usually work?

Yes. Treatment helps between 80% and 90% of people with depression.

Where can I get more information about depression?

You can find out more about depression and its treatment at the following websites:

- http://www.apa.org: The American Psychological Association has a public-access section with information on various mental health issues, including depression.

- http://www.depression-screening.org: The National Mental Health Association website has information on depression, screening for this disorder, education about treatment and resources. This site has a Spanish-language option.

- www.nimh.nih.gov/publicat/depressionmenu.cfm: The National Institute of Mental Health website has information on various aspects of depression, including types, causes and where to get help.

- http://www.psych.org: The American Psychiatric Association Web site includes a public information area with information on mental health issues.

Additional resources for more information about depression are listed in the end section of this book.

Chapter 49

Depression and HIV (Human Immunodeficiency Virus)

Depression can strike anyone. People with serious illnesses such as HIV may be at greater risk. Even when undergoing complicated treatment regimens for other illnesses, depression should always be treated.

Research has enabled many men and women, and young people living with HIV to lead fuller, more productive lives. As with other serious illnesses such as cancer, heart disease or stroke, however, HIV often can be accompanied by depression, an illness that can affect mind, mood, body and behavior. If left untreated, depression can increase the risk for suicide.

Although as many as one in three persons with HIV may suffer from depression, family and friends and even many primary care physicians often misinterpret depression's warning signs. They often mistake these symptoms for natural accompaniments to HIV in the same way that family members and doctors often erroneously assume that symptoms of depression are a natural accompaniment to growing old.

Depression can strike at any age. NIMH-sponsored studies estimate that six percent of 9- to 17-year olds, and seven percent of the entire U.S. adult population experience some form of depression every year—women at twice the rate of men. Although available therapies alleviate symptoms in over 80 percent of those treated, nearly two-thirds of those who suffer from depression don't get the help they need.

A fact sheet produced by the National Institute of Mental Health, updated August 2000; available online at www.nimh.nih.gov/publicat/hivdepression.cfm.

Treat Your Depression

Persons with depression and HIV must overcome stigma associated with both illnesses. Despite the enormous advances in brain research in the past 20 years, the stigma of mental illness remains. Even people who have access to good health care often fail or refuse to recognize their depression and seek treatment.

Depression is a disease that affects how a person relates to people around them, and if left untreated, can cause relationships to deteriorate. Some people respond to depression by becoming angry and abusive to people who care about them, or children who depend on them. Many choose to treat their depression themselves with alcohol or street drugs, which can quicken HIV's progression to AIDS. Others turn to herbal remedies. Recently scientists have discovered that St. John's wort, an herbal remedy sold over-the-counter to treat mild depression, reduces blood levels of the protease inhibitor indinavir (Crixivan®) and probably the other protease inhibitors as well. If taken together, the combination could allow the AIDS virus to rebound, perhaps in a drug-resistant form. (See the alert on the NIMH website: http://www.nimh.nih.gov/events/stjohnwort.cfm).

Prescription antidepressant medications are generally well tolerated and safe for people with HIV. There are, however, interactions among some of the drugs that require careful monitoring.

So, if you or someone you know with HIV is exhibiting the pattern of depressive symptoms described below, seek out the services of a health care provider. And make certain that he or she is experienced in diagnosing and treating depression in people with HIV.

Some of the symptoms of depression could be related to HIV, specific HIV-related disorders, or medication side effects. They could just be a normal part of living. Everyone has bad days.

Clinical Depression Is Different from Normal Ups and Downs

Depression

- The symptoms last all day every day for at least two weeks.

- The symptoms occur together during the same time period.

- The symptoms cause daily events such as work, self-care and child care, or social activities to be extremely difficult or impossible.

Taking the above characteristics into account, examine the symptoms listed below and see if they characterize you or someone you know living with HIV:

- Feelings of sadness, hopelessness

- Loss of interest in formerly enjoyable activities, including sex

- A sense that life is not worth living or that there is nothing to look forward to

- Feelings of excessive guilt, or a feeling that one is a worthless person

- Slowed or agitated movements (not in response to discomfort)

- Recurrent thoughts of dying or of ending one's own life, with or without a specific plan

- Significant, unintentional weight loss and decrease in appetite; or, less commonly, weight gain and increase in appetite

- Insomnia or excessive sleeping

- Fatigue and loss of energy

- A diminished ability to think, concentrate, or make decisions

- Physical symptoms of anxiety, including dry mouth, cramps, diarrhea, and sweating

Many therapies are available, but they must be carefully chosen by a trained professional, based on the particular circumstances of the patient and family. Recovery from depression takes time. Medications for depression can take several weeks to begin to work and may need to be combined with on-going psychotherapy. Not everyone responds to the medications in the same way. Dosing may need to be adjusted. Prescriptions may need to be changed.

Other mood disorders besides depression, such as various forms of manic-depression, also called bipolar disorder, may occur with HIV. Bipolar disorder is characterized by mood swings, from depression to mania.

Mania

Mania is characterized by abnormally and persistently elevated (high) mood or irritability accompanied by at least three of the following symptoms:

- Overly-inflated self-esteem
- Decreased need for sleep
- Increased talkativeness
- Racing thoughts
- Distractibility
- Increase in goal-directed activity such as shopping
- Physical agitation
- Excessive involvement in risky behaviors or activities

Anxiety

People with HIV also have a high incidence of anxiety disorders such as panic disorder. For more information on anxiety disorders visit the NIMH web site: (http://www.nimh.nih.gov/anxiety/anxietymenu.cfm). For free brochures on anxiety disorders and their treatment, phone 1-88-88-ANXIETY (1-888-826-9438) or use the online order form.

Staying Healthy

It takes more than access to good medical care for persons living with HIV to stay healthy. A positive outlook, determination and discipline are also required to deal with the extra stress: avoiding high-risk behaviors, keeping up with the latest scientific advances, adhering to complicated medication regimens, reshuffling schedules for doctor visits, and grieving over the death of loved ones.

The causes of depression are still not clear. It may result from an underlying genetic predisposition triggered by stress, or by the side effects of medications, or by viruses like HIV that can affect the brain. Whatever its origins, depression can sap the energy needed to keep focused on staying healthy, and research shows that it can accelerate HIV's progression to AIDS.

Depression can be treated in addition to whatever other illnesses a person might have, including HIV. If you or someone you know with HIV is depressed, seek help from a health care professional who is experienced in treating persons with both diseases. Don't lose hope.

Chapter 50

Insomnia

What is insomnia?

Insomnia is the perception or complaint of inadequate or poor-quality sleep because of one or more of the following:

- difficulty falling asleep
- waking up frequently during the night with difficulty returning to sleep
- waking up too early in the morning
- unrefreshing sleep

Insomnia is not defined by the number of hours of sleep a person gets or how long it takes to fall asleep. Individuals vary normally in their need for, and their satisfaction with, sleep. Insomnia may cause problems during the day, such as tiredness, a lack of energy, difficulty concentrating, and irritability.

Insomnia can be classified as transient (short term), intermittent (on and off), and chronic (constant). Insomnia lasting from a single night to a few weeks is referred to as transient. If episodes of transient insomnia occur from time to time, the insomnia is said to be intermittent. Insomnia is considered to be chronic if it occurs on most nights and lasts a month or more.

From the Office on Women's Health, Department of Health and Human Services (www.4woman.gov), 1998.

Who is likely to get insomnia?

Women, the elderly, and individuals with a history of depression are all more likely to experience insomnia. If other conditions (such as stress, anxiety, a medical problem, or the use of certain medications) occur along with the above conditions, insomnia is more likely.

What causes transient (temporary) or intermittent insomnia?

There are many causes of insomnia. Transient and intermittent insomnia generally occur in people who are temporarily experiencing one or more of the following:

- stress
- environmental noise
- extreme temperatures
- change in the surrounding environment
- sleep/wake schedule problems such as those due to jet lag
- medication side effects

What causes chronic insomnia?

Chronic insomnia is more complex and often results from a combination of factors, including underlying physical or mental disorders. One of the most common causes of chronic insomnia is depression. Other underlying causes include arthritis, kidney disease, heart failure, asthma, sleep apnea, narcolepsy, restless legs syndrome, Parkinson's disease, and hyperthyroidism. However, chronic insomnia may also be due to behavioral factors, including the misuse of caffeine, alcohol, or other substances; disrupted sleep/wake cycles as may occur with shift work or other nighttime activity schedules; and chronic stress.

Can insomnia be aggravated by certain behaviors?

Some behaviors may prolong existing insomnia, and they can also be responsible for causing the sleeping problem in the first place:

- expecting to have difficulty sleeping and worrying about it
- ingesting excessive amounts of caffeine
- drinking alcohol before bedtime
- smoking cigarettes before bedtime

- excessive napping in the afternoon or evening
- irregular or continually disrupted sleep/wake schedules

Stopping these behaviors may eliminate the insomnia altogether.

How do I know if I have insomnia?

Patients with insomnia are evaluated with the help of a medical history and a sleep history. The sleep history may be obtained from a sleep diary filled out by the patient or by an interview with the patient's bed partner concerning the quantity and quality of the patient's sleep. Specialized sleep studies may be recommended, but only if there is suspicion that the patient may have a primary sleep disorder such as sleep apnea or narcolepsy.

What kind of treatment is there for insomnia?

Transient and intermittent insomnia may not require treatment since episodes last only a few days at a time. For example, if insomnia is due to a temporary change in the sleep/wake schedule, as with jet lag, the person's biological clock will often get back to normal on its own. However, for some people who experience daytime sleepiness and impaired performance as a result of transient insomnia, the use of short-acting sleeping pills may improve sleep and next-day alertness. As with all drugs, there are potential side effects. The use of over-the-counter sleep medicines is not usually recommended for the treatment of insomnia.

Treatments for people diagnosed with chronic insomnia include identifying behaviors that may worsen insomnia and stopping (or reducing) them, possibly using sleeping pills (although the long-term use of sleeping pills for chronic insomnia is controversial), and trying behavioral techniques to improve sleep, such as relaxation therapy, sleep restriction therapy, and reconditioning.

For More Information

You can find out more about insomnia by contacting:

National Center on Sleep Disorders Research (NCSDR)
Two Rockledge Centre, Suite 7024
6701 Rockledge Drive, MSC 7920
Bethesda, MD 20892-7920
Phone: 301-435-0199

Fax: 301-480-3451
Website: http://www.nhlbi/nih.gov/about/ncsdr

A directory of depression-related resources is included in the end section of this book.

Chapter 51

Depression in Parkinson's Disease

Summary

Depression is present in approximately 40% of Parkinson's disease (PD) patients. It usually is an integral or intrinsic part of PD, unrelated to the degree or duration of physical symptoms. In 20% of PD patients who are depressed, the depression precedes the onset of physical symptoms.

Obviously, this is something appreciated only in retrospect—after the patient has been diagnosed with PD. In addition to an integral, intrinsic, or endogenous depression, PD patients may suffer from an exogenous depression, a depression related to external events such as job loss, retirement, or knowledge of a relative or friend with advanced PD with fear of becoming as disabled as the relative or friend with advanced PD.

In some patients depression is associated with anxiety and in some of these patients the anxiety is overwhelming and results in an agitated depression. In some patients, PD is complicated by autonomic nervous system symptoms: the autonomic nervous system controls regulates activities such as blood pressure, heart rate, breathing, swallowing, saliva flow, bowel movements, and bladder function.

In some patients PD is complicated by a sleep disorder. In some patients PD is complicated by selective intellectual (or cognitive)

"Depression in Parkinson's Disease," by Abraham N. Lieberman, M.D., Medical Director, National Parkinson Foundation, Inc. © 2000 National Parkinson Foundation, Inc.; reprinted with permission.

impairment. And in some patients PD is complicated by combinations of autonomic nervous system symptoms, a sleep disorder, and selective intellectual impairment. In such patients it may be difficult to diagnose depression.

Some PD patients, perhaps 20%, suffer from anergia (lack of energy, perpetual tiredness, or fatigue), anhedonia (an inability to receive or experience pleasure from activities from which they previously received or experienced pleasure), apathy, and passivity. These patients deny they are depressed and their anergia, anhedonia, apathy, and passivity are unaccompanied by feelings traditionally associated with depression such as feelings of gloom, guilt, hopelessness, pessimism, remorse, or sadness. These patients are usually not anxious. This syndrome of anergia, anhedonia, apathy and passivity which is separate from depression (but may be accompanied by depression) probably has a different basis than depression. This syndrome does not usually respond to conventional treatments for depression.

The Anatomy of Parkinson Disease and Depression

Depression is common in Parkinson disease (PD) patients. Depression accompanied by feelings of gloom, guilt, hopelessness, pessimism, remorse, or sadness occurs in approximately 40% of PD patients independently of their age or the duration or severity of their physical symptoms. The physical or motor symptoms of PD are characterized by the presence of two or more of the four cardinal, main, or primary symptoms that include bradykinesia (slowness and paucity of movement), rigidity (or stiffness), tremor, and postural instability (with difficulty walking). While the cause of PD is unknown, it's known that the physical or motor symptoms arise because of degeneration and loss of dopamine nerve cells in the substantia nigra—an area midway between the cortex, the thinking part of the brain, and the spinal cord. PD is also characterized by a degeneration and loss of norepinephrine nerve cells in the locus ceruleus—an area immediately below the substantia nigra, and acetyl-choline nerve cells in the nucleus basalis of Meynert—an area adjacent to the striatum, the area of above the substantia nigra. The degeneration and loss of nerve cells in the locus ceruleus, the nucleus basalis of Meynert and, to a lesser extent, the degeneration and loss of a specific subset of nerve cells in the substantia nigra, may be responsible for some of the non-motor symptoms of PD such as difficulty sleeping, intellectual impairment, and the syndrome of anergia, anhedonia, apathy, and passivity. The above mentioned degeneration may also contribute to depression.

The Difficulty of Diagnosing Depression in Parkinson Disease

The relation between PD and depression is confounded by the appearance of symptoms common to both disorders and trying to decide if the patient has PD, depression, or both. Thus a PD patient with hypomimia (an expressionless, immobile, sad, poker face), hypophonia (a barely audible, low, weepy voice), and stooped posture (bent as though he is bearing the weight of the world on his shoulder) may appear depressed—when he's not. Conversely, a depressed patient who moves slowly, speaks softly, and walks stooped over with her eyes on the ground to avoid contact with people, may appear to have PD—when she does not.

A detailed and structured interview with the patient, the spouse, and the caregiver supplemented by the use of a Depression and/or an Anxiety Rating Scale such as the Beck or Hamilton Scale is often helpful in distinguishing depressed from non-depressed PD patients. However, until a universal and specific test for depression is invented, one that is sensitive to moderate or marked depression while ignoring transient disappointment, loneliness, or sadness, there will be disagreement about the diagnosis of depression in PD.

Depression can be an integral, intrinsic, or primary component of PD—referred to as an endogenous depression. An endogenous depression is not a reaction to having PD: a chronic, progressive, and debilitating illness. The endogenous depression of PD is independent of the duration and severity of the physical or motor symptoms of PD. In 20% of PD patients who are depressed, the depression precedes the onset of physical or motor symptoms. Obviously, this is something appreciated only in retrospect—after the patient has been diagnosed with PD. In addition to an integral, intrinsic, primary, or endogenous depression, PD patients may suffer from an exogenous depression, a depression related to external events such as job loss, retirement, or knowledge of a relative or friend with advanced PD with fear of becoming as disabled as the relative or friend with advanced PD.

The Prevalence of Depression in Parkinson Disease

In a review of 24 studies, encompassing 3840 PD patients, 965 (25%) were judged to be moderately or markedly depressed. In most of the studies no distinction was made as to whether the depression was endogenous, exogenous, or both. There were 13 retrospective studies, studies in which the data were collected after the studies were completed, after the fact. There were 11 prospective studies, studies in which the data were collected during the study as an integral part of the study. In general, prospective studies give more reliable information on the prevalence of a condition than retrospective studies. The 11 prospective studies included 576 patients, or 15% of the 3840 patients. In these 11 prospective studies PD patients were evaluated using a detailed, structured interview often supplemented by a Depression Scale (the Beck or the Hamilton). In some of the prospective studies PD patients were compared with non-PD patients who were matched for age, sex, and severity of physical or motor disability. In the 11 prospective studies 38% of the PD patients (almost 40%) were depressed. In the 13 retrospective studies, 23% of PD patients were depressed. In the retrospective studies depression was often not diagnosed on the basis of a detailed structured interview and patients were usually not compared with non-PD patients who were matched for age, sex, and severity of physical or motor disability. The disparity between the prospective and the retrospective studies suggests depression, when sought, is more pervasive than thought. A caveat, however, is that investigators who seek depression are more likely to find it.

As an investigator who has participated in both prospective and retrospective studies on depression in PD, I believe the higher figure from the prospective studies, 38%, more accurately reflects the prevalence of depression in PD patients.

The Endogenous and the Exogenous Depression of Parkinson Disease

Depression can be an integral, intrinsic or primary component of PD—referred to as an endogenous depression. An endogenous depression is not a reaction to having PD. The endogenous depression of PD is independent of the duration and severity of the physical or motor symptoms of PD or the efficacy of anti-Parkinson drugs. In 20% of PD patients who are depressed, the depression precedes the onset of physical or motor symptoms. However, the endogenous depression may be complicated by an exogenous, external, or event-related depression or an exogenous depression may occur independently of an exogenous depression. An exogenous depression is likely to occur in:

1. A patient whose parent, grandparent, sibling, aunt, uncle, spouse, or close friend was or is disabled by PD.

2. A patient undergoing a mid-life crisis related to retirement, job loss, or spousal illness.

3. A patient who suffers loss of self-esteem related to his tremor, or his autonomic nervous system symptoms such as such as impotence, drooling, or urinary incontinence.

A skilled interviewer may separate the exogenous from the endogenous component of depression, and appropriate counseling may resolve the exogenous component.

Anxiety and Panic Attacks

Approximately 40% of PD patients are unduly anxious. This anxiety may be a manifestation of depression. Anxiety may be a reaction to PD or it may, conceivably, be part of PD, related to a loss of dopamine, norepinephrine, and serotonin nerve cells.

Panic attacks, episodic outbursts of anxiety triggered by fear are characterized by a variety of symptoms including fear of dying, fear of going insane, breathlessness, sweating, chest discomfort, choking, and dizziness. Panic attack may simulate a heart attack, and, occasionally, a panic attack must be distinguished from a heart attack. In many patients the panic attacks are situationally cued and may be linked to immobility. Thus, among patients with "on/off" fluctuations, panic attacks invariably occur during the "off" period. When panic attacks occur during the "off" period, their intensity parallels the difference in mobility between the "off" and the "on." In these patients treatment should be directed toward decreasing the fluctuations. In some patients, panic attacks may occur throughout the day, regardless of whether the patients are "on" or "off." Serotonin re-uptake inhibitors, a type of antidepressant, are also useful in treating panic attacks.

The Syndrome of Anergia, Anhedonia, Apathy, and Passivity

A syndrome of depression-like symptoms including anergia, anhedonia, apathy, and passivity occurs in perhaps as many as 20% (or more) of PD patients. Such patients deny they are depressed and often are able to distinguish their symptoms from depression. Thus some of the patients who in the past had been depressed (unrelated to PD) state that when, in the past, they had been depressed the depression was accompanied by feelings traditionally associated with depression such as gloom, guilt, hopelessness, pessimism, remorse, or sadness. Now, in their anergic, anhedonic, apathetic, passive state they were not gloomy nor guilt-stricken. The did not feel hopeless, nor pessimistic, nor remorseful, nor sad. These patients do not respond to counseling and may not respond to antidepressants.

Selective Intellectual Impairment

Many patients, the number is unknown but is probably greater than 20%, develop a selective impairment in intellectual or cognitive function. This selective impairment in intellectual function is distinct from dementia: a global deterioration in intellectual or cognitive function. Manifestations of the selective impairment in intellectual function may include slowness of information processing (usually referred to as bradyphrenia) and impairment in certain functions such as the ability to innovate, organize, plan, and sequence. It may be difficult to distinguish a PD patient who has a selective impairment in intellectual function from a PD patient who is depressed. Both patients may exhibit changes such as:

1. Declining job performance.

2. Erratic or inappropriate conduct.

3. Inability to accomplish previously learned tasks: balancing a checkbook or completing a crossword puzzle.

The syndrome of selective impairment of intellectual function may be associated with the syndrome of anergia, anhedonia, apathy, and passivity. Both syndromes may arise from damage to or loss of a specific subset of dopamine nerve cells in the substantia nigra, from damage to or loss of norepinephrine nerve cells in the locus ceruleus, from damage to or loss of serotonin nerve cells in the vicinity of the substantia nigra, and from damage to or loss of acetyl-choline nerve cells in the nucleus basalis of Meynert. The loss of these different nerve cells among PD patients who have the syndrome of selective impairment in intellectual function and/or the syndrome of anergia, anhedonia, apathy, and passivity overlaps the loss of nerve cells among PD patients who are depressed accounting for the difficulty in distinguishing among them.

The loss of dopamine, norepinephrine, serotonin, and acetyl-choline nerve cells produce the different symptoms by interfering with normal function in a number of brain circuits.

Autonomic Nervous System Malfunction

Symptoms arising from malfunction of the autonomic nervous system can include impotence, drooling, urinary frequency and hesitancy, excessive sweating, heat and cold intolerance, and orthostatic or postural hypotension: a drop in blood pressure upon going from a lying to a sitting or standing posture or position. The drop in blood pressure may be accompanied by symptoms of dizziness or lightheadedness. Autonomic nervous system symptoms may complicate PD independent of the duration or severity of motor symptoms or depression. Autonomic nervous system symptoms are similar to those in multisystem atrophy (MSA), the Shy-Drager syndrome, a Parkinson-like or Parkinson-plus syndrome—one that may, at times, be mistaken for PD. The Autonomic nervous system symptoms in PD (and in multisystem atrophy) result from the degeneration and loss of norepinephrine and acetyl-choline nerve cells. Some autonomic nervous system symptoms such as excessive sweating and heat and cold intolerance may be related not to malfunctioning of the autonomic nervous system but to thyroid disease. When symptoms such as excessive sweating or heat and cold intolerance are present, the thyroid should be evaluated. It's easier to treat and correct symptoms arising from thyroid disease than those arising from malfunction of the autonomic nervous system.

Some autonomic nervous system symptoms such as drooling, drop in blood pressure upon standing, urinary frequency and hesitancy, and impotence and may be helped with specific treatments. For example, the drop in blood pressure upon standing may be helped by midodrine, an alpha-1 agonist.

Sleep Disorder

PD patients may suffer from a sleep disorder including trouble falling asleep, trouble staying asleep, and daytime drowsiness The sleep disorder may be a primary, endogenous disorder, or may result from an inability to turn in bed related to bradykinesia and/or rigidity. The sleep disorder may include symptoms such as spasmodic or dystonic leg and, less commonly, arm cramps, restless legs, vivid dreams, hallucinations, agitation, and nocturnal hypervigilance. The nocturnal hypervigilance may alternate with excessive daytime drowsiness. Spasmodic or dystonic leg cramps and restless legs are usually related to a deficiency of dopamine and usually improvement with the administration of drugs for PD such as levodopa/carbidopa or a dopamine agonist. The other symptoms may be related to an excess of dopamine or a related chemical, serotonin. Drugs for PD, drugs that relieve dystonic leg cramps and restless legs, may provoke or aggravate the other symptoms. The anti-cholinergic drugs (Artane, Cogentin), amantadine (Symmetrel), selegiline (deprenyl or Eldepryl), the dopamine agonists (bromocriptine, pergolide, pramipexole, ropinirole), and levodopa/carbidopa in the order presented provoke or aggravate the other symptoms.

The sleep disorder in PD patients resembles that following von Economo's encephalitis: encephalitis lethargica, sleeping sickness. Von Economo's encephalitis appeared during the period 1917–1930, and then disappeared. Parkinsonism, a sleep disorder, depression, a syndrome of anergia, anhedonia, apathy, and passivity, and a syndrome of selective intellectual impairment alone or in combination occurred in approximately 70% of patients who had von Economo's encephalitis. The syndromes of parkinsonism, a sleep disorder, depression, anergia, anhedonia, apathy, passivity, and selective intellectual impairment among post-encephalitic Parkinson patients and idiopathic PD patients were similar reflecting the similarity of brain regions involved in the processes of von Economo's encephalitis and idiopathic PD.

Treatment of Depression in Parkinson Disease

In PD patients with an exogenous depression, one linked to being diagnosed as having PD or to another external life-situation, counseling may be sufficient. In patients with a sustained depression, endogenous or exogenous, several approaches may be used. In some counseling may be sufficient, but for others, antidepressants are needed.

The selective serotonin re-uptake inhibitors (SSRIs): fluoxetine, paroxetine, and sertraline have become the mainstays of treatment. The SSRIs, unlike the tricyclic antidepressants, the previous class of drugs used to treat depression, are activating or energizing rather than sedating. This may be desirable for those depressed patients who are withdrawn but may be undesirable for those depressed patients who are agitated. In treating the depression of PD, the dose of the SSRIs is equal to or less than that used in non-PD depression: fluoxetine 20–40 mg per day, paroxetine 20 mg per day, sertraline 50 mg per day. Concern has also been raised about adverse interaction between SSRIs and selegiline. This occurs but is unusual. Nonetheless, if possible, selegiline should be stopped when an SSRI is started.

The tricyclic antidepressant remain an alternative, in some patients, to the SSRIs. Amitriptyline, nortriptyline, imipramine, desipramine, and doxepin have different abilities to block the reuptake of noradrenalin and serotonin, different plasma half-lives and clearances, and different antidepressant, anti-cholinergic, and sedative properties. Because, in patients who have cognitive impairment without dementia, tricyclics may increase confusion or induce delirium, it's best to use those tricyclics with a short plasma half-life, a rapid clearance, and little anti-cholinergic activity.

Rarely, electroconvulsive therapy (ECT) may be needed to treat severely depressed patients who have failed to be helped by counseling and antidepressants. A side benefit of ECT is that it may, in some patients, lessen, temporarily, the rigidity and bradykinesia of PD.

More Information

For more information about Parkinson's disease, contact:

National Parkinson Foundation, Inc.
Bob Hope Parkinson Research Center
1501 N.W. 9th Avenue, Bob Hope Road
Miami, FL 33136-1494
Toll Free: 800-327-4545
Website: www.parkinson.org

A list of resources for more information about depression is included in the end section of this book.

Chapter 52

Co-Occurrence of Depression with Stroke

Depression is a common, serious, and costly illness that affects one in ten adults in the U.S. each year, costs the Nation between $30 and $44 billion annually, and causes impairment, suffering, and disruption of personal, family, and work life. Although 80 percent of depressed people can be effectively treated, nearly two out of three of those suffering from this illness do not seek or receive appropriate treatment. Effective treatments include both medication and psychotherapy, which are sometimes used in combination.

Depression Co-Occurs with Stroke

Of particular significance, depression often co-occurs with stroke. When this happens, the presence of the additional illness, depression, is frequently unrecognized, leading to serious and unnecessary consequences for patients and families.

Though depressed feelings can be a common reaction to a stroke, clinical depression is not the expected reaction. For this reason, when present, specific treatment should be considered for clinical depression even in the presence of a stroke.

Appropriate diagnosis and treatment of depression may bring substantial benefits to the patient through improved medical status,

"Co-Occurrence of Depression with Stroke: Awareness and Treatment Can Improve Overall Health and Reduce Suffering," a fact sheet produced by the National Institute of Mental Health, updated June 1999; available online at www.nimh.nih.gov/publicat/stroke.cfm.

enhanced quality of life, a reduction in the degree of pain and disability, and improved treatment compliance and cooperation.

More Facts

The association between depression and stroke has long been recognized for its negative impact on an individual's rehabilitation, family relationships, and quality of life. Appropriate diagnosis and treatment of depression can shorten the rehabilitation process and lead to more rapid recovery and resumption of routine. It can also save health care costs (for example, eliminate nursing home expenses).

Of the 600,000 Americans who experience a first or recurrent stroke each year, an estimated 10–27 percent experience major depression. An additional 15–40 percent experience depressive symptomatology (not major depression) within two months following the stroke.

Three-fourths of strokes occur in people 65 years of age and over. With stroke a leading cause of disability in older persons, proper recognition and treatment of depression in this population is particularly important.

The mean duration of major depression in stroke patients has been shown to be just under a year. Among the factors that effect the likelihood and severity of depression following a stroke are the location of the brain lesion, previous or family history of depression, and pre-stroke social functioning. Post-stroke patients who are also depressed, particularly those with major depressive disorder, are less compliant with rehabilitation, more irritable and demanding, and may experience personality change.

Symptoms of Depression

- Persistent sad or empty mood
- Loss of interest or pleasure in ordinary activities, including sex
- Decreased energy, fatigue, being slowed down
- Sleep disturbances (insomnia, early-morning waking or over-sleeping)
- Eating disturbances (loss of appetite and weight, or weight gain)
- Difficulty concentrating, remembering, making decisions
- Feelings of guilt, worthlessness, helplessness
- Thoughts of death or suicide; suicide attempts

- Irritability

- Excessive crying

- Chronic aches and pains that don't respond to treatment

If a person has five or more of these symptoms for more than two weeks, it is important that these symptoms be brought to the attention of the individual's health care provider.

Action Steps

Don't Ignore Symptoms: Health care professionals should always be aware of the possibility of depression co-occurring with stroke. Patients or family members with concerns about this possibility should discuss these issues with the individuals' physicians. A consultation with a psychiatrist or other mental health clinician may be recommended to clarify the diagnosis.

Get the Word Out: Emphasize the importance of professional and public awareness of the co-occurrence of depression with stroke and proper diagnosis and treatment of depression. Community, professional, advocacy organizations, and the media can help spread important messages about depression co-occurring with stroke.

Stay Informed: For free brochures on depression and its treatment, call the National Institute of Mental Health (800-421-4211) or visit the NIMH website at http://www.nimh.nih.gov.

Chapter 53

Depression and Thyroid Disease

Depression may be the first sign of an overactive or underactive thyroid. The nervousness, anxiety, and hyperactivity of hyperthyroidism often interfere with a person's ability to function in normal daily activities. Both anxiety and depression can be severe, but should improve once the hyperthyroidism is recognized and treated.

Depression is more commonly associated with hypothyroidism with its fatigue, mental dullness, and lethargy leading to depression which is often profound and severe enough that a physician may mistakenly treat the patient first for depression without testing for underlying hypothyroidism. Since most hypothyroidism begins after age fifty, the symptoms are often attributed to aging, menopause and/or depression.

Postpartum Depression

Approximately one in twenty women experience a change in thyroid function following pregnancy. Since this is a time when the responsibilities of the young mother are considerable, she may attribute the fatigue and emotional symptoms as a natural result of her increased duties and lack of sleep. Some physicians have suggested, however, that every young mother who experiences depression should have a TSH (thyroid-stimulating hormone) test to be sure her thyroid function is normal.

"Depression and Thyroid Illness," an undated document © Thyroid Foundation of America; reprinted with permission. This document is available online at http://www.allthyroid.org/docs/yf/famdep_iv.html, cited March 2002.

Bipolar Mood Disorders and Thyroid Disease

Bipolar is a term that psychiatrists are using to describe individuals whose emotions tend to swing from highs to lows, elation to the blues. A subgroup of this population experience rapid cycling, meaning that they have at least four major highs and lows per year. Studies of patients with rapid cycling bipolar disease, (80% of whom are women) have shown that 25–50% have evidence of thyroid deficiency. Some feel well, and their only evidence of thyroid failure is an increased level of TSH in their blood. Others are clearly hypothyroid.

Lithium: A Problem for Some Patients

Physicians have prescribed lithium in the treatment of depression for years. It has a low incidence of side effects and a high success rate in treating depression, especially bipolar disorders including the rapid cycling described above.

Unfortunately, in individuals with an underlying tendency toward thyroid dysfunction, lithium may cause hypothyroidism. Since most physicians are aware of this relationship, it is now common for a physician to first check the serum TSH levels of a patient before prescribing lithium, repeating the thyroid test periodically while the patient is on the medication.

Are You at Risk?

Not all individuals with depression have a thyroid problem. Nevertheless, because thyroid dysfunction can be so difficult to recognize yet so responsive to treatment, most physicians will order an initial serum TSH test to evaluate thyroid function.

You are at increased risk if you or a close relative have had a thyroid problem. Your risk is also increased if you have a related autoimmune condition such as diabetes requiring insulin treatment, pernicious anemia, or the white skin spots of vitiligo. You are also more likely to develop thyroid dysfunction if you or a close relative have had prematurely gray hair (one gray hair before thirty) or any degree of ambidexterity or left-handedness.

But why risk missing a thyroid problem if you are depressed. Discuss these concerns with your physicians and be sure that your TSH has been checked before you are treated for depression.

Part Five

Suicide

Chapter 54

Depressive Illness and Suicide Risk

Facts about Suicide

If depressive illnesses are left untreated, they can be fatal. 30,000 people kill themselves in the U.S. every year. It is estimated that the actual figure may be three times that number due to inaccurate reporting, that is, suicides recorded as accidental instead. The *Journal of the American Medical Association* has reported that 95% of all suicides occur at the peak of a depressive episode. Healthy people do not kill themselves. Depressive illnesses can distort a person's thinking, so they don't think clearly or rationally. They may not know they have a treatable illness, or they may think that they can't be helped. Their illness can cause thoughts of hopelessness and helplessness, which may then lead to suicidal thoughts. In order to save lives, it's critical that society recognize the warning signs of these biological diseases that cause suicide. But there is still stigma associated with these illnesses which prevents public education and early treatment for sufferers. The topic of suicide has always been taboo. It is a subject that is misunderstood by people, thereby allowing myths to be perpetuated. Education is the key to understanding this incredible tragedy that, in many cases, might be prevented.

Excerpted from "Depression and Related Depressive Illnesses: Facts You Should Know," an undated fact sheet compiled by Tracy Pierson, © SAVE: Suicide Awareness Voices for Education, available online at www.save.org/depfacts.shtml, cited March 2002; reprinted with permission.

What Are Depressive Illnesses?

They are total-body illnesses that affect a person's thoughts, feelings, behavior, and physical health and appearance. They affect all areas of a person's life—home, work, school, and social life. These illnesses are different from ordinary blues, which are normal feelings that eventually pass. Depressive illnesses last for months or years with varying patterns.

A person with a depressive illness cannot talk themselves into feeling good. They cannot snap themselves out of it. Suffering or not suffering from these illnesses does not have anything to do with a person's willpower. Many times, society assumes a person suffering from depression is just lazy, or lacks motivation to get his or her life together. One might be labeled as simply having a behavior problem. This simply is not true.

To determine whether a depressive illness is present or not, a thorough medical examination is essential:

- Many drugs used in the treatment of other illnesses, such as cancer, heart disease, high blood pressure, or arthritis, as well as oral contraceptives and some antibiotics, can trigger depressive illnesses.

- Long-term or sudden illnesses can also bring on or exacerbate a depressive illness. And neurological disorders, hormonal disorders, infections, and tumors can mimic the symptoms of depressive illnesses or anxiety. If all medical tests come out negative, or if chronic physical pain does not respond to treatment, there is a strong possibility a depressive illness exists.

Signs and/or Symptoms of Depression and Related Illnesses

It is important to understand what constitutes normal development in infants, children, and adolescents vs. what may be signs of a depressive illness. You may not see a drastic change in a child/adolescent's behavior or mood if they were born with a depressive illness. It may be part of their make-up, having been present from day one.

The following signs and/or symptoms may be a result of possible unipolar depression, bipolar illness, anxiety disorders, or attention deficit disorder with or without hyperactivity. A person may have as few as two or three symptoms or many of the symptoms. It is not uncommon to have a combination of illnesses with overlapping symptoms.

Infants

- Unresponsive when talked to or touched, never smile or cry, or may cry often being difficult to soothe.

- Failure to gain weight (not due to other medical illness).

- Unmotivated in play.

- Restless, oversensitive to noise or touch.

- Problems with eating or sleeping.

- Digestive disorders (constipation/diarrhea).

Children

- Persistent unhappiness, negativity, complaining, chronic boredom, no initiative.

- Uncontrollable anger with aggressive or destructive behavior, possibly hitting themselves or others, kicking, or self-biting, head banging. Harming animals.

- Continual disobedience.

- Easily frustrated, frequent crying, low self-esteem, overly sensitive.

- Inability to pay attention, remember, or make decisions, easily distracted, mind goes blank.

- Energy fluctuations from lethargic to frenzied activity, with periods of normalcy.

- Eating or sleeping problems.

- Bedwetting, constipation, diarrhea.

- Impulsiveness, accident-prone.

- Chronic worry and fear, clingy, panic attacks.

- Extreme self-consciousness.

- Slowed speech and body movements.

- Disorganized speech—hard to follow when telling you a story, etc.

- Physical symptoms such as dizziness, headaches, stomachaches, arms or legs ache, nail-biting, pulling out hair or eyelashes. (ruling out other medical causes)

- Suicidal talk or attempts.

In children, depressive illnesses and/or anxiety may be disguised as, or presented as school phobia or school avoidance, social phobia or social avoidance, excessive separation anxiety, running away, obsessions, compulsions, or everyday rituals, such as having to go to bed at the exact time each night for fear something bad might happen. Chronic illnesses may be present also since depression weakens the immune system.

Adolescents

- Physical symptoms such as dizziness, headaches, stomachaches, neck aches, arms or legs hurt due to muscle tension, digestive disorders. (ruling out other medical causes)
- Persistent unhappiness, negativity, irritability.
- Uncontrollable anger or outbursts of rage.
- Overly self-critical, unwarranted guilt, low self-esteem.
- Inability to concentrate, think straight, remember, or make decisions, possibly resulting in refusal to study in school or an inability (due to depression or attention deficit disorder) to do schoolwork.
- Slowed or hesitant speech or body movements, or restlessness (anxiety).
- Loss of interest in once pleasurable activities.
- Low energy, chronic fatigue, sluggishness.
- Change in appetite, noticeable weight loss or weight gain, abnormal eating patterns.
- Chronic worry, excessive fear.
- Preoccupation with death themes in literature, music, drawings, speaking of death repeatedly, fascination with guns/knives.
- Suicidal thoughts, plans, or attempts.

Depressive illnesses and/or anxiety may be disguised as, or presented as eating disorders such as anorexia or bulimia, drug/alcohol abuse, sexual promiscuity, risk-taking behavior such as reckless driving, unprotected sex, carelessness when walking across busy streets, or on bridges or cliffs. There may be social isolation, running away, constant disobedience, getting into trouble with the law, physical or sexual assaults against others, obnoxious behavior, failure to care about appearance or hygiene, no sense of self or of values or morals, difficulty cultivating relationships, inability to establish and stick with occupational and educational goals.

Adults

- Persistent sad or empty mood.

- Feelings of hopelessness, helplessness, guilt, pessimism, or worthlessness.

- Drug/alcohol abuse. (Often masks depression/anxiety.)

- Chronic fatigue, or loss of interest in ordinary activities, including sex.

- Disturbances in eating or sleeping patterns.

- Irritability, increased crying; generalized anxiety (may include chronic fear of dying or being convinced dying of incurable disease), panic attacks.

- Hypochondria—sufferer actually feels symptoms, they are real and not imagined.

- Difficulty concentrating, remembering, or making decisions.

- Thoughts of suicide; suicide plans or attempts.

- Persistent physical symptoms or pains that do not respond to treatment—headaches, stomach problems, neck and back pain, joint pain, mouth pain.

Many people feel that it is normal for elderly persons to be depressed. This is simply not true and is a very dangerous misconception. If you suspect a older adult is suffering from a depressive illness, he or she should have a thorough medical examination as soon as possible.

Symptoms of Mania

- Decreased need for sleep.
- Restless, agitated, can't sit still.
- Increased energy, or an inability to slow down.
- Racing, disorganized thoughts, easily distracted.

- Rapid, increased talking or laughing

- Grandiose ideas, increased creativity.

- Overly excited, euphoric, giddy, exhilarated.

- Excessive irritability, on edge.

- Increased sex drive, possibly resulting in affairs, inappropriate sexual behaviors.

- Poor judgment, impulsiveness, spending sprees.

- Embarrassing social behavior.

- Paranoia, delusions, hallucinations.

What Are the Danger Signs of Suicide?

- Talking or joking about suicide.

- Statements about being reunited with a deceased loved one.

- Statements about hopelessness, helplessness, or worthlessness. Example: "Life is useless." "Everyone would be better off without me." "It doesn't matter. I won't be around much longer anyway." "I wish I could just disappear."

- Preoccupation with death. Example: recurrent death themes in music, literature, or drawings.

- Writing letters or leaving notes referring to death or "the end."

- Suddenly happier, calmer.

- Loss of interest in things one cares about.

- Unusual visiting or calling people one cares about—saying their good-byes.

- Giving possessions away, making arrangements, setting one's affairs in order.

- Self-destructive behavior (alcohol/drug abuse, self-injury or mutilation, promiscuity).

- Risk-taking behavior (reckless driving/excessive speeding, carelessness around bridges, cliffs or balconies, or walking in front of traffic).

- Having several accidents resulting in injury. Close calls or brushes with death. Obsession with guns or knives.

Just because an individual is doing these things does not mean his mind is made up. He can be stopped. He has not chosen death, but is instead focusing only on easing the pain or ending the pain. Pain which is usually the result of an illness—a chemical imbalance in the brain that is, many times, treatable. If a person understood that he could have the life back that he once had, before the depressive illness, he would almost certainly chose life, not death.

What Should a Person Do If They Suspect Someone They Know Might Be Suicidal?

Ask him or her. That may sound absurd and very scary, but you must ask him if he ever feels so bad that he thinks of suicide. Don't worry about planting the idea in someone's head. Suicidal thoughts are common with depressive illnesses, although not all people have them. If a person has been thinking of suicide, he or she will be relieved and grateful that you were willing to be so open and non-judgmental. It shows a person you truly care and take him or her seriously.

If you get a yes to your question, question the individual further. Ask if he has a plan, or a method, or if he has decided when he will do it. This will give you an idea if he is in immediate danger. If you feel he is, do not leave him alone. The person must see a doctor or psychiatrist immediately. You may have to take him to the nearest hospital emergency room. Always take a suicide threat seriously and never keep it a secret.

You must never call a person's bluff, or try to minimize his problems by telling him he has everything to live for or how hurt his family would be. This will only increase his guilt and feelings of hopelessness. He needs to be reassured that there is help, that what he is feeling is treatable, and that his suicidal feelings are temporary.

If you feel the person isn't in immediate danger, you can say things like, "I can tell you're really hurting," and "I care about you and will do my best to help you." And follow through—help him find a doctor or a mental health professional. Be by his side when he makes that first phone call, or go along with him to his first appointment. A supportive person can mean so much to someone who's in pain. This is an opportunity to interrupt the long process that for many, leads to suicide. You may save a life.

Chapter 55

Suicide in America

Suicide is a tragic and potentially preventable public health problem. In 1997, suicide was the 8th leading cause of death in the U.S.[1] Specifically, 10.6 out of every 100,000 persons died by suicide. The total number of suicides was approximately 31,000, or 1.3 percent of all deaths. Approximately 500,000 people received emergency room treatment as a result of attempted suicide in 1996.[2] Taken together, the numbers of suicide deaths and attempts show the need for carefully designed prevention efforts.

Suicidal behavior is complex. Some risk factors vary with age, gender, and ethnic group and may even change over time. The risk factors for suicide frequently occur in combination. Research has shown that more than 90 percent of people who kill themselves have depression or another diagnosable mental or substance abuse disorder.[3] In addition, research indicates that alterations in neurotransmitters such as serotonin are associated with the risk for suicide.[4] Diminished levels of this brain chemical have been found in patients with depression, impulsive disorders, a history of violent suicide attempts, and also in postmortem brains of suicide victims.

Adverse life events in combination with other risk factors such as depression may lead to suicide. However, suicide and suicidal behavior are not normal responses to stress. Many people have one or more risk factors and are not suicidal. Other risk factors include: prior suicide

This chapter includes text from "In Harm's Way: Suicide in America," National Institute of Mental Health (NIMH), January 2001; and "Suicide Facts," NIMH, December 2001.

attempt; family history of mental disorder or substance abuse; family history of suicide; family violence, including physical or sexual abuse; firearms in the home; incarceration; and exposure to the suicidal behavior of others, including family members, peers, and even in the media.[5]

Suicide Facts

Research shows that almost all people who kill themselves have a diagnosable mental or substance abuse disorder or both, and that the majority have depressive illness. Studies indicate that the most promising way to prevent suicide and suicidal behavior is through the early recognition and treatment of depression and other psychiatric illnesses.

Most people who are depressed do not kill themselves. Suicide is considered a possible complication of depressive illness in combination with other risk factors because suicidal thoughts and behavior can be symptoms of moderate to severe depression. These symptoms typically respond to proper treatment, and usually can be avoided with early intervention for depressive illness. Any concerns about suicidal risk should always be taken seriously and evaluated by a qualified professional immediately.

Suicide Risk Factors

It is important to note that many people experience one or more risk factors and are not suicidal.

- One or more diagnosable mental or substance abuse disorder
- Impulsivity
- Adverse life events
- Family history of mental or substance abuse disorder
- Family history of suicide
- Family violence, including physical or sexual abuse
- Prior suicide attempt
- Firearm in the home
- Incarceration
- Exposure to the suicidal behavior of others, including family, peers, or in the news or fiction stories

Gender Differences

More than four times as many men than women die by suicide;[1] however, women report attempting suicide about two to three times as often as men.[6] Suicide by firearm is the most common method for both men and women, accounting for 58 percent of all suicides in 1997. Seventy-two percent of all suicides were committed by white men, and 79 percent of all firearm suicides were committed by white men. The highest suicide rate was for white men over 85 years of age—65 per 100,000 persons.

Children, Adolescents, and Young Adults

Over the last several decades, the suicide rate in young people has increased dramatically.[7] In 1997, suicide was the 3rd leading cause of death in 15 to 24 year olds—11.4 of every 100,000 persons—following unintentional injuries and homicide.[1] Suicide also was the 3rd leading cause in 10 to 14 year olds, with 303 deaths among 19,097,000 children in this age group. For adolescents aged 15 to 19, there were 1,802 suicide deaths among 19,146,000 adolescents. The gender ratio in this age group was about 4:1 (males: females). Among young people 20 to 24 years of age, there were 2,384 suicide deaths among 17,488,000 people in this age group. The gender ratio in this age range was about 6:1 (males: females).[8]

Attempted Suicides

There may be as many as eight attempted suicides to one completion;[9] the ratio is higher in women and youth and lower in men and the elderly. Risk factors for attempted suicide in adults include depression, alcohol abuse, cocaine use, and separation or divorce.[10,11] Risk factors for attempted suicide in youth include depression, alcohol or other drug use disorder, physical or sexual abuse, and aggressive or disruptive behaviors.[12-14] The majority of suicide attempts are expressions of extreme distress and not just harmless bids for attention. A suicidal person should not be left alone and needs immediate mental health treatment.

How to Help

It is not true that if a person talks about suicide, they will not attempt it. Seriously suicidal people make such comments for a variety of reasons—it is extremely important to take these remarks seriously and help that person seek a mental health evaluation and treatment. A person in crisis may not be aware that they are in need of help or be able to seek it on their own. They may also need to be reminded that effective treatment for depression is available, and that many people can very quickly begin to experience relief from depressive symptoms.

Prevention Programs

All suicide prevention programs need to be scientifically evaluated to demonstrate whether or not they work. Preventive interventions for suicide must also be complex and intensive if they are to have lasting effects. Most school-based, information-only, prevention programs focused solely on suicide have not been evaluated to see if they are effective, and research suggests that such programs may actually increase distress in the young people who are most vulnerable.[15] School and community prevention programs designed to address suicide and suicidal behavior as part of a broader focus on mental health, coping skills in response to stress, substance abuse, aggressive behaviors, etc., are more likely to be successful in the long run.

Recognition and appropriate treatment of mental and substance abuse disorders also hold great suicide prevention value. For example, because most elderly suicide victims—70 percent—have visited their primary care physician in the month prior to their suicides,[16] improving the recognition and treatment of depression in medical settings is a promising way to prevent suicide in older adults. Toward this goal, NIMH-funded researchers are currently investigating the effectiveness of a depression education intervention delivered to primary care physicians and their elderly patients.

If someone is suicidal, he or she must not be left alone. You may need to take emergency steps to get help, such as calling 911. It is also important to limit the person's access to firearms, large amounts of medication, or other lethal means of committing suicide.

References

1. Hoyert DL, Kochanek KD, Murphy SL. Deaths: final data for 1997. *National Vital Statistics Report*, 47(19). DHHS Publication No. 99-1120. Hyattsville, MD: National Center for Health Statistics, 1999. http://www.cdc.gov/nchs/data/nvs47_19.pdf

2. McCraig LF, Stussman BJ. National Hospital Ambulatory Care Survey: 1996. Emergency department summary. *Advance*

Data from Vital and Health Statistics, no. 293. Hyattsville, MD: National Center for Health Statistics, 1997. http://www.cdc.gov/nchs/data/ad293.pdf

3. Conwell Y, Brent D. Suicide and aging I: patterns of psychiatric diagnosis. *International Psychogeriatrics*, 1995; 7(2): 149-64.

4. Mann JJ, Oquendo M, Underwood MD, et al. The neurobiology of suicide risk: a review for the clinician. *Journal of Clinical Psychiatry*, 1999; 60(Suppl 2): 7-11; discussion 18-20, 113-6.

5. Blumenthal SJ. Suicide: a guide to risk factors, assessment, and treatment of suicidal patients. *Medical Clinics of North America*, 1988; 72(4): 937-71.

6. Weissman MM, Bland RC, Canino GJ, et al. Prevalence of suicide ideation and suicide attempts in nine countries. *Psychological Medicine*, 1999; 29(1): 9-17.

7. National Center for Injury Prevention and Control. *Fact book for the year 2000: suicide and suicide behavior*. http://www.cdc.gov/ncipc/pub-res/FactBook/suicide.htm

8. National Center for Injury Prevention and Control. *Suicide deaths and rates per 100,000: United States 1994-1997*. http://www.cdc.gov/ncipc/data/us9794/Suic.htm

9. Moscicki EK. Epidemiology of suicide. In: Jacobs D, ed. *The Harvard Medical School guide to suicide assessment and intervention*. San Francisco, CA: Jossey-Bass, 1999, 40-71.

10. Kessler RC, Borges G, Walters EE. Prevalence of and risk factors for lifetime suicide attempts in the National Comorbidity Survey. *Archives of General Psychiatry*, 1999; 56(7): 617-26.

11. Petronis KR, Samuels JF, Moscicki EK, et al. An epidemiologic investigation of potential risk factors for suicide attempts. *Social Psychiatry and Psychiatric Epidemiology*, 1990; 25(4): 193-9.

12. Gould MS, King R, Greenwald S, et al. Psychopathology associated with suicidal ideation and attempts among children and adolescents. *Journal of the American Academy of Child and Adolescent Psychiatry*, 1998; 37(9): 915-23.

13. Fergusson DM, Horwood LJ, Lynskey MT. Childhood sexual abuse and psychiatric disorder in young adulthood, II: psychiatric outcomes of childhood sexual abuse. *Journal of the American Academy of Child and Adolescent Psychiatry*, 1996; 35(10): 1365-74.

14. Kaplan SJ, Pelcovitz D, Salzinger S, et al. Adolescent physical abuse and suicide attempts. *Journal of the American Academy of Child and Adolescent Psychiatry*, 1997; 36(6): 799-808.

15. Vieland V, Whittle B, Garland A, et al. The impact of curriculum-based suicide prevention programs for teenagers: an 18-month follow-up. *Journal of the American Academy of Child and Adolescent Psychiatry*, 1991; 30(5): 811-5.

16. Conwell, Y. Suicide in elderly patients. In: Schneider LS, Reynolds CF III, Lebowitz, BD, Friedhoff AJ, eds. *Diagnosis and treatment of depression in late life*. Washington, DC: American Psychiatric Press, 1994; 397-418.

Chapter 56

Suicide Facts and Misconceptions

Common Misconceptions about Suicide

People who talk about suicide won't really do it.

Almost everyone who commits suicide has given some clue or warning. Do not ignore suicide threats. Statements like "You'll be sorry when I'm dead," or "I can't see any way out" —no matter how casually or jokingly said—may indicate serious suicidal feelings.

Anyone who tries to kill themselves must be crazy.

Most suicidal people are not psychotic or insane. They must be upset, grief-stricken, depressed, or despairing, but extreme distress and emotional pain are not necessarily signs of mental illness.

If a person is determined to kill themselves, nothing is going to stop them.

Even the most severely depressed person has mixed feelings about death, wavering until the very last moment between wanting to live and wanting to die. Most suicidal people do not want death; they want

Excerpted from "Suicide: Learn More, Learn to Help," August 1998, National Alliance for the Mentally Ill (NAMI), Colonial Place Three, 2107 Wilson Blvd., Suite 300, Arlington, VA 22201, Phone: 703-524-7600; NAMI HelpLine: 1-800-950-NAMI [6264]; www.nami.org. © 1998 NAMI; reprinted with permission.

the pain to stop. The impulse to end it all, however overpowering, does not last forever.

People who commit suicide are people who were unwilling to seek help.

Studies of suicide victims have shown that more than half had sought medical help within six months before their deaths.

Talking about suicide may give someone the idea.

You don't give a suicidal person morbid ideas by talking about suicide. The opposite is true—bringing up the subject of suicide and discussing it openly is one of the most helpful things you can do.

Facts about Suicide Risk

Persons Who May Be at High Risk for Suicide

- Persons who are severely depressed and feel hopeless
- Persons who have a past history of suicide attempts
- Persons who have made concrete plans or preparations for suicide

Don't be afraid to ask: "Do you sometimes feel so bad you think of suicide?"

Just about everyone has considered suicide, however fleetingly, at one time or another. There is no danger of "giving someone the idea." In fact, it can be a great relief if you bring the question of suicide into the open, and discuss it freely, without showing shock or disapproval. Raising the question of suicide shows you are taking the person seriously and responding to the potential of his/her distress.

If the answer is "Yes, I do think of suicide," you must take it seriously.

How to Find out If Someone Is Suicidal

Ask these questions—in the same order—to find out if the person is seriously considering suicide:

1. "Have you been feeling sad or unhappy?"

A "yes" response will confirm that the person has been feeling some depression.

2. *"Do you ever feel hopeless? Does it seem as if things can never get better?"*

Feelings of hopelessness are often associated with suicidal thoughts.

3. *"Do you have thoughts of death? Does it seem as if things can never get better?"*

A "yes" response indicates suicidal wishes but not necessarily suicidal plans. Many depressed people say they think they'd be better off dead and wish they'd die in their sleep or get killed in an accident. However, most of them say they have no intention of actually killing themselves.

4. *"Do you ever have any actual suicidal impulses? Do you have any urge to kill yourself?"*

A "yes" indicates an active desire to die. This is a more serious situation.

5. *"Do you have any actual plans to kill yourself?"*

If the answer is "yes," ask about their specific plans. What method have they chosen? Hanging? Jumping? Pills? A gun? Have they actually obtained the rope? What building do they plan to jump from? Although these questions may sound grotesque, they may save a life. The danger is greatest when the plans are clear and specific, when they have made actual preparations, and when the method they have chosen is clearly lethal.

6. *"When do you plan to kill yourself?"*

If the suicide attempt is a long way off (say, in five years) danger is clearly not imminent. If they plan to kill themselves soon, the danger is grave.

7. *"Is there anything that would hold you back, such as your family or your religious convictions?"*

If the person says that people would be better off without them, and if they have no deterrents, suicide is much more likely.

8. *"Have you ever made a suicide attempt in the past?"*

Previous suicide attempts indicate that future attempts are more likely. Even if a previous attempt did not seem serious, the next attempt may be fatal. All suicide attempts should be taken seriously. However, suicidal gestures can be more dangerous than they seem, since many people do kill themselves.

9. "Would you be willing to talk to someone or seek help if you felt desperate? Whom would you talk to?"

If the person who feels suicidal is cooperative and has a clear plan to reach out for help, the danger is less than if they are stubborn, secretive, hostile, and unwilling to ask for help.

For More Information

If you are suicidal and in immediate danger, or if you are with someone who is suicidal and in immediate danger, call 9-1-1.

For more information about suicide and mental illness, contact:

National Alliance for the Mentally Ill
Colonial Place Three
2107 Wilson Boulevard, Suite 300
Arlington, VA 22201-3042
Toll-free: 800-950-NAMI (6264)
Phone: 703-524-7600
TDD: 703-516-7227
Fax: 703-524-9094
Website: http://www.nami.org

Information about other resources for help in dealing with a mental health crisis are listed in the end section of this book.

Chapter 57

Frequently Asked Questions about Suicide

What should you do if someone tells you they are thinking about suicide?

If someone tells you they are thinking about suicide, you should take their distress seriously, listen nonjudgmentally, and help them get to a professional for evaluation and treatment. People consider suicide when they are hopeless and unable to see alternative solutions to problems. Suicidal behavior is most often related to a mental disorder (depression) or to alcohol or other substance abuse. Suicidal behavior is also more likely to occur when people experience stressful events (major losses, incarceration). If someone is in imminent danger of harming himself or herself, do not leave the person alone. You may need to take emergency steps to get help, such as calling 911. When someone is in a suicidal crisis, it is important to limit access to firearms or other lethal means of committing suicide.

What are the most common methods of suicide?

Firearms are the most commonly used method of suicide for men and women, accounting for 60 percent of all suicides. Nearly 80 percent of all firearm suicides are committed by white males. The second most common method for men is hanging; for women, the second most common method is self-poisoning including drug overdose. The

A fact sheet produced by the National Institute of Mental Health, December 1999, updated January 2000; available online at www.nimh.nih.gov/research/ suicidefaq.cfm.

presence of a firearm in the home has been found to be an independent, additional risk factor for suicide. Thus, when a family member or health care provider is faced with an individual at risk for suicide, they should make sure that firearms are removed from the home.

Why do men commit suicide more often than women do?

More than four times as many men as women die by suicide; but women attempt suicide more often during their lives than do men, and women report higher rates of depression. Several explanations have been offered:

- Completed suicide is associated with aggressive behavior that is more common in men, and which may in turn be related to some of the biological differences identified in suicidality.

- Men and women use different suicide methods. Women in all countries are more likely to ingest poisons than men. In countries where the poisons are highly lethal and/or where treatment resources scarce, rescue is rare and hence female suicides outnumber males.

More research is needed on the social-cultural factors that may protect women from completing suicide, and how to encourage men to recognize and seek treatment for their distress, instead of resorting to suicide.

Who is at highest risk for suicide in the U.S.?

There is a common perception that suicide rates are highest among the young. However, it is the elderly, particularly older white males that have the highest rates. And among white males 65 and older, risk goes up with age. White men 85 and older have a suicide rate that is six times that of the overall national rate.

Why are rates so high for this group?

White males are more deliberate in their suicide intentions; they use more lethal methods (firearms), and are less likely to talk about their plans. It may also be that older persons are less likely to survive attempts because they are less likely to recuperate. Over 70 percent of older suicide victims have been to their primary care physician within the month of their death, many with a depressive illness that was not detected. This has led to research efforts to determine how to best improve physicians' abilities to detect and treat depression in older adults.

Do school-based suicide awareness programs prevent youth suicide?

Despite good intentions and extensive efforts to develop suicide awareness and prevention programs for youth in schools, few programs have been evaluated to see if they work. Many of these programs are designed to reduce the stigma of talking about suicide and encourage distressed youth to seek help. Of the programs that were evaluated, none has proven to be effective. In fact, some programs have had unintended negative effects by making at-risk youth more distressed and less likely to seek help. By describing suicide and its risk factors, some curricula may have the unintended effect of suggesting that suicide is an option for many young people who have some of the risk factors and in that sense normalize it—just the opposite message intended. Prevention efforts must be carefully planned, implemented, and scientifically tested. Because of the tremendous effort and cost involved in starting and maintaining programs, we should be certain that they are safe and effective before they are further used or promoted.

There are number of prevention approaches that are less likely to have negative effects, and have broader positive outcomes in addition to reducing suicide. One approach is to promote overall mental health among school-aged children by reducing early risk factors for depression, substance abuse, and aggressive behaviors. In addition to the potential for saving lives, many more youth benefit from overall enhancement of academic performance and reduction in peer and family conflict. A second approach is to detect youth most likely to be suicidal by confidentially screening for depression, substance abuse, and suicidal ideation. If a youth reports any of these, further evaluation of the youth takes place by professionals, followed by referral for treatment as needed. Adequate treatment of mental disorder among youth, whether they are suicidal or not, has important academic, peer, and family relationship benefits.

Are gay and lesbian youth at high risk for suicide?

With regard to completed suicide, there are no national statistics for suicide rates among gay, lesbian or bisexual (GLB) persons. Sexual orientation is not a question on the death certificate, and to determine whether rates are higher for GLB persons, we would need to know the proportion of the U.S. population that considers themselves gay, lesbian, or bisexual. Sexual orientation is a personal characteristic that people can, and often do choose to hide, so that in psychological autopsy studies of suicide victims where risk factors are examined, it is difficult to know for certain the victim's sexual orientation. This is particularly a problem when considering GLB youth who may be less certain of their sexual orientation and less open. In the few studies examining risk factors for suicide where sexual orientation was assessed, the risk for gay or lesbian persons did not appear any greater than among heterosexuals, once mental and substance abuse disorders were taken into account.

With regard to suicide attempts, several state and national studies have reported that high school students who report to be homosexually and bisexually active have higher rates of suicide thoughts and attempts in the past year compared to youth with heterosexual experience. Experts have not been in complete agreement about the best way to measure reports of adolescent suicide attempts, or sexual orientation, so the data are subject to question. But they do agree that efforts should focus on how to help GLB youth grow up to be healthy and successful despite the obstacles that they face. Because school-based suicide awareness programs have not proven effective for youth in general, and in some cases have caused increased distress in vulnerable youth, they are not likely to be helpful for GLB youth either. Because young people should not be exposed to programs that do not work, and certainly not to programs that increase risk, more research is needed to develop safe and effective programs.

Are African American youth at great risk for suicide?

Historically, African Americans have had much lower rates of suicides compared to white Americans. However, beginning in the 1980s, the rates for African American male youth began to rise at a much faster rate than their white counterparts. The most recent trends suggest a decrease in suicide across all gender and racial groups, but health policy experts remain concerned about the increase in suicide by firearms for all young males. Whether African American male youth are more likely to engage in "victim-precipitated homicide" by deliberately getting in the line of fire of either gang or law enforcement activity, remains an important research question, as such deaths are not typically classified as suicides.

Is suicide related to impulsiveness?

Impulsiveness is the tendency to act without thinking through a plan or its consequences. It is a symptom of a number of mental disorders, and therefore, it has been linked to suicidal behavior usually through its association with mental disorders and/or substance abuse. The mental disorders with impulsiveness most linked to suicide include borderline personality disorder among young females, conduct disorder among young males and antisocial behavior in adult males, and alcohol and substance abuse among young and middle-aged males. Impulsiveness appears to have a lesser role in older adult suicides. Attention deficit hyperactivity disorder that has impulsiveness as a characteristic is not a strong risk factor for suicide by itself. Impulsiveness has been linked with aggressive and violent behaviors including homicide and suicide. However, impulsiveness without aggression or violence present has also been found to contribute to risk for suicide.

Is there such a thing as "rational" suicide?

Some right-to-die advocacy groups promote the idea that suicide, including assisted suicide, can be a rational decision. Others have argued that suicide is never a rational decision and that it is the result of depression, anxiety, and fear of being dependent or a burden. Surveys of terminally ill persons indicate that very few consider taking their own life, and when they do, it is in the context of depression. Attitude surveys suggest that assisted suicide is more acceptable by the public and health providers for the old who are ill or disabled, compared to the young who are ill or disabled. At this time, there is limited research on the frequency with which persons with terminal illness have depression and suicidal ideation, whether they would consider assisted suicide, the characteristics of such persons, and the context of their depression and suicidal thoughts, such as family stress, or availability of palliative care. Neither is it yet clear what effect other factors such as the availability of social support, access to care, and pain relief may have on end-of-life preferences. This public debate will be better informed after such research is conducted.

What biological factors increase risk for suicide?

Researchers believe that both depression and suicidal behavior can be linked to decreased serotonin in the brain. Low levels of a serotonin metabolite, 5-HIAA, have been detected in cerebral spinal fluid in persons who have attempted suicide, as well as by postmortem studies examining certain brain regions of suicide victims. One of the goals of understanding the biology of suicidal behavior is to improve treatments. Scientists have learned that serotonin receptors in the brain increase their activity in persons with major depression and suicidality, which explains why medications that desensitize or down-regulate these receptors (such as the serotonin reuptake inhibitors, or SSRIs) have been found effective in treating depression. Currently, studies are underway to examine to what extent medications like SSRIs can reduce suicidal behavior.

Can the risk for suicide be inherited?

There is growing evidence that familial and genetic factors contribute to the risk for suicidal behavior. Major psychiatric illnesses, including bipolar disorder, major depression, schizophrenia, alcoholism and substance abuse, and certain personality disorders, which run in families, increase the risk for suicidal behavior. This does not mean that suicidal behavior is inevitable for individuals with this family history; it simply means that such persons may be more vulnerable and should take steps to reduce their risk, such as getting evaluation and treatment at the first sign of mental illness.

Does depression increase the risk for suicide?

Although the majority of people who have depression do not die by suicide, having major depression does increase suicide risk compared to people without depression. The risk of death by suicide may, in part, be related to the severity of the depression. New data on depression that has followed people over long periods of time suggests that about 2% of those people ever treated for depression in an outpatient setting will die by suicide. Among those ever treated for depression in an inpatient hospital setting, the rate of death by suicide is twice as high (4%). Those treated for depression as inpatients following suicide ideation or suicide attempts are about three times as likely to die by suicide (6%) as those who were only treated as outpatients. There are also dramatic gender differences in lifetime risk of suicide in depression. Whereas about 7% of men with a lifetime history of depression will die by suicide, only 1% of women with a lifetime history of depression will die by suicide.

Another way about thinking of suicide risk and depression is to examine the lives of people who have died by suicide and see what proportion of them were depressed. From that perspective, it is estimated that about 60% of people who commit suicide have had a mood disorder (for example, major depression, bipolar disorder, dysthymia). Younger persons who kill themselves often have a substance abuse disorder in addition to being depressed.

Does alcohol and other drug abuse increase the risk for suicide?

A number of recent national surveys have helped shed light on the relationship between alcohol and other drug use and suicidal behavior. A review of minimum-age drinking laws and suicides among youths age 18 to 20 found that lower minimum-age drinking laws was associated with higher youth suicide rates. In a large study following adults who drink alcohol, suicide ideation was reported among persons with depression. In another survey, persons who reported that they had made a suicide attempt during their lifetime were more likely to have had a depressive disorder, and many also had an alcohol and/or substance abuse disorder. In a study of all non-traffic injury deaths associated with alcohol intoxication, over 20 percent were suicides.

In studies that examine risk factors among people who have completed suicide, substance use and abuse occurs more frequently among youth and adults, compared to older persons. For particular groups at risk, such as American Indians and Alaskan Natives, depression and alcohol use and abuse are the most common risk factors for completed suicide. Alcohol and substance abuse problems contribute to suicidal behavior in several ways. Persons who are dependent on substances often have a number of other risk factors for suicide. In addition to being depressed, they are also likely to have social and financial problems. Substance use and abuse can be common among persons prone to be impulsive, and among persons who engage in many types of high risk behaviors that result in self-harm. Fortunately, there are a number of effective prevention efforts that reduce risk for substance abuse in youth, and there are effective treatments for alcohol and substance use problems. Researchers are currently testing treatments specifically for persons with substance abuse problems who are also suicidal, or have attempted suicide in the past.

What does "suicide contagion" mean, and what can be done to prevent it?

Suicide contagion is the exposure to suicide or suicidal behaviors within one's family, one's peer group, or through media reports of suicide and can result in an increase in suicide and suicidal behaviors. Direct and indirect exposure to suicidal behavior has been shown to precede an increase in suicidal behavior in persons at risk for suicide, especially in adolescents and young adults.

The risk for suicide contagion as a result of media reporting can be minimized by factual and concise media reports of suicide. Reports of suicide should not be repetitive, as prolonged exposure can increase the likelihood of suicide contagion. Suicide is the result of many complex factors; therefore media coverage should not report oversimplified explanations such as recent negative life events or acute stressors. Reports should not divulge detailed descriptions of the method used to avoid possible duplication. Reports should not glorify the victim and should not imply that suicide was effective in achieving a personal goal such as gaining media attention. In addition, information such as hotlines or emergency contacts should be provided for those at risk for suicide.

Following exposure to suicide or suicidal behaviors within one's family or peer group, suicide risk can be minimized by having family members, friends, peers, and colleagues of the victim evaluated by a mental health professional. Persons deemed at risk for suicide should then be referred for additional mental health services.

Is it possible to predict suicide?

At the current time there is no definitive measure to predict suicide or suicidal behavior. Researchers have identified factors that place individuals at higher risk for suicide, but very few persons with these risk factors will actually commit suicide. Risk factors include mental illness, substance abuse, previous suicide attempts, family history of suicide, history of being sexually abused, and impulsive or aggressive tendencies. Suicide is a relatively rare event and it is therefore difficult to predict which persons with these risk factors will ultimately commit suicide.

Chapter 58

Suicide Prevention

Understanding Suicidal Thinking

Suicidal thoughts are temporary. Suicide is permanent. Don't give in to suicidal thoughts—you can overcome them.

If depression or bipolar disorder (also known as manic depression) affects you or someone you care about, you know that one symptom of these illnesses may be feelings of hopelessness and thoughts of suicide. If such thoughts occur, there are ways to respond with strength and courage. Suicide can be prevented with the right kind of care, treatment, and support.

Here are some facts to keep in mind:

- Mood disorders are not character flaws or signs of personal weakness, nor are they conditions that will just go away if a person thinks positive.

- Mood disorders are medical conditions caused by changes in the chemistry of the body and brain. Depression and bipolar disorder may cause symptoms such as intense sadness, hopelessness, low energy, loss of appetite, changes in sleep patterns, inability to concentrate, decreased ability to perform one's usual tasks,

Excerpted with permission from "Suicide Prevention and Mood Disorders," © 2002 National Depressive and Manic-Depressive Association, 730 N. Franklin Street, Suite 501, Chicago, IL 60610-7204; 800-826-3632 or 312-642-0049; Website: http://www.ndmda.org.

loss of interest in once-enjoyed activities and thoughts of death or suicide that can be difficult to ignore or overcome.

- Depression and bipolar disorder are treatable with medication, psychotherapy, support from others and changes in lifestyle. With the right treatment, all symptoms can improve, including suicidal thoughts.

- The act of suicide is often a desperate attempt to control the symptoms of a mood disorder. During severe depression, as brain chemicals become out of balance, a person can't help but focus on memories that are dark and sad, and feelings of hopelessness about the future. Remembering only the bad times or disappointments in life and believing only bad things will continue to happen is a symptom of the illness. It is not a part of a person's true self.

If You Are Feeling Suicidal

The belief that there is no hope is not the truth. When you feel this way, it's your illness talking—your mind is lying to you. Remind yourself that suicidal thoughts are not reality.

If you are thinking of suicide, it is important to recognize these thoughts for what they are: expressions of a treatable medical illness. They are not true and they are not your fault. Don't let fear, shame, or embarrassment stand in the way of communication with your physician, therapist, family, and friends; tell someone right away.

- Tell a trusted family member, friend, or other support person, someone you can talk with honestly. Try not to be alone when you feel this way. This may mean sitting quietly with a family member or friend, going to a support group, or going to a hospital.

- Get help. Tell your health professional. Suicidal thinking can be treated. When suicidal thoughts occur, they are your signal that, more than ever, you need help from a professional.

- Know that you can get through this. Promise yourself you will hang on for another day, hour, minute, or whatever you can manage.

Suicide Prevention

It's very helpful to have a plan of action ready before thoughts of suicide occur.

- Stay in contact with your doctor. Always have your doctor's phone number with you—an office number as well as a pager or after-hours number—and a back-up number such as an emergency room or suicide crisis line like (800) 442-HOPE.

- Stay in contact with trusted friends. Develop a list with phone numbers of dependable family members and friends who can give you support during a crisis, and keep the list with you.

- Make a Plan for Life (see Figure 58.1 for an example) and promise yourself that you will follow it when you start to have suicidal thoughts.

- Give a copy of your plan (including your lists of phone numbers) to family and friends before it's needed, so they can be prepared to act quickly if needed.

- Recognize symptoms for what they are. With your doctor, therapist (counselor), or trusted friends, identify the symptoms you are likely to experience when your depression is at its worst. Always remember: feelings are not facts. Suicidal feelings are not your fault; they are a symptom of your illness. They may not seem temporary, but they are. As you learn to manage your illness, you will be able to spot your warning signs sooner and get help earlier.

- Write down your thoughts. Spend a little time each day writing down your thoughts about the things and people you appreciate and value in your life, and your hopes for the future. Read what you've written when you need to remind yourself why your own life is important.

- Connect with other people socially. When you are feeling suicidal, don't be alone for long periods of time. Visit with family and friends who are caring and understanding, even if it's difficult. Attend meetings of your local support group, where you will meet others who understand what it's like to live with a mood disorder.

- Avoid drugs and alcohol. Many suicides result from sudden, uncontrolled impulses. Since drugs and alcohol can make you more impulsive, it is important to avoid them. Drugs and alcohol can also make your treatment less effective.

- Know when it's best to go to the hospital. There are times when depression becomes so severe that hospitalization is the best way to protect your health and safety. Discuss this possibility and your options with your doctor before the need arises.

- Understand your health coverage. Know whether your insurance, HMO, Medicaid, or Medicare plan provides psychiatric hospitalization coverage, and how much. Keep copies of policy numbers and important health care information in an easy-to-find place. If you don't have insurance coverage, find out what other options you have, such as community or state-run facilities.

- Keep yourself safe. Make sure you do not have access to weapons or anything you could use to hurt yourself. Have someone hold on to your car keys when you are feeling suicidal. Throw away all medications you are no longer taking.

- Give yourself time to get better. When you are first treated, or when you have recently had a severe depressive or manic episode, give your brain and body time to heal. Allow yourself to take life a little more slowly, and don't get discouraged if you aren't up to your previous activity and lifestyle levels right away. With continued treatment, you can feel better.

If You Are Worried that Someone Is Considering Suicide

With courage and understanding, you can help a friend or family member overcome thoughts of suicide. If you are prepared and informed, you will be better able to help.

It is extremely important for people with mood disorders to receive early, quality treatment from health care professionals. If you believe someone close to you is seriously depressed, help that person find and stick with effective treatment. Be supportive, reassuring, and willing to talk about suicidal feelings and thoughts.

Take any mention of death or suicide seriously. If someone you know talks about suicide, asking direct questions about how, when, and where he or she intends to commit suicide may help prevent the attempt.

It's natural to fear that a question about suicide may anger or offend someone you care for—or even that it may put the idea of suicide into a person's mind. However, you cannot make someone suicidal by asking straightforward, caring questions. A person considering suicide may welcome the chance to talk about these feelings.

Warning Signs that Someone May Be Considering Suicide

Take any mention of death or suicide seriously.

426

- Unbearable feelings: Depression causes some people to have powerful, extreme feelings of hopelessness, despair and self-doubt. The more intense these feelings become, and the more often they are described as "unbearable," the more likely it is that the idea of suicide may enter the person's mind.

- Taking care of business, making final plans, preparing wills or life insurance or arranging for the family's welfare is another warning sign. The person may give away valued possessions or make reference to what others will do "after I'm gone."

- Rehearsing suicide, seriously discussing one or more specific suicide methods, purchasing weapons, or collecting large quantities of medication are all signs. Even if the person's suicidal thoughts seem to come and go, it is important to step in early and help.

- Drug or alcohol abuse is often a separate, treatable condition that must be addressed along with the mood disorder in order for treatment to be successful. Intoxication may cause impulsive behavior and make a person more likely to act on suicidal thoughts.

- Isolation: If a person seems determined to cut off friendships and social connections, there is a chance that the person might be experiencing serious depression and/or preparing for suicide.

- Sudden sense of calm: A person with a mood disorder may be most likely to attempt suicide just when he or she seems to have passed an episode's lowest point and be on the way to recovery. If a person who was recently feeling upset or hopeless suddenly seems very calm and settled, it may be a sign that he or she has decided on a plan.

What You Can Do to Help

- Don't promise confidentiality. Support your loved one in getting professional help.

- Express understanding and concern. Severe depression usually causes a self-absorbed, uncommunicative, withdrawn state of mind. When you try to help, the person may be unwilling to talk. At such times it is important to let the person know you understand the reality and severity of the painful and hopeless feelings. If the person is not comfortable talking with you, encourage him or her to talk with someone else.

Figure 58. 1a. Plan for Life

I Promise Myself

If I start to think about suicide, I will contact these family members or friends:

Name: _____   Phone: _____
Name: _____   Phone: _____
Name: _____   Phone: _____

I Will Also

❑ Call my doctor, or a suicide hotline, or go to a hospital if necessary
❑ Remember that suicidal thoughts are a treatable symptom of my illness
❑ Remember that my life is valuable and worthwhile, even if it doesn't feel that way right now
❑ Stick with my prescribed treatment plan
❑ Remember to take my medications
❑ Remember to see my counselor/therapist/psychiatrist
❑ Remember to call my doctor if I don't feel safe or if I'm having problems
❑ Get in contact with other people who have a mood disorder
❑ Stay away from alcohol and illegal drugs
❑ Have someone take away my car keys and anything I could use to hurt myself
❑ Stay aware of my moods, know my warning signs and get help early
❑ Be kind to myself
❑ _____
❑ _____
❑ _____

My Contact Information

Name: _____
Address:_____
Phone Number(s):_____
Diagnosis: _____

My Doctors

Primary Care Provider

Name:_____
Address:_____
Phone: _____   Pager: _____

Figure 58. 1b. Plan for Life

Psychiatrist

Name: _____

Address: _____

Phone: _____ Pager: _____

Therapist

Name: _____

Address: _____

Phone: _____ Pager: _____

If My Doctors are Not Available, Contact these Health Care Professionals:

Name: _____ Phone: _____

Name: _____ Phone: _____

My Local Suicide Hotline   Phone: _____

National Hopeline Network   Phone: (800) 442-HOPE (800-442-4673)

My Health Care Information

My preferred hospital: _____

Address: _____

Phone: _____ Emergency room phone: _____

2nd choice hospital: _____

Address: _____

Phone: _____ Emergency room phone: _____

Health Insurance Company/HMO/Medicaid Provider (attach photocopy of ID card)

Name: _____

Phone: _____

Policy number: _____

Amount of hospitalization coverage: _____

My Support Group

Contact name: _____

Phone: _____

Medications I'm taking:

1. _____ Dosage: _____

2. _____ Dosage: _____

3. _____ Dosage: _____

- Describe specific behaviors and events that worry you. Don't be afraid to point out particular ways the person's behavior has changed, or things that lead you to think he or she may be considering suicide.

- Try to help him or her overcome feelings of guilt. Your friend or family member may be unwilling to communicate because of guilt or shame over the depression and suicidal thoughts. Remind the person that he or she is not alone, and that guilt is also a treatable symptom of the illness.

- Stress that the person's life is important to you and to others. Remind the person in specific terms why his or her life is important to you and makes your own life better.

- Don't take responsibility for making the person well. Be supportive and encouraging as you help the person find professional treatment and stick with it.

- During hospitalization, you can support someone by making regular visits or calls, and offering to take care of the person's errands, home, children or pets.

- Support the person as he or she recovers and help him or her stick to a treatment plan, make a Plan for Life, and connect with a support group.

If Someone Is Threatening to Commit Suicide

- Take the person seriously. Stay calm and let the person know you are willing to listen.

- Involve other people. Don't try to handle the crisis alone or put yourself in danger. Call 911 if necessary. Contact the person's family, psychiatrist, therapist or others who are trained to help.

- Express concern. Ask direct questions and listen. Try to find out if the person has a specific plan for suicide and what it is.

- Be understanding, not judgmental. Remind the person that suicide is a permanent solution to a temporary problem, and that there is help and hope.

- Never promise confidentiality. You may need to speak to the person's doctor in order to protect the person. Secrecy can endanger your loved one's life.

- If possible, don't leave the person alone until you are sure he or she is in the care of professionals.

Difficult Situations

It takes courage to help a person who is considering suicide. If the person is also abusing drugs or alcohol or is verbally or physically abusive, helping may seem impossible. You may have correctly decided that you cannot tolerate this behavior and want to keep your distance. However, even if you keep your distance or live far away, you can still help by informing the person's doctor or another friend or family member who lives nearby, of the person's suicidal thoughts. People with severe depression—no matter how unreasonable or angry they become—need help finding help.

When you are helping someone else, it is also important to take care of yourself. You may be feeling many difficult emotions as you support someone close to you who is considering suicide. Be honest with yourself about your own feelings, and be sure to let yourself feel them. Don't be afraid to ask for help. Even if you are not severely depressed, therapy and support from your family and friends can help.

If You Have Lost Someone to Suicide

- Give yourself time to grieve. You may have overwhelming feelings of anger, guilt, confusion, sadness, and forgetfulness, as well as physical aches and pains or trouble eating or sleeping. Allow yourself to feel these things and know that they are normal reactions. Try not to make any major changes in your life right away.

- Get support. Talk to other friends and family members about what you are feeling. Find a support group for survivors. Don't be afraid to seek professional help to get you through this difficult time. You may even have suicidal thoughts. If you do, get help right away.

- Don't blame yourself. You may have thoughts such as "What if I had done this?" or "Why didn't I say that?" A mood disorder is not the fault of the person who has it, or of anyone else, and no one is the sole influence in another person's life. Know that this was not your fault. Allow yourself to feel angry at the person or at yourself, but work to forgive yourself and the person, too.

- Reach out to others. When you are honest about how you feel and what you are going through, you can help others who are having similar experiences.

431

Support Groups: An Important Step on the Road to Wellness

National Depressive and Manic-Depressive Association (DMDA) support groups provide the kind of caring and help that is important to lasting recovery. Members are people with depression or bipolar disorder and their loved ones. Each group has a professional advisor and appointed facilitators. People attending support groups say their groups:

- Provide a safe and welcoming forum for mutual acceptance, understanding and self-discovery.

- Give them the opportunity to reach out to others and benefit from the experience of those who have been there.

- Motivate them to follow their treatment plans.

- Help them understand that mood disorders do not define who they are.

- Help them rediscover their strengths and humor.

The mission of the National Depressive and Manic-Depressive Association (National DMDA) is to educate patients, families, professionals, and the public concerning the nature of depressive and manic-depressive illnesses as treatable medical diseases; to foster self-help for patients and families; to eliminate discrimination and stigma; to improve access to care; and to advocate for research toward the elimination of these illnesses.

You can contact National DMDA to find a support group near you or learn more about starting one. Take the next step toward wellness for yourself or someone you love. There is help, and there is hope.

National Depressive and Manic-Depressive Association
730 N. Franklin St., Suite 501
Chicago, IL 60610-7204
Toll-Free: 800-826-3632
Phone: 312-642-0049
Fax: 312-642-7243
Website: http://www.ndmda.org

Directories of additional resources for locating support groups, assistance in mental health crisis situations, or further information about depression and other mood disorders are included in the end section of this book.

Chapter 59

Teenage Suicide

Now the eighth-leading cause of death overall in the U.S. and the third-leading cause of death for young people between the ages of 15 and 24 years, suicide has become the subject of much concern. U.S. Surgeon General David Satcher, for instance, announced his *Call to Action to Prevent Suicide, 1999*, an initiative intended to increase public awareness, promote intervention strategies, and enhance research. The media, too, has been paying very close attention to the subject of suicide, writing articles and books and running news stories. Suicide among our nation's youth, a population very vulnerable to self-destructive emotions, has perhaps received the most discussion of late. Maybe this is because teenage suicide seems the most tragic—lives lost before they've even started. Yet, while all of this recent focus is good, it's only the beginning. We cannot continue to lose so many lives unnecessarily.

Some Basic Facts

- In 1996, more teenagers and young adults died of suicide than from cancer, heart disease, AIDS, birth defects, stroke, pneumonia and influenza, and chronic lung disease combined.

Excerpted from "Teenage Suicide," November 1999, National Alliance for the Mentally Ill (NAMI), Colonial Place Three, 2107 Wilson Blvd., Suite 300, Arlington, VA 22201, Phone: 703-524-7600; NAMI HelpLine: 1-800-950-NAMI [6264]; www.nami.org. © 1999 NAMI; reprinted with permission.

- In 1996, suicide was the second-leading cause of death among college students, the third-leading cause of death among those aged 15 to 24 years, and the fourth-leading cause of death among those aged 10 to 14 years.

- From 1980 to 1996, the rate of suicide among African-American males aged 15 to 19 years increased by 105 percent.

- The incidence of suicide among adolescents and young adults nearly tripled from 1965 to 1987, but teen suicide rates in the past ten years have actually been declining, possibly due to increased recognition and treatment.

Suicide Signs

There are many behavioral indicators that can help parents or friends recognize the threat of suicide in a loved one. Since mental and substance-related disorders so frequently accompany suicidal behavior, many of the cues to be looked for are symptoms associated with such disorders as depression, bipolar disorder (manic depression), anxiety disorders, alcohol and drug use, disruptive behavior disorders, borderline personality disorder, and schizophrenia. Some common symptoms of these disorders include:

- Extreme personality changes
- Loss of interest in activities that used to be enjoyable
- Significant loss or gain in appetite
- Difficulty falling asleep or wanting to sleep all day
- Fatigue or loss of energy
- Feelings of worthlessness or guilt
- Withdrawal from family and friends
- Neglect of personal appearance or hygiene
- Sadness, irritability, or indifference
- Having trouble concentrating
- Extreme anxiety or panic
- Drug or alcohol use or abuse
- Aggressive, destructive, or defiant behavior
- Poor school performance
- Hallucinations or unusual beliefs

Tragically, many of these signs go unrecognized. And while suffering from one of these symptoms certainly does not necessarily mean that one is suicidal, it's always best to communicate openly with a loved one who has one or more of these behaviors, especially if they are unusual for that person.

There are also some more obvious signs of the potential for committing suicide. Putting one's affairs in order, such as giving or throwing away favorite belongings, is a strong clue. And it can't be stressed more strongly that any talk of death or suicide should be taken seriously and paid close attention to. It is a sad fact that while many of those who commit suicide talked about it beforehand, only 33 percent to 50 percent were identified by their doctors as having a mental illness at the time of their death and only 15 percent of suicide victims were in treatment at the time of their death. Any history of previous suicide attempts is also reason for concern and watchfulness. Approximately one-third of teens who die by suicide have made a previous suicide attempt. It should be noted as well that while more females attempt suicide, more males are successful in completing suicide.

Causes of Teenage Suicide

While the reasons that teens commit suicide vary widely, there are some common situations and circumstances that seem to lead to such extreme measures. These include major disappointment, rejection, failure, or loss such as breaking up with a girlfriend or boyfriend, failing a big exam, or witnessing family turmoil. Since the overwhelming majority of those who commit suicide have a mental or substance-related disorder, they often have difficulty coping with such crippling stressors. They are unable to see that their life can turn around, unable to recognize that suicide is a permanent solution to a temporary problem. Usually, the common reasons for suicide listed above are actually not the causes of the suicide, but rather triggers for suicide in a person suffering from a mental illness or substance-related disorder.

More recently, scientists have focused on the biology of suicide. Suicide is thought by some to have a genetic component—to run in families. And research has shown strong evidence that mental and substance-related disorders, which commonly affect those who end up committing suicide, do run in families. While the suicide of a relative is obviously not a direct cause of suicide, it does, perhaps, put certain individuals at more risk than others. Certainly, the suicide of one's parent or other close family member could lead to thoughts of such behavior in a teen with a mental or substance-related disorder.

Research has also explored the specific brain chemistry of those who take their own lives. Some studies indicate that those who have attempted suicide may also have low levels of the brain chemical serotonin. Serotonin helps control impulsivity, and low levels of the brain chemical are thought to cause more impulsive behavior. Suicides are often committed out of impulse. Antidepressant drugs affecting serotonin are used to treat depression, impulsivity, and suicidal thoughts. However, much more research is needed to confirm these hypotheses and, hopefully, eventually lead to more definite indicators of and treatment for those prone to suicide.

How to Help

Since people who are contemplating suicide feel so alone and helpless, the most important thing to do if you think a friend or loved one is suicidal is to communicate with him or her openly and frequently. Make it clear that you care; stress your willingness to listen. Also, be sure to take all talk of suicide seriously. Don't assume that people who talk about killing themselves won't really do it. An estimated 80 percent of all those who commit suicide give some warning of their intentions or mention their feelings to a friend or family member. And don't ignore what may seem like casual threats or remarks. Statements like "You'll be sorry when I'm dead" and "I can't see any way out," no matter how off-the-cuff or jokingly said, may indicate serious suicidal feelings.

One of the most common misconceptions about talking with someone who might be contemplating suicide is that bringing up the subject may make things worse. This is not true. There is no danger of "giving someone the idea." Rather, the opposite is correct. Bringing up the question of suicide and discussing it without showing shock or disapproval is one of the most helpful things you can do. This openness shows that you are taking the individual seriously and responding to the severity of his or her distress.

If you do find that your friend or loved one is contemplating suicide, it is essential to help him or her find immediate professional care. (Calling the NAMI HelpLine at 1-800-950-NAMI [6264] for more information or to help you locate your local NAMI for area assistance is one possible resource; others are listed in the end section of this book.) Don't make the common misjudgment that those contemplating suicide are unwilling to seek help. Studies of suicide victims show that more than half had sought medical help within six months before their deaths. And don't leave the suicidal person to find help alone—they usually aren't capable. Also, never assume that someone who is determined to end his or her life can't be stopped. Even the most severely depressed person has mixed feelings about death, wavering until the very last moment between wanting to live and wanting to die. Most suicidal people do not want death; they want the pain to stop. The impulse to end it all, though, no matter how overpowering, does not last forever.

If the threat is immediate, if your friend or loved one tells you he or she is going to commit suicide, you must act immediately. Don't leave the person alone, and don't try to argue. Instead, ask questions like, "Have you thought about how you'd do it?" "Do you have the means?" and "Have you decided when you'll do it?" If the person has a defined plan, the means are easily available, the method is a lethal one, and the time is set, the risk of suicide is obviously severe. In such an instance, you must take the individual to the nearest psychiatric facility or hospital emergency room. If you are together on the phone, you may even need to call 911 or the police. Remember, under such circumstances no actions on your part should be considered too extreme—you are trying to save a life.

An overwhelming majority of young people who hear a suicide threat from a friend or loved one don't report the threat to an adult. Take all threats seriously—you are not betraying someone's trust by trying to keep them alive.

Other Serious Considerations

Don't automatically assume that someone who was considering suicide and is now in treatment or tells you that he or she is feeling better is, in fact, doing better. Some who commit suicide actually do so just as they seem to be improving. One reason for this may be that they did not have enough energy to kill themselves when they were extremely depressed, but now have just enough energy to go through with their plan. Another reason for suicide during a seeming improvement is that resigning oneself to death can release anxiety. While it's not good to monitor every action of someone who is recovering from suicidal thoughts, it is important to make certain that the lines of communication between you and the individual remain open.

While it may seem a bit obvious, it should also be mentioned that it is extremely advisable to bar teens who are suicidal from access to firearms. Nearly 60 percent of all completed suicides are committed with a firearm. And while having a firearm does not in itself promote suicidal behavior, knowing that one is accessible may help a troubled teen formulate his or her suicidal plans.

Chapter 60

Older Adults: Depression and Suicide

Major depression, a significant predictor of suicide in older adults,[1] is a widely under-recognized and under-treated medical illness. In fact, several studies have found that many older adults who commit suicide have visited a primary care physician very close to the time of the suicide: 20 percent on the same day, 40 percent within one week, and 70 percent within one month of the suicide.[2] These findings point to the urgency of enhancing both the detection and the adequate treatment of depression as a means of reducing the risk of suicide among the elderly.

Older Americans are disproportionately likely to commit suicide. Comprising only 13 percent of the U.S. population, individuals ages 65 and older accounted for 19 percent of all suicide deaths in 1997. The highest rate is for white men ages 85 and older: 64.9 deaths per 100,000 persons in 1997, about 6 times the national U.S. rate of 10.6 per 100,000.[3]

An estimated six percent of Americans ages 65 and older in a given year, or approximately two million of the 34 million adults in this age group in 1998, have a diagnosable depressive illness (major depressive disorder, bipolar disorder, or dysthymic disorder).[4] In contrast to the normal emotional experiences of sadness, grief, loss, or passing mood states, depressive disorders can be extreme and persistent and can interfere significantly with an individual's ability to function. Dysthymic disorder as well as depressive symptoms that do not meet

"Older Adults: Depression and Suicide Facts," National Institute of Mental Health, NIH Pub. No. 01-4593, January 2001.

full diagnostic criteria for a disorder are common among the elderly and are associated with an increased risk of developing major depression.[5] In any of its forms, however, depression is not a normal part of aging.

Depression often co-occurs with other medical illnesses such as cardiovascular disease, stroke, diabetes, and cancer.[6] Because many older adults face such physical illnesses as well as various social and economic difficulties, individual health care professionals often mistakenly conclude that depression is a normal consequence of these problems—an attitude often shared by patients themselves.[7] These factors conspire to make the illness under diagnosed and under treated.

Both doctors and patients may have difficulty identifying the signs of depression. Researchers funded by the National Institute for Mental Health (NIMH) are currently investigating the effectiveness of a depression education intervention delivered in primary care clinics for improving recognition and treatment of depression and suicidal symptoms in elderly patients.

Talk to Your Doctor

Your doctor can only treat you if you say how you are really feeling. Before you say, "I'm fine," ask yourself if you feel:

- nervous or empty
- guilty or worthless
- very tired and slowed down
- you don't enjoy things the way you used to
- restless or irritable
- like no one loves you
- like life is not worth living

Or, ask your self if you are:

- sleeping more or less than usual
- eating more or less than usual
- having persistent headaches, stomach aches, or chronic pain

These may be symptoms of depression, a treatable medical illness. Depression is not a normal part of aging. Talk to your doctor.

Research and Treatment

Modern brain imaging technologies are revealing that in depression, neural circuits responsible for the regulation of moods, thinking, sleep, appetite, and behavior fail to function properly, and that critical neurotransmitters—chemicals used by nerve cells to communicate—are out of balance.[8] Genetics research indicates that vulnerability to depression results from the influence of multiple genes acting together with environmental factors.[9] Studies of brain chemistry and of mechanisms of action of antidepressant medications continue to inform the development of new and better treatments.

Antidepressant medications are widely used effective treatments for depression.[10] Existing antidepressant drugs are known to influence the functioning of certain neurotransmitters in the brain, primarily serotonin and norepinephrine, known as monoamines. Older medications—tricyclic antidepressants (TCAs) and monoamine oxidase inhibitors (MAOIs)—affect the activity of both of these neurotransmitters simultaneously. Their disadvantage is that they can be difficult to tolerate due to side effects or, in the case of MAOIs, dietary and medication restrictions. Newer medications, such as the selective serotonin reuptake inhibitors (SSRIs), have fewer side effects than the older drugs, making it easier for patients including older adults to adhere to treatment. Both generations of medications are effective in relieving depression, although some people will respond to one type of drug, but not another.

Certain types of psychotherapy also are effective treatments for depression. Cognitive-behavioral therapy (CBT) and interpersonal therapy (IPT) are particularly useful. Approximately 80 percent of older adults with depression improve when they receive appropriate treatment with medication, psychotherapy, or the combination.[11]

In fact, recent research has shown that a combination of psychotherapy and antidepressant medication is extremely effective for reducing recurrence of depression among older adults. Those who received both interpersonal therapy and the antidepressant drug nortriptyline (a TCA) were much less likely to experience recurrence over a three-year period than those who received medication only or therapy only.[12]

Studies are in progress on the efficacy of SSRIs and short-term specific psychotherapies for depression in older persons. Findings from these studies will provide important data regarding the clinical course and treatment of late-life depression. Further research will be needed to determine the role of hormonal factors in the development of depression, and to find out whether hormone replacement therapy with estrogens or androgens is of benefit in the treatment of depression in the elderly.

For More Information

National Institute of Mental Health (NIMH)
Office of Communications and Public Liaison
Public Inquiries: 301-443-4513
E-mail: nimhinfo@nih.gov
Website: http://www.nimh.nih.gov

References

1. Conwell Y, Brent D. Suicide and aging I: Patterns of psychiatric diagnosis, *International Psychogeriatrics*, 1995; 7(2): 149-64.

2. Conwell, Y. Suicide in elderly patients. In: Schneider, LS, Reynolds CF III, Lebowitz, BD, Friedhoff AJ, eds. *Diagnosis and treatment of depression in late life*. Washington, DC: American Psychiatric Press, 1994; 397-418.

3. Hoyert DL, Kochanek KD, Murphy SL. Deaths: final data for 1997. *National Vital Statistics Report*, 47(19). DHHS Publication No. 99-1120. Hyattsville, MD: National Center for Health Statistics, 1999. http://www.cdc.gov/nchs/data/nvs47_19.pdf

4. Narrow WE. One-year prevalence of depressive disorders among adults 18 and over in the U.S.: NIMH ECA prospective data. Population estimates based on U.S. Census estimated residential population age 18 and over on July 1, 1998. Unpublished.

5. Horwath E, Johnson J, Klerman GL, et al. Depressive symptoms as relative and attributable risk factors for first-onset major depression, *Archives of General Psychiatry*, 1992; 49(10): 817-23.

6. Depression Guideline Panel. *Depression in primary care: volume 1. Detection and diagnosis. Clinical practice guideline, number 5*. AHCPR Publication No. 93-0550. Rockville, MD: Agency for Health Care Policy and Research, 1993.

7. Lebowitz BD, Pearson JL, Schneider LS, et al. Diagnosis and treatment of depression in late life. Consensus statement update,

Journal of the American Medical Association, 1997; 278(14): 1186-90.

8.   Soares JC, Mann JJ. The functional neuroanatomy of mood disorders, *Journal of Psychiatric Research*, 1997; 31(4): 393-432.

9.   NIMH Genetics Workgroup. *Genetics and mental disorders*. NIH Publication No. 98-4268. Rockville, MD: National Institute of Mental Health, 1998.

10. Mulrow CD, Williams JW Jr., Trivedi M, et al. Evidence report on treatment of depression-newer pharmacotherapies, *Psychopharmacology Bulletin*, 1998; 34(4): 409-795.

11. Little JT, Reynolds CF III, Dew MA, et al. How common is resistance to treatment in recurrent, nonpsychotic geriatric depression? *American Journal of Psychiatry*, 1998; 155(8): 1035-8.

12. Reynolds CF III, Frank E, Perel JM, et al. Nortriptyline and interpersonal psychotherapy as maintenance therapies for recurrent major depression: a randomized controlled trial in patients older than 59 years, *Journal of the American Medical Association*, 1999; 281(1): 39-45.

Chapter 61

For Those Left Behind after a Suicide

When the worst has happened and you have lost a loved one to depression and suicide there is little that can be said to comfort you. We suggest reading *Suicide—Survivors: A Guide For Those Left Behind* by Adina Wrobleski (Minneapolis, MN: SA/VE, 1994; ISBN 0935585060). It does not take away the grieving, but it has helped us understand and correct some of the wrong information we all have about suicide. Reading this book might be a good first step for someone beginning the arduous journey of trying to work through suicide grief.

It's Okay

- **It's Okay to Grieve:** The death of a loved one is a reluctant and drastic amputation, without any anesthesia. The pain cannot be described, and no scale can measure the loss. We despise the truth that the death cannot be reversed. It hurts. It's okay to grieve.

- **It's Okay to Cry:** Tears release the flood of sorrow, of missing, and of love. Tears relieve the brute force of hurting, enabling us

---

"When The Worst Has Happened," including a section, "Why We Grieve Differently," by Jinny Tesik, M.A. Copyright © 2002 Suicide Awareness Voices of Education (SAVE); reprinted with permission. SAVE is an organization dedicated to educating the public about suicide prevention. Contact SAVE at 7317 Cahill Road, Suite 207, Minneapolis, MN 55439-0507, Phone: 952-946-7998; Toll Free 1-888-511-SAVE; Fax: 952-946-7998; Internet: http://www.save.org.

to level off, and continue our cruise along the stream of life. It's okay to cry.

- **It's Okay to Heal:** We do not need to prove we loved him or her. As the months pass, we are slowly able to move around with less outward grieving each day. We need not feel guilty, for this is not an indication that we love less. It means that, although we don't like it, we are learning to accept death. It's a healthy sign of healing. It's okay to heal.

- **It's Okay to Laugh:** Laughter is not a sign of less grief. Laughter is not a sign of less love. It's a sign that many of our thoughts and memories are happy ones. It's a sign that we know our memories are happy ones. It's a sign that we know our dear one would have us laugh again. It's okay to laugh.

Grief: If We Avoid It Will It Go Away?

Grief is as old as mankind but is one of the most neglected of human problems. As we become aware of this neglect, we come to realize the enormous cost that it has been to the individual, to the families, and to society, in terms of pain and suffering because we have neglected the healing of grief.

Essential to a grieving person is to have at least one person who will allow them, give them permission to grieve. Some people can turn to a friend or to a family member. Some find a support group that will allow one to be the way one needs to be at the present as they work through their grief.

Dealing appropriately with grief is important in helping to preserve healthy individuals and nurturing families, to avoid destroying bodies and their psyche, their marriages, and their relationships.

You can postpone grief but you cannot avoid it. As other stresses come along, one becomes less able to cope if one has other unresolved grief.

It requires a great deal of energy to avoid grief and robs one of energy for creative expression in relating to other people and in living a fulfilling life. It limits one's life potential.

Suppressing grief keeps one in a continual state of stress and shock, unable to move from it. Our body feels the effects of it in ailments. Our emotional life suffers. Our spiritual life suffers. We say that the person is "stuck in grief."

When a person faces his grief, allows his feeling to come, speaks of his grief, allows its expression, it is then that the focus is to move from death and dying and to promote life and living.

Why We Grieve Differently

We accept without question uniqueness in the physical world..... fingerprints, snowflakes, etc. But we often refuse that same reality in our emotional world. This understanding is needed, especially in the grieving process.

No two people will ever grieve the same way, with the same intensity, or for the same duration. It is important to understand this basic truth. Only then can we accept our own manner of grieving and be sensitive to another's response to loss. Only then are we able to seek out the nature of support we need for our own personalized journey back to wholeness and be able to help others on their own journey.

Not understanding the individuality of grief could complicate and delay whatever grief we might experience from our own loss. It could also influence us, should we attempt to judge the grieving of others— even those we might most want to help.

Each of us is a unique combination of diverse past experiences. We each have a different personality, style, various way of coping with stress situations, and our own attitudes influence how we accept the circumstances around us. We are also affected by the role and relationship that each person in a family system had with the departed, by circumstances surrounding the death, and by influences in the present.

Past Experience

Past experiences from childhood on, have a great impact on how we are able to handle loss in the present.

What other losses have we faced in our childhood, adolescence, adulthood? How frightening were these experiences? Was there good support? Were feelings allowed to be expressed in a secure environment? Has there been a chance to recover and heal from these earlier losses?

What other life stresses have been going on prior to this recent loss? Has there been a move to a new area? Were there financial difficulties, problems, or illness with another member of the family or with ourselves?

What has our previous mental health history been like? Have we had bouts with depression? Have we harbored suicidal thoughts? Have we experienced a nervous breakdown? Have we been treated with medication or been hospitalized?

How has our family cultural influences conditioned us to respond to loss and the emotions of grief (stoic father, emotional mother, etc.)?

Relationship with the Deceased

No outsider is able to determine the special bond that connects two people, regardless of the relationship, role, or length of time the relationship has been in existence.

Our relationship with the deceased has a great deal to do with the intensity and duration of our grief. What was that relationship? Was the deceased a spouse? A child? A parent? A friend? A sibling?

How strong was the attachment to the deceased? Was it a close, dependent relationship, or intermittent and independent? What was the degree of ambivalence (the love/hate balance) in that relationship?

It is not only the person, but also the role that person played in our life which is lost. How major was that role? Was that person the sole breadwinner, the driver, the handler of financial matters? The only one who could fix a decent dinner? Was that person a main emotional support, an only friend? How dependent were we on the role that person filled?

Circumstances Surrounding the Death

The circumstances surrounding the death, that is, how the death occurred, are extremely important in determining how we are going to come to an acceptance of the loss.

Was the loss in keeping with the laws of nature as when a person succumbs to old age? Or was order thrown into chaos, as when a parent lives to see a child die?

What warnings were there that there would be a loss? Was there time to prepare, time to gradually come to terms with the inevitable? Or did death come so suddenly that there was no anticipation of its arrival?

Do we feel that this death could have been prevented or forestalled? How much responsibility am I taking for this death?

Do we feel that the deceased accomplished what he or she was meant to fulfill in this lifetime? Was their life full and rewarding? How much was left unsaid or undone between ourselves and the deceased? Does the extent of unfinished business foster a feeling of guilt?

Influences in the Present

We have looked at the past, at the relationship, and how the loss occurred. Now we see how the influences in the present can impact how we are finally going to come to terms with a current loss.

Age and sex are important factors. Are we young enough and resilient enough to bounce back? Are we old enough and wise enough to accept the loss and to grow with the experience? Can our life be rebuilt again? What opportunities does life offer now? Is health a problem?

What are the secondary losses that are the result of this death? Loss of income? Home? Family breakup? What other stresses or crises are present?

Our personality, present stability of mental health, and coping behavior play a significant role in our response to the loss. What kind of role expectations do we have for ourselves? What are those imposed by friends, relatives, and others? Are we expected to be the strong one, or is it all right for us to break down and have someone else take care of us? Are we going to try to assume an unrealistic attempt to satisfy everyone's expectations, or are we going to withdraw from the entire situation?

What is there in our social, cultural and ethnic backgrounds that give us strength and comfort? What role do rituals play in our recovery? Do our religious or philosophical beliefs bring comfort or add sorrow and guilt? What kind of social support is there in our lives during this emotional upheaval?

Conclusion

When a person who is a part of our life dies, understanding the uniqueness of this loss can guide us in finding the support we will need and to recognize when help should come from outside family or friends.

When the loss is experienced by someone we would like to help or by someone under our care, this same understanding is essential. Thus we can guard against a temptation to compare or to judge their grief responses to our own. The awareness of those factors which affect the manner, intensity, and duration of grief, should enable us to guide the grieving person in seeking those forms of support suggested by the nature of their loss and the unique way it affects them.

—section by Jinny Tesik, M.A.

For More Information

For information on Suicide Survivors support groups in your area contact:

American Association of Suicidology
4201 Connecticut Avenue NW, Suite 408
Washington, DC 20008

American Association of Suicidology (continued)
Toll Free: 800-SUICIDE
Phone: 202-237-2280
Fax: 202-237-2282
Website: http://www.suicidology.org

For information about suicide, contact:

SAVE—Suicide Awareness Voices of Education
7317 Cahill Road, Suite 207
Minneapolis, MN 55439-0507
Toll-free 888-511-SAVE
Phone: 952-946-7998
Fax: 952-946 7998
Website: http://www.save.org

Directories of other resources for information about depression and suicide are included in the end section of this book.

Part Six

Depression-Related Research

Chapter 62

Depression Research

Depressive disorders affect approximately 19 million American adults. The suffering endured by people with depression and the lives lost to suicide attest to the great burden of this disorder on individuals, families, and society. Improved recognition, treatment, and prevention of depression are critical public health priorities. The National Institute of Mental Health (NIMH), the world's leading mental health biomedical organization, conducts and supports research on the causes, diagnosis, prevention, and treatment of depression.

Evidence from neuroscience, genetics, and clinical investigation demonstrate that depression is a disorder of the brain. Modern brain imaging technologies are revealing that in depression, neural circuits responsible for the regulation of moods, thinking, sleep, appetite, and behavior fail to function properly, and that critical neurotransmitters—chemicals used by nerve cells to communicate—are out of balance. Genetics research indicates that vulnerability to depression results from the influence of multiple genes acting together with environmental factors. Studies of brain chemistry and of mechanisms of action of antidepressant medications continue to inform the development of new and better treatments.

In the past decade, there have been significant advances in our ability to investigate brain function at multiple levels. NIMH is collaborating with various scientific disciplines to effectively utilize the

From "Depression Research at the National Institute of Mental Health," National Institute of Mental Health, NIH Pub. No. 00-4501, updated March 14, 2001.

tools of molecular and cellular biology, genetics, epidemiology, and cognitive and behavioral science to gain a more thorough and comprehensive understanding of the factors that influence brain function and behavior, including mental illness. This collaboration reflects the Institute's increasing focus on "translational research," whereby basic and clinical scientists are involved in joint efforts to translate discoveries and knowledge into clinically relevant questions and targets of research opportunity. Translational research holds great promise for disentangling the complex causes of depression and other mental disorders and for advancing the development of more effective treatments.

Symptoms and Types of Depression

Symptoms of depression include a persistent sad mood; loss of interest or pleasure in activities that were once enjoyed; significant change in appetite or body weight; difficulty sleeping or oversleeping; physical slowing or agitation; loss of energy; feelings of worthlessness or inappropriate guilt; difficulty thinking or concentrating; and recurrent thoughts of death or suicide. A diagnosis of major depressive disorder (or unipolar major depression) is made if an individual has five or more of these symptoms during the same two-week period. Unipolar major depression typically presents in discrete episodes that recur during a person's lifetime.

Bipolar disorder (or manic-depressive illness) is characterized by episodes of major depression as well as episodes of mania—periods of abnormally and persistently elevated mood or irritability accompanied by at least three of the following symptoms: overly inflated self-esteem; decreased need for sleep; increased talkativeness; racing thoughts; distractibility; increased goal-directed activity or physical agitation; and excessive involvement in pleasurable activities that have a high potential for painful consequences. While sharing some of the features of major depression, bipolar disorder is a different illness.

Dysthymic disorder (or dysthymia), a less severe yet typically more chronic form of depression, is diagnosed when depressed mood persists for at least two years in adults (one year in children or adolescents) and is accompanied by at least two other depressive symptoms. Many people with dysthymic disorder also experience major depressive episodes. While unipolar major depression and dysthymia are the primary forms of depression, a variety of other subtypes exist.

In contrast to the normal emotional experiences of sadness, loss, or passing mood states, depression is extreme and persistent and can interfere significantly with an individual's ability to function. In fact, a recent study sponsored by the World Health Organization and the World Bank found unipolar major depression to be the leading cause of disability in the United States and worldwide.

There is a high degree of variation among people with depression in terms of symptoms, course of illness, and response to treatment, indicating that depression may have a number of complex and interacting causes. This variability poses a major challenge to researchers attempting to understand and treat the disorder. However, recent advances in research technology are bringing NIMH scientists closer than ever before to characterizing the biology and physiology of depression in its different forms and to the possibility of identifying effective treatments for individuals based on symptom presentation.

One of the most challenging problems in depression research and clinical practice is refractory—hard to treat—depression. While approximately 80 percent of people with depression respond very positively to treatment, a significant number of individuals remain treatment refractory. Even among treatment responders, many do not have complete or lasting improvement, and adverse side effects are common. Thus, an important goal of NIMH research is to advance the development of more effective treatments for depression—especially treatment-refractory depression—that also have fewer side effects than currently available treatments.

Research on Treatments for Depression

Medication

Studies on the mechanisms of action of antidepressant medication comprise an important area of NIMH depression research. Existing antidepressant drugs are known to influence the functioning of certain neurotransmitters in the brain, primarily serotonin and norepinephrine, known as monoamines. Older medications—tricyclic antidepressants (TCAs) and monoamine oxidase inhibitors (MAOIs)—affect the activity of both of these neurotransmitters simultaneously. Their disadvantage is that they can be difficult to tolerate due to side effects or, in the case of MAOIs, dietary restrictions. Newer medications, such as the selective serotonin reuptake inhibitors (SSRIs), have fewer side effects than the older drugs, making it easier for patients to adhere to treatment. Both generations of medications are effective in relieving depression, although some people will respond to one type of drug, but not another.

455

Antidepressant medications take several weeks to be clinically effective even though they begin to alter brain chemistry with the very first dose. Research now indicates that antidepressant effects result from slow-onset adaptive changes within the brain cells, or neurons. Further, it appears that activation of chemical messenger pathways within neurons, and changes in the way that genes in brain cells are expressed, are the critical events underlying long-term adaptations in neuronal function relevant to antidepressant drug action. A current challenge is to understand the mechanisms that mediate, within cells, the long-term changes in neuronal function produced by antidepressants and other psychotropic drugs and to understand how these mechanisms are altered in the presence of illness.

Knowing how and where in the brain antidepressants work can aid the development of more targeted and potent medications that may help reduce the time between first dose and clinical response. Further, clarifying the mechanisms of action can reveal how different drugs produce side effects and can guide the design of new, more tolerable, treatments.

As one route toward learning about the distinct biological processes that go awry in different forms of depression, NIMH researchers are investigating the differential effectiveness of various antidepressant medications in people with particular subtypes of depression. For example, this research has revealed that people with atypical depression, a subtype characterized by reactivity of mood (mood brightens in response to positive events) and at least two other symptoms (weight gain or increased appetite, oversleeping, intense fatigue, or rejection sensitivity), respond better to treatment with MAOIs, and perhaps with SSRIs than with TCAs.

Many patients and clinicians find that combinations of different drugs work most effectively for treating depression, either by enhancing the therapeutic action or reducing side effects. Although combination strategies are used often in clinical practice, there is little research evidence available to guide psychiatrists in prescribing appropriate combination treatment. NIMH is in the process of revitalizing and expanding its program of clinical research, and combination therapy will be but one of numerous treatment interventions to be explored and developed.

Untreated depression often has an accelerating course, in which episodes become more frequent and severe over time. Researchers are now considering whether early intervention with medications and maintenance treatment during well periods will prevent recurrence of episodes. To date, there is no evidence of any adverse effects of long-term antidepressant use.

Psychotherapy

Like the process of learning, which involves the formation of new connections between nerve cells in the brain, psychotherapy works by changing the way the brain functions. NIMH research has shown that certain types of psychotherapy, particularly cognitive-behavioral therapy (CBT) and interpersonal therapy (IPT), can help relieve depression. CBT helps patients change the negative styles of thinking and behaving often associated with depression. IPT focuses on working through disturbed personal relationships that may contribute to depression.

Research on children and adolescents with depression supports CBT as a useful initial treatment, but antidepressant medication is indicated for those with severe, recurrent, or psychotic depression. Studies of adults have shown that while psychotherapy alone is rarely sufficient to treat moderate to severe depression, it may provide additional relief in combination with antidepressant medication. In one recent NIMH-funded study, older adults with recurrent major depression who received IPT in combination with an antidepressant medication during a three-year period were much less likely to experience a recurrence of illness than those who received medication only or therapy only. For mild depression, however, a recent analysis of multiple studies indicated that combination treatment is not significantly more effective than CBT or IPT alone.

Preliminary evidence from an ongoing NIMH-supported study indicates that IPT may hold promise in the treatment of dysthymia.

Electroconvulsive Therapy (ECT)

Electroconvulsive therapy (ECT) remains one of the most effective yet most stigmatized treatments for depression. Eighty to ninety percent of people with severe depression improve dramatically with ECT. ECT involves producing a seizure in the brain of a patient under general anesthesia by applying electrical stimulation to the brain through electrodes placed on the scalp. Repeated treatments are necessary to achieve the most complete antidepressant response. Memory loss and other cognitive problems are common, yet typically short-lived side effects of ECT. Although some people report lasting difficulties, modern advances in ECT technique have greatly reduced the side effects of this treatment compared to earlier decades. NIMH research on ECT has found that the dose of electricity applied and the placement of electrodes (unilateral or bilateral) can influence the degree of depression relief and the severity of side effects.

457

A current research question is how best to maintain the benefits of ECT over time. Although ECT can be very effective for relieving acute depression, there is a high rate of relapse when the treatments are discontinued. NIMH is currently sponsoring two multicenter studies on ECT follow-up treatment strategies. One study is comparing different medication treatments, and the other study is comparing maintenance medication to maintenance ECT. Results from these studies will help guide and improve follow-up treatment plans for patients who respond well to ECT.

Genetics Research

Research on the genetics of depression and other mental illnesses is a priority of NIMH and constitutes a critical component of the Institute's multi-level research effort. Researchers are increasingly certain that genes play an important role in vulnerability to depression and other severe mental disorders.

In recent years, the search for a single, defective gene responsible for each mental illness has given way to the understanding that multiple gene variants, acting together with yet unknown environmental risk factors or developmental events, account for the expression of psychiatric disorders. Identification of these genes, each of which contributes only a small effect, has proven extremely difficult.

However, new technologies, which continue to be developed and refined, are beginning to allow researchers to associate genetic variations with disease. In the next decade, two large-scale projects that involve identifying and sequencing all human genes and gene variants will be completed and are expected to yield valuable insights into the causes of mental disorders and the development of better treatments. In addition, NIMH is currently soliciting researchers to contribute to the development of a large-scale database of genetic information that will facilitate efforts to identify susceptibility genes for depression and other mental disorders.

Stress and Depression

Psychosocial and environmental stressors are known risk factors for depression. NIMH research has shown that stress in the form of loss, especially death of close family members or friends, can trigger depression in vulnerable individuals. Genetics research indicates that environmental stressors interact with depression vulnerability genes to increase the risk of developing depressive illness. Stressful life events may contribute to recurrent episodes of depression in some individuals, while in others depression recurrences may develop without identifiable triggers.

Other NIMH research indicates that stressors in the form of social isolation or early-life deprivation may lead to permanent changes in brain function that increase susceptibility to depressive symptoms.

Brain Imaging

Recent advances in brain imaging technologies are allowing scientists to examine the brain in living people with more clarity than ever before. Functional magnetic resonance imaging (fMRI), a safe, noninvasive method for viewing brain structure and function simultaneously, is one new technique that NIMH researchers are using to study the brains of individuals with and without mental disorders. This technique will enable scientists to evaluate the effects of a variety of treatments on the brain and to associate these effects with clinical outcome.

Brain imaging findings may help direct the search for microscopic abnormalities in brain structure and function responsible for mental disorders. Ultimately, imaging technologies may serve as tools for early diagnosis and subtyping of depression and other mental disorders, thus advancing the development of new treatments and evaluation of their effects.

Hormonal Abnormalities

The hormonal system that regulates the body's response to stress, the hypothalamic-pituitary-adrenal (HPA) axis, is overactive in many patients with depression, and NIMH researchers are investigating whether this phenomenon contributes to the development of the illness.

The hypothalamus, the brain region responsible for managing hormone release from glands throughout the body, increases production of a substance called corticotropin releasing factor (CRF) when a threat to physical or psychological well-being is detected. Elevated levels and effects of CRF lead to increased hormone secretion by the pituitary and adrenal glands which prepares the body for defensive action. The body's responses include reduced appetite, decreased sex drive, and heightened alertness. NIMH research suggests that persistent overactivation of this hormonal system may lay the groundwork for depression. The elevated CRF levels detectable in depressed patients are reduced by treatment with antidepressant drugs or ECT, and this reduction corresponds to improvement in depressive symptoms.

459

NIMH scientists are investigating how and whether the hormonal research findings fit together with the discoveries from genetics research and monoamine studies.

Co-Occurrence of Depression and Anxiety Disorders

NIMH research has revealed that depression often co-exists with anxiety disorders (panic disorder, obsessive-compulsive disorder, post-traumatic stress disorder, social phobia, or generalized anxiety disorder). In such cases, it is important that depression and each co-occurring illness be diagnosed and treated.

Several studies have shown an increased risk of suicide attempts in people with co-occurring depression and panic disorder—the anxiety disorder characterized by unexpected and repeated episodes of intense fear and physical symptoms, including chest pain, dizziness, and shortness of breath.

Rates of depression are especially high in people with post-traumatic stress disorder (PTSD), a debilitating condition that can occur after exposure to a terrifying event or ordeal in which grave physical harm occurred or was threatened. In one study supported by NIMH, more than 40 percent of patients with PTSD had depression when evaluated both at one month and four months following the traumatic event.

Co-Occurrence of Depression and Other Illnesses

Depression frequently co-occurs with a variety of other physical illnesses, including heart disease, stroke, cancer, and diabetes, and also can increase the risk for subsequent physical illness, disability, and premature death. Depression in the context of physical illness, however, is often unrecognized and untreated. Furthermore, depression can impair the ability to seek and stay on treatment for other medical illnesses. NIMH research suggests that early diagnosis and treatment of depression in patients with other physical illnesses may help improve overall health outcome.

The results of a recent NIMH-supported study provide the strongest evidence to date that depression increases the risk of having a future heart attack. Analysis of data from a large-scale survey revealed that individuals with a history of major depression were more than four times as likely to suffer a heart attack over a 12–13 year follow-up period, compared to people without such a history. Even people with a history of two or more weeks of mild depression were more than twice as likely to have a heart attack, compared to those who had had no such episodes. Although associations were found between certain psychotropic medications and heart attack risk, the researchers determined that the associations were simply a reflection of the primary relationship between depression and heart trouble. The question of whether treatment for depression reduces the excess risk of heart attack in depressed patients must be addressed with further research.

NIMH is planning to present a major conference with other NIH Institutes on depression and co-occurring illnesses. The outcomes of this conference will guide NIMH investigation of depression both as a contributing factor to other medical illnesses and as a result of these illnesses.

Women and Depression

Nearly twice as many women (12 percent) as men (7 percent) are affected by a depressive illness each year. At some point during their lives, as many as 20 percent of women have at least one episode of depression that should be treated. Although conventional wisdom holds that depression is most closely associated with menopause, in fact, the childbearing years are marked by the highest rates of depression, followed by the years prior to menopause.

NIMH researchers are investigating the causes and treatment of depressive disorders in women. One area of research focuses on life stress and depression. Data from a recent NIMH-supported study suggests that stressful life experiences may play a larger role in provoking recurrent episodes of depression in women than in men.

The influence of hormones on depression in women has been an active area of NIMH research. One recent study was the first to demonstrate that the troublesome depressive mood swings and physical symptoms of premenstrual syndrome (PMS), a disorder affecting three to seven percent of menstruating women, result from an abnormal response to normal hormone changes during the menstrual cycle. Among women with normal menstrual cycles, those with a history of PMS experienced relief from mood and physical symptoms when their sex hormones, estrogen and progesterone, were temporarily "turned off" by administering a drug that suppresses the function of the ovaries. PMS symptoms developed within a week or two after the hormones were re-introduced. In contrast, women without a history of PMS reported no effects of the hormonal manipulation. The study showed that female sex hormones do not cause PMS—rather, they trigger PMS symptoms in women with a preexisting vulnerability to the disorder. The researchers currently are attempting to determine what makes some women but not others susceptible to PMS. Possibilities include genetic differences in hormone sensitivity at the cellular level, differences in history of other mood disorders, and individual differences in serotonin function.

NIMH researchers also are currently investigating the mechanisms that contribute to depression after childbirth (postpartum depression), another serious disorder where abrupt hormonal shifts in the context of intense psychosocial stress disable some women with an apparent underlying vulnerability. In addition, an ongoing NIMH clinical trial is evaluating the use of antidepressant medication following delivery to prevent postpartum depression in women with a history of this disorder after a previous childbirth.

Child and Adolescent Depression

Large-scale research studies have reported that up to 2.5 percent of children and up to 8.3 percent of adolescents in the United States suffer from depression. In addition, research has discovered that depression onset is occurring earlier in individuals born in more recent decades. There is evidence that depression emerging early in life often persists, recurs, and continues into adulthood, and that early onset depression may predict more severe illness in adult life. Diagnosing and treating children and adolescents with depression is critical to prevent impairment in academic, social, emotional, and behavioral functioning and to allow children to live up to their full potential.

Research on the diagnosis and treatment of mental disorders in children and adolescents, however, has lagged behind that in adults. Diagnosing depression in these age groups is often difficult because early symptoms can be hard to detect or may be attributed to other causes. In addition, treating depression in children and adolescents remains a challenge, because few studies have established the safety and efficacy of treatments for depression in youth. Children and adolescents are going through rapid, age-related changes in their physiological states, and there remains much to be learned about brain development during the early years of life before treatments for depression in young people will be as successful as they are in older people. NIMH is pursuing brain-imaging research in children and adolescents to gather information about normal brain development and what goes wrong in mental illness.

Depression in children and adolescents is associated with an increased risk of suicidal behaviors. Over the last several decades, the suicide rate in young people has increased dramatically. In 1996, the most recent year for which statistics are available, suicide was the third leading cause of death in 15–24 year olds and the fourth leading cause among 10–14 year olds. NIMH researchers are developing and testing various interventions to prevent suicide in children and adolescents. However, early diagnosis and treatment of depression and other mental disorders, and accurate evaluation of suicidal thinking, possibly hold the greatest suicide prevention value.

Until recently, there were limited data on the safety and efficacy of antidepressant medications in children and adolescents. The use of antidepressants in this age group was based on adult standards of treatment. A recent NIMH-funded study supported fluoxetine, an SSRI, as a safe and efficacious medication for child and adolescent depression. The response rate was not as high as in adults, however, emphasizing the need for continued research on existing treatments and for development of more effective treatments, including psychotherapies designed specifically for children. Other complementary studies in the field are beginning to report similar positive findings in depressed young people treated with any of several newer antidepressants. In a number of studies, TCAs were found to be ineffective for treating depression in children and adolescents, but limitations of the study designs preclude strong conclusions.

NIMH is committed to developing an infrastructure of skilled researchers in the areas of child and adolescent mental health. In 1995, NIMH co-sponsored a conference that brought together more than 100 research experts, family and patient advocates, and representatives of mental health professional organizations to discuss and reach consensus on various recommendations for psychiatric medication research in children and adolescents. Outcomes of this conference included awarding additional funds to existing research grants to study psychotropic medications in children and adolescents and establishing a network of Research Units of Pediatric Psychopharmacology (RUPPs). Recently, a large, multi-site, NIMH-funded study was initiated to investigate both medication and psychotherapeutic treatments for adolescent depression.

Continuing to address and resolve the ethical challenges involved with clinical research on children and adolescents is an NIMH priority.

Older Adults and Depression

In a given year, between one and two percent of people over age 65 living in the community (that is, not living in nursing homes or other institutions) suffer from major depression and about two percent have dysthymia. Depression, however, is not a normal part of aging. Research has clearly demonstrated the importance of diagnosing and treating depression in older persons. Because major depression is typically a recurrent disorder, relapse prevention is a high priority for treatment research. As noted previously, a recent NIMH-supported study established the efficacy of combined antidepressant medication and interpersonal psychotherapy in reducing depressive relapses in older adults who had recovered from an episode of depression.

Additionally, recent NIMH studies show that 13 to 27 percent of older adults have subclinical depressions that do not meet the diagnostic criteria for major depression or dysthymia but are associated with increased risk of major depression, physical disability, medical illness, and high use of health services. Subclinical depressions cause considerable suffering, and some clinicians are now beginning to recognize and treat them.

Suicide is more common among the elderly than in any other age group. NIMH research has shown that nearly all people who commit suicide have a diagnosable mental or substance abuse disorder. In studies of older adults who committed suicide, nearly all had major depression, typically a first episode, though very few had a substance abuse disorder. Suicide among white males aged 85 and older was nearly six times the national U.S. rate (65 per 100,000 compared with 11 per 100,000) in 1996, the most recent year for which statistics are available. Prevention of suicide in older adults is a high priority area in the NIMH prevention research portfolio.

Alternative Treatments

There is high public interest in herbal remedies for various medical conditions including depression. Among the herbals is *Hypericum* or St. John's wort, promoted as having antidepressant effects. Adverse drug interactions have been reported between St. John's wort and drugs used to treat HIV infections as well as those used to reduce the risk of organ transplant rejection. In general, preparations of St. John's wort vary significantly.

The Future of NIMH Depression Research

Research on the causes, treatment, and prevention of all forms of depression will remain a high NIMH priority for the foreseeable future. Areas of interest and opportunity include the following:

- NIMH researchers will seek to identify distinct subtypes of depression characterized by various features including genetic risk, course of illness, and clinical symptoms. The aims of this research will be to enhance clinical prediction of onset, recurrence, and co-occurring illness; to identify the influence of environmental stressors in people with genetic vulnerability for major depression; and to prevent the development of co-occurring physical illnesses and substance use disorders in people with primary recurrent depression.

- Because many adult mental disorders originate in childhood, studies of development over time that uncover the complex interactions among psychological, social, and biological events are needed to track the persistence, chronicity, and pathways into and out of disorders in childhood and adolescence. Information about behavioral continuities that may exist between specific dimensions of child temperament and child mental disorder, including depression, may make it possible to ward off adult psychiatric disorders.

- Recent research on thought processes that has provided insights into the nature and causes of mental illness creates opportunities for improving prevention and treatment. Among the important findings of this research is evidence that points to the role of negative attentional and memory biases—selective attention to and memory of negative information—in producing and sustaining depression and anxiety. Future studies are needed to obtain a more precise account of the content and life course development of these biases, including their interaction with social and emotional processes, and their neural influences and effects.

- Advances in neurobiology and brain imaging technology now make it possible to see clearer linkages between research findings from different domains of emotion and mood. Such "maps" of depression will inform understanding of brain development, effective treatments, and the basis for depression in children and adults. In adult populations, charting physiological changes involved in emotion during aging will shed light on mood disorders in the elderly, as well as the psychological and physiological effects of bereavement.

- An important long-term goal of NIMH depression research is to identify simple biological markers of depression that, for example, could be detected in blood or with brain imaging. In theory, biological markers would reveal the specific depression profile of each patient and would allow psychiatrists to select treatments known to be most effective for each profile. Although such data-driven interventions can only be imagined today, NIMH already is investing in multiple research strategies to lay the groundwork for tomorrow's discoveries.

For More Information about NIMH

The Office of Communications and Public Liaison carries out educational activities and publishes and distributes research reports, press releases, fact sheets, and publications intended for researchers, health care providers, and the general public. A publications list may be obtained on the web at http://www.nimh.nih.gov/publist/puborder.cfm or by contacting:

Office of Communications and Public Liaison, NIMH
Information Resources and Inquiries Branch
6001 Executive Blvd., Room 8184, MSC 9663
Bethesda, MD 20892-9663
Toll-Free Depression Information: 1-800-421-4211
Phone: 301-443-4513
FAX: 301-443-4279
Mental Health FAX4U: 301-443-5158
NIMH home page address: http://www.nimh.nih.gov
E-mail: nimhinfo@nih.gov

Information about NIMH clinical studies can be obtained by accessing the NIMH home page at http://www.nimh.nih.gov or the National Library of Medicine clinical trials database at http://www.clinical trials.gov.

Chapter 63

Imaging Emotion in the Brain

In the last few years, there has been a revolution in the study of emotions. Our emotions—love, fear, anger, desire—give coloration and meaning to everything in life. Our emotions are indispensable whenever we choose to pursue one goal and not another. The derangement of emotions is what leads to the profound pain and much of the disability experienced in mental illness. The emotions were once thought to reside in the heart, but scientists know now that they originate in the brain.

New Imaging Tools

Scientists have learned to use neuroimaging to see the living, thinking, feeling human brain at work. Neuroimaging tools include functional magnetic resonance imaging (fMRI), which uses magnetic fields and radio waves to elicit signals from the brain, and positron emission tomography (PET), which uses low doses of a radioactive tracer to obtain signals from the brain. Both of these technologies have been designed to reveal signals that correlate with human brain activity. These approaches have been used to study the pathways in the brain involved in sensory processes such as vision, and in a variety of cognitive processes.

We are now at the dawn of an era when we can use these technologies to see pathways in the brain that underlie emotions such as fear

"Seeing Our Feelings: Imaging Emotion in the Brain," National Institute of Mental Health, NIH Pub. No. 01-4601, February 2001.

and desire. In the near future, these approaches will allow us to see precise abnormalities in brain pathways that produce mental illness.

Brain Pathways

Fear is the emotion that has been most successfully studied. Fear is required for our survival, but when it is not regulated, it becomes responsible for anxiety disorders and some of the symptoms of depression. We have learned that fear depends on very specific circuits in the brain. In fact, the way that the brain processes emotion is no different from the way it processes vision or voluntary movements, which also rely on their own specific circuitry.

The emotion of fear relies on pathways that involve a structure deep in our brains called the amygdala. The details of this circuitry have been worked out in rat models; however, a series of studies that began in 1996 and have become increasingly sophisticated have demonstrated that showing a fearful face to a normal subject while scanning his/her brain permits us to see activation of the amygdala and associated brain pathways.[1,2,3,4] Subsequent experiments have shown that if humans learn a connection between a neutral signal and something noxious, like a loud buzzing sound, we actually can observe the brain in the act of storing information about the signal that predicts danger.[5,6,7] We can see that the brain processes information about threat and fear even when the person is not concentrating on it and may not even consciously remember seeing the danger signal.

Although this research is still in its early phase, success to date in delineating specific fear pathways has encouraged the investigations of emotional pathways in mental illness. We are finding out, for example, whether phobias hitchhike on the same pathways used by normal fear. Soon we will have information about other emotions and conditions such as depression. Over time, these tools will be used to study the effects of medications and psychological therapies on mental illness.

References

1. Morris J, Frith C, Perrett D, et al. A differential neural response in the human amygdala to fearful and happy facial expressions. *Nature*, 1996; 383(6603): 812-15.

2. Breiter H, Etcoff N, Whalen P, et al. Response and habituation of the human amygdala during visual processing of facial expression. *Neuron*, 1996; 17(5): 875-87.

3. Whalen P, Rauch S, Etcoff N, et al. Masked presentations of emotional facial expressions modulate amygdala activity without explicit knowledge. *Journal of Neuroscience*, 1998; 18(1): 411-18.

4. Hariri A, Bookheimer S, Mazziotta J. Modulating emotional responses: effects of a neocortical network on the limbic system. *Neuroreport*, 2000; 11 (1): 43-8.

5. Buechel C, Dolan R. Classical fear conditioning in functional neuroimaging. *Current Opinion in Neurobiology*, 2000; 10(2): 219-23.

6. LaBar K, Gatenby J, Gore J, et al. Human amygdala activation during conditioned fear acquisition and extinction: a mixed-trial fMRI study. *Neuron*, 1998; 20(5): 937-45.

7. Morris J, Ohman A, Dolan R. Conscious and unconscious emotional learning in the human amygdala. *Nature*, 1998; 393(6684): 467-70.

Chapter 64

Repetitive Transcranial Magnetic Stimulation (rTMS)

What is rTMS?

rTMS stands for repetitive Transcranial Magnetic Stimulation, and this is a way of non-invasively stimulating the brain using magnetic fields that are applied to the scalp. rTMS is investigational at this point, meaning it's still an experimental procedure. A number of centers including ours at Columbia are doing research on whether rTMS might be helpful in treating depression and other psychiatric disorders.

How does it work to treat those ailments?

From imaging studies, like positron emission tomography, or PET, investigators have learned a good deal about what are some of the underlying abnormalities of disorders like depression. They involve a network of brain areas that seem to malfunction in depression. In particular, the lateral prefrontal cortex appears to have lowered activity. With rTMS, the opportunity is to use this noninvasive technique to stimulate that brain area, to try to change its activity in a lasting way, restoring proper functioning.

"Repetitive Transcranial Magnetic Stimulation (rTMS): An Interview with Sarah H. Lisanby, M.D.," Assistant Professor of Psychiatry, Columbia University, Director of the Magnetic Brain Stimulation Lab. Reprinted with permission from *NAFDI News* (Winter 2000). © 2000 National Foundation for Depressive Illness, Inc.

How long does this antidepressant effect last?

We don't have a whole lot of data about how long the effects last. In some of the early studies—by early I actually mean 1995 or 96—it looked like the antidepressant effects might begin to wear off after a few weeks. However, recently investigators have reported anecdotally that the effects might last longer. We really need more data. Obviously to be useful in treating depression we would want for it to be very long lasting. One of the ways that we've been using it at Columbia to try to prolong the effects is to combine rTMS with medication. rTMS might speed up the initial onset of action of the medication and then after rTMS stops, you would remain on that antidepressant drug to prevent relapse.

That's similar to some uses of ECT [Electroconvulsive Therapy]?

Exactly, yes.

Are there any differences between rTMS and ECT?

Yes, these two treatments are very different. First of all, ECT induces a seizure under anesthesia. rTMS is not a seizure. Basically with rTMS the patient is awake, there's no anesthesia, and they're sitting in a chair and alert during the whole procedure. The magnetic field is applied, usually for about half an hour daily for two to four weeks. The other major difference is that ECT often causes amnesia of varying degrees. Whereas rTMS does not cause the amnesia that one sees with ECT.

Are there any other dangers or side effects of rTMS?

Yes, the most common side effect is headache, which is usually well managed by a nonprescription painkiller. That's not very serious. The most serious risk we know of is possibly inducing a seizure if the small amount of electricity induced in the brain is too strong. We take precautions by screening out patients with a history of seizures, and by limiting the amount of stimulation that we give, tailoring it for each individual person.

What needs to be determined before this can be used clinically?

Basically, we need to determine if it is effective or not. It's as simple as that. Also, in whom is it effective, and how long does it last. There are several published studies now that have been done in a controlled fashion, but not all of the studies have been confirmatory. And once more people have been exposed to this treatment we'll know about potential longer-term side effects.

Do you have any predictions as to how long it might take before it would be approved for use?

Well it's really hard to say. Perhaps on the order of years. There are a growing list of groups across the world that are actively doing research with rTMS now and recruiting more and more patients, and I think that ought to really speed this process along.

Chapter 65

Depression: Clinical Trials

The following studies are sponsored by the National Institute of Mental Health (NIMH). Additional information, including criteria for study participation and contact information for study sites, can be found online at www.clinicaltrials.gov. Further information can also be obtained from NIMH. Contact:

NIMH Public Inquiries
601 Executive Blvd., Rm. 8184, MSC 9663
Bethesda, MD 20892
Phone: 301-443-4513
TTY: 301-443-8431
Fax: 301-443-4279
Website: www.nimh.nih.gov

Sequenced Treatment Alternatives to Relieve Depression (STAR*D)

Purpose

STAR*D focuses on non-psychotic major depressive disorder in adults who are seen in outpatient settings. The primary purpose of

The text in this chapter was compiled in March 2002 from descriptions of current studies on depression sponsored by the National Institute of Mental Health (NIMH) at www.clinicaltrials.gov, a service of the National Institutes of Health, developed by the National Library of Medicine. The full text of all study descriptions is available online at www.clinicaltrials.gov.

this research study is to determine which treatments work best if the first treatment with medication does not produce an acceptable response. Participants will first receive citalopram, an SSRI medication; if symptoms remain after 8–12 weeks of treatment, up to four other levels of treatment will be offered, including cognitive therapy and other medications. There are no placebo treatments. Some patients may require a combination of two or more treatments to obtain full benefit. Participation could last from 15 to 27 months and involve up to 30 clinic visits. Participants will be interviewed by telephone throughout the study about their symptoms, daily functioning, treatment side effects, use of the health care system, and satisfaction with treatment. There will be a one-year follow up for participants once their depression has been successfully treated.

Eligibility and Other Details

- **Ages eligible for study:** 18–75 years
- **Genders eligible for study:** Both
- **Expected total enrollment:** 4000
- **Study dates:** started July 2001; completion date October 2004
- **Location:** 40 locations across the U.S.

Treatment for Adolescents with Depression Study (TADS)

Purpose

TADS is designed to compare the effectiveness of established treatments for teenagers suffering from major depressive disorder (MDD). The treatments are: psychotherapy ("talking therapy"); medication; and the combination of psychotherapy and medication. Altogether, 432 teenagers (both males and females) ages 12 to 17, will take part in this study at 12 sites in the United States.

The TADS design will provide answers to the following questions: What is the long-term effectiveness of medication treatment of teenagers who have major depression? What is the long-term effectiveness of a specific psychotherapy ("talking therapy) in the treatment of teenagers who have major depression? How does medication treatment compare with psychotherapy in terms of effectiveness, tolerability, and teenager and family acceptance? And, What is the cost-effectiveness of medication, psychotherapy and combined treatments?

The medication being used in this study is called fluoxetine. Fluoxetine is also known as Prozac. Research has shown that medications like Prozac help depression in young persons. Fluoxetine has been approved by the FDA for use in the treatment of adult depression and is under study for children and teenagers.

The psychotherapy or "talking therapy" being used in this study is called Cognitive Behavioral Therapy (CBT). CBT is a talking therapy that will teach both the teenager and his or her family member (for example, a parent) new skills to cope better with depression. Specific topics include education about depression and the causes of depression, setting goals, monitoring mood, increasing pleasant activities, social problem-solving, correcting negative thinking, negotiation, compromise and assertiveness. CBT sessions may also help with resolving disagreements as they affect families.

Eligibility and Other Details

- **Ages eligible for study:** 12–17 years
- **Genders eligible for study:** Both
- **Expected total enrollment:** 432
- **Study dates:** Started September 1998; completion date March 2004
- **Location:** 12 locations across the U.S.

Effect of Fluoxetine on Attention and Memory in Anxious and Depressed Youth

Purpose

This study will use magnetic resonance imaging (fMRI) to examine how the brain changes in adolescents receiving fluoxetine (Prozac) for anxiety or depression and will evaluate whether this drug is effective in treating anxiety or depression in adolescents.

Normal, healthy adolescents between 9 and 17 years of age and adolescents of the same ages with anxiety or depression may be eligible for this study. However, only adolescents with an impairing anxiety or depressive disorder will receive fluoxetine (Prozac). All subjects—both patients and normal volunteers—will be screened for participation in the study with interviews to assess how the child is doing in general, including his or her general mood, degree of nervousness and behavior. The adolescent and one of his or her parents will be interviewed separately and together.

All those enrolled in the study will have a physical examination and blood tests, for which about six tablespoons of blood will be drawn.

A saliva sample will be collected to measure hormone levels. They will undergo tests involving problem-solving and memory and perform tasks that involve looking at pictures, remembering things, testing reaction times, or making simple choices. They may also, during this visit, have training in a MRI simulator to familiarize them with the MRI test procedure before returning for the actual exam.

MRI uses radio waves and a magnetic field to produce images of the brain that show changes in tissues. During the scan, the subject lies in a metal cylinder (the scanner) for 60 to 90 minutes, keeping still for 10 to 15 minutes at a time. Earplugs are used to muffle the sound of loud knocking sounds during the scanning. The subject can talk to the person running the test at all times during the procedure. Saliva samples will be taken before and after the scan to monitor hormone levels. During the scan, heart rate, and respiration and skin conduction response will be measured. In addition, the participant will perform two computer tasks while lying in the scanner—one involves making ratings about pictures of people or scenes that appear on the computer screen, and the other involves testing reaction times. Trying to guess where a token is hidden on the screen. Parents may stay with the child during the MRI procedure. When the normal volunteers complete the MRI, their participation in the study is ended.

The adolescents with anxiety or depression will then meet with a psychiatrist or psychologist for two weekly sessions of talk therapy. Those who remain anxious or depressed after these two weeks will be randomly assigned to receive treatment with fluoxetine or placebo (a non-active medicine) once a day for eight weeks. They will also be seen weekly by a doctor for talk therapy and to complete verbal and written exercises. Blood samples (approximately six tablespoons each) will be drawn for laboratory tests before drug treatment begins and again when it ends.

Children who have not improved by the end of the study will be offered other treatment for one to three months, after which another source of care will be found for them. Those who improved with treatment will continue therapy at the National Institutes of Health until a referral is made to an outside physician who will monitor the medication after the child leaves the study.

Eligibility

- **Ages eligible for study:** Adolescent must be ages 9–17
- **Genders eligible for study:** Both
- **Expected total enrollment:** 155

- **Study dates:** Started June 26, 2001
- **Location:** National Institute of Mental Health (NIMH), 9000 Rockville Pike, Bethesda, MD 20892; Patient Recruitment and Public Liaison Office: 800-411-1222

Treatment of Resistant Depression in Adolescents (TORDIA)

Purpose

This is a study of depression in adolescents, ages 12 to 18, who are currently taking a prescribed selective serotonin reuptake inhibitor (SSRI) antidepressant medication but are still experiencing depression. The purpose of the study is to determine how best to treat adolescents with depression that is "resistant" to the first SSRI they have tried. In addition to receiving a complete psychiatric evaluation, participants will be randomly assigned to receive one of three other antidepressant medications, either alone or in combination with cognitive behavioral therapy. Participants will be monitored for 24 weeks and will receive follow-up psychiatric evaluations for one year.

Eligibility and Other Details

- **Ages eligible for study:** 12–18 years
- **Genders eligible for study:** Both
- **Expected total enrollment:** 400
- **Study dates:** Started January 2001; completion date July 2004
- **Location:** Six locations (Los Angeles, CA; Portland, OR; Pittsburgh, PA; Providence, RI; Galveston, TX; and Dallas, TX)

Riluzole to Treat Major Depression

This study will examine the safety and effectiveness of the drug riluzole (Rilutek®) for short-term treatment of depression symptoms, such as depressed mood, psychomotor retardation, and excessive sleeping. Despite the availability of a wide range of antidepressant drugs, studies indicate that 30 to 40 percent of patients with major depression do not respond to first-line antidepressant treatment with drugs such as fluoxetine, bupropion, venlafaxine and others. Riluzole, which is approved by the Food and Drug Administration (FDA) for amyotrophic lateral sclerosis (ALS), causes chemical changes in the brain that may also have antidepressant properties.

Patients between 18 and 60 years of age with major depressive disorder without psychotic features may be eligible for this 2-stage 7-week study. Candidates will be screened with a medical history and physical examination, including an electrocardiogram (EKG), blood and urine tests, and a psychiatric evaluation. A blood or urine sample will be tested for illegal drugs. Women of childbearing potential will have a pregnancy test.

Participants will complete stage 1 of the study, which lasts 1 week, and may then continue with stage 2 for an additional six weeks. At the start of the study, patients will be tapered off all psychiatric medicines and will begin treatment with a placebo (a sugar pill formulated to look like the active drug). At some point, they will be switched from placebo to riluzole.

Eligibility and Other Details

* **Ages eligible for study:** 18–70 years
* **Genders eligible for study:** Both
* **Expected total enrollment:** 25
* **Study dates:** Started November 6, 2001
* **Location:** National Institute of Mental Health (NIMH), 9000 Rockville Pike, Bethesda, MD 20892; Patient Recruitment and Public Liaison Office: 800-411-1222

Evaluation of Repetitive Transcranial Magnetic Stimulation (rTMS) in the Treatment of Mood Disorders

Purpose

This study is designed to evaluate repetitive transcranial magnetic stimulation (rTMS) as a potential treatment for depression. In rTMS, a rapidly changing magnetic field passes through your scalp and skull and generates a small electrical pulses in your brain. rTMS at lower intensities has helped some people with depression but we do not know what the results will be in your case using higher intensities, or whether you will be randomized to 3 weeks of high frequency (20 cycles per second), low frequency (1 cycle per second), or inactive (sham) rTMS. You will be assigned to receive one of these types of rTMS over the left front part of your brain five times per week for the three weeks. Each rTMS treatment session should take between 20-30 minutes of actual stimulation, but weekly ratings, memory testing, and blood sampling may require several hours per week. We will also ask you to have brain imaging procedures to see if these will predict response to high vs. low frequency rTMS. If you are randomized to the 3 weeks of sham rTMS, you will have the opportunity to receive one of the active stimulation frequencies for an additional 3 weeks. Responders to any phase will be offered an additional month of rTMS prior to study termination and recommendations of alternative treatments.

Eligibility and Other Details

- **Genders eligible for study:** Both
- **Expected total enrollment:** 70
- **Study dates:** Started May 18, 1996
- **Location:** National Institute of Mental Health (NIMH), 9000 Rockville Pike, Bethesda, MD 20892; Patient Recruitment and Public Liaison Office: 800-411-1222

Serotonin Receptor Imaging in Mood Disorders

Purpose

This protocol will study serotonin function in the brain of patients with major depression and examine how the stress hormone, cortisol, affects serotonin receptor function. Serotonin is a natural chemical in the brain that attaches to brain cell receptors to regulate emotion, sleep, stress hormones, and other body functions that are disturbed in major depression.

People between the ages of 18 and 60 years with major mood disorder (MMD) or bipolar disorder (BP), normal healthy volunteers, and patients with Cushing's disease (CD) may be eligible for this study.

All participants will have an initial medical and psychiatric evaluation and magnetic resonance imaging (MRI) and positron emission tomography (PET) scans. In addition, some patients will have a dexamethasone-CRH stimulation test, mood stabilizing treatment, or lumbar puncture.

Initial evaluation includes a psychiatric and medical history; ratings of depression, anxiety, negative thinking and level of functioning; and battery of tests of general intelligence and cognitive abilities, including memory and concentration. In addition, a physical examination will be done, along with blood and urine tests and collection of a saliva sample. Menstruating women will also have a pregnancy test and tests to determine menstrual phase and time of ovulation.

Eligibility and Other Details

- **Ages eligible for study:** 18–60 years
- **Genders eligible for study:** Both
- **Expected total enrollment:** 130
- **Study dates:** Started October 4, 2001
- **Location:** National Institute of Mental Health (NIMH), 9000 Rockville Pike, Bethesda, MD 20892; Patient Recruitment and Public Liaison Office: 800-411-1222

Treatment of Mid-Life-Related Mood Disorders

Purpose

Dehydroepiandrosterone (DHEA) is a hormone produced by the adrenal gland. As humans grow older the levels of DHEA naturally decrease. Low levels of DHEA have been associated with a variety of harmful effects, including increased heart disease, decreased immune system function, decreased bone density (osteoporosis), high cholesterol, and increased fat to muscle ratio.

Blood levels of DHEA and its sulfate form, DHEA-S, begin dropping when humans are in their 20's. By the time humans are in their 40's and 50's, levels of DHEA and DHEA-S levels are at 50% of their peak. Previous studies have shown that levels of these hormones are associated with feelings of "well-being" and enjoyment of "leisure" activities.

In this study researchers are interested in the effects on mood and behavior of DHEA in men and women with mid-life related mood disorders. Specifically, researchers would like to find out if increasing levels of DHEA will lessen the symptoms associated with these disorders.

Eligibility and Other Details

- **Ages eligible for study:** Must be age 40–65.
- **Genders eligible for study:** Both
- **Expected total enrollment:** 60
- **Study dates:** Started June 30, 1995
- **Location:** National Institute of Mental Health (NIMH), 9000 Rockville Pike, Bethesda, MD 20892; Patient Recruitment and Public Liaison Office: 800-411-1222

Dynamics of Leptin and Endocrine Function

Purpose

This is a study investigating the hormones and substances important to the stress response. The hormone that is most directly responsible for stress response is called corticotropin-releasing hormone (CRH). CRH is produced in the hypothalamus of the brain and causes the pituitary gland to produce another hormone called ACTH. The hormone ACTH then acts on the adrenal glands causing them to produce the hormone cortisol.

Unfortunately, CRH levels are unable to be measured in simple blood samples. However, substances like cortisol and leptin can provide information as to the activity of the hypothalamus.

The hormone leptin is associated with the regulation of body weight and the normal maintenance of bodily functions (homeostasis). It is found in fat cell (adipocytes) and communicates the nutritional status of the body to the brain (central nervous system). Research using animals has shown that defects in the communication between leptin and the brain causes obesity (the state of being overweight). It has also been noted that obese humans tend to have high levels of leptin.

By studying patients with abnormal genes responsible for leptin production, researchers have found that a least one leptin gene must be intact for the normal secretion of hormones to proceed. These results show that the hormone leptin is produced outside of the brain in fat cells and acts directly on the function of the hypothalamus within the brain. Researchers believe that leptin plays a key role in the normal release of hormones from the HPA axis.

Researchers intend on continuing to study the role of leptin in fat distribution, and the activity of the HPA axis in normal volunteers. In addition, this study will focus on the role of leptin in depression, because depression is characterized by changes in food intake, body weight, and neuroendocrine function. Data gathered from this study will provide a better understanding of the causes and medical consequences of major depression.

Eligibility and Other Details

- **Ages eligible for study:** 18–62 years
- **Genders eligible for study:** Both
- **Expected total enrollment:** 230
- **Study dates:** Started March 16, 1996

- **Location:** National Institute of Mental Health (NIMH), 9000 Rockville Pike, Bethesda, MD 20892; Patient Recruitment and Public Liaison Office: 800-411-1222

Heart Disease Risk Factors in Major Depression

Purpose

Patients with major depression have an increased risk for coronary artery disease, independent of smoking and traditional cardiac risk factors. Several hormonal changes that occur with depression may be associated with this increased risk. Our hypothesis is that one of these is probably related to the decreased response to insulin (insulin resistance). This study will examine insulin resistance in patients with major depression and, how severe it is, and why it occurs.

Eligibility and Other Details

- **Ages eligible for study:** 18–65 years
- **Genders eligible for study:** Both
- **Expected total enrollment:** 80
- **Study dates:** Started December 30, 1999
- **Location:** National Institute of Mental Health (NIMH), 9000 Rockville Pike, Bethesda, MD 20892; Patient Recruitment and Public Liaison Office: 800-411-1222

Bone Loss in Premenopausal Women with Depression

Purpose

Depression may be a major risk factor for osteoporosis and abnormally elevated stress hormone levels may contribute to bone loss. Depression is associated with elevated stress hormone levels. This study will determine whether women with major depression lose bone mass at a faster rate than women without depression. This study will also determine if the drug alendronate (Fosamax) can maintain or increase bone mass in premenopausal women with major depression and osteoporosis.

This 12-month study requires six visits at the National Institutes of Health Clinical Center in Bethesda, Maryland. Participants will receive psychiatric, medical, dietary and stress hormone evaluations, including bone mineral density measurements.

Participants with depression and low bone mass will be randomly assigned to take either 70 mg of alendronate or a placebo (a look-alike tablet with no active medication) once a week. Alendronate works by reducing the activity of osteoclasts (cells that cause bone loss.) The Food and Drug Administration has approved alendronate for treating and preventing osteoporosis in postmenopausal women; its use in premenopausal women with low bone mass and major depression is considered investigational. They will also take calcium (500mg) and vitamin D (400IU) supplements. If participants are currently taking anti-depressant medications, they may continue to do so.

Participants with depression and normal bone mass will be compared to a control group of healthy, premenopausal women with normal bone mass.

Eligibility and Other Details

- **Ages eligible for study:** 21–45 years
- **Genders eligible for study:** Female
- **Expected total enrollment:** 160
- **Study dates:** Started August 10, 2000
- **Location:** National Institute of Mental Health (NIMH), 9000 Rockville Pike, Bethesda, MD 20892; Patient Recruitment and Public Liaison Office: 800-411-1222

Chapter 66

Bipolar Disorder: Clinical Trials

The following studies are sponsored by the National Institute of Mental Health (NIMH). Additional information, including criteria for study participation and contact information for study sites, can be found online at www.clinicaltrials.gov. Further information can also be obtained from NIMH. Contact:

NIMH Public Inquiries
601 Executive Blvd., Rm. 8184, MSC 9663
Bethesda, MD 20892
Phone: 301-443-4513
TTY: 301-443-8431
Fax: 301-443-4279
Website: www.nimh.nih.gov

A Double Blind Study Examining the Efficacy of Clozapine and a Study of the Pathophysiology in Treatment Resistant Mania

Purpose

A significant proportion of manic patients either do not respond adequately to conventional treatment (lithium, valproate, or carbamazepine

The text in this chapter was compiled in March 2002 from descriptions of current studies on bipolar disorder (manic-depression) sponsored by the National Institute of Mental Health (NIMH) at www.clinicaltrials.gov, a service of the National Institutes of Health, developed by the National Library of Medicine. The full text of all study descriptions is available online at www.clinicaltrials.gov.

with or without antipsychotic drugs), or cannot tolerate the adverse effects associated with therapeutic doses of these agents. Thus, a need exists for additional effective treatments. Preliminary studies group suggest that clozapine may have antimanic actions and be effective in treatment-resistant bipolar disorder. However, the efficacy of clozapine as an alternative therapy in treatment-resistant mania has never been subjected to definitive study with an adequate numbers of subjects. Thus, we propose to conduct the largest and only double-blind, placebo-controlled trial to date, of clozapine, in bipolar manic patients who were unresponsive or intolerant to six weeks of treatment with lithium, valproate, carbamazepine, and at least one antipsychotic drug. The specific aims of this investigation are to 1) assess the acute treatment efficacy of clozapine in treatment-resistant mania, 2) to investigate the functional anatomical correlates of mania, and 3) to investigate the effects of clozapine treatment on cerebral glucose metabolism and metabolic correlates of effective antimanic, clozapine treatment.

Eligibility and Other Details

- **Ages eligible for study:** 18–60 years
- **Genders eligible for study:** Both
- **Expected total enrollment:** 42
- **Study dates:** Started January 2, 2002
- **Location:** National Institute of Mental Health (NIMH), 9000 Rockville Pike, Bethesda, MD 20892; Patient Recruitment and Public Liaison Office: 800-411-1222

Systematic Treatment Enhancement Program for Bipolar Disorder (STEP-BD)

Purpose

STEP-BD is the largest treatment study ever conducted for bipolar disorder. It is a long-term outpatient study (5 years) that aims to find out which treatments, or combinations of treatments, are most effective for treating episodes of depression and mania and for preventing recurrent episodes. In addition, the study will evaluate treatment effectiveness in terms of quality of life, adherence to treatment, ability to work, social functioning, and treatment cost-effectiveness. While many treatments are used currently for bipolar disorder, including medications and psychotherapies, doctors are uncertain which of these treatments or combination of treatments actually work best. Findings from STEP-BD will help improve the treatment standards used by doctors in everyday clinical practice.

Eligibility and Other Details

- **Ages eligible for study:** 15 years and above
- **Genders eligible for study:** Both
- **Expected total enrollment:** 5000
- **Study dates:** Started September 1998; Study Completion Date September 2003
- **Location:** 17 locations across the United States

An Investigation of the Efficacy of a Dopamine Agonist with Neurotrophic Properties in Bipolar Disorder

Purpose

Bipolar affective disorder (BPD; manic-depressive illness) is a common, severe, chronic, and often life-threatening illness. Increasingly, it is being recognized that it is the depressive phase of the illness, which contributes much of the morbidity and mortality. Impairment in physical and social functioning resulting from depression can be just as severe as other chronic medical illnesses. Suicide is the cause of death in 10–20% of individuals with either bipolar or recurrent depressive disorders.

The treatments for acute unipolar depression have been extensively researched. However, despite the availability of a wide range of antidepressant drugs, clinical trails indicate that 30% to 40% of (unipolar) depressed patients fail to respond to first-line antidepressant treatment, despite adequate dosage, duration, and compliance. Very few studies have examined the efficacy of somatic treatments for the acute phase of bipolar depression. Thus, there is a clear need to develop novel and improved therapeutics for bipolar depression. A deficiency of dopamine systems stands as a prime candidate for involvement in the pathophysiology of depression.

Preliminary studies suggest that pramipexole (Mirapex), a dopaminergic-agent that is FDA-approved Parkinson's Disease, may have antidepressant properties in unipolar patients as well as neurotrophic properties. This is a 6-week randomized double-blind, placebo-controlled add-on study that will examine the efficacy of pramipexole in acutely depressed Bipolar II patients.

Eligibility and Other Details

- **Ages eligible for study:** 18–70 years
- **Genders eligible for study:** Both
- **Expected total enrollment:** 120
- **Study dates:** Started October 22, 2001
- **Location:** National Institute of Mental Health (NIMH), 9000 Rockville Pike, Bethesda, MD 20892; Patient Recruitment and Public Liaison Office: 800-411-1222

Tamoxifen to Treat Acute Mania

Purpose

This study will examine how the drug tamoxifen affects the brain's protein kinase C (PKC) signaling pathway in patients with bipolar 1 (manic depressive) disorder. It will also examine whether the chemical changes that occur in the brain result in improvement of manic symptoms. A potent inhibitor of the PKC pathway, tamoxifen is better known for its use in treating breast and other cancers. Its effects on the PKC signaling pathway are similar to those of lithium and valproate (mood stabilizers widely used to treat bipolar disorder), but occur more quickly. In a recent study, seven patients with mania who were given 20 to 80 milligrams per day of tamoxifen for 4 to 15 days had a significant decrease in manic symptoms within 3 to 7 days.

Males 18 years of age and older with bipolar 1 disorder may be eligible for this study. Women are not included in the study because the risk of endometrial cancer with short-term exposure to tamoxifen is not known.

Eligibility and Other Details

- **Ages eligible for study:** 18–60 years
- **Genders eligible for study:** Male
- **Expected total enrollment:** 50
- **Study dates:** Started November 9, 2001
- **Location:** National Institute of Mental Health (NIMH), 9000 Rockville Pike, Bethesda, MD 20892; Patient Recruitment and Public Liaison Office: 800-411-1222

Symptoms and Causes of Bipolar Disease in Children and Adolescents

Purpose

The purpose of this study is to learn more about bipolar disease in children. Bipolar disease is a type of mood disorder that involves frequent changes in mood and activity level. The study will describe the symptoms, that is, the moods and behaviors, of children with bipolar disease over time and try to learn what happens in the brain to produce these symptoms. This is not a treatment study; children will not receive any new or experimental therapies.

Children and adolescents ages 6 through 17 with bipolar disorder and normal healthy volunteers (controls) of the same age group may participate in this study. Candidates will have a telephone interview and review of medical records to determine eligibility. Additional screening will include a medical and psychiatric history of the patient and extended family members, and a physical and neurological evaluation. The medical history interviews will be videotaped and kept confidential.

After evaluation, control subjects will have completed their participation in the study. Follow-up evaluations will be scheduled for patients only as follows: at the end of two months, then every three months until a year has passed from the first visit, then every six months for four years. Some visits will involve only interviews and questionnaires, some will also include a physical exam, and urine test and others will also include a blood tests. A MRI brain scan will be done at two and four years. Patients, their parents and siblings will also be asked to have blood drawn to obtain a DNA sample for genetic studies.

Eligibility and Other Details

- **Ages eligible for study:** 6–17 years
- **Genders eligible for study:** Both
- **Expected total enrollment:** 120
- **Study dates:** Started August 9, 2000
- **Location:** National Institute of Mental Health (NIMH), 9000 Rockville Pike, Bethesda, MD 20892; Patient Recruitment and Public Liaison Office: 800-411-1222

Chapter 67

Clinical Trials: Mood Disorders Associated with the Menstrual Cycle, Pregnancy, and Menopause

The following studies are sponsored by the National Institute of Mental Health (NIMH). Additional information, including criteria for study participation and contact information for study sites, can be found online at www.clinicaltrials.gov. Further information can also be obtained from NIMH. Contact:

NIMH Public Inquiries
601 Executive Blvd., Rm. 8184, MSC 9663
Bethesda, MD 20892
Phone: 301-443-4513
TTY: 301-443-8431
Fax: 301-443-4279
Website: www.nimh.nih.gov

Study of Menstrually-Regulated Mood and Behavioral Disorder

Purpose

The purpose of this research study is to identify a population of women who experience menstrually-related mood or behavior difficulties

The text in this chapter was compiled in March 2002 from descriptions of current studies on mood disorders associated with the menstrual cycle, pregnancy, and menopause sponsored by the National Institute of Mental Health (NIMH) at www.clinicaltrials.gov, a service of the National Institutes of Health, developed by the National Library of Medicine. The full text of all study descriptions is available online at www.clinicaltrials.gov.

(MRMD), and to describe the symptoms in the group and their relationship to menstruation. This will be accomplished by conducting clinical interviews, asking patients to complete self-rating scales, and conducting scheduled evaluations of mood and endocrine function.

In addition, researchers would like to identify a subgroup of women with menstrually-related mood disorder for participation in other research studies. These other studies will focus on:

1. Identifying the endocrinologic or physiologic causes responsible for the changes in mood and behavior.

2. Distinguishing women with MRMD from women without MRMD of the same age.

3. Developing a subgroup definition based on how patients respond to different medications.

4. Identify hereditary factors in women with MRMD.

Finally, researchers would like to identify a group of women with recurrent brief depression, who will serve as an additional group to compare against women with MRMD.

Eligibility and Other Details

*   **Ages eligible for study:** 18–50 years
*   **Genders eligible for study:** Female
*   **Expected total enrollment:** 1100
*   **Study dates:** Started August 24, 1981
*   **Location:** National Institute of Mental Health (NIMH), 9000 Rockville Pike, Bethesda, MD 20892; Patient Recruitment and Public Liaison Office: 800-411-1222

Evaluating Women with Perimenopause-Related Mood and Behavioral Disorders

Purpose

This study was designed to investigate the relationship between changes in mood and behavior and perimenopause/menopause.

Menopause is the time when women stop having menstrual periods, and represents the time when the ovaries stop making the two hormones estrogen and progesterone. As a result of low levels of estrogen, some women experience symptoms of menopause like hot flushes and vaginal dryness. Perimenopause refers to the time prior to actual menopause.

Researchers will first identify groups of women who are in the perimenopause, with and without depressive symptoms. The patients and controls (women without symptoms of depression) will be compared based on the presence of menopausal symptoms, like hot flashes. Patient subjects may also participate in other studies testing the antidepressant effectiveness of estrogen (estradiol) and testosterone (DHEA).

Eligibility and Other Details

- **Ages eligible for study:** 40–60 years
- **Genders eligible for study:** Female
- **Expected total enrollment:** 600
- **Study dates:** Started July 12, 1988
- **Location:** National Institute of Mental Health (NIMH), 9000 Rockville Pike, Bethesda, MD 20892; Patient Recruitment and Public Liaison Office: 800-411-1222

Progestin Induced Dysphoria

Purpose

Often women are prescribed hormone replacement therapy (HRT) during the perimenopause or menopause.

Hormone replacement therapy includes both estrogen and progesterone. The estrogen component of HRT helps to relieve the symptoms and has a beneficial effect on the heart and bones, but estrogen also increases the risk of uterine cancer. The progesterone component of the HRT (progestin) works to prevent the increased risk of uterine cancer.

There is evidence that some women experience unpleasant mood symptoms (such as irritability, depressed mood, and anxiety) while receiving hormone replacement therapy (HRT) while taking the progestin / progesterone component of the HRT.

This study is designed to evaluate the ability of progestins to produce negative mood symptoms in women. Researchers intend on doing this by comparing the effects of medroxyprogesterone acetate (Provera) and a placebo inactive sugar pill. Patient's moods will be monitored based on their response to questionnaires answered in the outpatient clinic and at home.

This research will attempt to answer the following questions:

1. Are progestins associated with changes in mood during hormone replacement therapy?

2. If progestins are associated with mood disturbance, is it because they are blocking the beneficial effects of estrogen?

Eligibility and Other Details

* **Ages eligible for study:** 40–65 years
* **Genders eligible for study:** Female
* **Expected total enrollment:** 50
* **Study dates:** Started March 14, 1998
* **Location:** National Institute of Mental Health (NIMH), 9000 Rockville Pike, Bethesda, MD 20892; Patient Recruitment and Public Liaison Office: 800-411-1222

An Endocrine Model for Postpartum Mood Disorders

Purpose

Depression can occur in the time immediately following delivery (post partum depression). While there are many speculations as to the causes of post partum depression, none has ever been confirmed.

This study is designed to create a "scaled down" hormonal state of pregnancy and the 6-week period following delivery (puerperium). This will help researchers determine whether women who have experienced a postpartum mood disorder will have signs and symptoms of a depressed mood compared to women who have never experienced a post-partum mood disorder (controls).

Researchers will raise blood levels of the hormones estrogen and progesterone, maintain them at higher than menstrual cycle levels, and then rapidly lower levels to simulate the action of hormones that occur during a normal pregnancy.

Women participating in this study will first be pretreated with Lupron. Lupron acts by blocking the release of the pituitary hormones FSH (follicle stimulating hormone) and LH (luteinizing hormone). FSH and LH are normally released from the pituitary in response to GnRH released from the hypothalamus in the brain. FSH and LH are responsible for stimulating the ovaries to release estrogen and progesterone.

Following pretreatment with Lupron, patients will be given doses of estrogen (estradiol) and progesterone for eight weeks. After eight weeks, estrogen and progesterone will be stopped causing a sudden drop in the level of hormones in the blood.

Mood symptoms and hormone levels will be measured during the study.

Eligibility and Other Details

- **Ages eligible for study:** 18–40 years
- **Genders eligible for study:** Female
- **Expected total enrollment:** 80
- **Study dates:** Started March 31, 1995
- **Location:** National Institute of Mental Health (NIMH), 9000 Rockville Pike, Bethesda, MD 20892; Patient Recruitment and Public Liaison Office: 800-411-1222

Chapter 68

Researching Gender Differences in Depression

Depression Can Differ in Men and Women

The National Institute of Mental Health (NIMH) conducts research to determine gender differences in various mental illnesses. To educate the public on this topic, it cosponsored a Smithsonian Resident Associates seminar entitled "Depression in Women and Men: What's the Difference?" Phyllis Greenberger, president of the Society for Women's Health Research (SWHR), and Dr. Steven Hyman, director of NIMH, presided over the meeting, which explored gender differences in depression from a variety of perspectives.

Depression in both women and men is a debilitating disorder that disrupts relationships and daily lives and affects nearly 10 percent of the population. Despite the fact that depression is very common, only about 10 percent of cases receive clinical attention. Once a person has a single episode of depression, the chances of recurrence are high. The disease is twice as common in women as in men, although both sexes suffer its debilitating effects.

A summary of the meeting follows.

This chapter contains excerpts from "Depression Can Differ in Men and Women," *NIH Record*, National Institutes of Health, May 15, 2001 and "Depression in Women and Men: What's the Difference?" National Institute of Mental Health, March 2001, updated: September 07, 2001. The full text of this document is available online at www.nimh.nih.gov/research/differencesummary.cfm.

Depression in Women and Men: What's the Difference?

Introduction: Phyllis Greenberger, SWHR Executive Director

As more and more researchers are investigating sex differences, they are noting that males and females often have different reactions to drugs, experience different patterns of diseases, and show different symptoms for the same disease. Depression is an area with an abundance of gender differences not only at the biological and physiological level but at the sociological level as well. Depression in both women and men is a debilitating disorder that disrupts relationships and daily lives and affects nearly ten percent of the population. Though depression is a treatable disease, about eighty percent of episodes of depression are not diagnosed and treated.

Ms. Greenberger highlighted these issues relating to women and depression:

- We are just beginning to learn about the ways in which medications are processed differently in women and men and how this affects treatment choices—such as dosages—and outcomes.

- Serotonin is a neurotransmitter used by the brain for mood balance. Males and females process this neurochemical and others, such as estrogen, in different ways.

- Suicide attempts are more common in women. Men are more successful in taking their own lives, but more women attempt it.

- Men are more likely to be diagnosed with alcohol problems, but women are at higher risk for developing alcohol problems following an episode of depression. Women experiencing depression are more likely to develop alcohol problems within a few years of their first depressive episode.

- Treatment issues during pregnancy and postpartum are particularly challenging.

- Under the age of 13, approximately equal numbers of girls and boys experience depression. Once children reach the age of 13, more girls than boys become depressed.

Understanding why these sex differences occur undoubtedly will help in understanding the biological basis of depression, and how better to treat it in both women and men, concluded Ms. Greenberger.

The Burden of Depression: Steven E. Hyman, M.D., Director of NIMH

Despite its remarkable prevalence (almost 10 percent of the U.S. population), depression—like many mental disorders—has been swept under the rug by misunderstanding. The brain is by far the body's most complex organ, yet it is invisible. Because depression is invisible in the sense that it does not leave obvious markers on the body, it is more difficult to diagnose than physical illness. Its effects are clear, however, and often tragically so. Mental disorders have been marginalized because we measure the burden of illness in a society primarily by mortality, and while mental disorders can be lethal, from suicide for example, they are not lethal as often as some other illnesses, like cancer. Nevertheless, they can destroy lives.

Certain mental illnesses have particularly strong genetic components: autism, bipolar disorder, and schizophrenia. The genetic risk of depression, though less than these other mental illnesses, is about the same as type II diabetes.

In terms of risk of mental illnesses, males and females differ. Boys are much more likely to have autism and attention deficit hyperactivity disorder (ADHD). As males get older, their risk for alcoholism is twice that of women, and men experience onset of schizophrenia earlier in life than women do.

Women are twice as likely to suffer from depression, panic disorder, and other anxiety disorders. While women and men are equally likely to develop bipolar disorder, women are more likely to be diagnosed with "rapid cycling" —as many as three episodes in a year. Dr. Hyman also noted, as Ms. Greenberger had, that women are more likely to attempt suicide, and men are more likely to complete it.

Before puberty, he noted, the gender ratio for depression is one to one, but later, women are at greater risk. There also are differences in depression across the reproductive cycle and mood symptoms associated with the menstrual cycle. There is postpartum depression and there are mood symptoms associated with perimenopause. "Gender is not a political issue. It is a true biological issue that affects the frequency and expression of mental illnesses," said Dr. Hyman.

While one may wonder if these differences are an artifact of society, research suggests that is not the case. Across many different societies, the rates of schizophrenia and bipolar disorder are the same. And while depression occurs in different societies at different times at different rates, the symptoms are always the same and the gender ratio is always two to one. "There is some profound biological message we need to decode," concluded Dr. Hyman.

Defining and Understanding Depression: Ellen Leibenluft, M.D., Chief of the Unit on Affective Disorders in NIMH's Pediatrics and Developmental Neuropsychiatry Branch

To receive a diagnosis of major depressive disorder, an individual must experience depressed mood or anhedonia (the inability to experience pleasure) for two weeks, in addition to five or more of the following symptoms: weight loss or gain, insomnia or excessive sleep, fatigue, feelings of worthlessness, difficulty concentrating, or suicidal thoughts. Most people who seek treatment have experienced symptoms for several months or longer.

Dr. Leibenluft noted that many people think that depression is more common in women than men because women are more likely than men to admit to feeling depressed, while men are more likely to deny their symptoms or even to forget them. Her conclusion, based on the data she has reviewed, is that men who are currently depressed are not more likely to deny symptoms than women who are currently depressed, but that men may be somewhat more likely to minimize or forget past episodes. These differences, however, cannot account for the gender differences in depression, she emphasized.

The major gender difference is that women are at higher risk than men to experience a first episode of depression. After that, there is no consistent gender difference in the severity or course of depression—in other words, depressed men and women don't differ in the extent to which depression interferes with their ability to function, or in the length or frequency of their depressive episodes. Women, however, are more likely than men to report a high number of depressive symptoms (seven or eight). And pure depression—in which the person has no other psychiatric illness, such as substance abuse or anxiety—is more common in women than men.

Most depressed patients, however, do not have pure depression; instead, they also suffer from other psychiatric illnesses. These other mental disorders often appear before the clinical depression. In women, depression often follows anxiety disorders, while in men it often follows substance abuse disorders or conduct disorder (antisocial behaviors). Although women overall have a lower risk for substance abuse than do men, depressed women are more likely than depressed men to develop substance abuse disorder after they become depressed. Women also tend to develop brain and liver damage relatively early

502

in the course of alcoholism. Dr. Leibenluft suggested that this may relate to body size or rate of metabolism.

Few men or women who have suicidal thoughts get treatment. Suicidal thinking and behavior is particularly common among adolescents and the elderly. More women attempt suicide, but more men complete suicide attempts, partly because they tend to use more lethal methods such as guns rather than medication overdoses.

These important gender differences could have implications for treatment and prevention of depression, concluded Dr. Leibenluft.

Risk Factors for Depression: Carolyn M. Mazure, Ph.D., Professor of Psychiatry at the Yale University School of Medicine and Director of Women's Health Research at Yale.

A risk factor is a condition or behavior that precedes the onset of depression and is found at a higher rate in persons with depression than without depression. Risk factors also can provide a profile of those for whom depression is more likely and, consequently, can serve as targets for treatment and prevention strategies.

One of the most consistently determined risk factors for depression is female gender. It has been shown in many well-conducted studies that lifetime rates of depression are higher for women than men and that the relative difference in the rates between women and men are maintained essentially over the life span.

Some of the other factors that increase risk for depression include prior episodes of depression, family history of depression in first-degree relatives (parents and siblings), and chronic medical illness. With regard to sex differences in these risk factors, prior episodes are not more predictive of depression for women than men. Because women have more first episodes of depression, however, there are more women in the "pool" of those who could have a recurrence. Women are six times more likely than men to develop depression after physical illness or injury; specifically, some data suggest that women are twice as likely to develop depression after myocardial infarction.

Certain cognitive styles—ways of thinking and viewing the world— also can be risk factors for depression. For example, those who focus extensively on pleasing others to avoid disapproval and those who have an exaggerated need for control have an increased risk for depression. People with these needs establish unattainable goals that make them feel more hopeless. While both women and men with these styles have a higher risk for depression, the first style seems to be more pronounced in women than in men. Another cognitive style is rumination, or replaying negative experiences and their possible meanings and consequences. This ineffective search for control is more common in women than men; it increases negative thinking and impairs problem solving, worsens mood, and promotes depression. With cognitive behavioral therapy, some of these styles can be modified.

Finally, a very important risk factor is life stress, or exposure to adverse experience, and the effect of this factor might be particularly helpful in explaining the gender disparity in rates of depression. Life stress greatly increases risk for depression, and women are preferentially affected by life stress and have more event-related depression than men. Dr. Mazure emphasized that future studies need to translate these findings into treatment strategies that reduce risk for depression.

The Neuroscience of Depression: Richard Davidson, Ph.D., Vilas Professor of Psychology and Psychiatry in the Department of Psychology at the University of Wisconsin-Madison

Positron emission tomography (PET) scanning allows us to visualize the biochemistry of the brain. Functional magnetic resonance imaging (fMRI) does not involve exposing individuals to ionizing radiation and is responsible for the advances in exploring the human brain as it undergoes different emotions and mood changes. As research progresses, scientists are finding that apparently the mechanisms involved in the regulation of emotions may be different from the circuits in the brain involved in the initial generation of that emotion.

Dr. Davidson reviewed several slides depicting the ventral side of the brain, or the "underbelly" of the prefrontal cortex. Patients with damage to this area show aberrant behavior and have difficulty anticipating the emotional consequences of their behaviors. Asked to contemplate a specific choice, these patients are unable to feel the emotion that may be associated with a poor choice and use that to guide their behavior, especially when faced with complex choices.

The old-fashioned view, Dr. Davidson said, is that emotions are disrupters of behavior. In fact, in many ways, the appropriate use of emotions is important to our lives. If the parts of our brain that help us anticipate these emotions are damaged, then our decision-making ability also is damaged. The left prefrontal cortex is an area of the brain that appears to be particularly important for representing positive goals and organizing behavior toward the acquisition of such goals. Damage to this area of the brain impairs an individual's ability to implement goals and can result in depressive-like behavior when goals are not pursued. The amygdala, in a different part of the brain, responds to signals in the environment that represent potential threats. This area of the brain is hyperactive or fails to turn off with certain types of mood or anxiety disorders.

In general, Dr. Davidson explained, research has shown that depression is more prevalent in patients with lesions on the left side of the brain while mania is associated with lesions on the right side. In studies of patients who have suffered a stroke, those with the most severe depression have left prefrontal lesions, leading researchers to hypothesize that areas in the left prefrontal area of the brain play a role in positive emotion and damage to this area may contribute to a deficit in one's capacity to experience pleasure.

In a study of people with no brain damage, researchers exposed participants to pictures designed to elicit either little emotion, positive emotion, or negative emotion and recorded brain activity with PET. Positive pictures tended to activate responses in the prefrontal region in the left hemisphere. Negative pictures tended to activate responses in the right hemisphere, in a different region of the prefrontal cortex.

Dr. Davidson suggested that there may be differences among people in their ability to respond to negative and positive stimuli, an ability based on a complex mix of genetics and environment. Referring to Dr. Mazure's discussion of rumination, Dr. Davidson said that scientists speculate that rumination is the failure to attenuate negative emotion after a negative event occurs, resulting in it persisting in that part of the brain. This notion of persistence of mood beyond the point at which it typically falls off in a nondepressed person may relate to the machinery in the brain involved in the regulation of negative emotion. There also may be a relationship between hormonal changes and changes in brain activity.

Dr. Davidson concluded by emphasizing that understanding the brain machinery responsible for persistence of emotions may eventually help researchers understand what may be responsible for gender differences in mood disorders since there is some evidence to suggest that women and men ruminate to different degrees.

505

Stress and Depression: Ned Kalin, M.D., Hedberg Professor and Chair of the Department of Psychiatry at the University of Wisconsin Medical School in Madison

The stress response is important for survival and adaptation. The stress response, which involves both emotional and physiological changes, is an adaptive response that motivates our behavior so we can protect ourselves. It is turned on by the brain working in specific neural circuits modulated by neurotransmitters and hormones.

There are important individual differences in humans. Some people may have the ability to shut down quickly their emotional, behavioral, and hormonal responses to stressful situations, while others may have prolonged responses. Over time, these prolonged responses could affect physiology and brain function. For example, increased release of cortisol over a long time could affect glucose regulation, bone density, immune function, and the function of specific brain cells. These individuals could become vulnerable to developing physical and mental diseases. Evidence suggests that overactivity of corticotropin-releasing factor, a brain neurochemical, may play a role in why some people become excessively anxious and depressed. For example, about 50 percent of depressed patients have overactivity of the stress hormone response, which is regulated by corticotropin-releasing factor. Whether this overactivity causes or contributes to depression is unclear. It is also possible that overactivity of this system may play a role in altering the structure and function of certain brain cells.

Dr. Kalin described studies of childhood experiences that may reveal a connection between stress hormone levels and depression. A study in 1945 by Spitz examined the psychological condition of orphans who were hospitalized and provided with a clean and healthy environment but with very little contact or comfort by the nurses. These children were described as withdrawn, and social interactions with them became increasingly difficult. In more recent studies, data suggests that children who have been deprived of contact or comfort develop alterations in their stress hormonal responses.

Studies of monkeys also can provide some insight into the relationship between stress hormones and depression, Dr. Kalin said. One long-ago experiment by Harlow focused on monkeys who were raised apart from their mothers with little or no physical contact with other animals. When these monkeys became mothers, they were either indifferent and withdrawn or violent and abusive to their offspring; they were unable to regulate their own emotions. This suggests that their early experience promoted the development of a vulnerability that proved to be very important when they became adults.

The offspring of these motherless mothers, moreover, began to exhibit similar abnormal behavior. The fact that some of the motherless monkeys were withdrawn and others were abusive reflects the differences among individuals who experience trauma, said Dr. Kalin. "We can't give a complete answer as to why one individual responds in one way and another responds in a completely different manner," he said. "We're dealing with very complicated brain systems involving numerous brain chemicals interacting across many brain regions."

Scientists hope that by studying how the stress response system relates to development and depression they may be able to develop early recognition and new treatment strategies, perhaps targeting early environmental factors as well as the hormonal systems that may be affected.

The Limbic System and Depression: Huda Akil, Ph.D., Gardner Quarton Distinguished University Professor of Neuroscience in the Department of Psychiatry at the University of Michigan and Co-director of the University's Mental Health Research Institute

Depression is a complex genetic disorder. Patterns of gene activity or "gene expression" in specific brain circuits are the result not only of genetic endowment, but also of the impact of experience on the brain. Thus, the brain is where genes and environment meet, and their interaction results in unique patterns of genetic activity that mediate specific behaviors. Hormones play a role in modulating these patterns of activity in the emotional circuitry. Women and men differ physically and psychologically, and they differ in the social demands made upon them. Women and men perceive social stress differently, and that stress, in turn, differs in its impact on their brains.

The limbic system, essential to processing emotions and handling stress, is a part of the brain relevant to depression. The component that interfaces between emotional processing and higher order cognition is the prefrontal cortex. The combination of thinking and feeling is important for mediating language, remembering, and anticipating. Humans do not live only moment-to-moment; emotions can persist from the past, and we can project them into the future. It is this ability to sustain emotions over long periods of time that represents a hallmark of human emotional responsiveness, and distinguishes immediate emotional reactions that might be shared with animals from long-standing changes in mood and affect.

In her studies of hamsters, Dr. Akil has identified brain circuits that are critical to psychosocial emotions, including social defeat. These circuits are not only generic stress circuits, but also they are quite specific and readily distinguishable from circuits that are activated during fighting that results in winning. Interestingly, these defeat circuits found in rodents parallel the circuits found to be disrupted in human depression. Though they are primitive, they represent a fundamental circuitry that encodes emotion and affect. This circuitry is further modulated in humans by the higher-order cortical information.

Dr. Akil described some possible future directions for research. Microarray technology involves placing on a small slide an entire genome of an animal or human. If a specific gene is expressed in a particular part of the brain, it will be detected by researchers using a dye of a particular color. When comparing two individuals and using a different color dye for each individual, researchers can use the interaction between the colors to detect whether the genes are active to a same or a different extent between the two subjects. This allows researchers to compare patterns of gene expression in particular brain regions across two groups of animals or two sets of human subjects. Since the entire genome is being examined, this not only focuses on the genes we already know, but allows us to discover the potential alterations in novel or previously unstudied genes. Such information can be applied to humans in an effort to understand psychiatric disorders that are not easily modeled in animals. Dr. Akil and her collaborators (members of the Conte Center Grant and the Pritzker Consortium: Drs. W. E. Bunney, E. Jones, D. Cox, S.J. Watson, A. Schatzberg) are beginning to use this microarray technology to uncover the unique patterns of gene expression in severely depressed individuals. They are studying differences between men and women as well as the differences among depressed and nondepressed men and women. The ultimate goal is to develop novel therapeutic targets. Using the human genome, Dr. Akil said, "We can come up with new directions on how to treat and think about depression."

Treating Depression: Kimberly Ann Yonkers, M.D., Associate Professor in the Department of Psychiatry at the Yale School of Medicine

Among available treatments are antidepressant agents, including tricyclics (Elavil®, Tofranil®), monoamine oxidase inhibitors (Nardil®,

Parnate®), and selective serotonin reuptake inhibitors (Paxil®, Prozac®, Zoloft®); psychotherapy; and electroconvulsive therapy (ECT). Alternative therapies include herbals (such as St. John's wort) and acupuncture.

Studying sex differences in treatment response may lead to an increased understanding of illness mechanisms; sex differences may provide a window into understanding the pathophysiology of psychiatric disorders, Dr. Yonkers said. Gender may influence depression treatment responses because:

- Sex-specific processes may be associated with the cause of subtypes of mood disorders, such as premenstrual dysphoric disorder and postpartum depression

- Sex-specific processes may affect the ways treatments work

- Differences in brain function or structure may relate to responses

- Some medications are absorbed, distributed, or metabolized differently in men and women

- Hormone receptors could be interacting with other receptors and could reflect differences in treatment responses

Sex-specific responses are related to certain mood disorders. Women experience premenstrual dysphoria, postpartum depression, and perimenopausal depression. Men manifest late-life minor depression and hypogonadal depression.

In the past ten years or so, new federal guidelines mandate that researchers conducting clinical trials compare how women and men respond to medications instead of just comparing the efficacy of a medication versus a placebo. Research suggests that men respond better to tricyclics than monoamine oxidase inhibitors, while younger women respond better to monoamine oxidase inhibitors. In postmenopausal women, however, tricyclics and monoamine oxidase inhibitors work equally well. Women are more likely to respond to ECT. Men and women are equally likely to respond either to cognitive behavior therapy or interpersonal psychotherapy.

Panel Discussion

Mary Blehar, Ph.D., Chief of the Women's Mental Health Program at NIMH, moderated a panel that addressed questions from the audience. Presenters were joined by Peter Schmidt, M.D., Chief, Unit on

Reproductive Endocrinology, in the Behavioral Endocrinology Branch, NIMH. Questions and answers were wide ranging.

Could depression be contagious?

There is evidence that depression is increasing in younger age groups, which has led some researchers to suggest a role for a changing incidence of environmental triggers, such as use of street drugs or environmental stress. There is no evidence, however, that depression is "contagious" in the sense of being caused by a specific pathogen such as a germ or virus. There is evidence that some pediatric obsessive-compulsive disorders might result from the response of the autoimmune system to streptococcal infections. It is highly likely that infections that affect the immune system also can impact the brain and mood, but the precise cause-and-effect relationship has not been established.

What do we know about the contribution of genetic factors to depression? Is there any evidence of a gender difference in these factors? Is a daughter more likely to inherit depression than a son? Does it matter whether depression is inherited from a mother or a father?

Family and twin studies indicate that major depression tends to run in families. Beyond that, we know little as yet about specific genetic factors predisposing to depression, so we also know little about possible gender differences. Twin studies indicate that depression is heritable in both women and men, and there is some evidence from these studies that the extent of heritability may differ between the sexes. These studies also suggest that somewhat different constellations of genetic, biological, and environmental risk factors may predispose to depression in men and women. NIMH currently is funding molecular genetic studies to identify vulnerability genes in one form of highly heritable depression—recurrent early-onset depression. This work also may further elucidate the role of gender differences in depression.

If women are twice as likely as men to suffer from depression, are women also twice as likely as men to become depressed as a reaction to life events?

This is a complicated question. Approximately 70% of episodes of major depression are preceded close in time by a stressful life event, so we know that stress plays some role in triggering depression. And there is evidence suggesting that women and men may differ in their behavioral—and even biological—responses to stress. Therefore, researchers are investigating the mechanisms by which stress contributes to depression and the role that gender plays in this.

Some evidence shows that women and men differ in the life events they perceive as highly stressful, and there are some studies indicating that women develop depression following a greater range of stressful events than men. For example, one study found that women and men are likely to report events as stressful that occur to their immediate family, but women also are adversely affected by events occurring to a range of people in their social network. Differences, then, in stress potential of different events also may contribute to gender differences in rates of depression.

Are there developmental or lifespan differences in risk for depression? How do these play out in the two sexes?

The childbearing years are the time of highest risk for depression in women. This is particularly important not only for the affected women but also for families because maternal depression, such as postpartum depression, is reported to have a negative impact on child mental health. Although fewer men than women are diagnosed with depression, men with depression are at higher risk for completed suicide and the risk is particularly high in older men. However, women with depression are more likely to attempt suicide than are men. A recent report suggests that women with early-onset chronic depression may have poorer occupational and social functional outcomes relative to other women with depression or men with early-onset chronic depression.

How about depression following the onset and diagnosis of an illness such as cancer? What do we know about gender differences here?

Women are more likely to seek health care both for mental health problems in specialized settings and for physical conditions in primary care settings. We know that depression accompanying other medical conditions is the most common mental illness in primary care settings, and we know that women are more likely to be diagnosed as having depression in these settings. Thus, co-occurring depression in general medical settings does exhibit a pattern of gender differences similar to that found in community settings. We also know that it is important to identify depression in primary care settings because untreated depression that accompanies other medical conditions has a worse outcome than conditions that are uncomplicated by depression.

People with undiagnosed depression may report physical symptoms that are, in fact, a manifestation of their depression. This may lead to higher health care costs for unnecessary medical screening tests. There is also some evidence that in primary care settings women are more likely than men to manifest forms of depression characterized by bodily complaints (for example, fatigue, aches, and pains).

How does exercise help combat depression?

Exercise, when it causes the body to release endorphins, seems to have a beneficial effect on mood, but very little is known about its effects in persons with clinical major depression. One practical obstacle to using exercise for the treatment of depression is that many people who are depressed do not have the energy or motivation to initiate exercise so they never get to the point where they can recognize this effect. We need to do more research to determine what role exercise can play in preventing and treating depression and for which types of depression it may be more appropriate. Some animal studies suggest that exercise can contribute to increasing the production of new brain cells, so it is possible that exercise has real salutary effects on mood and cognition.

Does treatment of depression in adolescent females differ from treatment of depression in adolescent males?

Unfortunately, we have very little information about the treatment of adolescent depression in terms of the most effective medications and/or therapy. There are currently only a few pharmacological studies of depression in adolescent samples and a few studies of psychotherapies. Although these studies indicate that both of these treatments are effective, they have not reported on gender differences in outcome. We do know that adolescent depression has more frequent comorbidity with conduct disorders and substance abuse in males and with anxiety disorders and eating disorders in females. A good direction for future study might well be to focus on devising treatments that address these differing comorbid conditions in the course of treating depression in adolescent males and females.

Do people develop a tolerance for an antidepressant so that the medication they take becomes less effective?

People taking antidepressants over a period of time following an acute episode of depression are at less risk for a relapse or recurrent episode than those who discontinue medication after the acute episode, but new relapses and recurrences happen even in those on medication. In that sense, an antidepressant's effects may wear off over time. Researchers are looking at strategies to prevent this from happening, but at this point we do not know if this lessening of effectiveness is a counter-response to the medication—that is, the systems that were out of balance over-respond—or if the lessening of effectiveness is a result of the patient's metabolism. NIMH research is currently focusing not only on acute treatment of an episode of depression but also on maintenance and relapse prevention strategies, which may be different than the interventions used for acute phase treatment.

We are learning that depression is more complex than we realized. Currently, we conceive of depression as a single illness; ten years from now, we may see it as ten different illnesses. Depression may be more like fever, a nonspecific condition that tells us that something is severely wrong in the emotional-cognitive interface.

Can we realistically speak of "curing" depression?

Just as we have many types of respiratory conditions ranging from acute infections to chronic or recurrent conditions such as asthma and bronchitis, we have different manifestations of mood disorders. Some individuals report only one episode of depression over a lifetime; more people with depression have a chronic course or recurrent episodes. The prevalence of chronic depression, including dysthymia, chronic major depression, and major depression with incomplete symptomatic recovery is more than 5%. Recurrent depression is also common. One study found that after one year, 30% of persons with depression had not recovered completely. Of those who recovered, 60% had a relapse within five years. Other data suggest that each recurrence increases the likelihood of another episode. Some research suggests that depression actually changes the brain circuitry, so becoming depressed makes us more vulnerable to further episodes of depression. In these cases, clinicians are coming to view depression as a chronic condition to be managed using strategies used for the treatment of other chronic conditions.

What is the most exciting research going on now?

NIMH's budget is about $1.1 billion. Of that, about $140 million is going to depression research; this disorder affects 20 million Americans, and we have some promising scientific leads.

One of those is research into identifying genes that increase vulnerability to depression. Identifying vulnerability factors will provide us with novel targets for developing treatments. We would like to be able to ask, "What is it about this version of this gene that puts you at risk? At what point does it affect the developing brain? Could understanding this gene lead us to behavioral prevention?"

We also are finding that emotional tuning is controlled by very precise circuitry, just as motor control and vision are controlled by precise circuitry.

Finally, we are convinced that more research into potential commonalities in human societies could help account for the similar ratios in depression and other mood disorders across cultures.

Chapter 69

Depression, Bone Mass, and Osteoporosis

The National Institute of Mental Health (NIMH) has launched a new study of women ages 21 to 45 who are suffering from major depression to find out whether low bone mass is related to depression or stress hormones, such as cortisol. During a 12-month period, researchers will monitor bone loss and the effects of depression and stress on physical health. The trial involves six visits to NIMH, where participants will receive a psychological evaluation, a bone mineral density test, and measurements of stress hormones.

In a review of published research, NIMH-funded scientists report a strong association between depression and osteoporosis. The literature suggests that depression may be a significant risk factor for osteoporosis, a progressive decrease in bone density that makes bones fragile and more likely to break. Low bone mineral density (BMD), a major risk factor for fracture, is more common in depressed people than in the general population.

"Using different data, all of the studies point to the same conclusion," said NIMH researcher and first author Giovanni Cizza, M.D., Ph.D. "Depression is not only a disease of the brain, but it also has long-term consequences for other medical conditions, such as osteoporosis."

Both the clinical trial and research review underscore the seriousness of depression, a treatable illness that affects five to nine percent of women and one to two percent of men. Although its causes are unclear,

"Depression, Bone Mass, and Osteoporosis," National Institute of Mental Health, Press Release, June 29, 2001, updated October 2, 2001.

major depression is associated with hormonal abnormalities that can lead to changes in tissue, such as bone. Research suggests that higher cortisol levels, often found in depressed patients, may contribute to bone loss and changes in body composition. Fragile bones and increased risk of fracture are signs of osteoporosis. When one or more risk factors occur, such as low BMD, family history, previous fracture, thinness, or smoking, a clinical evaluation for osteoporosis is recommended. Identifying depression as a risk factor would improve patient diagnosis and treatment.

In one study, evidence revealed that bone density at the lumbar spine was 15% lower in 80 men and women older than 40 with major depression compared to 57 men and women who were not depressed. Factors such as smoking, a history of excessive or inadequate exercise, or estrogen treatment did not affect the study, implying that depression per se had an effect on bone mass.

Another study measured bone mineral density at the spine, hip, and radius in 22 pre- and two postmenopausal women with previous or current major depression. The 24 controls were matched by age, menopausal status, race, and body mass index. BMD was 6% lower at the spine and 14% lower at the hip in the depressed women. No premenopausal women in the control group had such a deficit.

The association between depression, BMD, falls, and risk of fracture was examined in a study of 7,414 elderly women. Depression prevalence was 6%. Depressed women were more likely to fall (70% versus 59%) and had more vertebral (11% versus 5%) and non-vertebral (28% versus 21%) fractures compared with controls. This research underlines depression as a risk factor for osteoporotic fractures.

The relationship between osteoporosis and mental health was evaluated in a sample of 102 middle-aged Portuguese women. Osteoporosis had a 47% prevalence, and depression was significantly more common in women with osteoporosis than in women without it (77% versus 54%). Women with the disorder had depressive scores 25–35% higher than those with normal bone mass. This study did not find a link between depressive symptoms and low BMD, suggesting that only fully developed depression is a risk factor for osteoporosis.

In their summary, the researchers show a consistent association between depression and osteoporosis, suggesting that depression is a substantial risk factor. Some bone-loss studies combined actively depressed subjects with those who had a previous diagnosis, so it is unknown whether current depression and past diagnoses affect bone loss equally. With major depression as the threshold, most studies revealed a clear association between depression and osteoporosis.

Cizza and colleagues concluded that a clinical evaluation of subjects with unexplained bone loss, especially premenopausal women and young or middle-aged men, should include an assessment of depression. Conversely, non-traumatic fractures in a depressed patient should alert the physician to the possibility of osteoporosis.

The current NIMH study will determine whether women with major depression and normal BMD lose bone mass faster than women without depression and if the drug alendronate (Fosamax) can maintain or increase bone mass in premenopausal women with major depression and low bone mass. It is open to women 21 to 45 years old in treatment for major depression within the year and no history of schizophrenia, bipolar or eating disorders, or suicide risk and to healthy control women with no history of major depression or major organ disease.

The trial will be conducted at the National Institute of Mental Health, 9000 Rockville Pike, Bethesda, Maryland, 20892. For more information on the study of women, depression, and osteoporosis, call 1-800-411-1222 or 301-496-5645, e-mail prpl@mail.cc.nih.gov or write to Dr. Giovanni Cizza, Principle Investigator, NIH, Building 10, Room 2D 47, 10 Center Drive, Bethesda, MD 20892.

The National Institute of Mental Health (NIMH) is part of the National Institutes of Health (NIH), the Federal Government's primary agency for biomedical and behavioral research. NIH is a component of the U.S. Department of Health and Human Services. For more information about NIMH and its research programs, visit the NIMH Web site http://www.nimh.nih.gov.

Chapter 70

Estrogen Lifts Mood in Perimenopause

Women who suffer depression as they enter the early stages of menopause (perimenopause) may find estrogen to be an alternative to traditional antidepressants, suggest National Institute of Mental Health (NIMH) researchers. The efficacy of the female hormone was comparable to that usually reported with antidepressants in the first controlled study of its direct effects on mood in perimenopausal women meeting standardized criteria for depression. Drs. Peter Schmidt, David Rubinow of the NIMH Behavioral Endocrinology Branch, and colleagues, report on the findings of this preliminary study in the August 2000 *American Journal of Obstetrics and Gynecology.*

Estrogen levels, body thermostats, and mood often fluctuate in the perimenopause. But only a minority of women become clinically depressed. Although researchers had long suspected that estrogen might lift mood in such women, controlled studies were lacking. Additionally, they hadn't ruled out the possibility that any antidepressant effect could be secondary to the hormone's known ability to reduce hot flushes. The night sweats, experienced by most perimenopausal women, often disturb sleep and may worsen mood, thus confounding assessment of the hormone's antidepressant properties. Might estrogen simply afford a good night's sleep?

To find out, Schmidt and Rubinow studied 34 women, ages 44–55, who experienced onset of depression coinciding with perimenopause, as confirmed by hormone measures and standardized diagnostic interviews.

"Estrogen Lifts Mood in Perimenopause," National Institute of Mental Health, Press Release, August 28, 2000, updated: October 2, 2001.

In controlled, randomized fashion, the women received either estrogen or placebo for 3–6 weeks. Using standardized symptom rating scales and structured interviews, the researchers confirmed that estrogen significantly boosted mood in 80 percent of the depressed women, independent of hot flushes. This level of relief, and the time required to achieve a therapeutic effect, about three weeks, are comparable to that seen with antidepressant drugs. Only 20% of the women responded to placebo. Among depression symptoms that improved with the hormone were early morning awakening, loss of enjoyment, sadness, and irritability. Among symptoms that failed to improve were sexual interest and disturbed sleep.

Blood concentrations of estrogen (estradiol) prior to the study or after hormone treatment did not predict therapeutic response. This suggests that the beneficial effects of estrogen aren't mediated by correcting abnormally low levels of the hormone. Rather, Schmidt and Rubinow suggest that some women may be especially sensitive to changing hormone levels. As with disorders like PMS and postpartum depression, such hormonal changes appear to be necessary, but not sufficient, to trigger perimenopausal depression, say the researchers, who are attempting to identify the still unknown underlying predisposing factors. Long-term use of estrogen replacement may increase a woman's risk of breast and uterine cancer. In the future, more specific-acting medications that work through estrogen receptors may be engineered to selectively enhance bone, blood lipids and brain tissue without adversely affecting breast and uterine tissue, the researchers suggest.

Also participating in the study were: Dr. Lynnette Nieman, National Institute of Child Health and Human Development; Merry Danaceau, NIH Clinical Center Nursing Department; Jean Murphy, and Drs. Marie Tobin and Catherine Roca, NIMH Behavioral Endocrinology Branch.

For information about participating in NIMH studies on menopause-related mood problems, call 301-496-5645.

Reference

Schmidt PJ, Nieman L, Danaceau MA, Tobin MB, Roca CA, Murphy JH, Rubinow DR, Estrogen replacement in perimenopause-related depression: a preliminary report. *American Journal of Obstetrics and Gynecology*, August 2000.

Chapter 71

RU-486 May Relieve Psychotic Depression

Preliminary trials suggest that the controversial drug RU-486, a recently approved abortifacient and emergency contraceptive, may provide sudden relief for psychotic depression, a disease normally very difficult to treat. Related findings suggest that hydrocortisone may also speed up treatment of non-psychotic depression.

"Some psychotically depressed patients are dramatically better within a few days," said Alan Schatzberg, MD, Kenneth T. Norris Junior Professor and chairman of the department of psychology and behavioral sciences at Stanford University. "They stop hearing voices and having pessimistic kinds of delusions, like they're dying or the world is ending. We've seen the response within a four-day study. This is fairly dramatic."

Traditionally, patients with psychotic depression receive one of two treatments: an anti-depressant administered in conjunction with an anti-psychotic drug, or electroconvulsive therapy (ECT). Even when effective, both treatments are relatively slow, and can leave residual symptoms that last for months.

"With mifepristone (RU-486) there's a very quick intervention, the patients often feel better, and then we can put them on conventional anti-depressants without the anti-psychotics or ECT," Schatzberg said. "What's interesting is that the results are not effervescent. The patients feel better and it lasts. Nobody's had to come back, nobody's had to undergo ECT." The social implications of the treatment are profound,

From "RU-486 May Dramatically Relieve Psychotic Depression," *Stanford Report*, November 8, 2000. Reprinted with permission.

Schatzberg said, both because mifepristone might eliminate the need for shock treatments and because it comes from a drug with other uses that some people don't like.

Originally mifepristone was developed as a steroid treatment for Cushing's disease, to block the adrenal hormone cortisol. But since progesterone receptors and cortisol receptors are structurally related, mifepristone also blocks progesterone, an effect that makes it useful as an abortifacient and, in smaller doses, as an emergency contraceptive.

Research over the last 17 years has revealed that cortisol is extremely elevated in psychotically depressed patients. As a "stress" hormone, cortisol is released during times of significant stress as part of humans' "fight or flight" behaviors. In psychotic depression, the natural feedback loop involving cortisol is thought to be awry, with sustained levels of the hormone creating a chronic stress reaction. This in turn may cause the serious symptoms of psychotic depression, including hallucinations, sleep disturbances, and memory problems.

"We believe that the cortisol receptor is involved in the cognitive problems of severely depressed patients, particularly those with psychosis," said Schatzberg. "And so blocking those receptors, we think, may be associated with a relatively rapid response to treatment."

In a preliminary trial, five psychotically depressed patients were treated with mifepristone and four showed marked improvement within about four days. Further studies are now underway and in need of volunteers.

One study, being conducted in conjunction with the company Corcept, tests dosing levels of mifepristone for psychotic depression. Over the next year, 70 patients will be studied upon receiving mifepristone for about a week.

"Usually we get a good sense after a week whether mifepristone's going to be useful or not," said Charles DeBattista, MD, assistant professor of psychiatry and director of the Depression Research Clinic. "For some patients it's been dramatically helpful in two or three days. For instance, one gentleman went from being severely depressed, with suicidal thoughts, severe fatigue, daily hallucinations, hearing voices that wouldn't stop, to being free of all those symptoms within a week. It's happened enough that we're pretty excited."

A second trial underway, also involving mifepristone, is designed to shed light on the biologic basis of psychotic depression, as distinguished from milder or non-depressive states.

About 90 patients will be studied over five years—30 individuals each from the psychotically depressed, non-psychotically depressed, and control categories. The landmark study, funded by the NIH, should provide crucial data for differentiating psychotic and non-psychotic depressions, which are thought to be distinct illnesses. As many as 15% of depressed patients suffer psychotic depression.

In the study, only psychotically depressed patients will receive mifepristone. Non-psychotically depressed patients will be eligible to participate in a second phase of the trial, testing whether the administration of hydrocortisone speeds up the response of a standard antidepressant called Effexor. "One of our earlier studies suggested that non-psychotically depressed patients can have a rapid improvement in symptoms just with the administration of hydrocortisone," said DeBattista. The trial will be the first of its kind to study whether something as common as hydrocortisone can speed up response to antidepressants.

"These are really innovative studies that may greatly impact the way we treat depression in the future," DeBattista added. Volunteers who feel they may qualify for the study as depressed or psychotically depressed individuals and are interested in participating should contact the Depression Research Clinic at (650) 725-4620 for an initial over-the-phone assessment.

Along with Schatzberg and DeBattista, the depression group includes Joseph Belanoff, a Stanford postdoctoral fellow working with Corcept; Steve Lindley, MD, PhD, clinical instructor in psychiatry at the Palo Alto VA; David Lyons, PhD, associate professor at the Stanford Primate Center; and psychiatry fellows Ben Flores, MD, and Shelly Flemming, PhD.

—by Charles Clawson

Part Seven

Additional Help and Information

Chapter 72

Glossary of Depression-Related Terms

affective: Pertaining to mood, emotion, feeling, sensibility, or a mental state.

agitated depression: Depression with excitement and restlessness.

anaclitic depression: Impairment of an infant's physical, social, and intellectual development following separation from its mother or from a mothering surrogate; characterized by listlessness, withdrawal, and anorexia.

anhedonia: Absence of pleasure from the performance of acts that would ordinarily be pleasurable.

antidepressant: 1. Counteracting depression. 2. An agent used in treating depression.

bipolar disorder: An affective disorder characterized by the occurrence of alternating periods of euphoria (mania) and depression.

catatonia: A syndrome of psychomotor disturbances characterized by periods of physical rigidity, negativism, or stupor; may occur in schizophrenia, mood disorders, or organic mental disorders.

Terms excerpted from *Stedman's Medical Dictionary, 27th Edition*, copyright © 2000 Lippincott Williams & Wilkins. All rights reserved; reprinted with permission.

cognition: 1. Generic term embracing the mental activities associated with thinking, learning, and memory. 2. Any process whereby one acquires knowledge.

comorbidity: A concomitant but unrelated pathologic or disease process; usually used in epidemiology to indicate the coexistence of two or more disease processes.

cyclothymia: A mental disorder characterized by marked swings of mood from depression to hypomania but not to the degree that occurs in bipolar disorder.

depression: A temporary mental state or chronic mental disorder characterized by feelings of sadness, loneliness, despair, low self-esteem, and self-reproach; accompanying signs include psychomotor retardation or less frequently agitation, withdrawal from social contact, and vegetative states such as loss of appetite and insomnia.

dysphoria: A mood of general dissatisfaction, restlessness, depression, and anxiety; a feeling of unpleasantness or discomfort.

dysthymia: A chronic mood disorder manifested as depression for most of the day, more days than not, accompanied by some of the following symptoms: poor appetite or overeating, insomnia or hypersomnia, low energy or fatigue, low self-esteem, poor concentration, difficulty making decisions, and feelings of hopelessness.

electroconvulsive therapy (ECT): A form of treatment of mental disorders in which convulsions are produced by the passage of an electric current through the brain.

etiology: 1. The science and study of the causes of disease and their mode of operation. 2. The science of causes, causality; in common usage, cause.

euphoria: A feeling of well-being, commonly exaggerated and not necessarily well founded.

Hamilton depression rating scale: A list of specific symptoms used as a measure of severity of depression.

hypersomnia: A condition in which sleep periods are excessively long, but the person responds normally in the intervals.

hypomania: A mild degree of mania.

insomnia: Inability to sleep, in the absence of external impediments, such as noise, a bright light, etc., during the period when sleep should normally occur; may vary in degree from restlessness or disturbed slumber to a curtailment of the normal length of sleep or to absolute wakefulness.

labile: Unstable; unsteady, not fixed; in psychology or psychiatry, denoting free and uncontrolled mood or behavioral expression of the emotions.

libido: 1. Conscious or unconscious sexual desire. 2. Any passionate interest or form of life force. 3. In jungian psychology, synonymous with psychic energy.

mania: An emotional disorder characterized by euphoria or irritability, increased psychomotor activity, rapid speech, flight of ideas, decreased need for sleep, distractibility, grandiosity, and poor judgment; usually occurs in bipolar disorder.

melancholia: 1. A severe form of depression marked by anhedonia, insomnia, psychomotor changes, and guilt. 2. A symptom occurring in other conditions, marked by depression of spirits and by a sluggish and painful process of thought.

melatonin: A substance formed by the pineal gland, which appears to depress gonadal function; a precursor is serotonin; melatonin is rapidly metabolized and is taken up by all tissues; it is involved in circadian rhythms. Melatonin secretion is linked to both the sleep-wakefulness and light-dark cycles.

monoamine oxidase inhibitor (MAOI): A class of chemical compounds that exert antidepressant effect by the reversible or irreversible inhibition of monoamine oxidase A.

mood disorders: A group of mental disorders involving a disturbance of mood, accompanied by either a full or partial manic or depressive syndrome that is not due to any other mental disorder. Mood refers to a prolonged emotion that colors the whole psychic life; it generally involves either depression or elation; for example, manic episode, major depressive episode, bipolar disorders, and depressive disorder.

morbidity: 1. A diseased state. 2. The ratio of sick to well in a community. 3. The frequency of the appearance of complications following a surgical procedure or other treatment.

mortality: 1. The state of being mortal. 2. death rate. 3. A fatal outcome.

neurotransmitter: Any specific chemical agent released by a presynaptic cell, upon excitation, that crosses the synapse to stimulate or inhibit the postsynaptic cell. More than one may be released at any given synapse.

norepinephrine: A catecholamine hormone; it is stored in the adrenal medulla and secreted in response to hypotension and physical stress; in contrast to epinephrine it has little effect on bronchial smooth muscle, metabolic processes, and cardiac output, but has strong vasoconstrictive effects.

personality disorder: General term for a group of behavioral disorders characterized by usually lifelong ingrained maladaptive patterns of subjective internal experience and deviant behavior, lifestyle, and social adjustment, which patterns may manifest in impaired judgement, affect, impulse control, and interpersonal functioning.

pharmacokinetic: Relating to the disposition of drugs in the body (their absorption, distribution, metabolism, and elimination).

pharmacotherapy: Treatment of disease by means of drugs.

premenstrual syndrome (PMS): In women of reproductive age, a constellation of emotional, behavioral, and physical symptoms that occur in the luteal (premenstrual) phase of the menstrual cycle and subside with the onset of menstruation; characterized by swelling and weight gain due to fluid retention, breast tenderness, irritability, mood swings, anxiety, depression, drowsiness, fatigue, difficulty concentrating, and changes in appetite and libido.

psychiatrist: A physician who specializes in psychiatry.

psychosis: A mental and behavioral disorder causing gross distortion or disorganization of a person's mental capacity, affective response, and capacity to recognize reality, communicate, and relate to others to the degree of interfering with the person's capacity to cope with the ordinary demands of everyday life.

psychotherapist: A person, usually a psychiatrist or clinical psychologist, professionally trained and engaged in psychotherapy. Currently, the term is also applied to social workers, nurses, and others whose state-licensed practice acts include psychotherapy.

psychotherapy: Treatment of emotional, behavioral, personality, and psychiatric disorders based primarily upon verbal or nonverbal communication and interventions with the patient, in contrast to treatments utilizing chemical and physical measures.

reactive depression: A psychological state occasioned directly by an intensely sad external situation (frequently loss of a loved person), relieved by the removal of the external situation (for example, reunion with a loved person).

refractory: Resistant to treatment.

seasonal affective disorder (SAD): A depressive mood disorder that occurs at approximately the same time year after year and spontaneously remits at the same time each year. The most common type is winter depression and it is characterized by morning hypersomnia, low energy, increased appetite, weight gain, and carbohydrate craving, all of which remit in the spring.

selective serotonin reuptake inhibitor (SSRI): A class of chemical compounds that selectively, to varying degrees, inhibit the reuptake of serotonin by presynaptic neurons and are posited to exert their antidepressant effect by this mechanism.

serotonin: A vasoconstrictor, liberated by blood platelets, that inhibits gastric secretion and stimulates smooth muscle; present in relatively high concentrations in some areas of the central nervous system (hypothalamus, basal ganglia), and occurring in many peripheral tissues and cells and in carcinoid tumors.

social therapy: A psychiatric rehabilitative therapy to improve a patient's social functioning.

St. John's wort: A shrubby perennial (*Hypericum perforatum*) with numerous orange-yellow flowers whose petals may be speckled black along their margins; a herbal antidepressant that compares favorably with standard synthetic psychopharmaceutical agents in the treatment of mild to moderate depression.

synapse: The functional membrane-to-membrane contact of the nerve cell with another nerve cell, an effector (muscle, gland) cell, or a sensory receptor cell. The synapse subserves the transmission of nerve impulses.

tardive dyskinesia: Involuntary movements of the facial muscles and tongue, often persistent, that develop as a late complication of some neuroleptic therapy, more likely with typical antipsychotics.

titration: Volumetric analysis by means of the addition of definite amounts of a test solution to a solution of the substance being examined.

tricyclic antidepressant (TCA): A chemical group of antidepressant drugs that share a 3-ringed nucleus; for example, amitriptyline, imipramine, desipramine, and nortriptyline.

Chapter 73

Additional Reading about Depression

In order to make topics more readily apparent, the books in this chapter are listed alphabetically by title within the following categories:

- Books about Depressive Illnesses
- Books for Children and Teens
- Books for Parents

Depressive Illnesses

The American Medical Association Essential Guide to Depression, New York: Pocket Books, 2000. ISBN: 0743403592

Behind the Smile: My Journey out of Postpartum Depression, by Marie Osmond, Marcia Wilkie, and Judith Moore, New York: Warner Books, Inc., 2002. ISBN: 044667852X

The Bipolar Disorder Survival Guide: What You and Your Family Need to Know, by David J. Miklowitz, New York: Guilford Publications, Inc. 2002. ISBN: 1572307129

The Broken Brain: The Biological Revolution in Psychiatry, by Nancy Andreasen, New York: Harper and Row, 1985. ISBN 0060 912723

The list of books in this chapter was compiled from many different sources. Inclusion does not constitute endorsement. Check your local library or favorite bookstore for current prices and availability.

Concise Guide to Mood Disorders, by Steven L. Dubovsky and Amelia N. Dubovsky, Washington: American Psychiatric Publishing Group, Inc., 2002. ISBN: 1585620564

Conquering the Beast Within: How I Fought Depression and Won... and How You Can, Too, by Cait Irwin, New York: Times Books, 1999. ISBN: 0812932471

The Deepest Blue: How Women Face and Overcome Depression, by Lauren Dockett Matthew McKay, Oakland, CA: New Harbinger Publications, 2001. ISBN: 1572242531

Depression and Women: An Integrative Treatment Approach, by Susan L. Simonds, New York : Springer Publishing Co., 2001. ISBN: 0826114458

Depression in Late Life, Third edition, by Dan G. Blazer, New York: Springer Publishing Co., 2001. ISBN: 0826114520

The Depression Workbook: A Guide for Living with Depression and Manic Depression, Second edition, by Mary Ellen Copeland and Matthew McKay, Oakland, CA: New Harbinger Publications, 2002. ISBN: 157224268X

Getting Your Life Back: The Complete Guide to Recovery from Depression, Jesse Wright and Monica Ramirez Basco, New York: Simon and Schuster, 2001. ISBN: 0743200500

The Hand-Me-Down Blues: How to Stop Depression from Spreading in Families, Michael D. Yapko, New York: St. Martin's Press, 2000. ISBN: 0312263325

Helping Someone With Mental Illness: A Compassionate Guide for Family, Friends and Caregivers, by Rosalyn Carter and Susan K. Golant, New York: Times Books, 1999. ISBN: 0812928989

How You Can Survive when They're Depressed: Living and Coping with Depression Fallout, by Anne Sheffield, New York: Random House, 1999. ISBN 0609804154

I Can See Tomorrow: A Guide for Living with Depression, Second edition, by Patricia Owen, Center City, MN: Hazelden Information and Educational Services, 2000. ISBN: 1568385684

I Don't Walk to Talk about It: Overcoming the Secret Legacy of Male Depression, by Terrence Real, New York: Simon and Schuster, 1997. ISBN: 0684831023

Living Longer Depression Free: A Family Guide to Recognizing, Treating, and Preventing Depression in Later Life, by Mark D. Miller and Charles F. Reynolds, Baltimore: Johns Hopkins University Press, 2002. ISBN: 0801869420

The Loneliness Workbook: A Guide to Developing and Maintaining Lasting Connections, by Mary Ellen Copeland, Oakland, CA: New Harbinger Publications, 2000. ISBN: 1572242035

Mayo Clinic on Depression, edited by John E. King, Broomall, PA: Mason Crest Publishers, 2002. ISBN: 1590842375

Mood Disorders Throughout the Lifespan, edited by Kenneth I. Shulman, Mauricio Tohen, and Stanley P. Kutcher, New York: Wiley-Liss, 1996. ISBN: 0471104779

Moodswing, Second edition, by Ronald R. Fieve, New York: Bantam Books, 1989. ISBN: 0553279831

Night Falls Fast: Understanding Suicide, by Kay Redfield Jamison, New York: Vintage Books, 2000. ISBN: 037570478

Overcoming Depression, Third edition, by Demitri Papolos, New York: HarperCollins Publishers, 1998. ISBN: 0060931779

Overcoming Depression: A Step-by-Step Approach to Gaining Control Over Depression, Second edition, by Paul Gilbert, New York: Oxford University Press, 2001, ISBN: 0195143116

Postnatal Depression: Facing the Paradox of Loss, Happiness and Motherhood, by Paula Nicolson, New York: John Wiley and Sons, Inc., 2001. ISBN: 0471485276

Seasonal Affective Disorder: Practice and Research, edited by Timo Partonen and Andres Magnusson, New York: Oxford University Press, Inc., 2001. ISBN: 0192632256

Treatment Works for Major Depressive Disorder: A Patient and Family Guide, Washington: American Psychiatric Press, Inc., 2000. ISBN: 0890422885

Understanding Depression: What We Know and What You Can Do about It, by J. Raymond DePaulo and Leslie Alan Horvitz, Hoboken, NJ: John Wiley and Sons, Inc., 2002. ISBN: 0471395528

An Unquiet Mind: A Memoir of Moods and Madness, by Kay Redfield. Jamison New York: Random House, Inc., 1996. ISBN: 0679 443746

The Van Gogh Blues: The Creative Person's Path Through Depression, by Eric Maisel, Emmaus, PA: Rodale Press, Inc., 2002. ISBN: 157954570X

What to Do when Someone You Love is Depressed: A Practical, Compassionate, and Helpful Guide for Caregivers, by Mitch Golant and Susan K. Golant, New York: Henry Holt and Co., 1998. ISBN: 080505829X

Willow Weep for Me, A Black Woman's Journey Through Depression, by Meri Nana-Ama Dumquah, New York: Ballantine Books, 1999. ISBN: 0345432134

Winter Blues: Seasonal Affective Disorder—What It Is and How to Overcome It, by Norman E. Rosenthal, New York: Guilford Publications, Inc., 1998. ISBN 1572303956

Working in the Dark: Keeping Your Job While Dealing with Depression, by Fawn Fitter and Beth Gulas, Center City, MN: Hazelden Information and Educational Services, 2002. ISBN: 1568387903.

Your Depression Map: Find the Source of Your Depression and Chart Your Own Recovery, by Randy J. Paterson, Oakland: New Harbinger Publications, 2002. ISBN: 1572243007

Books for Children and Teens

Antidepressants, by Judy Monroe, Berkeley Heights, NJ: Enslow Publishers, Inc., 2001. ISBN: 0766019179

Bipolar Disorder and Depression, by Susan Dudley Gold, Berkeley Heights, NJ: Enslow Publishers, Inc., 2000. ISBN: 0766016544

Bipolar Disorder, Depression, and Other Mood Disorders, by Helen A. Demetriades, Berkeley Heights, NJ: Enslow Publishers, Inc., 2002. ISBN: 0766018989

Body Blues: Weight and Depression, by Laura Weeldreyer, New York: Rosen Publishing Group, 1998. ISBN: 082392761X

Depression: What It Is, How to Beat It, by Linda Wasmer Smith, Berkeley Heights, NJ: Enslow Publishers, Inc., 2000. ISBN: 076601 357X

Everything You Need to Know about Depression, by Eleanor H. Ayer, New York: Rosen Publishing Group, Inc., 2001. ISBN: 082393 439X

Mommy Stayed in Bed This Morning: Helping Children Understand Depression, by Mary Wenger Weaver, illustrated by Mary Chambers, Scottdale, PA: Herald Press, 2002. ISBN: 0836191501

Teens, Depression and the Blues, by Kathleen Winkler, Berkeley Heights, NJ: Enslow Publishers, Inc., 2000. ISBN: 0766013693

When Nothing Matters Anymore: A Survival Guide for Depressed Teens, by Bev Cobain, Minneapolis: Free Spirit Publishing, Inc., 1998. ISBN: 1575420368

Why Are You So Sad? A Child's Book about Parental Depression, by Beth Andrews, illustrated by Nicole A. Wong, Washington: Magination Press, 2002. ISBN: 1557988366

Books for Parents

Adolescent Depression: A Guide for Parents, by Francis Mark Mondimore, Baltimore: Johns Hopkins University Press, 2002. ISBN: 0801870585

The Bipolar Child: The Definitive and Reassuring Guide to Childhood's Most Misunderstood Disorder, by Demitri Papolos and Janice Papolos, New York: Broadway Books, 2000. ISBN: 0767903161

But I Didn't Say Goodbye: For Parents and Professionals Helping Child Suicide Survivors, by Barbara Rubel, Kendall Park, NJ: Griefwork Center, Inc., 2000. ISBN: 1892906007

The Depressed Child: A Parent's Guide for Rescuing Kids, by Douglas A. Riley, Lanham, MD: Taylor Publishing Co., 2001. ISBN: 0878331875

Growing up Sad: Childhood Depression and Its Treatment, by Leon H. Cytryn and Donald McKnew, Jr., New York: W. W. Norton and Company, Inc., 1998. ISBN: 0393317889

Help Me, I'm Sad: Recognizing, Treating and Preventing Childhood and Adolescent Depression, by David G. Fassler, New York: Penguin Putnam, Inc., 1998. ISBN: 0140267638

Helping Your Teen Overcome Depression: A Guide for Parents, by Miriam Kaufman, Buffalo: Firefly Books, Ltd., 2000. ISBN: 155263 2784

Lonely, Sad and Angry: How to Help Your Unhappy Child, by Barbara D. Ingersoll and Sam Goldstein, Plantation, FL: Specialty Press, Inc., 2001. ISBN: 1886941459

Out of the Darkened Room: When a Parent Is Depressed: Protecting the Children and Strengthening the Family, by William R. Beardslee, New York : Little, Brown and Company, 2002. ISBN: 0316085499

Understanding Teenage Depression: A Guide to Diagnosis, Treatment, and Management, by Maureen Empfield and Nick Bakalar, New York: Owl Paperback Books, 2001. ISBN: 0805067612

Chapter 74

Resources for Further Information on Depression

Resources on Depression and Related Mental Health Concerns

American Academy of Child and Adolescent Psychiatry
3615 Wisconsin Ave., N.W.
Washington, DC 20016-3007
Toll Free: 800-333-7636
Phone: 202-966-7300
Fax: 202-966-2891
Website: http://www.aacap.org

American Academy of Family Physicians
11400 Tomahawk Creek Parkway
Leawood, KS 66211-2672
Toll Free: 800-274-2237
Phone 913-906-6000
Website: http://www.aafp.org
E-mail: fp@aafp.org

American Association for Geriatric Psychiatry
7910 Woodmont Ave.,
Suite 1050
Bethesda, MD 20814-3004
Phone: 301-654-7850
Fax: 301-654-4137
Website: http://
www.aagponline.org
E-mail: main@aagponline.org

American Association of Pastoral Counselors
9504A Lee Highway
Fairfax, VA 22031-2303
Phone: 703-385-6967
Fax: 703-352-7725
Website: http://www.aapc.org
E-mail: info@aapc.org

The information in this chapter was compiled from many sources. All contact information was updated and verified in July 2002.

539

American Psychiatric Association
1400 K Street N.W.
Washington, DC 20005
Toll-free: 888-852-8330
Fax: 202-682-6850
Website: http://www.psych.org
E-mail: apa@psych.org

American Psychological Association
750 First Street, N.E.
Washington, DC 20002-4242
Toll-free: 800-374-2721
Phone: 202-336-5510
TDD/TTY: 202-336-6123
Website: http://www.apa.org

Center for Mental Health Services Knowledge Exchange Network
SAMHSA, DHHS
P.O. Box 42490
Washington, DC 20015
Toll-free: 800-789-2647
TDD: 866-889-2647 TDD (toll-free)
International TDD: 301-443-9006
Fax: 301-984-8796
Website: http://www.mental health.org
E-mail: ken@mentalhealth.org

Centre for Addiction and Mental Health
33 Russell Street
Toronto, ON M5S 2S1 CANADA
Toll Free: 800-463-6273
Phone: 416-535-8501
Website: http://www.camh.net
E-mail: public affairs@camh.net

Child and Adolescent Bipolar Foundation
1187 Willmette Avenue
PMB #331
Willmette, IL 60091
Phone: 847-256-8525
Fax: 847-920-9498
Website: http://www.bpkids.org
E-mail: support@bpkids.org

Council on Family Health
1155 Connecticut Avenue, N.W., Suite 400
Washington, DC 20036
Phone: 202-331-7373
Website: http://www.cfhinfo.org
E-mail: inbox@cfinfo.org

Depression and Related Affective Disorders Association
Johns Hopkins Hospital
Meyer 3-181
600 North Wolfe Street
Baltimore, MD 21287-7381
Phone: 410-955-4647 or 202-955-5800
Website: http:// www.med.jhu.edu/drada
E-mail: drada@jhmi.edu

Depression Central
Ivan Goldberg, MD
1556 Third Avenue
Suite 407
New York, NY 10128
Phone: 212-876-7800
Website: www.psycom.net/ depression.central.html
E-mail: psydoc@psycom.net

Depression Week

Website: www.depressionweek.org
E-mail: info@depressionweek.org

Family Support America

20 North Wacker Dr.
Suite 1100
Chicago, IL 60606
Phone: 312-341-0900
Fax: 312-338-1522
Website: http://www.family
support.america.org

Federation of Families for Children's Mental Health

1101 King Street
Suite 420
Alexandria, VA 22314
Phone: 703-684-7710
Fax: 703-836-1040
Website: http://www.ffcmh.org
E-mail: ffcmh@ffcmh.org

Lithium Information Center

Madison Institute of Medicine
7617 Mineral Point Road
Suite 300
Madison, WI 53717
Phone: 608-827-2470
Fax: 608-827-2479
Website: http://www.miminc.org/
aboutlithinfoctr.html
E-mail: mim@miminc.org

Mental Health Sanctuary

PMB 200
Yakima, WA 98907
Website: http://
www.mhsanctuary.com

National Alliance for Research on Schizophrenia and Depression

60 Cutter Mill Road
Suite 404
Great Neck, NY 11021
Toll Free: 800-829-8289
Phone: 516-829-0091
Fax: 516-487-6930
Website: http://www.mhsource.
com/narsad
E-mail: info@narsad.org

National Alliance for the Mentally Ill

Colonial Place Three
2107 Wilson Boulevard
Suite 300
Arlington, VA 22201-3042
Toll-free: 800-950-NAMI (6264)
Phone: 703-524-7600
TDD: 703-516-7227
Fax: 703-524-9094
Website: http://www.nami.org

National Consortium on Alternatives for Youth at Risk

5250 17th Street
Suite 107
Sarasota, FL 34235
Toll-free: 800-245-7133
Phone: 941-378-4793
Fax: 941-377-6807
Website: http://www.ncayar.org
E-mail: ncayar@worldnet.att.net

National Depressive and Manic-Depressive Association
730 North Franklin Street, Suite 501
Chicago, IL 60610-7204
Toll-free: 800-826-3632
Phone: 312-642-0049
Fax: 312-642-7243
Website: http://www.ndmda.org
E-mail: questions@ndmda.org

National Foundation for Depressive Illness, Inc.
P.O. Box 2257
New York, NY 10116
Toll-Free: 800-239-1265
Phone: 212-696-1088
Website: http://www.depression.org

National Heart, Lung, and Blood Institute
Information Center
P.O. Box 30105
Bethesda, MD 20824-0105
Phone: 301-592-8573
TTY: 240-629-3255
Fax: 301-592-8563
Website: http://www.nhlbi.nih.gov
E-mail: NHLBIinfo@rover.nhlbi.nih.gov

National Information Center for Children and Youth with Disabilities
P.O. Box 1492
Washington, DC 20013
Toll Free: 800-695-0285
Phone: 202-884-8200 (Voice/TTY)
Fax: 202-884-8441
Website: http://www.nichcy.org
E-mail: nichcy@aed.org

National Institute of Mental Health
6001 Executive Blvd.
Room 8184, MSC 9663
Bethesda, MD 20892-9663
Toll-free: 800-421-4211
Phone: 301-443-4513
TTY: 301-443-8431
Fax: 301-443-4279
Website: http://www.nimh.nih.gov
E-mail: nimhinfo@nih.gov

National Institute on Aging Information Center
31 Center Drive
Building 31, Room 5C27
MSC 2292
Bethesda, MD 20892
Toll-free: 800-222-2225
Phone: 301-496-1752
Website: http://www.nih.gov/nia

National Mental Health Association
1021 Prince Street
Alexandria, VA 22314-2971
Toll-Free: 800-969-NMHA (6642)
Phone: 703-684-7722
TTY: 800-433-5959
Fax: 703-684-5968
Website: http://www.nmha.org
E-mail: infoctr@nmha.org

National Mental Health Consumer's Self-Help Clearinghouse
1211 Chestnut Street
Suite 1207
Philadelphia, PA 19107
Toll Free: 800-553-4539
Phone: 215-751-1810
Fax: 215-636-6312
Website: http://mhselfhelp.org
E-mail: info@mhselfhelp.org

National Resource Center on Homelessness and Mental Illness
345 Delaware Avenue
Delmar, NY 12054
Toll-free: 800-444-7415
Phone: 518-439-7415
Fax: 518-439-7612
Website: http://www.nrchmi.com
E-mail: nrc@prainc.com

Resources for Depression-Related Women's Issues

American College of Obstetricians and Gynecologists
409 12th Street, SW
Washington, DC 20090-6920
Phone: (202) 484-3321
Fax: (202) 479-6826
Website: http://www.acog.com

Association for Post-Natal Illness
145 Dawes Road
Fulham, London SW6 7EB
England
Phone: 011-44-171-020-7386-0868
Fax: 011-44-171- 020-7386-8885
Website: http://www.apni.org
E-mail: info@apni.org

Depression After Delivery
91 East Somerset Street
Raritan, NJ 08869
Toll-free: 800-944-4473
Website: http://
www.depressionafterdelivery.com

National Women's Health Information Center
8550 Arlington Blvd., Suite 300
Fairfax, VA 22031
Toll-free: 800-994-WOMAN
(800-994-9662)
TDD: 1-888-220-5446 (toll-free)
Website: http://www.4woman.gov
E-mail: listserve@list.nih.gov

National Women's Health Network
514 10th St. NW, Suite 400
Washington, DC 20004
Phone: 202-347-1140
Fax: 202-347-1168
Website: http://
www.womenshealthnetwork.org

Office on Women's Health
Office of the Secretary, DHHS
200 Independence Avenue, S.W.,
Rm 730B
Washington, DC 20201
Phone: 202-690-7650
Fax: 202-690-7172
Website: http://www.4woman.
gov/owh/about/index.htm

Pacific Post Partum Support Society
1416 Commercial Drive, #104
Vancouver, BC, CANADA V5L 3X9
Phone: 604-255-7999
Fax: 604-255-7588
Website: http://
www.postpartum.org
E-mail: pps@postpartum.org

Postpartum Adjustment Support Services—Canada
460 Woody Road, #3
Oakville, ON CANADA L6K 3T6
Phone: 905-844-9009
Parent Info Line: 905-897-2662
Fax: 905-844-5973
Website: http://www.passcan.ca
E-mail: info@passcan.ca

Postpartum Education for Parents
P.O. Box 6154
Santa Barbara, CA 93160
Website: http://www.sbpep.org
E-mail: pepmail@yahoo.com

Postpartum Support International
927 North Kellogg Avenue
Santa Barbara, CA 93111
Phone: 805-967-7636
Fax: 805-967-0608
Website: http://
www.chss.iup.edu/postpartum

Chapter 75

Finding Help in a Mental Health Crisis

Many local areas offer help for people in crisis. Numbers may be listed in the front of your telephone directory or in the white or yellow pages under listings such as: suicide prevention; crisis intervention; community crisis centers; or mental health centers. Additional resources are listed below.

Suicide Prevention

If you are suicidal and in immediate danger, or if you are with someone who is suicidal and in immediate danger, call 9-1-1.

American Association of Suicidology
4201 Connecticut Avenue NW, Suite 408
Washington, DC 20008
Toll Free: 800-SUICIDE
Phone: 202-237-2280
Fax: 202-237-2282
Website: http://www.suicidology.org

American Foundation for Suicide Prevention
120 Wall Street, 22nd Floor
New York, NY 10005
Toll Free: 888-333-AFSP
Phone: 212-363-3500
Fax: 212-363-6237
Website: http://www.afsp.org
E-mail: inquiry@afsp.org

The information in this chapter was compiled from many sources. All contact information was updated and verified in July 2002.

Crisis Intervention and Suicide Prevention Center of Mateo County
1860 El Camino Real
Suite 400
Burlingame, CA 94010
Phone: 650-692-6662
E-mail: crisiscenter@yfa.org
Website: http://www.yfa.org

National Hopeline
Toll-free 1-800-SUICIDE (24 hours a day, 7 days a week)
Website: http://1-800-suicide.com

SAVE—Suicide Awareness Voices of Education
7317 Cahill Road, Suite 207
Minneapolis, MN 55439-0507
Toll-free 888-511-SAVE
Phone: 952-946-7998
Fax: 952-946 7998
Website: http://www.save.org
E-mail: save@winternet.com

Suicide and Rape
Toll Free: 800-333-444 (24 hour emergency services)

Suicide Crisis Center
Website: http://www.suicidecrisiscenter.com

Suicide Prevention Advocacy Network
SPAN USA, Inc.
5034 Odins Way
Marietta, GA 30068
Toll Free: 888-649-1366
Phone: 770-998-8819
Fax: 770-649-1366
Web site: http://www.spanusa.org

Suicide Prevention Center
Didi Hirsch Community Mental Health Center
4760 South Sepulveda Boulevard
Culver City, CA 90230-4888
Toll Free: 877-7CRISIS
Phone: 310-391-1253
Fax: 310-398-5690
Website: http://www.suicidecrisisline.org
E-mail: spcdh@pacificnet.net

Resources for Young People in Crisis

Center for Children and Families, Inc.
295 Lafayette Street, Suite 920
New York, NY 11432
Phone: 212-226-3536
Phone: 212-226-1918
Website: http://www.kidsuccess.com
E-mail: safespace@safespace nyc.org

Covenant House New York
460 W. 41st Street
New York, NY 10036
Toll-Free Nineline: 800-999-9999
Phone: 212-613-0300
Fax: 212-629-3756
Website: http://www.covenanthouseny.org
E-mail: chny@covenanthouse.org

Girls and Boys Town USA
Toll Free: 800-448-3000 (Girls and Boys Town National Hotline)
TTY: 800-448-1833
Website: http://www.girlsand boystown.org
E-mail: hotline@boystown.org

Kids Help
439 University Avenue
Suite 300
Toronto, ON CANADA M5G 1Y8
Toll Free: 800-668-6868
Website: http://www.kidshelp.
sympatico.ca

National Runaway Switchboard
3080 North Lincoln Ave.
Chicago, IL 60657
Toll Free: 800-621-4000
Phone: 773-880-9860
Fax: 773-929-5150
Website: http://
www.nrscriisiline.org
E-mail: info@nrscrisisline.org

National Teen Crisis Hotline
Toll Free: 800-999-9999

National Youth Crisis Hotline
Toll Free: 800-448-4663

United Methodist Youth Organization
P.O. Box 340003
Nashville, TN 37203-0003
Toll Free: 877-899-2780 ext. 7184
Phone: 615-340-7184
Fax: 615-340-1764
Website: http://www.umyouth.org
E-mail: umyouthorg@gbod.org

Youth Development International
5331 Mt. Alifan Drive
San Diego, CA 92177-8408
Toll Free: 800-448-4663 (National Youth Crisis Hotline)
Phone: 858-292-5683
Fax: 858-292-9197
Website: http://www.1800hit
home.com

Other Crisis Help

Alcohol and Drug Helpline
107 Lincoln St.
Worcester, MA 01605
Toll Free: 800-ALCOHOL (662-4357)
Drug-Free Workplace Hotline:
800-843-4571
Website: www.adcare.com

Elder Abuse Hotline
Toll Free: 800-392-0210

Gay/Lesbian/Bisexual/ Transgender/Transexual Helpline
Toll Free: 800-549-1749

Grief Recovery Helpline
Toll Free: 800-445-4808

Help Line USA, Inc.
Toll Free: 866-334-HELP
Phone: 561-615-4029
Website: www.thehelpline.net or
www.thehelplineusa.com
E-mail: crisiscounselors@hot
mail.com

National Domestic Violence Hotline
P.O. Box 161810
Austin, Texas 78716
Toll Free: 800-799-SAFE (7233)
800-787-3224 (TTY)
Fax: 512-453-8541
Website: http://www.ndvh.org

National Victim Center
Phone: 800-FYI-CALL
Website: http://www.ncvc.org
E-mail: gethelp@ncvc.org

Parents Anonymous Help Line
675 W. Foothill Blvd.
Suite 220
Claremont, CA 91711
Phone: 909-621-6184
Fax: 909-625-6304
Website: http://www.parents
anonymous.org
E-mail: parentsanonymous@
parentsanonymous.org

Rape, Abuse, and Incest National Network (RAINN)
635-B Pennsylvania Ave., SE
Washington, DC 20003
Toll Free: 800-656-HOPE
Fax: 202-544-3556
Website: http://www.rainn.org
E-mail: rainnmail@aol.com

SAFE (Self Abuse Finally Ends)
Toll Free: 800-DONT-CUT (366-8288)
Website: http://
www.selfinjury.com

United Way Crisis Help Line
Toll Free: 800-233-4357
Website: http://www.infoline.org

Chapter 76

Locating Depression-Related Support Groups

To locate support groups for depression and other mental health concerns:

- Check the front pages of your local phone book.
- Check with your local mental health associations.
- Call your local hospital and ask for a referral.

Other resources are listed below.

National Organizations

The following national organizations and agencies can also help direct you to sources of support in your local community.

National Alliance for the Mentally Ill
Colonial Place Three
2107 Wilson Boulevard, Suite 300
Arlington, VA 22201-3042
Toll-free: 800-950-NAMI
Phone: 703-524-7600; TDD: 703-516-7227; Fax: 703-524-9094
Affiliate Finder online at:
http://www.nami.org/cfapps/Affiliate_Finder/affiliate_ finder.cfm

---

The information in this chapter was compiled from many sources. All contact information was updated and verified in July 2002.

National Association of Social Workers

750 Front Street, NE
Suite 700
Washington DC, 20002-4241
Toll-free: 800-638-8799
Phone: 202-408-8600
Website: http://www.naswdc.org

National Depressive and Manic-Depressive Association

730 North Franklin Street, Suite 501
Chicago, IL 60610-7204
Toll-free: 800-826-3632
Phone: 312-642-0049
Fax: 312-642-7243
Chapter and Support Group Directory online at: http://www.ndmda.org/findsupport.html

National Mental Health Association

1021 Prince Street
Alexandria, VA 22314-2971
Toll-Free: 800-969-NMHA (6642)
Phone: 703-684-7722
Fax: 703-684-5968
TTY: 800-443-5959
Affiliate Directory online at http://www.nmha.org/affliates/directory/index.cfm
E-mail: infoctr@nmha.org

National Institute of Mental Health

6001 Executive Blvd.
Room 8184, MSC 9663
Bethesda, MD 20892-9663
Toll-free: 800-421-4211
Phone: 301-443-4513
Fax: 301-443-4279
TTY: 301-443-8431
Website: http://www.nimh.nih.gov
E-mail: nimhinfo@nih.gov

Other Sources of Support

The following organizations sponsor or help coordinate local support groups or provide support or referrals on the internet.

Alcoholics Anonymous

General Service Office
475 Riverside Drive, 11th Floor
New York, NY 10115
Phone: 212-870-3400
Website: http://www.alcoholics-anonymous.org

American Self-Help Group Clearinghouse

100 E. Hanover Ave, Suite 202
Cedar Knolls, NJ 07927-2020
Phone: 973-326-7893
TTY: 973-326-9467
Website: http://www.selfhelpgroups.org
E-mail: ashc@cybernex.net

Depressed Anonymous
P.O. Box 17414
Louisville, KY 40217
Phone: 502-569-1989
Website:
www.depressedanon.com
E-mail: info@depressedanon.com

**Depression After Delivery—
National**
91 East Somerset Street
Raritan, NJ 08869
Phone: 800-944-4773
Website: http://www.depression
afterdelivery.com

Depression Support Group
Toll Free: 800-784 2433
Website: http://
members.aol.com/_ht_a/lkhix/
index.html?mtbrand=AOL_US

Emotions Anonymous
P.O. Box 4245
St. Paul, MN 55104
Phone: 651-647-9712
Fax: 651-647-1593
Website: http://www.emotions
anonymous.org
E-mail: info@emotions
anonymous.org

**Families for Depression
Awareness**
118 Waltham Street, Second Floor
Watertown, MA 02472-4808
Phone: 617-924-9383
Fax: 617-924-9192
Website: www.familyaware.org
E-mail: info@familyaware.org

Freedom From Fear
308 Seaview Avenue
Staten Island, New York 10305
Phone: 718-351-1717
Fax: 718-667-8893
Website: http://www.freedom
fromfear.com

**Mental Health Association
of the Heartland**
739 Minnesota Ave.
Kansas City, KS 66101
Compassionate Ear Warmline:
913-281-2251 (non-crisis listen-
ing service)
Phone: 913-281-1234 (Mental
Help line)
Phone: 913-281-2299 (Teen con-
nection hotline)
Phone: 913-281-2221 (Office)
Fax: 913-281-3977

**Michigan Self-Help
Clearinghouse**
Michigan Protection and
Advocacy Service, Inc.
106 West Allegan Ave.
Suite 300
Lansing, MI 48933-1706
Toll-free: 800-777-5556 (Michi-
gan only)
Phone: 517-484-7373
Fax: 517-487-0827
Website: http://
www.laurushealth.com
E-mail: LaurusInfo@Laurus
Health.com

Mood Disorders Support Group
P.O. Box 30377
New York, NY 10011
Phone: 212-533-6374
Fax: 212-675-0218
24 Hour Suicide Hotline: 212-673-3000
Website: http://www.mdsg.org
E-mail: info@mdsg.org

Mood Disorders Support Group of Guelph
P.O. Box 873
Guelph, ON CANADA N1H 6M6
Phone 519-766-4477
Website: www.mooddisorders guelph.org
E-mail: webmaster@mood disordersguelph.org

National Self-Help Clearinghouse
Graduate School and University Center
City University of New York
365 5th Avenue
Suite 3300
New York, NY 10016
Phone: 212-817-1822
Website: www.selfhelpweb.org
E-mail: info@selfhelpweb.org

REACH (Reassurance to Each)
Mental Health Association of Minnesota
205 W. 2nd Street., Suite 412
Duluth, MN 55802
Phone: 218-726-0793
Fax: 218-727-1468
Website: http://www.mental health.org
E-mail: info@mentalhealth mn.org

Samaritans
The Upper Mill
Kingston Road
Ewell, Surrey KT17 2AF
England
Phone: 011-44-020-8394-8300
Fax: 011-44-020-8394-8301
Website: http://www.Samaritans. org.uk
E-mail: admin@Samaritans.org

Self-Help Center
405 South State Street
Champaign IL 61820
Phone: 217-352-0099
Website: http:// www.prairienet.org/selfhelp/ homepage.phtml
E-mail: selfhelp@prairienet.org

Self-Help Clearinghouse
Mental Health Association of the Mid-South
200 Jefferson Avenue, Suite #1107
Memphis, TN 38103-2328
Phone: 901-323-0633
Fax: 901-323-0858
Website: http://www.nmha.org
E-mail: mha@netten.net

Self-Help Clearinghouse

1211 Chestnut Street
Suite 1207
Philadelphia, PA 19107
Toll Free: 800-553-4539
Phone: 215-751-1810
Fax: 215-636-6312
Website: http://www.mhself
help.org
E-mail: info@mhselfhelp.org

Self-Help Information Network Exchange (SHINE)

538 Spruce St.
Suite 420
Scranton, PA 18503
Phone: 507-961-1234
(Lackawanna County, 24 hours)
Phone: 570-347-5616 (Adminis-
tration)
Fax: 570-341-5816
Website: http://www.vacnepa.org
E-mail: shinevacnepa.org

Self-Help Resource Center (Broome County)

Mental Health Association
82 Oak St.
Binghamton, NY 13905
Phone: 607-771-8888
Fax: 607-771-8892
Website: yalenwhavnhealth.org
E-mail: mha@stny.rr.com

Self-Help Resource Center for Greater Houston

Mental Health Association in
Houston and Harris County
c/o MHA of Houston
2211 Norfolk, Suite 810
Houston, TX 77098
Phone: 713-522-5161 (Informa-
tion and Referral)
Phone: 713-522-8963 (Adminis-
tration)
Fax: 713-522-0698
Website: http://www.mhagh.org

Support4Hope

P.O. Box 184
Deer Lodge, TN 37726
Website: http://support4hope.com
E-mail: webmaster@Support
4Hope.com

Texas Self-Help Information and Referral Service

Mental Health Association in
Texas
c/o Mental Health Association
8401 Shoal Creek Blvd.
Austin, TX 78757
Phone: 512-454-3706 ext.202
Fax: 512-454-3725
Website: http://
www.LaurusHealth.com

Walkers in Darkness, Inc.

P.O. Box 2187
Columbia, MD 21045-1187
Website: http://www.walkers.org
E-mail: walkrweb@walker.org

Chapter 77

Medication Assistance Programs for People with Depressive Illnesses

Many people are faced with the crushing despair of their depressive illness and flattened finances as well. One may find oneself without health insurance, without any money to spare, only able to handle a simple, minimally paying job, perhaps out of work.

In these situations, one may be able to obtain medications free of charge through Indigent Patient Assistance Programs, which are usually sponsored by drug manufacturers. One must make arrangements through a doctor, it takes some paperwork, and it takes some processing time; but, these programs may give some respite to improve and stabilize one's mood and one's financial prospects.

Most of the programs require that:

- you have no insurance coverage for outpatient prescription drugs

- purchasing the medication at its retail price would be a hardship for you due to your income and/or expenses

- you do not qualify for a government or third-party program that can pay for the prescription.

Maximum allowed income levels vary by program and by medical condition(s). Some require income levels no higher than the federal

"Indigent Patient Programs," reprinted with permission from *NAFDI News* (Spring/Summer 2000). © Copyright 2000 National Foundation for Depressive Illness, Inc. The version presented here includes updates made by the editor in 2002.

poverty level, but some allow somewhat higher income levels, and/or will decide on a case-by-case basis.

A month or so after the application is made, a qualified applicant will receive a two or three month supply of medication, which would be delivered to a doctor's office. After that, more can generally be had through a re-submittal of the paperwork.

Kim Frawley at Pfizer Inc., manufacturer of a popular SSRI anti-depressant, reported that their program has been in operation for 18 years, and that in 1999 Pfizer donated nearly $105 million dollars (suggested retail value) of medications to more than 500,000 uninsured low-income patients across the U.S. Ms. Frawley stated that the program makes "most of Pfizer's outpatient products for chronic conditions available... to those patients who were falling through the cracks."

Free Medication Available through Patient Assistance Programs

For more information, you or your doctor can contact a company directly to ask about its indigent assistance program. Some details are available at The Pharmaceutical Research and Manufacturers' Association's website: www.phrma.org/patients. If the manufacturer of your medication is not listed here, please contact the National Foundation for Depressive Illness (800-239-1265 or online at http://www. depression.org). Please note that generic versions of medications are not usually offered through these programs. Also, note that programs, medications available, and indeed corporations may change without notice.

This list includes commonly prescribed medications available through indigent patient assistance programs, the manufacturer, and program phone number:

Asendin (amoxapine): Wyeth Pharmaceuticals 800-568-9938

BuSpar (buspirone): Bristol Myers Squibb 800-736-0003

Carbatrol (carbamazepine): Shire Richwood 800-536-7878

Celexa (citalopram): Forest 800-678-1605

Clozapine (generic): Mylan 888-823-7835

Clozaril (clozapine): Novartis 800-277-2254

Compazine (prochlorperazine): SmithKline Beecham Pharmaceuticals 800-546-0420

Depakote (valproic acid/divalproex): Abbott Laboratories 800 222-6885 (touchtone option 1)

Desyrel (trazodone): Bristol-Meyers Squibb Company 800-736-0003

Dilantin (phenytoin): Parke Davis 908-725-1247

Effexor (venlafaxine): Wyeth Pharmaceuticals 800-568-9938

Elavil (amitriptyline): AstraZeneca Pharmaceuticals 800-424-3727

Eskalith (lithium): Scios, Inc. 800-972-4670

Etrafon (amitriptyline + perphenazine): Schering Labs/Key Pharmaceuticals 800-656-9485

Haldol (haloperidol): Ortho-McNeil Pharmaceuticals 800-682-6532 (touchtone option 1)

Isoptin (verapamil): Abbott Laboratories Pharmaceutical 800 222-6885 (touchtone option 1)

Klonopin (clonazepam): Roche Laboratories 800-285-4484

Lamictal (lamotrigine): GlaxoWellcome 800-722-9294

Levoxyl (levothyroxine): King Pharmaceutical 314-576-6100 (touchtone option 7)

Lithobid (lithium): Solvay 800-241-1643 (touchtone option 6, then touchtone option 4)

Loxitane (loxapine): Wyeth Pharmaceuticals 800-568-9938

Ludiomil (maprotiline): Ciba Pharmaceuticals 800-257-3273 (touchtone option 2)

Luvox (fluvoxamine): Solvay 800-241-1643 (touchtone option 6, then touchtone option 4)

Mysoline (primidone): Elan Pharmaceuticals 800-511-2120

Navane (thiothixene): Pfizer 800-646-4455

Neurontin (gabapentin): Parke Davis 908-725-1247

Norpramin (desipramine): Aventis Pharmaceuticals 800-221-4025

Orap (pimozide): Gate 800-292-4283

Parnate (tranylcypromine): Scios, Inc. 800-972-4670

Paxil (paroxetine): SmithKline Beecham Pharmaceuticals 800-546-0420

Prozac (fluoxetine): Lilly Cares Program 800-545-6962

Remeron (mirtazapine): Organon 973-325-4946

Risperdal (risperidone): Janssen Pharmaceutical 800 652-6227

Serentil (mesoridazine): Boehringer Ingleheim 800-556-8317

Seroquel (quetiapine): AstraZeneca Pharmaceuticals 800-424-3727

Serzone (nefazodone): Bristol Myers Squibb 800-736-0003

Sinequan (doxepin): Pfizer 800-646-4455

Stelazine (trifluoperazine): Scios, Inc. 800-972-4670

Surmontil (trimipramine): Wyeth Pharmaceuticals 800-568-9938

Synthroid (levothyroxine): Knoll Pharmaceutical 800-526-0710

Tarka (verapamil): Knoll Pharmaceutical 800-526-0710

Tegretol (carbamazepine): Novartis 800-277-2254

Thorazine (chlorpromazine): Scios, Inc. 800-972-4670

Topamax (topiramate): Ortho-McNeil Pharmaceuticals 800-682-6532 (touchtone option 1)

Trilafon (perphenazine): Schering Labs/Key Pharmaceuticals 800-656-9485

Valium (diazepam): Roche Laboratories 800-285-4484

Vistaril (hydroxyzine): Pfizer 800-646-4455

Vivactil (protriptyline): Merck 800 994-2111

Wellbutrin (bupropion): GlaxoWellcome 800-722-9294

Zarontin (ethosuximide): Parke Davis 908-725-1247

Zoloft (sertraline): Pfizer 800-646-4455

Zyprexa (olanzapine): Lilly Cares Program 800-545-6962

Index

Index

Diagnostic and Statistical Manual of Mental Disorders, Fourth Edition (DSM-IV)
cyclothymic disorder 32–33
described 25
dysthymic disorder 28–31
major depressive episode 26–28
manic episode 31–32
Diamond, Jed 143
diazepam 232, 558
diet and nutrition
depression 140
monoamine oxidase inhibitors 11, 226, 441
Dietary Supplement Health and Education Act (1994) 292
Dilantin (phenytoin) 557
diltiazem 92
disopyramide 93
disulfiram 91, 93
divalproex 231, 557
divalproex sodium 231, 320–21
dopamine
antidepressant medications 10, 20
bipolar disorder 489–90
depression 125
Dopar (levodopa) 91
Dott, Andrew B. 139n
Dott, Caroline 139n
doxepin 147, 222, 250, 387, 558
drinking diary 85–86
drug abuse
antidepressant medications 11
bipolar disorder 61
college students 111–12
depression 7
dual diagnosis 77–82
libido 193
mood disorders 265–68
suicide 421
"Drug Interactions: What You Should Know" (FDA) 259n
drugs *see* medications
dual diagnosis, substance abuse 77–82
dysphoria
defined 528
described 25

dysthymia
college students 109
defined 4, 279, 528
described 52, 118, 454
overview 28–29, 45–47
"Dysthymic Disorder: When Depression Lingers" (AAFP) 45n

E

EAP *see* employee assistance programs
eating disorders
adolescents 121
depression 357–59
ECT *see* electroconvulsive therapy
"The Effects of Depression in the Workplace" (NIMH) 151n
Effexor (venlafaxine) 147, *148,* 222, 251, 557
Elavil (amitriptyline) 147, 222, 249, 508, 557
Elder Abuse Hotline, contact information 547
elderly
antidepressant medications 246
antipsychotic medications 238
depression 7–8, 124, 157–65
depression research 463–64
drug-induced depression 92
suicide 439–43
electroconvulsive therapy (ECT)
bipolar disorder 60
defined 528
depression 10, 327
depression research 457–58, 509
described 281–83
elderly people 163
Parkinson disease 387
schizoaffective disorder 75
women 128
Elspar (asparaginase) 92
emotional disorders, *versus* substance abuse 79
Emotions Anonymous, contact information 551
employee assistance programs (EAP) 154–55
empty nest syndrome, described 124

O

Health Reference Series
COMPLETE CATALOG

Adolescent Health Sourcebook

Basic Consumer Health Information about Common Medical, Mental, and Emotional Concerns in Adolescents, Including Facts about Acne, Body Piercing, Mononucleosis, Nutrition, Eating Disorders, Stress, Depression, Behavior Problems, Peer Pressure, Violence, Gangs, Drug Use, Puberty, Sexuality, Pregnancy, Learning Disabilities, and More

Along with a Glossary of Terms and Other Resources for Further Help and Information

Edited by Chad T. Kimball. 658 pages. 2002. 0-7808-0248-9. $78.

■

AIDS Sourcebook, 1st Edition

Basic Information about AIDS and HIV Infection, Featuring Historical and Statistical Data, Current Research, Prevention, and Other Special Topics of Interest for Persons Living with AIDS

Along with Source Listings for Further Assistance

Edited by Karen Bellenir and Peter D. Dresser. 831 pages. 1995. 0-7808-0031-1. $78.

"One strength of this book is its practical emphasis. The intended audience is the lay reader . . . useful as an educational tool for health care providers who work with AIDS patients. Recommended for public libraries as well as hospital or academic libraries that collect consumer materials."
— *Bulletin of the Medical Library Association, Jan '96*

"This is the most comprehensive volume of its kind on an important medical topic. Highly recommended for all libraries." — *Reference Book Review, '96*

"Very useful reference for all libraries."
— *Choice, Association of College and Research Libraries, Oct '95*

"There is a wealth of information here that can provide much educational assistance. It is a must book for all libraries and should be on the desk of each and every congressional leader. Highly recommended."
— *AIDS Book Review Journal, Aug '95*

"Recommended for most collections."
— *Library Journal, Jul '95*

■

AIDS Sourcebook, 2nd Edition

Basic Consumer Health Information about Acquired Immune Deficiency Syndrome (AIDS) and Human Immunodeficiency Virus (HIV) Infection, Featuring Updated Statistical Data, Reports on Recent Research and Prevention Initiatives, and Other Special Topics of Interest for Persons Living with AIDS, Including New Antiretroviral Treatment Options, Strategies for Com- bating Opportunistic Infections, Information about Clinical Trials, and More

Along with a Glossary of Important Terms and Resource Listings for Further Help and Information

Edited by Karen Bellenir. 751 pages. 1999. 0-7808-0225-X. $78.

"Highly recommended."
— *American Reference Books Annual, 2000*

"Excellent sourcebook. This continues to be a highly recommended book. There is no other book that provides as much information as this book provides."
— *AIDS Book Review Journal, Dec-Jan 2000*

"Recommended reference source."
— *Booklist, American Library Association, Dec '99*

"A solid text for college-level health libraries."
— *The Bookwatch, Aug '99*

Cited in *Reference Sources for Small and Medium-Sized Libraries, American Library Association, 1999*

■

Alcoholism Sourcebook

Basic Consumer Health Information about the Physical and Mental Consequences of Alcohol Abuse, Including Liver Disease, Pancreatitis, Wernicke-Korsakoff Syndrome (Alcoholic Dementia), Fetal Alcohol Syndrome, Heart Disease, Kidney Disorders, Gastrointestinal Problems, and Immune System Compromise and Featuring Facts about Addiction, Detoxification, Alcohol Withdrawal, Recovery, and the Maintenance of Sobriety

Along with a Glossary and Directories of Resources for Further Help and Information

Edited by Karen Bellenir. 613 pages. 2000. 0-7808-0325-6. $78.

"This title is one of the few reference works on alcoholism for general readers. For some readers this will be a welcome complement to the many self-help books on the market. Recommended for collections serving general readers and consumer health collections."
— *E-Streams, Mar '01*

"This book is an excellent choice for public and academic libraries."
— *American Reference Books Annual, 2001*

"Recommended reference source."
— *Booklist, American Library Association, Dec '00*

"Presents a wealth of information on alcohol use and abuse and its effects on the body and mind, treatment, and prevention." — *SciTech Book News, Dec '00*

"Important new health guide which packs in the latest consumer information about the problems of alcoholism." — *Reviewer's Bookwatch, Nov '00*

SEE ALSO *Drug Abuse Sourcebook, Substance Abuse Sourcebook*

Allergies Sourcebook, 1st Edition

Basic Information about Major Forms and Mechanisms of Common Allergic Reactions, Sensitivities, and Intolerances, Including Anaphylaxis, Asthma, Hives and Other Dermatologic Symptoms, Rhinitis, and Sinusitis

Along with Their Usual Triggers Like Animal Fur, Chemicals, Drugs, Dust, Foods, Insects, Latex, Pollen, and Poison Ivy, Oak, and Sumac; Plus Information on Prevention, Identification, and Treatment

Edited by Allan R. Cook. 611 pages. 1997. 0-7808-0036-2. $78.

Allergies Sourcebook, 2nd Edition

Basic Consumer Health Information about Allergic Disorders, Triggers, Reactions, and Related Symptoms, Including Anaphylaxis, Rhinitis, Sinusitis, Asthma, Dermatitis, Conjunctivitis, and Multiple Chemical Sensitivity

Along with Tips on Diagnosis, Prevention, and Treatment, Statistical Data, a Glossary, and a Directory of Sources for Further Help and Information

Edited by Annemarie S. Muth. 598 pages. 2002. 0-7808-0376-0. $78.

Alternative Medicine Sourcebook, First Edition

Basic Consumer Health Information about Alternatives to Conventional Medicine, Including Acupressure, Acupuncture, Aromatherapy, Ayurveda, Bioelectromagnetics, Environmental Medicine, Essence Therapy, Food and Nutrition Therapy, Herbal Therapy, Homeopathy, Imaging, Massage, Naturopathy, Reflexology, Relaxation and Meditation, Sound Therapy, Vitamin and Mineral Therapy, and Yoga, and More

Edited by Allan R. Cook. 737 pages. 1999. 0-7808-0200-4. $78.

"Recommended reference source."
—*Booklist, American Library Association, Feb '00*

"A great addition to the reference collection of every type of library." —*American Reference Books Annual, 2000*

Alternative Medicine Sourcebook, Second Edition

Basic Consumer Health Information about Alternative and Complementary Medical Practices, Including Acupuncture, Chiropractic, Herbal Medicine, Homeopathy, Naturopathic Medicine, Mind-Body Interventions, Ayurveda, and Other Non-Western Medical Traditions

Along with Facts about such Specific Therapies as Massage Therapy, Aromatherapy, Qigong, Hypnosis, Prayer, Dance, and Art Therapies, a Glossary, and Resources for Further Information

Edited by Dawn D. Matthews. 618 pages. 2002. 0-7808-0605-0. $78.

Alzheimer's, Stroke & 29 Other Neurological Disorders Sourcebook, 1st Edition

Basic Information for the Layperson on 31 Diseases or Disorders Affecting the Brain and Nervous System, First Describing the Illness, Then Listing Symptoms, Diagnostic Methods, and Treatment Options, and Including Statistics on Incidences and Causes

Edited by Frank E. Bair. 579 pages. 1993. 1-55888-748-2. $78.

"Nontechnical reference book that provides reader-friendly information."
—*Family Caregiver Alliance Update, Winter '96*

"Should be included in any library's patient education section." —*American Reference Books Annual, 1994*

"Written in an approachable and accessible style. Recommended for patient education and consumer health collections in health science center and public libraries." —*Academic Library Book Review, Dec '93*

"It is very handy to have information on more than thirty neurological disorders under one cover, and there is no recent source like it." —*Reference Quarterly, American Library Association, Fall '93*

SEE ALSO Brain Disorders Sourcebook

Alzheimer's Disease Sourcebook, 2nd Edition

Basic Consumer Health Information about Alzheimer's Disease, Related Disorders, and Other Dementias, Including Multi-Infarct Dementia, AIDS-Related Dementia, Alcoholic Dementia, Huntington's Disease, Delirium, and Confusional States

Along with Reports Detailing Current Research Efforts in Prevention and Treatment, Long-Term Care Issues, and Listings of Sources for Additional Help and Information

Edited by Karen Bellenir. 524 pages. 1999. 0-7808-0223-3. $78.

"Provides a wealth of useful information not otherwise available in one place. This resource is recommended for all types of libraries."
—*American Reference Books Annual, 2000*

"Recommended reference source."
—*Booklist, American Library Association, Oct '99*

Arthritis Sourcebook

Basic Consumer Health Information about Specific Forms of Arthritis and Related Disorders, Including Rheumatoid Arthritis, Osteoarthritis, Gout, Polymyalgia Rheumatica, Psoriatic Arthritis, Spondyloarthropathies, Juvenile Rheumatoid Arthritis, and Juvenile Ankylosing Spondylitis

Along with Information about Medical, Surgical, and Alternative Treatment Options, and Including Strategies for Coping with Pain, Fatigue, and Stress

Edited by Allan R. Cook. 550 pages. 1998. 0-7808-0201-2. $78.

"... accessible to the layperson."
—*Reference and Research Book News, Feb '99*

Asthma Sourcebook

Basic Consumer Health Information about Asthma, Including Symptoms, Traditional and Nontraditional Remedies, Treatment Advances, Quality-of-Life Aids, Medical Research Updates, and the Role of Allergies, Exercise, Age, the Environment, and Genetics in the Development of Asthma

Along with Statistical Data, a Glossary, and Directories of Support Groups, and Other Resources for Further Information

Edited by Annemarie S. Muth. 628 pages. 2000. 0-7808-0381-7. $78.

"A worthwhile reference acquisition for public libraries and academic medical libraries whose readers desire a quick introduction to the wide range of asthma information." — *Choice, Association of College & Research Libraries, Jun '01*

"Recommended reference source."
— *Booklist, American Library Association, Feb '01*

"Highly recommended." — *The Bookwatch, Jan '01*

"There is much good information for patients and their families who deal with asthma daily."
— *American Medical Writers Association Journal, Winter '01*

"This informative text is recommended for consumer health collections in public, secondary school, and community college libraries and the libraries of universities with a large undergraduate population."
— *American Reference Books Annual, 2001*

Attention Deficit Disorder Sourcebook, First Edition

Basic Consumer Health Information about Attention Deficit/Hyperactivity Disorder in Children and Adults, Including Facts about Causes, Symptoms, Diagnostic Criteria, and Treatment Options Such as Medications, Behavior Therapy, Coaching, and Homeopathy

Along with Reports on Current Research Initiatives, Legal Issues, and Government Regulations, and Featuring a Glossary of Related Terms, Internet Resources, and a List of Additional Reading Material

Edited by Dawn D. Matthews. 470 pages. 2002. 0-7808-0624-7. $78.

Back & Neck Disorders Sourcebook

Basic Information about Disorders and Injuries of the Spinal Cord and Vertebrae, Including Facts on Chiropractic Treatment, Surgical Interventions, Paralysis, and Rehabilitation

Along with Advice for Preventing Back Trouble

Edited by Karen Bellenir. 548 pages. 1997. 0-7808-0202-0. $78.

"The strength of this work is its basic, easy-to-read format. Recommended."
— *Reference and User Services Quarterly, American Library Association, Winter '97*

Blood & Circulatory Disorders Sourcebook

Basic Information about Blood and Its Components, Anemias, Leukemias, Bleeding Disorders, and Circulatory Disorders, Including Aplastic Anemia, Thalassemia, Sickle-Cell Disease, Hemochromatosis, Hemophilia, Von Willebrand Disease, and Vascular Diseases

Along with a Special Section on Blood Transfusions and Blood Supply Safety, a Glossary, and Source Listings for Further Help and Information

Edited by Karen Bellenir and Linda M. Shin. 554 pages. 1998. 0-7808-0203-9. $78.

"Recommended reference source."
—*Booklist, American Library Association, Feb '99*

"An important reference sourcebook written in simple language for everyday, non-technical users. "
— *Reviewer's Bookwatch, Jan '99*

Brain Disorders Sourcebook

Basic Consumer Health Information about Strokes, Epilepsy, Amyotrophic Lateral Sclerosis (ALS/Lou Gehrig's Disease), Parkinson's Disease, Brain Tumors, Cerebral Palsy, Headache, Tourette Syndrome, and More

Along with Statistical Data, Treatment and Rehabilitation Options, Coping Strategies, Reports on Current Research Initiatives, a Glossary, and Resource Listings for Additional Help and Information

Edited by Karen Bellenir. 481 pages. 1999. 0-7808-0229-2. $78.

"Belongs on the shelves of any library with a consumer health collection." — *E-Streams, Mar '00*

"Recommended reference source."
— *Booklist, American Library Association, Oct '99*

SEE ALSO *Alzheimer's, Stroke & 29 Other Neurological Disorders Sourcebook, 1st Edition*

Breast Cancer Sourcebook

Basic Consumer Health Information about Breast Cancer, Including Diagnostic Methods, Treatment Options, Alternative Therapies, Self-Help Information, Related Health Concerns, Statistical and Demographic Data, and Facts for Men with Breast Cancer

Along with Reports on Current Research Initiatives, a Glossary of Related Medical Terms, and a Directory of Sources for Further Help and Information

Edited by Edward J. Prucha and Karen Bellenir. 580 pages. 2001. 0-7808-0244-6. $78.

"Recommended reference source."
— *Booklist, American Library Association, Jan '02*

"This reference source is highly recommended. It is quite informative, comprehensive and detailed in nature, and yet it offers practical advice in easy-to-read language. It could be thought of as the 'bible' of breast cancer for the consumer." — *E-Streams, Jan '02*

"The broad range of topics covered in lay language make the *Breast Cancer Sourcebook* an excellent addition to public and consumer health library collections." — *American Reference Books Annual 2002*

"From the pros and cons of different screening methods and results to treatment options, *Breast Cancer Sourcebook* provides the latest information on the subject." — *Library Bookwatch, Dec '01*

"This thoroughgoing, very readable reference covers all aspects of breast health and cancer. . . . Readers will find much to consider here. Recommended for all public and patient health collections." — *Library Journal, Sep '01*

SEE ALSO Cancer Sourcebook for Women, 1st and 2nd Editions, Women's Health Concerns Sourcebook

■

Breastfeeding Sourcebook

Basic Consumer Health Information about the Benefits of Breastmilk, Preparing to Breastfeed, Breastfeeding as a Baby Grows, Nutrition, and More, Including Information on Special Situations and Concerns Such as Mastitis, Illness, Medications, Allergies, Multiple Births, Prematurity, Special Needs, and Adoption

Along with a Glossary and Resources for Additional Help and Information

Edited by Jenni Lynn Colson. 388 pages. 2002. 0-7808-0332-9. $78.

SEE ALSO Pregnancy & Birth Sourcebook

■

Burns Sourcebook

Basic Consumer Health Information about Various Types of Burns and Scalds, Including Flame, Heat, Cold, Electrical, Chemical, and Sun Burns

Along with Information on Short-Term and Long-Term Treatments, Tissue Reconstruction, Plastic Surgery, Prevention Suggestions, and First Aid

Edited by Allan R. Cook. 604 pages. 1999. 0-7808-0204-7. $78.

"This is an exceptional addition to the series and is highly recommended for all consumer health collections, hospital libraries, and academic medical centers." — *E-Streams, Mar '00*

"This key reference guide is an invaluable addition to all health care and public libraries in confronting this ongoing health issue." — *American Reference Books Annual, 2000*

"Recommended reference source." — *Booklist, American Library Association, Dec '99*

SEE ALSO Skin Disorders Sourcebook

■

Cancer Sourcebook, 1st Edition

Basic Information on Cancer Types, Symptoms, Diagnostic Methods, and Treatments, Including Statistics on Cancer Occurrences Worldwide and the Risks Associated with Known Carcinogens and Activities

Edited by Frank E. Bair. 932 pages. 1990. 1-55888-888-8. $78.

Cited in *Reference Sources for Small and Medium-Sized Libraries, American Library Association, 1999*

"Written in nontechnical language. Useful for patients, their families, medical professionals, and librarians." — *Guide to Reference Books, 1996*

"Designed with the non-medical professional in mind. Libraries and medical facilities interested in patient education should certainly consider adding the *Cancer Sourcebook* to their holdings. This compact collection of reliable information . . . is an invaluable tool for helping patients and patients' families and friends to take the first steps in coping with the many difficulties of cancer." — *Medical Reference Services Quarterly, Winter '91*

"Specifically created for the nontechnical reader . . . an important resource for the general reader trying to understand the complexities of cancer." — *American Reference Books Annual, 1991*

"This publication's nontechnical nature and very comprehensive format make it useful for both the general public and undergraduate students." — *Choice, Association of College and Research Libraries, Oct '90*

■

New Cancer Sourcebook, 2nd Edition

Basic Information about Major Forms and Stages of Cancer, Featuring Facts about Primary and Secondary Tumors of the Respiratory, Nervous, Lymphatic, Circulatory, Skeletal, and Gastrointestinal Systems; and Specific Organs; Statistical and Demographic Data; Treatment Options; and Strategies for Coping

Edited by Allan R. Cook. 1,313 pages. 1996. 0-7808-0041-9. $78.

"An excellent resource for patients with newly diagnosed cancer and their families. The dialogue is simple, direct, and comprehensive. Highly recommended for patients and families to aid in their understanding of cancer and its treatment."

—Booklist Health Sciences Supplement, American Library Association, Oct '97

"The amount of factual and useful information is extensive. The writing is very clear, geared to general readers. Recommended for all levels."   *—Choice, Association of College & Research Libraries, Jan '97*

■

Cancer Sourcebook, 3rd Edition

Basic Consumer Health Information about Major Forms and Stages of Cancer, Featuring Facts about Primary and Secondary Tumors of the Respiratory, Nervous, Lymphatic, Circulatory, Skeletal, and Gastrointestinal Systems, and Specific Organs

Along with Statistical and Demographic Data, Treatment Options, Strategies for Coping, a Glossary, and a Directory of Sources for Additional Help and Information

Edited by Edward J. Prucha. 1,069 pages. 2000. 0-7808-0227-6. $78.

"This title is recommended for health sciences and public libraries with consumer health collections."

—E-Streams, Feb '01

". . . can be effectively used by cancer patients and their families who are looking for answers in a language they can understand. Public and hospital libraries should have it on their shelves."

—American Reference Books Annual, 2001

"Recommended reference source."

—Booklist, American Library Association, Dec '00

■

Cancer Sourcebook for Women, 1st Edition

Basic Information about Specific Forms of Cancer That Affect Women, Featuring Facts about Breast Cancer, Cervical Cancer, Ovarian Cancer, Cancer of the Uterus and Uterine Sarcoma, Cancer of the Vagina, and Cancer of the Vulva; Statistical and Demographic Data; Treatments, Self-Help Management Suggestions, and Current Research Initiatives

Edited by Allan R. Cook and Peter D. Dresser. 524 pages. 1996. 0-7808-0076-1. $78.

". . . written in easily understandable, non-technical language. Recommended for public libraries or hospital and academic libraries that collect patient education or consumer health materials."

—Medical Reference Services Quarterly, Spring '97

"Would be of value in a consumer health library. . . . written with the health care consumer in mind. Medical jargon is at a minimum, and medical terms are explained in clear, understandable sentences."

—Bulletin of the Medical Library Association, Oct '96

"The availability under one cover of all these pertinent publications, grouped under cohesive headings, makes this certainly a most useful sourcebook."   *—Choice, Association of College & Research Libraries, Jun '96*

"Presents a comprehensive knowledge base for general readers. Men and women both benefit from the gold mine of information nestled between the two covers of this book. Recommended."

—Academic Library Book Review, Summer '96

"This timely book is highly recommended for consumer health and patient education collections in all libraries."   *— Library Journal, Apr '96*

SEE ALSO *Breast Cancer Sourcebook, Women's Health Concerns Sourcebook*

■

Cancer Sourcebook for Women, 2nd Edition

Basic Consumer Health Information about Gynecologic Cancers and Related Concerns, Including Cervical Cancer, Endometrial Cancer, Gestational Trophoblastic Tumor, Ovarian Cancer, Uterine Cancer, Vaginal Cancer, Vulvar Cancer, Breast Cancer, and Common Non-Cancerous Uterine Conditions, with Facts about Cancer Risk Factors, Screening and Prevention, Treatment Options, and Reports on Current Research Initiatives

Along with a Glossary of Cancer Terms and a Directory of Resources for Additional Help and Information

Edited by Karen Bellenir. 604 pages. 2002. 0-7808-0226-8. $78.

SEE ALSO *Breast Cancer Sourcebook, Women's Health Concerns Sourcebook*

■

Cardiovascular Diseases & Disorders Sourcebook, 1st Edition

Basic Information about Cardiovascular Diseases and Disorders, Featuring Facts about the Cardiovascular System, Demographic and Statistical Data, Descriptions of Pharmacological and Surgical Interventions, Lifestyle Modifications, and a Special Section Focusing on Heart Disorders in Children

Edited by Karen Bellenir and Peter D. Dresser. 683 pages. 1995. 0-7808-0032-X. $78.

". . . comprehensive format provides an extensive overview on this subject."   *—Choice, Association of College & Research Libraries, Jun '96*

". . . an easily understood, complete, up-to-date resource. This well executed public health tool will make valuable information available to those that need it most, patients and their families. The typeface, sturdy non-reflective paper, and library binding add a feel of quality found wanting in other publications. Highly recommended for academic and general libraries. "

—Academic Library Book Review, Summer '96

SEE ALSO *Healthy Heart Sourcebook for Women, Heart Diseases & Disorders Sourcebook, 2nd Edition*

Caregiving Sourcebook

Basic Consumer Health Information for Caregivers, Including a Profile of Caregivers, Caregiving Responsibilities and Concerns, Tips for Specific Conditions, Care Environments, and the Effects of Caregiving

Along with Facts about Legal Issues, Financial Information, and Future Planning, a Glossary, and a Listing of Additional Resources

Edited by Joyce Brennfleck Shannon. 600 pages. 2001. 0-7808-0331-0. $78.

"Essential for most collections."
— *Library Journal, Apr 1, 2002*

"An ideal addition to the reference collection of any public library. Health sciences information professionals may also want to acquire the *Caregiving Sourcebook* for their hospital or academic library for use as a ready reference tool by health care workers interested in aging and caregiving."   —*E-Streams, Jan '02*

"Recommended reference source."
—*Booklist, American Library Association, Oct '01*

◾

Colds, Flu & Other Common Ailments Sourcebook

Basic Consumer Health Information about Common Ailments and Injuries, Including Colds, Coughs, the Flu, Sinus Problems, Headaches, Fever, Nausea and Vomiting, Menstrual Cramps, Diarrhea, Constipation, Hemorrhoids, Back Pain, Dandruff, Dry and Itchy Skin, Cuts, Scrapes, Sprains, Bruises, and More

Along with Information about Prevention, Self-Care, Choosing a Doctor, Over-the-Counter Medications, Folk Remedies, and Alternative Therapies, and Including a Glossary of Important Terms and a Directory of Resources for Further Help and Information

Edited by Chad T. Kimball. 638 pages. 2001. 0-7808-0435-X. $78.

"A good starting point for research on common illnesses. It will be a useful addition to public and consumer health library collections."
—*American Reference Books Annual 2002*

"Will prove valuable to any library seeking to maintain a current, comprehensive reference collection of health resources. . . . Excellent reference."
—*The Bookwatch, Aug '01*

"Recommended reference source."
—*Booklist, American Library Association, July '01*

◾

Communication Disorders Sourcebook

Basic Information about Deafness and Hearing Loss, Speech and Language Disorders, Voice Disorders, Balance and Vestibular Disorders, and Disorders of Smell, Taste, and Touch

Edited by Linda M. Ross. 533 pages. 1996. 0-7808-0077-X. $78.

"This is skillfully edited and is a welcome resource for the layperson. It should be found in every public and medical library."   — *Booklist Health Sciences Supplement, American Library Association, Oct '97*

◾

Congenital Disorders Sourcebook

Basic Information about Disorders Acquired during Gestation, Including Spina Bifida, Hydrocephalus, Cerebral Palsy, Heart Defects, Craniofacial Abnormalities, Fetal Alcohol Syndrome, and More

Along with Current Treatment Options and Statistical Data

Edited by Karen Bellenir. 607 pages. 1997. 0-7808-0205-5. $78.

"Recommended reference source."
— *Booklist, American Library Association, Oct '97*

SEE ALSO *Pregnancy & Birth Sourcebook*

◾

Consumer Issues in Health Care Sourcebook

Basic Information about Health Care Fundamentals and Related Consumer Issues, Including Exams and Screening Tests, Physician Specialties, Choosing a Doctor, Using Prescription and Over-the-Counter Medications Safely, Avoiding Health Scams, Managing Common Health Risks in the Home, Care Options for Chronically or Terminally Ill Patients, and a List of Resources for Obtaining Help and Further Information

Edited by Karen Bellenir. 618 pages. 1998. 0-7808-0221-7. $78.

"Both public and academic libraries will want to have a copy in their collection for readers who are interested in self-education on health issues."
—*American Reference Books Annual, 2000*

"The editor has researched the literature from government agencies and others, saving readers the time and effort of having to do the research themselves. Recommended for public libraries."
— *Reference and User Services Quarterly, American Library Association, Spring '99*

"Recommended reference source."
— *Booklist, American Library Association, Dec '98*

◾

Contagious & Non-Contagious Infectious Diseases Sourcebook

Basic Information about Contagious Diseases like Measles, Polio, Hepatitis B, and Infectious Mononucleosis, and Non-Contagious Infectious Diseases like Tetanus and Toxic Shock Syndrome, and Diseases Occurring as Secondary Infections Such as Shingles and Reye Syndrome

Along with Vaccination, Prevention, and Treatment Information, and a Section Describing Emerging Infectious Disease Threats

Edited by Karen Bellenir and Peter D. Dresser. 566 pages. 1996. 0-7808-0075-3. $78.

Death & Dying Sourcebook

Basic Consumer Health Information for the Layperson about End-of-Life Care and Related Ethical and Legal Issues, Including Chief Causes of Death, Autopsies, Pain Management for the Terminally Ill, Life Support Systems, Insurance, Euthanasia, Assisted Suicide, Hospice Programs, Living Wills, Funeral Planning, Counseling, Mourning, Organ Donation, and Physician Training

Along with Statistical Data, a Glossary, and Listings of Sources for Further Help and Information

Edited by Annemarie S. Muth. 641 pages. 1999. 0-7808-0230-6. $78.

"Public libraries, medical libraries, and academic libraries will all find this sourcebook a useful addition to their collections."
— *American Reference Books Annual, 2001*

"An extremely useful resource for those concerned with death and dying in the United States."
— *Respiratory Care, Nov '00*

"Recommended reference source."
— *Booklist, American Library Association, Aug '00*

"This book is a definite must for all those involved in end-of-life care." — *Doody's Review Service, 2000*

■

Depression Sourcebook

Basic Consumer Health Information about Unipolar Depression, Bipolar Disorder, Postpartum Depression, Seasonal Affective Disorder, and Other Types of Depression in Children, Adolescents, Women, Men, the Elderly, and Other Selected Populations

Along with Facts about Causes, Risk Factors, Diagnostic Criteria, Treatment Options, Coping Strategies, Suicide Prevention, a Glossary, and a Directory of Sources for Additional Help and Information

Edited by Karen Belleni. 602 pages. 2002. 0-7808-0611-5. $78.

■

Diabetes Sourcebook, 1st Edition

Basic Information about Insulin-Dependent and Noninsulin-Dependent Diabetes Mellitus, Gestational Diabetes, and Diabetic Complications, Symptoms, Treatment, and Research Results, Including Statistics on Prevalence, Morbidity, and Mortality

Along with Source Listings for Further Help and Information

Edited by Karen Bellenir and Peter D. Dresser. 827 pages. 1994. 1-55888-751-2. $78.

". . . very informative and understandable for the layperson without being simplistic. It provides a comprehensive overview for laypersons who want a general understanding of the disease or who want to focus on various aspects of the disease."
— *Bulletin of the Medical Library Association, Jan '96*

Diabetes Sourcebook, 2nd Edition

Basic Consumer Health Information about Type 1 Diabetes (Insulin-Dependent or Juvenile-Onset Diabetes), Type 2 (Noninsulin-Dependent or Adult-Onset Diabetes), Gestational Diabetes, and Related Disorders, Including Diabetes Prevalence Data, Management Issues, the Role of Diet and Exercise in Controlling Diabetes, Insulin and Other Diabetes Medicines, and Complications of Diabetes Such as Eye Diseases, Periodontal Disease, Amputation, and End-Stage Renal Disease

Along with Reports on Current Research Initiatives, a Glossary, and Resource Listings for Further Help and Information

Edited by Karen Bellenir. 688 pages. 1998. 0-7808-0224-1. $78.

"An invaluable reference." — *Library Journal, May '00*

Selected as one of the 250 "Best Health Sciences Books of 1999." — *Doody's Rating Service, Mar-Apr 2000*

"This comprehensive book is an excellent addition for high school, academic, medical, and public libraries. This volume is highly recommended."
— *American Reference Books Annual, 2000*

"Provides useful information for the general public."
— *Healthlines, University of Michigan Health Management Research Center, Sep/Oct '99*

". . . provides reliable mainstream medical information . . . belongs on the shelves of any library with a consumer health collection." — *E-Streams, Sep '99*

"Recommended reference source."
— *Booklist, American Library Association, Feb '99*

■

Diet & Nutrition Sourcebook, 1st Edition

Basic Information about Nutrition, Including the Dietary Guidelines for Americans, the Food Guide Pyramid, and Their Applications in Daily Diet, Nutritional Advice for Specific Age Groups, Current Nutritional Issues and Controversies, the New Food Label and How to Use It to Promote Healthy Eating, and Recent Developments in Nutritional Research

Edited by Dan R. Harris. 662 pages. 1996. 0-7808-0084-2. $78.

"Useful reference as a food and nutrition sourcebook for the general consumer." — *Booklist Health Sciences Supplement, American Library Association, Oct '97*

"Recommended for public libraries and medical libraries that receive general information requests on nutrition. It is readable and will appeal to those interested in learning more about healthy dietary practices."
— *Medical Reference Services Quarterly, Fall '97*

"An abundance of medical and social statistics is translated into readable information geared toward the general reader." — *Bookwatch, Mar '97*

"With dozens of questionable diet books on the market, it is so refreshing to find a reliable and factual reference book. Recommended to aspiring professionals, librari-

ans, and others seeking and giving reliable dietary advice. An excellent compilation." —Choice, Association of College and Research Libraries, Feb '97

SEE ALSO Digestive Diseases & Disorders Sourcebook, Gastrointestinal Diseases & Disorders Sourcebook

∎

Diet & Nutrition Sourcebook, 2nd Edition

Basic Consumer Health Information about Dietary Guidelines, Recommended Daily Intake Values, Vitamins, Minerals, Fiber, Fat, Weight Control, Dietary Supplements, and Food Additives

Along with Special Sections on Nutrition Needs throughout Life and Nutrition for People with Such Specific Medical Concerns as Allergies, High Blood Cholesterol, Hypertension, Diabetes, Celiac Disease, Seizure Disorders, Phenylketonuria (PKU), Cancer, and Eating Disorders, and Including Reports on Current Nutrition Research and Source Listings for Additional Help and Information

Edited by Karen Bellenir. 650 pages. 1999. 0-7808-0228-4. $78.

"This book is an excellent source of basic diet and nutrition information." —Booklist Health Sciences Supplement, American Library Association, Dec '00

"This reference document should be in any public library, but it would be a very good guide for beginning students in the health sciences. If the other books in this publisher's series are as good as this, they should all be in the health sciences collections."
—American Reference Books Annual, 2000

"This book is an excellent general nutrition reference for consumers who desire to take an active role in their health care for prevention. Consumers of all ages who select this book can feel confident they are receiving current and accurate information." —Journal of Nutrition for the Elderly, Vol. 19, No. 4, '00

"Recommended reference source."
—Booklist, American Library Association, Dec '99

SEE ALSO Digestive Diseases & Disorders Sourcebook, Gastrointestinal Diseases & Disorders Sourcebook

∎

Digestive Diseases & Disorders Sourcebook

Basic Consumer Health Information about Diseases and Disorders that Impact the Upper and Lower Digestive System, Including Celiac Disease, Constipation, Crohn's Disease, Cyclic Vomiting Syndrome, Diarrhea, Diverticulosis and Diverticulitis, Gallstones, Heartburn, Hemorrhoids, Hernias, Indigestion (Dyspepsia), Irritable Bowel Syndrome, Lactose Intolerance, Ulcers, and More

Along with Information about Medications and Other Treatments, Tips for Maintaining a Healthy Digestive Tract, a Glossary, and Directory of Digestive Diseases Organizations

Edited by Karen Bellenir. 335 pages. 2000. 0-7808-0327-2. $78.

"This title would be an excellent addition to all public or patient-research libraries."
—American Reference Books Annual, 2001

"This title is recommended for public, hospital, and health sciences libraries with consumer health collections." —E-Streams, Jul-Aug '00

"Recommended reference source."
—Booklist, American Library Association, May '00

SEE ALSO Diet & Nutrition Sourcebook, 1st and 2nd Editions, Gastrointestinal Diseases & Disorders Sourcebook

∎

Disabilities Sourcebook

Basic Consumer Health Information about Physical and Psychiatric Disabilities, Including Descriptions of Major Causes of Disability, Assistive and Adaptive Aids, Workplace Issues, and Accessibility Concerns

Along with Information about the Americans with Disabilities Act, a Glossary, and Resources for Additional Help and Information

Edited by Dawn D. Matthews. 616 pages. 2000. 0-7808-0389-2. $78.

"It is a must for libraries with a consumer health section." —American Reference Books Annual 2002

"A much needed addition to the Omnigraphics Health Reference Series. A current reference work to provide people with disabilities, their families, caregivers or those who work with them, a broad range of information in one volume, has not been available until now. . . . It is recommended for all public and academic library reference collections." —E-Streams, May '01

"An excellent source book in easy-to-read format covering many current topics; highly recommended for all libraries." —Choice, Association of College and Research Libraries, Jan '01

"Recommended reference source."
—Booklist, American Library Association, Jul '00

"An involving, invaluable handbook."
—The Bookwatch, May '00

∎

Domestic Violence & Child Abuse Sourcebook

Basic Consumer Health Information about Spousal/ Partner, Child, Sibling, Parent, and Elder Abuse, Covering Physical, Emotional, and Sexual Abuse, Teen Dating Violence, and Stalking; Includes Information about Hotlines, Safe Houses, Safety Plans, and Other Resources for Support and Assistance, Community Initiatives, and Reports on Current Directions in Research and Treatment

Along with a Glossary, Sources for Further Reading, and Governmental and Non-Governmental Organizations Contact Information

Edited by Helene Henderson. 1,064 pages. 2001. 0-7808-0235-7. $78.

"This is important information. The Web has many resources but this sourcebook fills an important societal need. I am not aware of any other resources of this type." —*Doody's Review Service, Sep '01*

"Recommended for all libraries, scholars, and practitioners." —*Choice, Association of College & Research Libraries, Jul '01*

"Recommended reference source." —*Booklist, American Library Association, Apr '01*

"Important pick for college-level health reference libraries." —*The Bookwatch, Mar '01*

"Because this problem is so widespread and because this book includes a lot of issues within one volume, this work is recommended for all public libraries." —*American Reference Books Annual, 2001*

◼

Drug Abuse Sourcebook

Basic Consumer Health Information about Illicit Substances of Abuse and the Diversion of Prescription Medications, Including Depressants, Hallucinogens, Inhalants, Marijuana, Narcotics, Stimulants, and Anabolic Steroids

Along with Facts about Related Health Risks, Treatment Issues, and Substance Abuse Prevention Programs, a Glossary of Terms, Statistical Data, and Directories of Hotline Services, Self-Help Groups, and Organizations Able to Provide Further Information

Edited by Karen Bellenir. 629 pages. 2000. 0-7808-0242-X. $78.

"Containing a wealth of information, this book will be useful to the college student just beginning to explore the topic of substance abuse. This resource belongs in libraries that serve a lower-division undergraduate or community college clientele as well as the general public." —*Choice, Association of College and Research Libraries, Jun '01*

"Recommended reference source." —*Booklist, American Library Association, Feb '01*

"Highly recommended." —*The Bookwatch, Jan '01*

"Even though there is a plethora of books on drug abuse, this volume is recommended for school, public, and college libraries." —*American Reference Books Annual, 2001*

SEE ALSO *Alcoholism Sourcebook, Substance Abuse Sourcebook*

◼

Ear, Nose & Throat Disorders Sourcebook

Basic Information about Disorders of the Ears, Nose, Sinus Cavities, Pharynx, and Larynx, Including Ear Infections, Tinnitus, Vestibular Disorders, Allergic and Non-Allergic Rhinitis, Sore Throats, Tonsillitis, and Cancers That Affect the Ears, Nose, Sinuses, and Throat

Along with Reports on Current Research Initiatives, a Glossary of Related Medical Terms, and a Directory of Sources for Further Help and Information

Edited by Karen Bellenir and Linda M. Shin. 576 pages. 1998. 0-7808-0206-3. $78.

"Overall, this sourcebook is helpful for the consumer seeking information on ENT issues. It is recommended for public libraries." —*American Reference Books Annual, 1999*

"Recommended reference source." —*Booklist, American Library Association, Dec '98*

◼

Eating Disorders Sourcebook

Basic Consumer Health Information about Eating Disorders, Including Information about Anorexia Nervosa, Bulimia Nervosa, Binge Eating, Body Dysmorphic Disorder, Pica, Laxative Abuse, and Night Eating Syndrome

Along with Information about Causes, Adverse Effects, and Treatment and Prevention Issues, and Featuring a Section on Concerns Specific to Children and Adolescents, a Glossary, and Resources for Further Help and Information

Edited by Dawn D. Matthews. 322 pages. 2001. 0-7808-0335-3. $78.

"Recommended for health science libraries that are open to the public, as well as hospital libraries. This book is a good resource for the consumer who is concerned about eating disorders." —*E-Streams, Mar '02*

"This volume is another convenient collection of excerpted articles. Recommended for school and public library patrons; lower-division undergraduates; and two-year technical program students." —*Choice, Association of College & Research Libraries, Jan '02*

"Recommended reference source." —*Booklist, American Library Association, Oct '01*

◼

Emergency Medical Services Sourcebook

Basic Consumer Health Information about Preventing, Preparing for, and Managing Emergency Situations, When and Who to Call for Help, What to Expect in the Emergency Room, the Emergency Medical Team, Patient Issues, and Current Topics in Emergency Medicine

Along with Statistical Data, a Glossary, and Sources of Additional Help and Information

Edited by Jenni Lynn Colson. 494 pages. 2002. 0-7808-0420-1. $78.

Endocrine & Metabolic Disorders Sourcebook

Basic Information for the Layperson about Pancreatic and Insulin-Related Disorders Such as Pancreatitis, Diabetes, and Hypoglycemia; Adrenal Gland Disorders Such as Cushing's Syndrome, Addison's Disease, and Congenital Adrenal Hyperplasia; Pituitary Gland Disorders Such as Growth Hormone Deficiency, Acromegaly, and Pituitary Tumors; Thyroid Disorders Such as Hypothyroidism, Graves' Disease, Hashimoto's Disease, and Goiter; Hyperparathyroidism; and Other Diseases and Syndromes of Hormone Imbalance or Metabolic Dysfunction

Along with Reports on Current Research Initiatives

Edited by Linda M. Shin. 574 pages. 1998. 0-7808-0207-1. $78.

"Omnigraphics has produced another needed resource for health information consumers."
—*American Reference Books Annual, 2000*

"Recommended reference source."
—*Booklist, American Library Association, Dec '98*

■

Environmentally Induced Disorders Sourcebook

Basic Information about Diseases and Syndromes Linked to Exposure to Pollutants and Other Substances in Outdoor and Indoor Environments Such as Lead, Asbestos, Formaldehyde, Mercury, Emissions, Noise, and More

Edited by Allan R. Cook. 620 pages. 1997. 0-7808-0083-4. $78.

"Recommended reference source."
—*Booklist, American Library Association, Sep '98*

"This book will be a useful addition to anyone's library." —*Choice Health Sciences Supplement, Association of College and Research Libraries, May '98*

". . . a good survey of numerous environmentally induced physical disorders . . . a useful addition to anyone's library."
—*Doody's Health Sciences Book Reviews, Jan '98*

". . . provide[s] introductory information from the best authorities around. Since this volume covers topics that potentially affect everyone, it will surely be one of the most frequently consulted volumes in the *Health Reference Series*." —*Rettig on Reference, Nov '97*

■

Ethnic Diseases Sourcebook

Basic Consumer Health Information for Ethnic and Racial Minority Groups in the United States, Including General Health Indicators and Behaviors, Ethnic Diseases, Genetic Testing, the Impact of Chronic Diseases, Women's Health, Mental Health Issues, and Preventive Health Care Services

Along with a Glossary and a Listing of Additional Resources

Edited by Joyce Brennfleck Shannon. 664 pages. 2001. 0-7808-0336-1. $78.

"Recommended for health sciences libraries where public health programs are a priority."
—*E-Streams, Jan '02*

"Not many books have been written on this topic to date, and the *Ethnic Diseases Sourcebook* is a strong addition to the list. It will be an important introductory resource for health consumers, students, health care personnel, and social scientists. It is recommended for public, academic, and large hospital libraries."
—*American Reference Books Annual 2002*

"Recommended reference source."
—*Booklist, American Library Association, Oct '01*

"Will prove valuable to any library seeking to maintain a current, comprehensive reference collection of health resources. . . . An excellent source of health information about genetic disorders which affect particular ethnic and racial minorities in the U.S."
—*The Bookwatch, Aug '01*

■

Family Planning Sourcebook

Basic Consumer Health Information about Planning for Pregnancy and Contraception, Including Traditional Methods, Barrier Methods, Hormonal Methods, Permanent Methods, Future Methods, Emergency Contraception, and Birth Control Choices for Women at Each Stage of Life

Along with Statistics, a Glossary, and Sources of Additional Information

Edited by Amy Marcaccio Keyzer. 520 pages. 2001. 0-7808-0379-5. $78.

"Recommended for public, health, and undergraduate libraries as part of the circulating collection."
—*E-Streams, Mar '02*

"Information is presented in an unbiased, readable manner, and the sourcebook will certainly be a necessary addition to those public and high school libraries where Internet access is restricted or otherwise problematic." —*American Reference Books Annual 2002*

"Recommended reference source."
—*Booklist, American Library Association, Oct '01*

"Will prove valuable to any library seeking to maintain a current, comprehensive reference collection of health resources. . . . Excellent reference."
—*The Bookwatch, Aug '01*

SEE ALSO Pregnancy & Birth Sourcebook

■

Fitness & Exercise Sourcebook, 1st Edition

Basic Information on Fitness and Exercise, Including Fitness Activities for Specific Age Groups, Exercise for People with Specific Medical Conditions, How to Begin a Fitness Program in Running, Walking, Swimming, Cycling, and Other Athletic Activities, and Recent Research in Fitness and Exercise

Edited by Dan R. Harris. 663 pages. 1996. 0-7808-0186-5. $78.

"A good resource for general readers." — *Choice, Association of College and Research Libraries, Nov '97*

"The perennial popularity of the topic ... make this an appealing selection for public libraries."
— *Rettig on Reference, Jun/Jul '97*

Fitness & Exercise Sourcebook, 2nd Edition

Basic Consumer Health Information about the Fundamentals of Fitness and Exercise, Including How to Begin and Maintain a Fitness Program, Fitness as a Lifestyle, the Link between Fitness and Diet, Advice for Specific Groups of People, Exercise as It Relates to Specific Medical Conditions, and Recent Research in Fitness and Exercise

Along with a Glossary of Important Terms and Resources for Additional Help and Information

Edited by Kristen M. Gledhill. 646 pages. 2001. 0-7808-0334-5. $78.

"This work is recommended for all general reference collections."
— *American Reference Books Annual 2002*

"Highly recommended for public, consumer, and school grades fourth through college."
— *E-Streams, Nov '01*

"Recommended reference source." — *Booklist, American Library Association, Oct '01*

"The information appears quite comprehensive and is considered reliable. . . . This second edition is a welcomed addition to the series."
— *Doody's Review Service, Sep '01*

"This reference is a valuable choice for those who desire a broad source of information on exercise, fitness, and chronic-disease prevention through a healthy lifestyle." — *American Medical Writers Association Journal, Fall '01*

"Will prove valuable to any library seeking to maintain a current, comprehensive reference collection of health resources. . . . Excellent reference."
— *The Bookwatch, Aug '01*

Food & Animal Borne Diseases Sourcebook

Basic Information about Diseases That Can Be Spread to Humans through the Ingestion of Contaminated Food or Water or by Contact with Infected Animals and Insects, Such as Botulism, E. Coli, Hepatitis A, Trichinosis, Lyme Disease, and Rabies

Along with Information Regarding Prevention and Treatment Methods, and Including a Special Section for International Travelers Describing Diseases Such as Cholera, Malaria, Travelers' Diarrhea, and Yellow Fever, and Offering Recommendations for Avoiding Illness

Edited by Karen Bellenir and Peter D. Dresser. 535 pages. 1995. 0-7808-0033-8. $78.

"Targeting general readers and providing them with a single, comprehensive source of information on selected topics, this book continues, with the excellent caliber of its predecessors, to catalog topical information on health matters of general interest. Readable and thorough, this valuable resource is highly recommended for all libraries."
— *Academic Library Book Review, Summer '96*

"A comprehensive collection of authoritative information." — *Emergency Medical Services, Oct '95*

Food Safety Sourcebook

Basic Consumer Health Information about the Safe Handling of Meat, Poultry, Seafood, Eggs, Fruit Juices, and Other Food Items, and Facts about Pesticides, Drinking Water, Food Safety Overseas, and the Onset, Duration, and Symptoms of Foodborne Illnesses, Including Types of Pathogenic Bacteria, Parasitic Protozoa, Worms, Viruses, and Natural Toxins

Along with the Role of the Consumer, the Food Handler, and the Government in Food Safety; a Glossary, and Resources for Additional Help and Information

Edited by Dawn D. Matthews. 339 pages. 1999. 0-7808-0326-4. $78.

"This book is recommended for public libraries and universities with home economic and food science programs." — *E-Streams, Nov '00*

"Recommended reference source."
— *Booklist, American Library Association, May '00*

"This book takes the complex issues of food safety and foodborne pathogens and presents them in an easily understood manner. [It does] an excellent job of covering a large and often confusing topic."
— *American Reference Books Annual, 2000*

Forensic Medicine Sourcebook

Basic Consumer Information for the Layperson about Forensic Medicine, Including Crime Scene Investigation, Evidence Collection and Analysis, Expert Testimony, Computer-Aided Criminal Identification, Digital Imaging in the Courtroom, DNA Profiling, Accident Reconstruction, Autopsies, Ballistics, Drugs and Explosives Detection, Latent Fingerprints, Product Tampering, and Questioned Document Examination

Along with Statistical Data, a Glossary of Forensics Terminology, and Listings of Sources for Further Help and Information

Edited by Annemarie S. Muth. 574 pages. 1999. 0-7808-0232-2. $78.

"Given the expected widespread interest in its content and its easy to read style, this book is recommended for most public and all college and university libraries."
— *E-Streams, Feb '01*

"Recommended for public libraries."
— *Reference & User Services Quarterly, American Library Association, Spring 2000*

"Recommended reference source."
—*Booklist, American Library Association, Feb '00*

"A wealth of information, useful statistics, references are up-to-date and extremely complete. This wonderful collection of data will help students who are interested in a career in any type of forensic field. It is a great resource for attorneys who need information about types of expert witnesses needed in a particular case. It also offers useful information for fiction and nonfiction writers whose work involves a crime. A fascinating compilation. All levels." —*Choice, Association of College and Research Libraries, Jan 2000*

"There are several items that make this book attractive to consumers who are seeking certain forensic data. . . . This is a useful current source for those seeking general forensic medical answers."
—*American Reference Books Annual, 2000*

Gastrointestinal Diseases & Disorders Sourcebook

Basic Information about Gastroesophageal Reflux Disease (Heartburn), Ulcers, Diverticulosis, Irritable Bowel Syndrome, Crohn's Disease, Ulcerative Colitis, Diarrhea, Constipation, Lactose Intolerance, Hemorrhoids, Hepatitis, Cirrhosis, and Other Digestive Problems, Featuring Statistics, Descriptions of Symptoms, and Current Treatment Methods of Interest for Persons Living with Upper and Lower Gastrointestinal Maladies

Edited by Linda M. Ross. 413 pages. 1996. 0-7808-0078-8. $78.

". . . very readable form. The successful editorial work that brought this material together into a useful and understandable reference makes accessible to all readers information that can help them more effectively understand and obtain help for digestive tract problems."
—*Choice, Association of College & Research Libraries, Feb '97*

SEE ALSO *Diet & Nutrition Sourcebook, 1st and 2nd Editions, Digestive Diseases & Disorders*

Genetic Disorders Sourcebook, 1st Edition

Basic Information about Heritable Diseases and Disorders Such as Down Syndrome, PKU, Hemophilia, Von Willebrand Disease, Gaucher Disease, Tay-Sachs Disease, and Sickle-Cell Disease, Along with Information about Genetic Screening, Gene Therapy, Home Care, and Including Source Listings for Further Help and Information on More Than 300 Disorders

Edited by Karen Bellenir. 642 pages. 1996. 0-7808-0034-6. $78.

"Recommended for undergraduate libraries or libraries that serve the public."
—*Science & Technology Libraries, Vol. 18, No. 1, '99*

"Provides essential medical information to both the general public and those diagnosed with a serious or fatal genetic disease or disorder." —*Choice, Association of College and Research Libraries, Jan '97*

"Geared toward the lay public. It would be well placed in all public libraries and in those hospital and medical libraries in which access to genetic references is limited." —*Doody's Health Sciences Book Review, Oct '96*

Genetic Disorders Sourcebook, 2nd Edition

Basic Consumer Health Information about Hereditary Diseases and Disorders, Including Cystic Fibrosis, Down Syndrome, Hemophilia, Huntington's Disease, Sickle Cell Anemia, and More; Facts about Genes, Gene Research and Therapy, Genetic Screening, Ethics of Gene Testing, Genetic Counseling, and Advice on Coping and Caring

Along with a Glossary of Genetic Terminology and a Resource List for Help, Support, and Further Information

Edited by Kathy Massimini. 768 pages. 2001. 0-7808-0241-1. $78.

"Recommended for public libraries and medical and hospital libraries with consumer health collections."
—*E-Streams, May '01*

"Recommended reference source."
—*Booklist, American Library Association, Apr '01*

"Important pick for college-level health reference libraries." —*The Bookwatch, Mar '01*

Head Trauma Sourcebook

Basic Information for the Layperson about Open-Head and Closed-Head Injuries, Treatment Advances, Recovery, and Rehabilitation

Along with Reports on Current Research Initiatives

Edited by Karen Bellenir. 414 pages. 1997. 0-7808-0208-X. $78.

Headache Sourcebook

Basic Consumer Health Information about Migraine, Tension, Cluster, Rebound and Other Types of Headaches, with Facts about the Cause and Prevention of Headaches, the Effects of Stress and the Environment, Headaches during Pregnancy and Menopause, and Childhood Headaches

Along with a Glossary and Other Resources for Additional Help and Information

Edited by Dawn D. Matthews. 362 pages. 2002. 0-7808-0337-X. $78.

592

Health Insurance Sourcebook

Basic Information about Managed Care Organizations, Traditional Fee-for-Service Insurance, Insurance Portability and Pre-Existing Conditions Clauses, Medicare, Medicaid, Social Security, and Military Health Care

Along with Information about Insurance Fraud

Edited by Wendy Wilcox. 530 pages. 1997. 0-7808-0222-5. $78.

"Particularly useful because it brings much of this information together in one volume. This book will be a handy reference source in the health sciences library, hospital library, college and university library, and medium to large public library."
—Medical Reference Services Quarterly, Fall '98

Awarded "Books of the Year Award"
—American Journal of Nursing, 1997

"The layout of the book is particularly helpful as it provides easy access to reference material. A most useful addition to the vast amount of information about health insurance. The use of data from U.S. government agencies is most commendable. Useful in a library or learning center for healthcare professional students."
—Doody's Health Sciences Book Reviews, Nov '97

■

Health Reference Series Cumulative Index 1999

A Comprehensive Index to the Individual Volumes of the Health Reference Series, Including a Subject Index, Name Index, Organization Index, and Publication Index

Along with a Master List of Acronyms and Abbreviations

Edited by Edward J. Prucha, Anne Holmes, and Robert Rudnick. 990 pages. 2000. 0-7808-0382-5. $78.

"This volume will be most helpful in libraries that have a relatively complete collection of the Health Reference Series." —American Reference Books Annual, 2001

"Essential for collections that hold any of the numerous Health Reference Series titles."
—Choice, Association of College and Research Libraries, Nov '00

■

Healthy Aging Sourcebook

Basic Consumer Health Information about Maintaining Health through the Aging Process, Including Advice on Nutrition, Exercise, and Sleep, Help in Making Decisions about Midlife Issues and Retirement, and Guidance Concerning Practical and Informed Choices in Health Consumerism

Along with Data Concerning the Theories of Aging, Different Experiences in Aging by Minority Groups, and Facts about Aging Now and Aging in the Future; and Featuring a Glossary, a Guide to Consumer Help, Additional Suggested Reading, and Practical Resource Directory

Edited by Jenifer Swanson. 536 pages. 1999. 0-7808-0390-6. $78.

"Recommended reference source."
—Booklist, American Library Association, Feb '00

SEE ALSO Physical & Mental Issues in Aging Sourcebook

■

Healthy Heart Sourcebook for Women

Basic Consumer Health Information about Cardiac Issues Specific to Women, Including Facts about Major Risk Factors and Prevention, Treatment and Control Strategies, and Important Dietary Issues

Along with a Special Section Regarding the Pros and Cons of Hormone Replacement Therapy and Its Impact on Heart Health, and Additional Help, Including Recipes, a Glossary, and a Directory of Resources

Edited by Dawn D. Matthews. 336 pages. 2000. 0-7808-0329-9. $78.

"A good reference source and recommended for all public, academic, medical, and hospital libraries."
—Medical Reference Services Quarterly, Summer '01

"Because of the lack of information specific to women on this topic, this book is recommended for public libraries and consumer libraries."
—American Reference Books Annual, 2001

"Contains very important information about coronary artery disease that all women should know. The information is current and presented in an easy-to-read format. The book will make a good addition to any library." —American Medical Writers Association Journal, Summer '00

"Important, basic reference."
—Reviewer's Bookwatch, Jul '00

SEE ALSO Cardiovascular Diseases & Disorders Sourcebook, 1st Edition, Heart Diseases & Disorders Sourcebook, 2nd Edition, Women's Health Concerns Sourcebook

■

Heart Diseases & Disorders Sourcebook, 2nd Edition

Basic Consumer Health Information about Heart Attacks, Angina, Rhythm Disorders, Heart Failure, Valve Disease, Congenital Heart Disorders, and More, Including Descriptions of Surgical Procedures and Other Interventions, Medications, Cardiac Rehabilitation, Risk Identification, and Prevention Tips

Along with Statistical Data, Reports on Current Research Initiatives, a Glossary of Cardiovascular Terms, and Resource Directory

Edited by Karen Bellenir. 612 pages. 2000. 0-7808-0238-1. $78.

"This work stands out as an imminently accessible resource for the general public. It is recommended for the reference and circulating shelves of school, public, and academic libraries."
—American Reference Books Annual, 2001

"Recommended reference source."
—Booklist, American Library Association, Dec '00

"Provides comprehensive coverage of matters related to the heart. This title is recommended for health sciences and public libraries with consumer health collections."
— E-Streams, Oct '00

SEE ALSO *Cardiovascular Diseases & Disorders Sourcebook, 1st Edition; Healthy Heart Sourcebook for Women*

Household Safety Sourcebook

Basic Consumer Health Information about Household Safety, Including Information about Poisons, Chemicals, Fire, and Water Hazards in the Home

Along with Advice about the Safe Use of Home Maintenance Equipment, Choosing Toys and Nursery Furniture, Holiday and Recreation Safety, a Glossary, and Resources for Further Help and Information

Edited by Dawn D. Matthews. 606 pages. 2002. 0-7808-0338-8. $78.

Immune System Disorders Sourcebook

Basic Information about Lupus, Multiple Sclerosis, Guillain-Barré Syndrome, Chronic Granulomatous Disease, and More

Along with Statistical and Demographic Data and Reports on Current Research Initiatives

Edited by Allan R. Cook. 608 pages. 1997. 0-7808-0209-8. $78.

Infant & Toddler Health Sourcebook

Basic Consumer Health Information about the Physical and Mental Development of Newborns, Infants, and Toddlers, Including Neonatal Concerns, Nutrition Recommendations, Immunization Schedules, Common Pediatric Disorders, Assessments and Milestones, Safety Tips, and Advice for Parents and Other Caregivers

Along with a Glossary of Terms and Resource Listings for Additional Help

Edited by Jenifer Swanson. 585 pages. 2000. 0-7808-0246-2. $78.

"As a reference for the general public, this would be useful in any library." — E-Streams, May '01

"Recommended reference source."
— Booklist, American Library Association, Feb '01

"This is a good source for general use."
—American Reference Books Annual, 2001

Injury & Trauma Sourcebook

Basic Consumer Health Information about the Impact of Injury, the Diagnosis and Treatment of Common and Traumatic Injuries, Emergency Care, and Specific Injuries Related to Home, Community, Workplace, Transportation, and Recreation

Along with Guidelines for Injury Prevention, a Glossary, and a Directory of Additional Resources

Edited by Joyce Brennfleck Shannon. 696 pages. 2002. 0-7808-0421-X. $78.

Kidney & Urinary Tract Diseases & Disorders Sourcebook

Basic Information about Kidney Stones, Urinary Incontinence, Bladder Disease, End Stage Renal Disease, Dialysis, and More

Along with Statistical and Demographic Data and Reports on Current Research Initiatives

Edited by Linda M. Ross. 602 pages. 1997. 0-7808-0079-6. $78.

Learning Disabilities Sourcebook

Basic Information about Disorders Such as Dyslexia, Visual and Auditory Processing Deficits, Attention Deficit/Hyperactivity Disorder, and Autism

Along with Statistical and Demographic Data, Reports on Current Research Initiatives, an Explanation of the Assessment Process, and a Special Section for Adults with Learning Disabilities

Edited by Linda M. Shin. 579 pages. 1998. 0-7808-0210-1. $78.

Named "Outstanding Reference Book of 1999."
— New York Public Library, Feb 2000

"An excellent candidate for inclusion in a public library reference section. It's a great source of information. Teachers will also find the book useful. Definitely worth reading."
— Journal of Adolescent & Adult Literacy, Feb 2000

"Readable . . . provides a solid base of information regarding successful techniques used with individuals who have learning disabilities, as well as practical suggestions for educators and family members. Clear language, concise descriptions, and pertinent information for contacting multiple resources add to the strength of this book as a useful tool." — Choice, Association of College and Research Libraries, Feb '99

"Recommended reference source."
— Booklist, American Library Association, Sep '98

"A useful resource for libraries and for those who don't have the time to identify and locate the individual publications." — Disability Resources Monthly, Sep '98

Liver Disorders Sourcebook

Basic Consumer Health Information about the Liver and How It Works; Liver Diseases, Including Cancer, Cirrhosis, Hepatitis, and Toxic and Drug Related Diseases; Tips for Maintaining a Healthy Liver; Laboratory Tests, Radiology Tests, and Facts about Liver Transplantation

Along with a Section on Support Groups, a Glossary, and Resource Listings

Edited by Joyce Brennfleck Shannon. 591 pages. 2000. 0-7808-0383-3. $78.

"A valuable resource."
—American Reference Books Annual, 2001

"This title is recommended for health sciences and public libraries with consumer health collections."
—E-Streams, Oct '00

"Recommended reference source."
—Booklist, American Library Association, Jun '00

Lung Disorders Sourcebook

Basic Consumer Health Information about Emphysema, Pneumonia, Tuberculosis, Asthma, Cystic Fibrosis, and Other Lung Disorders, Including Facts about Diagnostic Procedures, Treatment Strategies, Disease Prevention Efforts, and Such Risk Factors as Smoking, Air Pollution, and Exposure to Asbestos, Radon, and Other Agents

Along with a Glossary and Resources for Additional Help and Information

Edited by Dawn D. Matthews. 678 pages. 2002. 0-7808-0339-6. $78.

Medical Tests Sourcebook

Basic Consumer Health Information about Medical Tests, Including Periodic Health Exams, General Screening Tests, Tests You Can Do at Home, Findings of the U.S. Preventive Services Task Force, X-ray and Radiology Tests, Electrical Tests, Tests of Blood and Other Body Fluids and Tissues, Scope Tests, Lung Tests, Genetic Tests, Pregnancy Tests, Newborn Screening Tests, Sexually Transmitted Disease Tests, and Computer Aided Diagnoses

Along with a Section on Paying for Medical Tests, a Glossary, and Resource Listings

Edited by Joyce Brennfleck Shannon. 691 pages. 1999. 0-7808-0243-8. $78.

"Recommended for hospital and health sciences libraries with consumer health collections."
—E-Streams, Mar '00

"This is an overall excellent reference with a wealth of general knowledge that may aid those who are reluctant to get vital tests performed."
—Today's Librarian, Jan 2000

"A valuable reference guide."
—American Reference Books Annual, 2000

Men's Health Concerns Sourcebook

Basic Information about Health Issues That Affect Men, Featuring Facts about the Top Causes of Death in Men, Including Heart Disease, Stroke, Cancers, Prostate Disorders, Chronic Obstructive Pulmonary Disease, Pneumonia and Influenza, Human Immunodeficiency Virus and Acquired Immune Deficiency Syndrome, Diabetes Mellitus, Stress, Suicide, Accidents and Homicides; and Facts about Common Concerns for Men, Including Impotence, Contraception, Circumcision, Sleep Disorders, Snoring, Hair Loss, Diet, Nutrition, Exercise, Kidney and Urological Disorders, and Backaches

Edited by Allan R. Cook. 738 pages. 1998. 0-7808-0212-8. $78.

"This comprehensive resource and the series are highly recommended."
—American Reference Books Annual, 2000

"Recommended reference source."
—Booklist, American Library Association, Dec '98

Mental Health Disorders Sourcebook, 1st Edition

Basic Information about Schizophrenia, Depression, Bipolar Disorder, Panic Disorder, Obsessive-Compulsive Disorder, Phobias and Other Anxiety Disorders, Paranoia and Other Personality Disorders, Eating Disorders, and Sleep Disorders

Along with Information about Treatment and Therapies

Edited by Karen Bellenir. 548 pages. 1995. 0-7808-0040-0. $78.

"This is an excellent new book . . . written in easy-to-understand language."
—Booklist Health Sciences Supplement, American Library Association, Oct '97

". . . useful for public and academic libraries and consumer health collections."
—Medical Reference Services Quarterly, Spring '97

"The great strengths of the book are its readability and its inclusion of places to find more information. Especially recommended." *—Reference Quarterly, American Library Association, Winter '96*

". . . a good resource for a consumer health library."
—Bulletin of the Medical Library Association, Oct '96

"The information is data-based and couched in brief, concise language that avoids jargon. . . . a useful reference source." *—Readings, Sep '96*

"The text is well organized and adequately written for its target audience." *—Choice, Association of College and Research Libraries, Jun '96*

". . . provides information on a wide range of mental disorders, presented in nontechnical language."
—Exceptional Child Education Resources, Spring '96

"Recommended for public and academic libraries."
—Reference Book Review, 1996

Mental Health Disorders Sourcebook, 2nd Edition

Basic Consumer Health Information about Anxiety Disorders, Depression and Other Mood Disorders, Eating Disorders, Personality Disorders, Schizophrenia, and More, Including Disease Descriptions, Treatment Options, and Reports on Current Research Initiatives

Along with Statistical Data, Tips for Maintaining Mental Health, a Glossary, and Directory of Sources for Additional Help and Information

Edited by Karen Bellenir. 605 pages. 2000. 0-7808-0240-3. $78.

"Well organized and well written."
—*American Reference Books Annual, 2001*

"Recommended reference source."
—*Booklist, American Library Association, Jun '00*

∎

Mental Retardation Sourcebook

Basic Consumer Health Information about Mental Retardation and Its Causes, Including Down Syndrome, Fetal Alcohol Syndrome, Fragile X Syndrome, Genetic Conditions, Injury, and Environmental Sources

Along with Preventive Strategies, Parenting Issues, Educational Implications, Health Care Needs, Employment and Economic Matters, Legal Issues, a Glossary, and a Resource Listing for Additional Help and Information

Edited by Joyce Brennfleck Shannon. 642 pages. 2000. 0-7808-0377-9. $78.

"Public libraries will find the book useful for reference and as a beginning research point for students, parents, and caregivers."
—*American Reference Books Annual, 2001*

"The strength of this work is that it compiles many basic fact sheets and addresses for further information in one volume. It is intended and suitable for the general public. This sourcebook is relevant to any collection providing health information to the general public."
—*E-Streams, Nov '00*

"From preventing retardation to parenting and family challenges, this covers health, social and legal issues and will prove an invaluable overview."
—*Reviewer's Bookwatch, Jul '00*

∎

Obesity Sourcebook

Basic Consumer Health Information about Diseases and Other Problems Associated with Obesity, and Including Facts about Risk Factors, Prevention Issues, and Management Approaches

Along with Statistical and Demographic Data, Information about Special Populations, Research Updates, a Glossary, and Source Listings for Further Help and Information

Edited by Wilma Caldwell and Chad T. Kimball. 376 pages. 2001. 0-7808-0333-7. $78.

"The book synthesizes the reliable medical literature on obesity into one easy-to-read and useful resource for the general public."
—*American Reference Books Annual 2002*

"This is a very useful resource book for the lay public."
—*Doody's Review Service, Nov '01*

"Well suited for the health reference collection of a public library or an academic health science library that serves the general population." —*E-Streams, Sep '01*

"Recommended reference source."
—*Booklist, American Library Association, Apr '01*

" Recommended pick both for specialty health library collections and any general consumer health reference collection." —*The Bookwatch, Apr '01*

∎

Ophthalmic Disorders Sourcebook

Basic Information about Glaucoma, Cataracts, Macular Degeneration, Strabismus, Refractive Disorders, and More

Along with Statistical and Demographic Data and Reports on Current Research Initiatives

Edited by Linda M. Ross. 631 pages. 1996. 0-7808-0081-8. $78.

∎

Oral Health Sourcebook

Basic Information about Diseases and Conditions Affecting Oral Health, Including Cavities, Gum Disease, Dry Mouth, Oral Cancers, Fever Blisters, Canker Sores, Oral Thrush, Bad Breath, Temporomandibular Disorders, and other Craniofacial Syndromes

Along with Statistical Data on the Oral Health of Americans, Oral Hygiene, Emergency First Aid, Information on Treatment Procedures and Methods of Replacing Lost Teeth

Edited by Allan R. Cook. 558 pages. 1997. 0-7808-0082-6. $78.

"Unique source which will fill a gap in dental sources for patients and the lay public. A valuable reference tool even in a library with thousands of books on dentistry. Comprehensive, clear, inexpensive, and easy to read and use. It fills an enormous gap in the health care literature." —*Reference and User Services Quarterly, American Library Association, Summer '98*

"Recommended reference source."
—*Booklist, American Library Association, Dec '97*

∎

Osteoporosis Sourcebook

Basic Consumer Health Information about Primary and Secondary Osteoporosis and Juvenile Osteoporosis and Related Conditions, Including Fibrous Dysplasia, Gaucher Disease, Hyperthyroidism, Hypophosphatasia, Myeloma, Osteopetrosis, Osteogenesis Imperfecta, and Paget's Disease

Along with Information about Risk Factors, Treatments, Traditional and Non-Traditional Pain Management, a Glossary of Related Terms, and a Directory of Resources

Edited by Allan R. Cook. 584 pages. 2001. 0-7808-0239-X. $78.

"This would be a book to be kept in a staff or patient library. The targeted audience is the layperson, but the therapist who needs a quick bit of information on a particular topic will also find the book useful."
—Physical Therapy, Jan '02

"This resource is recommended as a great reference source for public, health, and academic libraries, and is another triumph for the editors of Omnigraphics."
—American Reference Books Annual 2002

"Recommended for all public libraries and general health collections, especially those supporting patient education or consumer health programs."
—E-Streams, Nov '01

"Will prove valuable to any library seeking to maintain a current, comprehensive reference collection of health resources. . . . From prevention to treatment and associated conditions, this provides an excellent survey."
—The Bookwatch, Aug '01

"Recommended reference source."
—Booklist, American Library Association, July '01

SEE ALSO Women's Health Concerns Sourcebook

Pain Sourcebook, 1st Edition

Basic Information about Specific Forms of Acute and Chronic Pain, Including Headaches, Back Pain, Muscular Pain, Neuralgia, Surgical Pain, and Cancer Pain

Along with Pain Relief Options Such as Analgesics, Narcotics, Nerve Blocks, Transcutaneous Nerve Stimulation, and Alternative Forms of Pain Control, Including Biofeedback, Imaging, Behavior Modification, and Relaxation Techniques

Edited by Allan R. Cook. 667 pages. 1997. 0-7808-0213-6. $78.

"The text is readable, easily understood, and well indexed. This excellent volume belongs in all patient education libraries, consumer health sections of public libraries, and many personal collections."
—American Reference Books Annual, 1999

"A beneficial reference." —Booklist Health Sciences Supplement, American Library Association, Oct '98

"The information is basic in terms of scholarship and is appropriate for general readers. Written in journalistic style . . . intended for non-professionals. Quite thorough in its coverage of different pain conditions and summarizes the latest clinical information regarding pain treatment." —Choice, Association of College and Research Libraries, Jun '98

"Recommended reference source."
—Booklist, American Library Association, Mar '98

Pain Sourcebook, 2nd Edition

Basic Consumer Health Information about Specific Forms of Acute and Chronic Pain, Including Muscle and Skeletal Pain, Nerve Pain, Cancer Pain, and Disorders Characterized by Pain, Such as Fibromyalgia, Shingles, Angina, Arthritis, and Headaches

Along with Information about Pain Medications and Management Techniques, Complementary and Alternative Pain Relief Options, Tips for People Living with Chronic Pain, a Glossary, and a Directory of Sources for Further Information

Edited by Karen Bellenir. 670 pages. 2002. 0-7808-0612-3. $78.

Pediatric Cancer Sourcebook

Basic Consumer Health Information about Leukemias, Brain Tumors, Sarcomas, Lymphomas, and Other Cancers in Infants, Children, and Adolescents, Including Descriptions of Cancers, Treatments, and Coping Strategies

Along with Suggestions for Parents, Caregivers, and Concerned Relatives, a Glossary of Cancer Terms, and Resource Listings

Edited by Edward J. Prucha. 587 pages. 1999. 0-7808-0245-4. $78.

"An excellent source of information. Recommended for public, hospital, and health science libraries with consumer health collections." —E-Streams, Jun '00

"Recommended reference source."
—Booklist, American Library Association, Feb '00

"A valuable addition to all libraries specializing in health services and many public libraries."
—American Reference Books Annual, 2000

Physical & Mental Issues in Aging Sourcebook

Basic Consumer Health Information on Physical and Mental Disorders Associated with the Aging Process, Including Concerns about Cardiovascular Disease, Pulmonary Disease, Oral Health, Digestive Disorders, Musculoskeletal and Skin Disorders, Metabolic Changes, Sexual and Reproductive Issues, and Changes in Vision, Hearing, and Other Senses

Along with Data about Longevity and Causes of Death, Information on Acute and Chronic Pain, Descriptions of Mental Concerns, a Glossary of Terms, and Resource Listings for Additional Help

Edited by Jenifer Swanson. 660 pages. 1999. 0-7808-0233-0. $78.

"This is a treasure of health information for the layperson." — Choice Health Sciences Supplement, Association of College & Research Libraries, May 2000

"Recommended for public libraries."
—American Reference Books Annual, 2000

"Recommended reference source."
—Booklist, American Library Association, Oct '99

SEE ALSO Healthy Aging Sourcebook

597

Podiatry Sourcebook

Basic Consumer Health Information about Foot Conditions, Diseases, and Injuries, Including Bunions, Corns, Calluses, Athlete's Foot, Plantar Warts, Hammertoes and Clawtoes, Clubfoot, Heel Pain, Gout, and More

Along with Facts about Foot Care, Disease Prevention, Foot Safety, Choosing a Foot Care Specialist, a Glossary of Terms, and Resource Listings for Additional Information

Edited by M. Lisa Weatherford. 380 pages. 2001. 0-7808-0215-2. $78.

"Recommended reference source."
— *Booklist, American Library Association, Feb '02*

"There is a lot of information presented here on a topic that is usually only covered sparingly in most larger comprehensive medical encyclopedias."
— *American Reference Books Annual 2002*

■

Pregnancy & Birth Sourcebook

Basic Information about Planning for Pregnancy, Maternal Health, Fetal Growth and Development, Labor and Delivery, Postpartum and Perinatal Care, Pregnancy in Mothers with Special Concerns, and Disorders of Pregnancy, Including Genetic Counseling, Nutrition and Exercise, Obstetrical Tests, Pregnancy Discomfort, Multiple Births, Cesarean Sections, Medical Testing of Newborns, Breastfeeding, Gestational Diabetes, and Ectopic Pregnancy

Edited by Heather E. Aldred. 737 pages. 1997. 0-7808-0216-0. $78.

"A well-organized handbook. Recommended."
— *Choice, Association of College and Research Libraries, Apr '98*

"Recommended reference source."
— *Booklist, American Library Association, Mar '98*

"Recommended for public libraries."
— *American Reference Books Annual, 1998*

SEE ALSO *Congenital Disorders Sourcebook, Family Planning Sourcebook*

■

Prostate Cancer Sourcebook

Basic Consumer Health Information about Prostate Cancer, Including Information about the Associated Risk Factors, Detection, Diagnosis, and Treatment of Prostate Cancer

Along with Information on Non-Malignant Prostate Conditions, and Featuring a Section Listing Support and Treatment Centers and a Glossary of Related Terms

Edited by Dawn D. Matthews. 358 pages. 2001. 0-7808-0324-8. $78.

"Recommended reference source."
— *Booklist, American Library Association, Jan '02*

"A valuable resource for health care consumers seeking information on the subject....All text is written in a clear, easy-to-understand language that avoids technical jargon. Any library that collects consumer health resources would strengthen their collection with the addition of the *Prostate Cancer Sourcebook."*
— *American Reference Books Annual 2002*

■

Public Health Sourcebook

Basic Information about Government Health Agencies, Including National Health Statistics and Trends, Healthy People 2000 Program Goals and Objectives, the Centers for Disease Control and Prevention, the Food and Drug Administration, and the National Institutes of Health

Along with Full Contact Information for Each Agency

Edited by Wendy Wilcox. 698 pages. 1998. 0-7808-0220-9. $78.

"Recommended reference source."
— *Booklist, American Library Association, Sep '98*

"This consumer guide provides welcome assistance in navigating the maze of federal health agencies and their data on public health concerns."
— *SciTech Book News, Sep '98*

■

Reconstructive & Cosmetic Surgery Sourcebook

Basic Consumer Health Information on Cosmetic and Reconstructive Plastic Surgery, Including Statistical Information about Different Surgical Procedures, Things to Consider Prior to Surgery, Plastic Surgery Techniques and Tools, Emotional and Psychological Considerations, and Procedure-Specific Information

Along with a Glossary of Terms and a Listing of Resources for Additional Help and Information

Edited by M. Lisa Weatherford. 374 pages. 2001. 0-7808-0214-4. $78.

"An excellent reference that addresses cosmetic and medically necessary reconstructive surgeries. . . . The style of the prose is calm and reassuring, discussing the many positive outcomes now available due to advances in surgical techniques."
— *American Reference Books Annual 2002*

"Recommended for health science libraries that are open to the public, as well as hospital libraries that are open to the patients. This book is a good resource for the consumer interested in plastic surgery."
— *E-Streams, Dec '01*

"Recommended reference source."
— *Booklist, American Library Association, July '01*

■

Rehabilitation Sourcebook

Basic Consumer Health Information about Rehabilitation for People Recovering from Heart Surgery, Spinal Cord Injury, Stroke, Orthopedic Impairments, Amputation, Pulmonary Impairments, Traumatic Injury, and More, Including Physical Therapy, Occupa-

tional Therapy, Speech/ Language Therapy, Massage Therapy, Dance Therapy, Art Therapy, and Recreational Therapy

Along with Information on Assistive and Adaptive Devices, a Glossary, and Resources for Additional Help and Information

Edited by Dawn D. Matthews. 531 pages. 1999. 0-7808-0236-5. $78.

"This is an excellent resource for public library reference and health collections."
— *American Reference Books Annual, 2001*

"Recommended reference source."
— *Booklist, American Library Association, May '00*

Respiratory Diseases & Disorders Sourcebook

Basic Information about Respiratory Diseases and Disorders, Including Asthma, Cystic Fibrosis, Pneumonia, the Common Cold, Influenza, and Others, Featuring Facts about the Respiratory System, Statistical and Demographic Data, Treatments, Self-Help Management Suggestions, and Current Research Initiatives

Edited by Allan R. Cook and Peter D. Dresser. 771 pages. 1995. 0-7808-0037-0. $78.

"Designed for the layperson and for patients and their families coping with respiratory illness. . . . an extensive array of information on diagnosis, treatment, management, and prevention of respiratory illnesses for the general reader." — *Choice, Association of College and Research Libraries, Jun '96*

"A highly recommended text for all collections. It is a comforting reminder of the power of knowledge that good books carry between their covers."
— *Academic Library Book Review, Spring '96*

"A comprehensive collection of authoritative information presented in a nontechnical, humanitarian style for patients, families, and caregivers."
— *Association of Operating Room Nurses, Sep/Oct '95*

Sexually Transmitted Diseases Sourcebook, 1st Edition

Basic Information about Herpes, Chlamydia, Gonorrhea, Hepatitis, Nongonoccocal Urethritis, Pelvic Inflammatory Disease, Syphilis, AIDS, and More

Along with Current Data on Treatments and Preventions

Edited by Linda M. Ross. 550 pages. 1997. 0-7808-0217-9. $78.

Sexually Transmitted Diseases Sourcebook, 2nd Edition

Basic Consumer Health Information about Sexually Transmitted Diseases, Including Information on the Diagnosis and Treatment of Chlamydia, Gonorrhea, Hepatitis, Herpes, HIV, Mononucleosis, Syphilis, and Others

Along with Information on Prevention, Such as Condom Use, Vaccines, and STD Education; And Featuring a Section on Issues Related to Youth and Adolescents, a Glossary, and Resources for Additional Help and Information

Edited by Dawn D. Matthews. 538 pages. 2001. 0-7808-0249-7. $78.

"Recommended for consumer health collections in public libraries, and secondary school and community college libraries."
— *American Reference Books Annual 2002*

"Every school and public library should have a copy of this comprehensive and user-friendly reference book."
— *Choice, Association of College & Research Libraries, Sep '01*

"This is a highly recommended book. This is an especially important book for all school and public libraries." — *AIDS Book Review Journal, Jul-Aug '01*

"Recommended reference source."
— *Booklist, American Library Association, Apr '01*

"Recommended pick both for specialty health library collections and any general consumer health reference collection." — *The Bookwatch, Apr '01*

Skin Disorders Sourcebook

Basic Information about Common Skin and Scalp Conditions Caused by Aging, Allergies, Immune Reactions, Sun Exposure, Infectious Organisms, Parasites, Cosmetics, and Skin Traumas, Including Abrasions, Cuts, and Pressure Sores

Along with Information on Prevention and Treatment

Edited by Allan R. Cook. 647 pages. 1997. 0-7808-0080-X. $78.

". . . comprehensive, easily read reference book."
— *Doody's Health Sciences Book Reviews, Oct '97*

SEE ALSO Burns Sourcebook

Sleep Disorders Sourcebook

Basic Consumer Health Information about Sleep and Its Disorders, Including Insomnia, Sleepwalking, Sleep Apnea, Restless Leg Syndrome, and Narcolepsy

Along with Data about Shiftwork and Its Effects, Information on the Societal Costs of Sleep Deprivation, Descriptions of Treatment Options, a Glossary of Terms, and Resource Listings for Additional Help

Edited by Jenifer Swanson. 439 pages. 1998. 0-7808-0234-9. $78.

"This text will complement any home or medical library. It is user-friendly and ideal for the adult reader."
—*American Reference Books Annual, 2000*

"A useful resource that provides accurate, relevant, and accessible information on sleep to the general public. Health care providers who deal with sleep disorders patients may also find it helpful in being prepared to answer some of the questions patients ask."
— *Respiratory Care, Jul '99*

"Recommended reference source."
— *Booklist, American Library Association, Feb '99*

Sports Injuries Sourcebook, First Edition

Basic Consumer Health Information about Common Sports Injuries, Prevention of Injury in Specific Sports, Tips for Training, and Rehabilitation from Injury

Along with Information about Special Concerns for Children, Young Girls in Athletic Training Programs, Senior Athletes, and Women Athletes, and a Directory of Resources for Further Help and Information

Edited by Heather E. Aldred. 624 pages. 1999. 0-7808-0218-7. $78.

"While this easy-to-read book is recommended for all libraries, it should prove to be especially useful for public, high school, and academic libraries; certainly it should be on the bookshelf of every school gymnasium."
— *E-Streams, Mar '00*

"Public libraries and undergraduate academic libraries will find this book useful for its nontechnical language."
—*American Reference Books Annual, 2000*

Sports Injuries Sourcebook, Second Edition

Basic Consumer Health Information about the Diagnosis, Treatment, and Rehabilitation of Common Sports-Related Injuries in Children and Adults

Along with Suggestions for Conditioning and Training, Information and Prevention Tips for Injuries Frequently Associated with Specific Sports and Special Populations, a Glossary, and a Directory of Additional Resources

Edited by Joyce Brennfleck Shannon. 614 pages. 2002. 0-7808-0604-2. $78.

Stress-Related Disorders Sourcebook

Basic Consumer Health Information about Stress and Stress-Related Disorders, Including Stress Origins and Signals, Environmental Stress at Work and Home, Mental and Emotional Stress Associated with Depression, Post-Traumatic Stress Disorder, Panic Disorder, Suicide, and the Physical Effects of Stress on the Cardiovascular, Immune, and Nervous Systems

Along with Stress Management Techniques, a Glossary, and a Listing of Additional Resources

Edited by Joyce Brennfleck Shannon. 610 pages. 2002. 0-7808-0560-7. $78.

Substance Abuse Sourcebook

Basic Health-Related Information about the Abuse of Legal and Illegal Substances Such as Alcohol, Tobacco, Prescription Drugs, Marijuana, Cocaine, and Heroin; and Including Facts about Substance Abuse Prevention Strategies, Intervention Methods, Treatment and Recovery Programs, and a Section Addressing the Special Problems Related to Substance Abuse during Pregnancy

Edited by Karen Bellenir. 573 pages. 1996. 0-7808-0038-9. $78.

"A valuable addition to any health reference section. Highly recommended."
— *The Book Report, Mar/Apr '97*

". . . a comprehensive collection of substance abuse information that's both highly readable and compact. Families and caregivers of substance abusers will find the information enlightening and helpful, while teachers, social workers and journalists should benefit from the concise format. Recommended."
— *Drug Abuse Update, Winter '96/'97*

SEE ALSO Alcoholism Sourcebook, Drug Abuse Sourcebook

Surgery Sourcebook

Basic Consumer Health Information about Inpatient and Outpatient Surgeries, Including Cardiac, Vascular, Orthopedic, Ocular, Reconstructive, Cosmetic, Gynecologic, and Ear, Nose, and Throat Procedures and More

Along with Information about Operating Room Policies and Instruments, Laser Surgery Techniques, Hospital Errors, Statistical Data, a Glossary, and Listings of Sources for Further Help and Information

Edited by Annemarie S. Muth and Karen Bellenir. 596 pages. 2002. 0-7808-0380-9. $78.

Transplantation Sourcebook

Basic Consumer Health Information about Organ and Tissue Transplantation, Including Physical and Financial Preparations, Procedures and Issues Relating to Specific Solid Organ and Tissue Transplants, Rehabilitation, Pediatric Transplant Information, the Future of Transplantation, and Organ and Tissue Donation

Along with a Glossary and Listings of Additional Resources

Edited by Joyce Brennfleck Shannon. 628 pages. 2002. 0-7808-0322-1. $78.

Traveler's Health Sourcebook

Basic Consumer Health Information for Travelers, Including Physical and Medical Preparations, Transportation Health and Safety, Essential Information about Food and Water, Sun Exposure, Insect and Snake Bites, Camping and Wilderness Medicine, and Travel with Physical or Medical Disabilities

Along with International Travel Tips, Vaccination Recommendations, Geographical Health Issues, Disease Risks, a Glossary, and a Listing of Additional Resources

Edited by Joyce Brennfleck Shannon. 613 pages. 2000. 0-7808-0384-1. $78.

"**Recommended reference source.**"
— *Booklist, American Library Association, Feb '01*

"**This book is recommended for any public library, any travel collection, and especially any collection for the physically disabled.**"
—*American Reference Books Annual, 2001*

Vegetarian Sourcebook

Basic Consumer Health Information about Vegetarian Diets, Lifestyle, and Philosophy, Including Definitions of Vegetarianism and Veganism, Tips about Adopting Vegetarianism, Creating a Vegetarian Pantry, and Meeting Nutritional Needs of Vegetarians, with Facts Regarding Vegetarianism's Effect on Pregnant and Lactating Women, Children, Athletes, and Senior Citizens

Along with a Glossary of Commonly Used Vegetarian Terms and Resources for Additional Help and Information

Edited byChad T. Kimball. 360 pages. 2002. 0-7808-0439-2. $78.

Women's Health Concerns Sourcebook

Basic Information about Health Issues That Affect Women, Featuring Facts about Menstruation and Other Gynecological Concerns, Including Endometriosis, Fibroids, Menopause, and Vaginitis; Reproductive Concerns, Including Birth Control, Infertility, and Abortion; and Facts about Additional Physical, Emotional, and Mental Health Concerns Prevalent among Women Such as Osteoporosis, Urinary Tract Disorders, Eating Disorders, and Depression

Along with Tips for Maintaining a Healthy Lifestyle

Edited by Heather E. Aldred. 567 pages. 1997. 0-7808-0219-5. $78.

"**Handy compilation. There is an impressive range of diseases, devices, disorders, procedures, and other physical and emotional issues covered . . . well organized, illustrated, and indexed.**" — *Choice, Association of College and Research Libraries, Jan '98*

SEE ALSO *Breast Cancer Sourcebook, Cancer Sourcebook for Women, 1st and 2nd Editions, Healthy Heart Sourcebook for Women, Osteoporosis Sourcebook*

Workplace Health & Safety Sourcebook

Basic Consumer Health Information about Workplace Health and Safety, Including the Effect of Workplace Hazards on the Lungs, Skin, Heart, Ears, Eyes, Brain, Reproductive Organs, Musculoskeletal System, and Other Organs and Body Parts

Along with Information about Occupational Cancer, Personal Protective Equipment, Toxic and Hazardous Chemicals, Child Labor, Stress, and Workplace Violence

Edited by Chad T. Kimball. 626 pages. 2000. 0-7808-0231-4. $78.

"**As a reference for the general public, this would be useful in any library.**" —*E-Streams, Jun '01*

"**Provides helpful information for primary care physicians and other caregivers interested in occupational medicine. . . . General readers; professionals.**"
— *Choice, Association of College & Research Libraries, May '01*

"**Recommended reference source.**"
— *Booklist, American Library Association, Feb '01*

"**Highly recommended.**" — *The Bookwatch, Jan '01*

Worldwide Health Sourcebook

Basic Information about Global Health Issues, Including Malnutrition, Reproductive Health, Disease Dispersion and Prevention, Emerging Diseases, Risky Health Behaviors, and the Leading Causes of Death

Along with Global Health Concerns for Children, Women, and the Elderly, Mental Health Issues, Research and Technology Advancements, and Economic, Environmental, and Political Health Implications, a Glossary, and a Resource Listing for Additional Help and Information

Edited by Joyce Brennfleck Shannon. 614 pages. 2001. 0-7808-0330-2. $78.

"**Named an Outstanding Academic Title.**"
—*Choice, Association of College & Research Libraries, Jan '02*

"**Yet another handy but also unique compilation in the extensive Health Reference Series, this is a useful work because many of the international publications reprinted or excerpted are not readily available. Highly recommended.**"
—*Choice, Association of College & Research Libraries, Nov '01*

"**Recommended reference source.**"
—*Booklist, American Library Association, Oct '01*

Teen Health Series

Helping Young Adults Understand, Manage, and Avoid Serious Illness

Diet Information for Teens
Health Tips about Diet and Nutrition

Including Facts about Nutrients, Dietary Guidelines, Breakfasts, School Lunches, Snacks, Party Food, Weight Control, Eating Disorders, and More

Edited by Karen Bellenir. 399 pages. 2001. 0-7808-0441-4. $58.

"Full of helpful insights and facts throughout the book. . . . An excellent resource to be placed in public libraries or even in personal collections."
—*American Reference Books Annual 2002*

"Recommended for middle and high school libraries and media centers as well as academic libraries that educate future teachers of teenagers. It is also a suitable addition to health science libraries that serve patrons who are interested in teen health promotion and education."
— *E-Streams, Oct '01*

"This comprehensive book would be beneficial to collections that need information about nutrition, dietary guidelines, meal planning, and weight control. . . . This reference is so easy to use that its purchase is recommended." — *The Book Report, Sep-Oct '01*

"This book is written in an easy to understand format describing issues that many teens face every day, and then provides thoughtful explanations so that teens can make informed decisions. This is an interesting book that provides important facts and information for today's teens." —*Doody's Health Sciences Book Review Journal, Jul-Aug '01*

"A comprehensive compendium of diet and nutrition. The information is presented in a straightforward, plain-spoken manner. This title will be useful to those working on reports on a variety of topics, as well as to general readers concerned about their dietary health."
— *School Library Journal, Jun '01*

Drug Information for Teens
Health Tips about the Physical and Mental Effects of Substance Abuse

Including Facts about Alcohol, Anabolic Steroids, Club Drugs, Cocaine, Depressants, Hallucinogens, Herbal Products, Inhalants, Marijuana, Narcotics, Stimulants, Tobacco, and More

Edited by Karen Bellenir. 452 pages. 2002. 0-7808-0444-9. $58.

Mental Health Information for Teens
Health Tips about Mental Health and Mental Illness

Including Facts about Anxiety, Depression, Suicide, Eating Disorders, Obsessive-Compulsive Disorders, Panic Attacks, Phobias, Schizophrenia, and More

Edited by Karen Bellenir. 406 pages. 2001. 0-7808-0442-2. $58.

"In both language and approach, this user-friendly entry in the *Teen Health Series* is on target for teens needing information on mental health concerns." — *Booklist, American Library Association, Jan '02*

"Readers will find the material accessible and informative, with the shaded notes, facts, and embedded glossary insets adding appropriately to the already interesting and succinct presentation."
—*School Library Journal, Jan '02*

"This title is highly recommended for any library that serves adolescents and parents/caregivers of adolescents." — *E-Streams, Jan '02*

"Recommended for high school libraries and young adult collections in public libraries. Both health professionals and teenagers will find this book useful."
— *American Reference Books Annual 2002*

"This is a nice book written to enlighten the society, primarily teenagers, about common teen mental health issues. It is highly recommended to teachers and parents as well as adolescents."
— *Doody's Review Service, Dec '01*

Sexual Health Information for Teens
Health Tips about Sexual Development, Human Reproduction, and Sexually Transmitted Diseases

Including Facts about Puberty, Reproductive Health, Chlamydia, Human Papillomavirus, Pelvic Inflammatory Disease, Herpes, AIDS, Contraception, Pregnancy, and More

Edited by Deborah A. Stanley. 400 pages. 2003. 0-7808-0445-7. $58.

Health Reference Series

Adolescent Health Sourcebook

AIDS Sourcebook, 1st Edition

AIDS Sourcebook, 2nd Edition

Alcoholism Sourcebook

Allergies Sourcebook, 1st Edition

Allergies Sourcebook, 2nd Edition

Alternative Medicine Sourcebook, 1st Edition

Alternative Medicine Sourcebook, 2nd Edition

Alzheimer's, Stroke & 29 Other Neurological Disorders Sourcebook, 1st Edition

Alzheimer's Disease Sourcebook, 2nd Edition

Arthritis Sourcebook

Asthma Sourcebook

Attention Deficit Disorder Sourcebook

Back & Neck Disorders Sourcebook

Blood & Circulatory Disorders Sourcebook

Brain Disorders Sourcebook

Breast Cancer Sourcebook

Breastfeeding Sourcebook

Burns Sourcebook

Cancer Sourcebook, 1st Edition

Cancer Sourcebook (New), 2nd Edition

Cancer Sourcebook, 3rd Edition

Cancer Sourcebook for Women, 1st Edition

Cancer Sourcebook for Women, 2nd Edition

Cardiovascular Diseases & Disorders Sourcebook, 1st Edition

Caregiving Sourcebook

Childhood Diseases & Disorders Sourcebook

Colds, Flu & Other Common Ailments Sourcebook

Communication Disorders Sourcebook

Congenital Disorders Sourcebook

Consumer Issues in Health Care Sourcebook

Contagious & Non-Contagious Infectious Diseases Sourcebook

Death & Dying Sourcebook

Depression Sourcebook

Diabetes Sourcebook, 1st Edition

Diabetes Sourcebook, 2nd Edition

Diet & Nutrition Sourcebook, 1st Edition

Diet & Nutrition Sourcebook, 2nd Edition

Digestive Diseases & Disorder Sourcebook

Disabilities Sourcebook

Domestic Violence & Child Abuse Sourcebook

Drug Abuse Sourcebook

Ear, Nose & Throat Disorders Sourcebook

Eating Disorders Sourcebook

Emergency Medical Services Sourcebook

Endocrine & Metabolic Disorders Sourcebook

Environmentally Induced Disorders Sourcebook

Ethnic Diseases Sourcebook

Eye Care Sourcebook, 2nd Edition

Family Planning Sourcebook

Fitness & Exercise Sourcebook, 1st Edition

Fitness & Exercise Sourcebook, 2nd Edition

Food & Animal Borne Diseases Sourcebook

Food Safety Sourcebook

Forensic Medicine Sourcebook